Adaptation-Level Theory

Harry Helson

Adaptation-Level Theory

A SYMPOSIUM

Edited by M. H. APPLEY

GRADUATE SCHOOL
UNIVERSITY OF MASSACHUSETTS
AMHERST, MASSACHUSETTS

1971

ACADEMIC PRESS   New York and London

ACADEMIC PRESS, INC.
111 Fifth Avenue, New York, New York 10003

United Kingdom Edition published by
ACADEMIC PRESS, INC. (LONDON) LTD.
24/28 Oval Road, London NW1 7DD

LIBRARY OF CONGRESS CATALOG CARD NUMBER: 70-154394

PRINTED IN THE UNITED STATES OF AMERICA

To Harry Helson

CONTENTS

Section I   Harry Helson and Adaptation-Level Theory

Section II   Psychophysics and Scaling

Section VII   Tributes to Harry Helson

Appendix

List of Contributors

Numbers in parentheses indicate the pages on which the authors' contributions begin.

Robert Adamson, *Department of Psychology, Florida Atlantic University, Boca Raton, Florida* (159)

M. H. Appley, *Graduate School, University of Massachusetts, Amherst, Massachusetts* (1, 285)

Lloyd L. Avant, *Department of Psychology, Iowa State University, Ames, Iowa* (19, 101)

William Bevan, *American Association for the Advancement of Science, Washington, D.C.* (101, 307)

Gordon H. Bower, *Department of Psychology, Stanford University, Stanford, California* (175)

Philip Brickman, *Department of Psychology, Northwestern University, Evanston, Illinois* (287)

Donald R. Brown, *Department of Psychology, University College of London, London, England* (215)

Donald T. Campbell, *Department of Psychology, Northwestern University, Evanston, Illinois* (287)

John F. Corso, *Department of Psychology, State University of New York at Cortland, Cortland, New York* (27)

Dorothy Dinnerstein, *Institute for Cognitive Studies, Newark College of Arts and Sciences, Rutgers University, Newark, New Jersey* (81)

Alice H. Eagly, *Department of Psychology, University of Massachusetts, Amherst, Massachusetts* (257)

Howard Egeth, *Department of Psychology, The Johns Hopkins University, Baltimore, Maryland* (233)

xi

Howard R. Flock, *Department of Psychology, York University, Downsview, Toronto, Ontario, Canada* (129)

Alberta Steinman Gilinsky, *Department of Psychology, University of Bridgeport, Bridgeport, Connecticut* (71)

Sanford Goldstone, *Department of Psychiatry, Cornell University Medical College, White Plains, New York* (263)

J. P. Guilford, *Department of Psychology, University of Southern California, Los Angeles, California* (311)

John A. Hebert, *Department of Psychology, Colorado State University, Fort Collins, Colorado* (97, 325)

Harry Helson, *Department of Psychology, University of Massachusetts, Amherst, Massachusetts* (5)

Wayne H. Holtzman, *The Hogg Foundation for Mental Health, The University of Texas, Austin, Texas* (203)

Francis W. Irwin, *Department of Psychology, University of Pennsylvania, Philadelphia, Pennsylvania* (157)

Deane B. Judd, *Office of Colorimetry, Institute for Applied Technology, National Bureau of Standards, Washington, D.C.* (147, 305)

William T. Lhamon, *Cornell University Medical College, New York, New York* (263)

Melvin Manis, *Department of Social Psychology, University of Michigan, Ann Arbor, Michigan* (237)

David C. McClelland, *Department of Social Relations, Harvard University, Cambridge, Massachusetts* (303)

Carol M. Reich, *Department of Psychology, University College of London, London, England* (215)

Frank Restle, *Department of Psychology, Indiana University, Bloomington, Indiana* (55)

Ross Stagner, *Department of Psychology, Wayne State University, Detroit, Michigan* (207)

Joseph A. Steger, *Department of Psychology, State University of New York at Albany, Albany, New York* (281)*

* Present address: Department of Management, Rensselaer Polytechnic Institute, Troy, New York.

John A. Swets, *Bolt Beranek & Newman, Inc., Cambridge, Massachusetts* (49)

Richard Trumbull, *American Association for the Advancement of Science, Washington, D.C.* (123)

Arnold Well, *Department of Psychology, University of Massachusetts, Amherst, Massachusetts* (95)

Martha Wilson, *Department of Psychology, University of Connecticut, Storrs, Connecticut* (169)

PREFACE

This volume is based in part on a Symposium on Adaptation-Level (AL) Theory held at the University of Massachusetts at Amherst, on May 7–9, 1970.

The idea for the Symposium grew out of discussions between William Bevan and the editor on ways in which Harry Helson and his significant contributions to psychology could be honored. We first thought of soliciting contributions for a *Festschrift* from Professor Helson's former students and colleagues. However, this prospect seemed too retrospective for a man and a theory so currently active and so widely influential. We settled instead on a symposium format and decided to focus upon only one area of Professor Helson's work—albeit the most pervasive.

The AL Theory Symposium was designed to permit the display of the wide range of applicability of Helson's concept. To this end, we invited a sampling of the persons who have made use of the theory in different areas of psychology. With a few exceptions—where prior commitments could not be changed—our invitations were enthusiastically accepted. We regretted only that the symposium format (as well as financial constraints) did not allow us to extend the participant list to many others who have contributed significantly to AL theory literature.

The reader may recall that the spring of 1970, when the Symposium was held, was the time of the Cambodian invasion, the Kent State and Jackson State Universities student killings, and national campus strikes. Because of responsibilities on their own campuses, several of the intended participants were forced to cancel their appearances at the last minute, and adjustments in program had to be made. We were nevertheless fortunate in being able to obtain replacements on short notice, thus having a series of excellent papers presented and hearing some lively and fruitful discussions.

Because of the expected time lag between presentation and publication, it was decided not to faithfully reproduce the transcript of the Symposium but to invite each author to modify his manuscript to include new data and/or changes suggested in the formal and informal discussions which followed the papers. Many chose to do so (in at least two cases with new collaborators). In addition, a few of the comments included in this volume were not actually presented at the Symposium, but were later invited by the editor.*

We had originally intended to include direct transcriptions of the general discussions in each section. These turned out to be too varied in length and quality for this purpose, however. (This was not so much a function of the intrinsic merits of the papers themselves as a result of such irrelevant factors as schedule constraints, extraneous interruptions, and, in one session, an overzealous and unmodifiable air-conditioning system.) The several symposium session chairmen were therefore provided with transcripts of the discussions and asked to include those which could be appropriately summarized in their introductory remarks.

Amherst   *M. H. A.*
October, 1971

* Bevan's and Guilford's appreciations, Steger's and McClelland's comments, and Hebert's memorial note on Jack Capehart.

ACKNOWLEDGMENTS

Dr. Harry Helson will, by the time this volume appears, have retired from his Professorship at the University of Massachusetts, but not from a continuing writing and speaking career. At my insistence, he overcame his natural reluctance to participate actively in a symposium honoring himself and provided the keynote paper, one which sees both the limits and the prospects of his earlier thinking and sets direction for the future. As friend and colleague, he has been most helpful to me in any number of ways, and I am pleased to acknowledge his generous—though never intrusive—advice and assistance from the beginning of this project.

Dr. William Bevan collaborated with the editor in planning the Symposium but was prevented from attending at the last minute because of his responsibility as Provost of Johns Hopkins University at the time of the campus strike. He later had to withdraw from joint editorship upon assuming major new duties as Executive Officer of the American Association for the Advancement of Science. I am nevertheless indebted to him for his helpful consultation from time to time throughout the project.

Henry Odbert and James Brown of the National Science Foundation are to be thanked for their advice in my preparation of the application for Foundation support and their appreciation of the value the Symposium would have.

Appreciation is due to Dr. William Venman and Karen Kells of the University's Continuing Education Division for the excellence of the physical arrangements for the symposium.

My secretary and girl Friday, Sharon Wielgus, gave continuity to pre-Symposium and Symposium arrangements, even to running a private airport shuttle service for participants, and my appreciation of her thoughtfulness "beyond the call of duty" is shared, I know, by all who participated in the Symposium.

Leslie Thayer, with assistance from Dorothy Thayer, did the tedious job of transcribing the Symposium tapes and trying to unravel voice upon voice. I much appreciate their patience and the conscientiousness of their labors.

Patricia Lemon, more than anyone else, has been responsible for translating raw manuscript materials into edited publisher-ready copy. She corresponded with all of the participants on editorial matters, carefully guarded deadlines, painstakingly checked and corrected bibliographic materials, and made many substantive contributions to the editing process. Press of my other duties would have kept this exciting volume from ever reaching the reader had it not been for Mrs. Lemon's excellent assistance. I am happy to acknowledge my gratitude for it.

The Symposium was supported through grants from the National Science Foundation (GB-19643) and the Research Council of the University of Massachusetts (FR-S11-70(1)). Significant assistance was also provided by many of the participants and their institutions in the form of underwritten travel expenses and by the Department of Psychology and the Graduate School of the University of Massachusetts in the form of secretarial service to the editor in organizing both the Symposium itself and this volume.

Amherst   *M. H. A.*
October, 1971

Adaptation-Level Theory

A SYMPOSIUM

Harry Helson
and Adaptation-Level Theory

INTRODUCTION

M. H. Appley

Since its formulation by Helson in 1947, adaptation-level (AL) theory has been extended from its origin in psychophysics and perception to such varied fields as learning (Bevan & Adamson, 1960; Capehart & Pease, 1968; and others); cognitive processes (Helson, Dworkin, & Michels, 1956; Brown, 1969; McBrearty, Kanfer, Merston, & Evander, 1963); motivation and affectivity McClelland, Atkinson, Clark, & Lowell, 1953); transposition and the intermediate size problem (James, 1953; Zeiler, 1963a, b; DiLollo & Beez, 1966); stimulus generalization (Thomas & Jones, 1962; Helson & Avant, 1967); personality (Young, Holtzman, & Bryant, 1954); intelligence testing (Heim, 1955); social psychology (Manis, 1965, 1967); clinical psychology (Block, 1962a, b, 1963; Goldstone 1967; Goldstone & Goldfarb, 1964; Hunt, Campbell, & Lewis, 1957); and mathematical model building (Restle, 1968) to name but a few.

The importance of AL theory in present-day psychology is attested not only by the numerous studies in the literature using this paradigm, but also by the fact that chapters in various texts have been devoted to it, in whole or in part, e.g., in general experimental psychology (Corso, 1967); social psychology (Bieri, Atkins, Scott, Leaman, Miller, & Tripodi, 1966); and motivation (Cofer & Appley, 1964; DiLollo, Beez, & Allison, 1965; Helson & Bevan, 1966). In addition, AL has received attention and incited work abroad, e.g., in Japan (Noguchi & Ohishi, 1961; A. Kozaki, 1965; T. Kozaki, 1968); Finland (von Wright & Mikkonen, 1963, 1964); and Germany (Sarris, 1967; Witte, 1960a, b). Increasingly, psychologists in various areas are finding the AL paradigm useful not only in designing experiments, but also in interpreting experimental, test, and clinical data.

The purpose of the present volume is to report the findings and views of a group of active investigators and theoreticians in various fields of psychology who have employed the concept or paradigm of AL theory, particularly in the past five years. The papers and comments herein provide a reasonably comprehensive evaluation of the present state of theoretical development and offer provocative suggestions for further extensions of the theory into new areas of application.

Three statements of appreciation of Harry Helson by distinguished colleagues who have known him and his work intimately over many years are given at the end of the volume. They speak eloquently of the contribution Helson has made to the development of psychological science. Although each refers to his own experience in association with Helson, all attest to the scope of his concerns, the persistence of his efforts, and the lasting influence his research and thinking have had and are likely to continue to have across the whole spectrum of psychology and beyond.

Helson offers his own assessment of the future of AL theory and its uses in a forward-looking paper subtitled "1970 — and After." He places AL theory in historic perspective and, in his own inimitable way, deals with his critics as well as his supporters in showing how AL theory has, when properly understood, withstood the widest range of tests in varied empirical settings. Anticipating the final section of the book, he predicts that AL theory will have its most important impact in investigations of "the norms men live by,"[1] their origins and determinants, and the means by which such norms affect perception of social, political, and economic conditions. Correctly used, he feels, such knowledge could lead to better understanding of "what is going on in the world about us as well as in the contrived world of the psychological laboratory."

REFERENCES

Bevan, W., & Adamson, R. Reinforcers and reinforcement: Their relation to maze performance. *Journal of Experimental Psychology,* 1960, **59**, 226–232.
Bieri, J., Atkins, A. L., Scott, B., Leaman, R. L., Miller, H., & Tripodi, T. *Clinical and social judgment: The discrimination of behavioral information.* New York: Wiley, 1966.
Block, W. E. Adaptation-level theory: Paradigmatic application to projective testing. *Journal of Clinical Psychology,* 1962, **18**, 466–468.   (a)
Block, W. E. Preliminary study of adaptation-level theory as a framework for projective testing. *Perceptual and Motor Skills,* 1962, **15**, 366.   (b)
Block, W. E. Clinical validation of adaptation-level theory as a framework for projective testing. *Journal of Clinical Psychology,* 1963, **19**, 304–309.
Brown, D. R. Personal communication. 1969.
Capehart, J., & Pease, V. An application of adaptation-level theory to transposition responses in a conditional discrimination. *Psychonomic Science,* 1968, **10**, 147–148.
Cofer, C. N., & Appley, M. H. *Motivation: Theory and research.* New York: Wiley, 1964.
Corso, J. F. Adaptation-level theory. In Corso, J. F. (Ed.) *The experimental psychology of sensory behavior.* New York: Holt, 1967. Pp. 508–549.

[1] This is the tentative title of a book addressed to a lay audience that Helson has currently in preparation.

DiLollo, V., & Beez, V. Negative contrast effect as a function of magnitude of reward decrement. *Psychonomic Science,* 1966, **5**, 99–100.

DiLollo, V., Beez, V., & Allison, J. An adaptation-level model for incentive motivation. Personal communication. 1965.

Goldstone, S. The human clock: A framework for the study of healthy and deviant time perception. *Annals of the New York Academy of Sciences,* 1967, **138**, 767–783.

Goldstone, S., & Goldfarb, J. L. Adaptation level, personality theory, and psychopathology. *Psychological Bulletin,* 1964, **61**, 176–187.

Heim, A. W. Adaptation to level of difficulty in intelligence testing. *British Journal of Psychology,* 1955, **46**, 211–224.

Helson, H., & Avant, L. L. Stimulus generalization as a function of contextual stimuli. *Journal of Experimental Psychology,* 1967, **73**, 565–567.

Helson, H., & Bevan, W. (Eds.) *Contemporary approaches to psychology.* Princeton, New Jersey: Van Nostrand, 1966.

Helson, H., Dworkin, R. S., & Michels, W. C. Quantitative denotations of common terms as a function of background. *American Journal of Psychology,* 1956, **69**, 194–208.

Hunt, W. A., Campbell, D. T., & Lewis, N. A. The effect of assimilation and contrast in judgments of clinical materials. *American Journal of Psychology,* 1957, **70**, 347–360.

James, H. An application of Helson's theory of adaptation level to the problem of transposition. *Psychological Review,* 1953, **60**, 345–352.

Kozaki, A. The effect of co-existent stimuli other than test stimulus on brightness constancy. *Japanese Psychological Research,* 1965, **7**, 138–147.

Kozaki, T. Background effects on contrast and assimilation. Personal communication, 1968.

McBrearty, J. F., Kanfer, J. H., Merston, A. R., & Evander, D. Focal and contextual stimulus variables in verbal conditioning. *Psychological Reports,* 1963, **13**, 115–124.

McClelland, D. C., Atkinson, J. W., Clark, R. A., & Lowell, E. L. *The achievement motive.* New York: Appleton, 1953.

Manis, M. Immunization, delay, and the interpretation of persuasive messages. *Journal of Personality and Social Psychology,* 1965, **1**, 541–550.

Manis, M. Context effects in communication. *Journal of Personality and Social Psychology,* 1967, **5**, 324–326.

Noguchi, K., & Ohishi, A. An experimental study on the system of reference in social judgment. *Japanese Psychological Research,* 1961, **3**, 71–89.

Restle, F. Personal communication to Professor Helson. 1968.

Sarris, V. Die Abhängigkeit des Adaptation-Niveaus von Ankerreizen. *Zeitschrift für experimentelle und angewandte Psychologie,* 1967, **14**, 1–51.

Thomas, D. R., & Jones, C. G. Stimulus generalization as a function of the frame of reference. *Journal of Experimental Psychology,* 1962, **64**, 77–80.

von Wright, J. M., & Mikkonen, V. Changes in reproduction as a function of adaptation level. I. *The Institute of Psychology,* University of Turku, 1963, No. 1, 1–10.

von Wright, J. M., & Mikkonen, V. Changes in repeated reproduction of weight as a function of adaptation level. *Scandinavian Journal of Psychology,* 1964, **5**, 239–248.

Witte, W. Experimentelle Untersuchungen von Bezugssystemen. I. Struktur, Dynamik und Genese von Bezugssystemen. *Psychologische Beiträge,* 1960, **4**, 218–252. (a)

Witte, W. Über Phänomenskalen. *Psychologische Beiträge,* 1960, **4**, 643–674. (b)

Young, H. H., Holtzman, W. H., & Bryant, N. D. Effects of item context and order on personality ratings. *Educational and Psychological Measurement,* 1954, **14**, 499–517.

Zeiler, M. D. New dimensions of the intermediate size problem: Neither absolute nor relational response. *Journal of Experimental Psychology,* 1963, **70**, 516–533. (a)

Zeiler, M. D. The ratio theory of intermediate size discrimination. *Psychological Review,* 1963, **70**, 516–533. (b)

ADAPTATION-LEVEL THEORY

1970 – AND AFTER

Harry Helson

It is now generally accepted that adaptation is one of the most important phenomena in behavior. Originally used by psychologists to denote merely the decrement in sensory responses following prolonged exposure to stimulation, adaptation is now seen to play a wider role in all types of behavior. Thus Krech, Crutchfield, and Levison (1969) list under "Adaptive Behavior" the various types of learning (images, language, and thought), the development of language and thinking, and creative problem solving. The adaptive nature of communication has also been stressed by MacKay (1969) in his attempt to broaden classical information theory so as to include meaning as well as uncertainty in its definition. Many other sources can be cited to show that the concept of adaptation is no longer restricted to sensory processes (see Helson, 1964, pp. 36–63).

More specifically, considering adaptation-level (AL) theory, we can regard a theory or concept as accepted when it has found its way into the literature, particularly into elementary texts, without being labeled with any one person's name. We no longer speak of Hartley's or Bain's associationism, Watson's behaviorism, or Wertheimer's concept of Gestalt. We speak of association, stimulus–response (S–R) theory, and Gestalt theory. So it is happening with AL theory. Even the weighted-mean model of AL theory has been taken over by various workers without reference to papers published as long ago as 1938 and 1947. Since we are primarily interested in the advancement of knowledge, and only secondarily in creating eponyms, reference to concepts rather than names is a natural development in the growth of a science.

From the title of this article it might be inferred that it was my intention to survey the various areas in which the theory of AL has been used and to indicate its further developments, but this was not my purpose. While new applications of AL theory have been made since the appearance of my book (Helson, 1964), the main areas in which it has been applied were spelled out quite well in it, and space does not permit a survey of what has happened in the last six years. What I would like to do here is to reemphasize certain features of AL theory to correct some misconceptions about it and to indicate some directions in which the theory may be fruitfully extended and applied.

COMPATIBILITY OF ADAPTATION-LEVEL THEORY

The first thing that should perhaps be emphasized is that unlike theories that begin by attacking other approaches (compare psychoanalysis versus academic psychology; behaviorism versus mentalism; Gestalt versus atomism), AL theory is compatible with other theories and positions, even with purely empirical or nontheoretical approaches, so long as they take into account the role of AL in whatever type of behavior they deal with. This insistence on the inclusion of AL in any approach springs from essentially two considerations: First, something as ubiquitous and important as adaptation simply must not, cannot, be left out of account. Second, AL theory has proved to be capable of explaining many phenomena with fewer assumptions than alternative explanations, and thus it has contributed to the economy of thinking about many problems.

Let us now turn to some basic issues raised by certain critics of AL theory. There is, of course, nothing to say to those would-be critics who dismiss our position with mere *ad hominem* arguments, since they betray a total lack of acquaintance with the vast literature now extant supporting AL theory. But alternative theories can be examined, tested, and evaluated in the light of experimental findings and with whatever scientific acumen we may have at our command. Fortunately, new experimental evidence from our own and other laboratories has not weakened our fundamental assumptions.

LOCUS OF CONTEXT EFFECTS

One of the main issues confronting investigators concerns the locus of context effects. Here there is a clear division: Adaptation-level theorists maintain that with changes in stimulation accompanying focal stimuli the quality, magnitude, and other dimensions of the stimuli also change more or less. Critics of AL theory assert that the changes under such conditions reported by the subjects do not reflect changes in *perceived* attributes but are merely verbal, semantic, or judgmental artifacts. It is interesting that such critics now grant that a neutral stimulus in a chromatic field really takes on the color complementary to the hue and brightness of the surround (though Helmholtz held to a judgmental theory of this phenomenon), but they hold to a Helmholtzian type of theory in denying that a 300-gm weight hefted following a 900-gm weight really feels lighter than when hefted alone. Anchor effects are explained as due only to a change in the response, not in the perception! One reason for the belief that background, contextual, and anchor effects merely represent semantic changes is to be found in our use of category rating scales. When the subjects change their response from heavy to light in the case of lifted weights, or from soft to loud with tones, as a result of anchor effects, it seems plausible to assert that the perception of the stimuli has not really changed and that only the categories have been varied due to a change of scale modulus. To test this explanation an *experimentum crucis* was performed (Helson & A. Kozaki, 1968) satisfying the following conditions: First, the stimuli and judgmental task were as simple as possible to minimize play of verbal factors. Second, the response language was in terms of cardinal numbers learned once and for all. Third, the numbers expressing responses were restricted in range and were relatively small so that when shifts due to anchors occurred, they could not reasonably be ascribed to change of modulus of the judgmental scale. Stimuli consisted of random patterns of 10, 12, 14, 16, and 18 dots exposed for .30 sec. Four groups of 5 Ss each were used: One group was shown an anchor of 4 dots, another an anchor of 13 dots, a third an anchor of 32 dots. The anchors were exposed before each of the stimuli, but were not judged as such. A fourth group served as the control, judging the series stimuli without anchor.

The results are shown in Fig. 1, wherein it is seen that the small anchor (4 dots) reliably resulted in increasing the number of dots perceived, while the

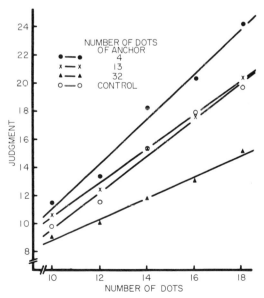

Fig. 1. Numerical estimates of numbers of dots in random patterns by independent groups with anchors of 4, 13, and 32 dots and by a control group that judged without any anchor (from Helson & T. Kozaki, 1968).

large anchor (32 dots) reliably resulted in a decrease. The judgments of the control group are close to the objective number as are those of the group with the 13-dot anchor, as expected. The 13-dot AL is close to the geometric mean of the series stimuli. Thus anchor effects using category rating scales are also found with numbers. The shifts in judgments with the 4- and 32-dot anchors, while highly significant statistically, are not large enough to be attributed to changes in the scale modulus as Stevens (1958) has maintained. Still other arguments showing that the "change in semantics-scale modulus" theory is clearly untenable are given in the original publication of these data (Helson & A. Kozaki, 1968) and in references cited therein.

ADAPTATION-LEVEL THEORY, ASSIMILATION, AND CONTRAST

Turning to another issue, it is sometimes said that AL theory is a theory of contrast effects only, with the implication that it cannot account for assimilation effects. I have already pointed out that assimilation and contrast are not antithetical phenomena (Helson, 1964). If the subjects use a finite scale, there must be compression (assimilation) in some parts of the scale if there is spread (contrast) of judgments in other parts. Perceptually, extensive investigations of von Bezold assimilation (reversal of classical lightness contrast) have shown that when the width of black and white stripes on gray background is systematically varied, there is a continuum from classical contrast (light lines darken and dark lines lighten intervening gray areas) to assimilation (light lines lighten and dark lines darken intervening gray areas), with a neutral region in which intermediate widths of lines neither lighten nor darken adjacent gray areas (Helson & Rohles, 1959; Helson & Joy, 1962). A physiological hypothesis (Helson, 1963) advanced to account for these findings, including the case where only assimilation is found with near-white and near-black intervening areas, has found support in experiments by Steger (1969). Assimilation and contrast effects are found concurrently whenever strong anchors raise or depress perceived magnitudes and qualities of stimuli. For example, with very heavy anchor weights judgments are predominantly on the light side, while with very light anchor weights judgments are predominantly on the heavy side of the judgment scale—a phenomenon of compression. On the other hand, the shift in judgments of stimuli near the anchor can be regarded as a contrast effect (see Helson & Nash, 1960). Hence, background and anchor effects result in both contrast and assimilation. Furthermore, as inspection of curves showing anchor effects proves (Helson, 1964), functions embodying AL fitted to data involving contrast and assimilation effects in judgment reveal no need for different equations for the two phenomena.

But even if AL theory were merely a theory of contrast effects, we would still have to ask if this theory and classical contrast theory give the same answers to critical cases. Before proceeding to answer this question, it should be pointed out that classical contrast theory (e.g., in vision) has extreme difficulty in dealing with a number of interacting reflectances or luminances, since it deals with the action of part on part of complex fields. Calculating the contrast effect from a weighted average of the different parts of the field proves to yield a much more manageable treatment than does the classical approach, as Marimont (1962) has shown and as Flock and Judd show in this volume. Returning to the question asked above, we must answer that AL theory and classical contrast theory do not give the same answers or predictions in critical cases. Thus, early in the history of AL theory (Helson, 1948) it was pointed out that when an anchor much heavier than any of the series stimuli was used, none of the stimuli should be judged heavy if only simple contrast effects were at the basis of the judgments. Since the top stimuli in the series were judged heavy, they must have been judged with respect to a neutral point lighter than the anchor.

Evidence that contrast effects can be predicted correctly only by reference to a prevailing level also comes from a recent experiment (Helson & T. Kozaki, 1968, unpublished study). Three groups of 6 Ss each judged a series of squares with sides 36, 45, 54, 63, and 72 mm. long, using a 9-point rating scale ranging from very, very small to very, very large. In one group, all the squares except the largest were exposed for .25 sec. and the largest was exposed for 1.0 sec.; in the second group, all the squares except the smallest were exposed for .25 sec. and the smallest was exposed for 1.0 sec.; in the third (control) group, all squares were exposed for .25 sec. It was found that when one square was exposed longer than the others in the series, it exerted greater weight in the pooling process, pulling prevailing AL upwards in the one case and downwards in the other. Simple contrast theory cannot predict the results obtained, particularly the judgments of the overexposed stimuli themselves. As seen from Fig. 2, when the largest stimulus was overexposed, judgments of all the stimuli were shifted downward, and when the smallest stimulus was overexposed, they were shifted upward as compared with the control group's judgments. We can account for these results only by reference to the shifts of AL. The fact that the judgments of the overexposed stimuli themselves were shifted downward in the one case and upward in the other is especially noteworthy because, according to the well-established relation between duration and size, we would have expected just the opposite results (see Helson & A. Kozaki, 1968). Contrast might explain the shifts in judgments of all the stimuli *except* the overexposed ones, for they cannot be said to contrast with themselves. If they contrasted with the rest of the series, the shifts should have been in the opposite direction: The largest stimulus should have been judged larger and the smallest judged smaller than in the control-group judgments. Only if the judgments of all the stimuli are made with respect to a prevailing level can we understand the judgments of the overexposed as well as the underexposed stimuli.

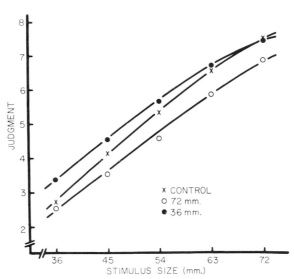

Fig. 2. This shows that longer duration of the largest stimulus (72 mm.) causes a downward shift in judgments of size of the other series stimuli, while longer duration of the smallest stimulus (36 mm.) causes an upward shift in the judgments (from Helson & T. Kozaki, unpublished data).

The Weighted Log Mean Formula for Adaptation Level

Perhaps at this point, I should clarify some misconceptions about the weighted log mean formula for AL. The statement, whether in words or in mathematical symbols, is a definition, and as it stands it is neither true nor false. In Bertrand Russell's terminology, it is a propositional function; it does not become a true or false proposition until specific values are given the weighting coefficients in the definition. Thus the truth of

$$AL = (\bar{X}_i^p \cdot B^q \cdot R^r)^{1/p+q+r}$$

where B is background stimulus, R is residual stimulus, and $\bar{X}_i$ is series stimuli, depends upon the values assigned to p, q, and r. Sarris (1967) has made much of the fact that p, q, and r are not constant when a very wide range of anchors is used with a given set of stimuli—a fact previously acknowledged by Helson and Masters (1966). This definition, like all definitions, is empirical; the values of the weighting coefficients must be determined experimentally. Unfortunately, Sarris, in his criticism of an admittedly empirical formula, did not advance our knowledge, since he has no theory for the problems he discusses. In one case he uses *four* empirical constants where we used *one* (Sarris, 1967, p. 338), and in another case he merely substitutes another empirical constant for the constant we had taken to represent the step interval between series stimuli, asserting that this empirical constant "cannot be further *theoretically* [sic] interpreted in the present experimental-scientific stage [p. 341]". Suffice it here to state that in limiting cases the step interval between stimuli can be shown to be important, since, if stimuli are made indiscriminable (by making the step interval too small), they will be judged identically (or almost so) and they will not be differentiated from prevailing AL. Here is a possible starting point for a theoretically based derivation of the influence of the step interval that others besides ourselves have found to be important, Sarris to the contrary notwithstanding (see Helson, 1964).

Due to the use of negatively accelerated functions for fitting data in much of our work, some people believe that AL theory stands or falls with the goodness of fit to these particular types of curves. That this does not follow can be shown by deriving values of AL and fitting to data by means of other types of functions. Thus, in the classical method of constant stimulus differences, the data are fitted by ogive functions, and the point of subjective equality (PSE) derived from percentages of judgments is the same as the value of AL (Furth, 1960; Helson, 1964). Even the method of paired comparisons yields ALs as shown by Guilford's data reproduced in my book (Helson, 1964). Almost any kind of transformation can be used legitimately to fit data and to derive values of AL.

THE PROBLEM OF ORGANIZATION

A critical problem for psychology in general, and perception and judgment in particular, is that of organization or Gestalt. A great advance was made by the Gestalt psychologists in their emphasis on problems of organization in perception, learning, and personality (Angyal, 1965). It would be surprising if further advances had not been made in psychology over the last few decades, and we now know that the concept of Gestalt must be broadened to include cognitive–affective as well as perceptual wholes. We perceive objects not only as figures against their backgrounds, but as possessing various attributes in varying degrees—some sensory, some cognitive, some affective—which position them in various classes. Thus we see a man as tall or short, bright or dull, black or white, radical or conservative, kind or cruel, and so on through countless categories. I do not mean by these examples to imply that we perceive only extremes; on the contrary, we assign very fine gradations in our judgments. How we rate objects depends upon their relations to our internal norms or ALs. It is at this point that AL theory differs from Gestalt theory, for the latter makes organization a primitive concept and regards its job of explaining as done when it refers perceived differences of any kind to differences in organization. A concrete case

Up to this point, I have dealt with problems for which different solutions have been proposed by adherents to AL theory and by some of its critics who, I might add, have been fairly few in number. I come now to the future, although I have not attempted to give complete coverage of the past or present. Interesting and fruitful work is still being done in various areas using the AL paradigm which I would have liked to discuss but cannot on this occasion. Suffice it to say here that new applications have been made in old, established fields—such as psychophysics, learning, and perception—by various workers. We may now ask: What of the future? While it is not possible to foretell how the theory will develop or how it will be used in specific areas, some guesses may be hazarded regarding further applications.

There are signs that AL theory may play a larger role in psychophysics as internal factors are brought into more sophisticated mathematical models. Until now psychophysics has been mostly concerned with functions embodying only stimulus relations with hardly more than a nod at the contribution of the organism. That this is changing is shown by classical signal-detection theory (SDT), with its concern for the criterion of judgment, and by incorporation of internal factors, including AL (Durlach & Braida, 1969), in more recent developments of SDT. Similarly, advances are being made in older areas, such as learning and perception utilizing the AL paradigm, for example, the Bevan–Adamson (1960) reinforcement model; the transposition model of Capehart and Pease (1968); the treatment of various illusions by Restle and his co-workers (Restle, 1970; Restle & Merryman, 1968); the influence of anchor effects in organization (Bell & Bevan, 1968); and many others too numerous to mention. These are but illustrative of fresh approaches to classical, well-worked areas.

ADAPTATION-LEVEL THEORY AND DEVELOPMENTAL PSYCHOLOGY

Relatively new areas in which AL theory may be fruitfully applied would seem to be first of all developmental psychology. It is probably to the infant and young child that we must turn in order to study the most important phases of the learning process. We need to know how internal norms become established, how they are modified and develop, and, finally, how they become more or less fixed in the adult. We need to find out, as mentioned above, how objects are grouped into classes and what determines the limits of class membership. This, in turn, determines what will or will not be relevant to any class of objects. Studies of this sort may reveal more about learning mechanisms than investigations of so-called learning in adults whose learning patterns were established long before in early life. It is not unlikely that, by the time most studies of learning are made, what is really being studied is not learning but *strategies* adopted by individuals to meet or adapt to highly specific and artificial types of tasks in the laboratory. It may be too late to study the learning process, even in adult subhuman species. The field of developmental psychology, whether human or subhuman, can well give new impetus to the study of really significant learning mechanisms hitherto untouched by traditional approaches.

Affects and Motivation

Affects and motivation offer another fertile field for the application of AL concepts, since adaptive effects are even greater in this area than in sensory processes where they have been studied most assiduously. Everyday life furnishes many such examples of AL: in the liking for foods, in appreciation of art, in striving for goals, and in the arousal and decay of motives. In the laboratory, we have been able to show the influence of anchors on the pleasantness of musical chords and of visual materials (Helson, 1964). These studies demonstrate the feasibility of further work on motivation and affectivity. Indeed, McClelland and Clark have proposed an AL theory of motivation (in McClelland, Atkinson, Clark, & Lowell, 1953) that throws light on some vexing problems in this area. Probably, central-neural adaptations are more important in affective and motivational processes than in sensory processes where adaptation is largely peripheral, but we may expect the former to behave very much like those we have encountered in the study of the latter. The importance of internal norms in motivational processes can perhaps best be expressed in the dictum: There is no basic change in behavior without there being first a change in the internal norm underlying that behavior. Explicit recognition of this principle can have important implications for counseling and psychotherapy.

Social and Interpersonal Relations

Finally, let me mention but one other area in which I believe advances are to be made within the AL framework, namely, that of social and interpersonal relations. In the Texas "action" studies of conformity (see Helson, 1964, for references) we attempted to show that by varying the strength of focal, background, and residual stimuli, lawful relations could be found comparable to those in the older areas of sensation and learning. Thus far, social psychologists have shown little disposition to continue studies in this vein, perhaps because of their desire to come out with results seeming to have practical value. It is possible, as we showed, to produce social interactions having all the flavor of real-life situations yet yielding quantitative data. Variables for study can be isolated in social interactions without oversimplification or undue artificiality in the laboratory situation. Certainly this is one of the most fertile fields for further work along the lines advocated here.

It is to be expected that a theory that stresses the role of internal norms in behavior must have relevance for ethical and moral questions. What has value for an individual—the ethical and moral bases of his behavior—must be sought in his internal norms. Investigation of the norms men live by, the manner in which they arise and develop, is one of the most important areas for psychological investigation. At this very moment, we are living in a time of crisis, the causes of which are rooted in psychological mechanisms such as we have been studying for years in both human and subhuman subjects. We know that relative rather than absolute values and quantities determine reaction patterns. The presence of extreme contrasts has accentuated the dissatisfactions and disequilibria that are found in our society today. Contrast the superabundance of wealth with extreme poverty almost side by side; contrast the billions poured into a far-off war with the curtailment of funds for education, medical care, research, and slum removal; and contrast what can be achieved by violence as against peaceful exhortation, and you can see why we have the problems we do. The perception of these contrasts in modern media of communication, most of them visual, affects every individual who watches television, goes to the movies, or looks into the popular magazines. The facts learned about the role of anchors and much else concerned with internal norms carry directly over to our perception of social, political, and economic conditions. Using this knowledge rightly may show that psychology is more than a purely academic subject and that our experiments and theories can enable us to understand what is going on in the world about us as well as in the contrived world of the psychology laboratory.

REFERENCES

Angyal, A. *Neurosis and treatment: A holistic theory.* New York: Wiley, 1965.
Bell, R. A., & Bevan, W. Influence of anchors upon the operation of certain Gestalt organizing principles. *Journal of Experimental Psychology,* 1968, **78**, 670–678.
Bevan, W., & Adamson, R. Reinforcers and reinforcement: Their relation to maze performance. *Journal of Experimental Psychology,* 1960, **59**, 226–232.
Bevan, W., & Pritchard, J. F. The anchor effect and the problem of relevance in the judgment of shape. *Journal of General Psychology,* 1963, **69**, 147–161.   (a)
Bevan, W., & Pritchard, J. F. Effect of "subliminal" tones upon the judgment of loudness. *Journal of Experimental Psychology,* 1963, **66**, 23–29.   (b)
Black, R. W., & Bevan, W. The effect of subliminal shock upon the judged intensity of weak shock. *American Journal of Psychology,* 1960, **73**, 262–267.
Boardman, W. K., & Goldstone, S. Effects of subliminal anchors upon judgments of size. *Perceptual and Motor Skills,* 1962, **14**, 475–482.

Brown, D. R. Stimulus-similarity and the anchoring of subjective scales. *American Journal of Psychology,* 1953, **66**, 199–214.

Capehart, J., & Pease, V. An application of adaptation-level theory to transposition responses in a conditional discrimination. *Psychonomic Science,* 1968, **10**, 147–148.

Durlach, N. I., & Braida, L. D. Intensity perception. I. Preliminary theory of intensity resolution. *Journal of the Acoustical Society of America,* 1969, **46**, 372–383.

Furth, H. G. The effect of the size–weight illusion on adaptation level. *Journal of Experimental Psychology,* 1960, **60**, 150–154.

Helson, H. Adaptation-level as frame of reference for prediction of psychophysical data. *American Journal of Psychology,* 1947, **60**, 1–29.

Helson, H. Adaptation-level as a basis for a quantitative theory of frames of reference. *Psychological Review,* 1948, **55**, 297–313.

Helson, H. Studies of anomalous contrast and assimilation. *Journal of the Optical Society of America,* 1963, **53**, 179–184.

Helson, H. *Adaptation-level theory: An experimental and systematic approach to behavior.* New York: Harper, 1964.

Helson, H., & Joy, V. L. Domains of lightness assimilation and contrast. *Psychologische Beiträge,* 1962, **6**, 405–415.

Helson, H., & Kozaki, A. Anchor effects using numerical estimates of simple dot patterns. *Perception and Psychophysics,* 1968, **4**, 163–164.

Helson, H., & Kozaki, T. Effects of duration of series and anchor-stimuli on judgments of perceived size. *American Journal of Psychology,* 1968, **81**, 291–302.

Helson, H., & Masters, H. G. A study of inflection-points in the locus of adaptation levels as a function of anchor stimuli. *American Journal of Psychology,* 1966, **79**, 400–408

Helson, H., & Nash, M. C. Anchor, contrast, and paradoxical distance effects. *Journal of Experimental Psychology,* 1960, **59**, 113–121.

Helson, H., & Rohles, F. H., Jr. A quantitative study of reversal of classical lightness-contrast. *American Journal of Psychology,* 1959, **72**, 530–538.

Helson, H., Bevan, W., & Masters, H. G. A quantitative study of relevance in the formation of adaptation levels. *Perceptual and Motor Skills,* 1966, **22**, 743–749.

Krech, D., Crutchfield, R. S., & Levison, N. *Elements of psychology.* New York: Knopf, 1969.

McClelland, D. C., Atkinson, J. W., Clark, R. A., & Lowell, E. L. *The achievement motive.* New York: Appleton, 1953.

MacKay, D. M. *Information, mechanism and meaning.* Cambridge, Massachusetts: MIT Press, 1969.

Marimont, R. B. Model for visual response to contrast. *Journal of the Optical Society of America,* 1962, **52**, 800–806.

Restle, F. Moon illusion explained on the basis of relative size. *Science,* 1970, **167**, 1092–1096.

Restle, F., & Merryman, C. T. An adaptation-level theory account of a relative-size illusion. *Psychonomic Science,* 1968, **12**, 229–230.

Sarris, V. Adaptation-level theory: Two critical experiments on Helson's weighted-average model. *American Journal of Psychology,* 1967, **80**, 331–344.

Steger, J. A. Visual lightness assimilation and contrast as a function of differential stimulation. *American Journal of Psychology,* 1969, **82**, 56–72.

Stevens, S. S. Adaptation-level vs. the relativity of judgment. *American Journal of Psychology,* 1958, **71**, 633–646.

Psychophysics and Scaling

INTRODUCTION

Lloyd L. Avant

There have been, since Fechner's law and his classical methods (see, for example, Boring, 1929, 1942), four major developments in the field of psychophysics: Thurstone's law of comparative judgment (1927); Stevens' power law (e.g., 1961); Swets, Tanner, and Birdsall's theory of signal detection (e.g., 1961); and Helson's adaptation-level theory (1964).

In Fechner's classical psychophysics, sensory phenomena directly depended upon the neurophysiology of peripheral sense organs, and no emphasis was given to events occurring in the central nervous system. Each perceived dimension had its origin at an absolute threshold, and, as Weber had pointed out, detection of change along a stimulus dimension depended upon the ratios between stimulus magnitudes rather than their absolute values. The universal law describing the psychophysical relationship between each stimulus magnitude and its directly associated response was that perceived intensity is determined by the product of some constant of proportionality and the logarithm of stimulus magnitude. The stimulus unit was the differential threshold value. Stevens, the modern representative of traditional psychophysics, claims the just noticeable difference (JND) to be a measure of variability or error which varies, as a constant proportion, with stimulus magnitude. Thus, Stevens argues that while Fechner was correct in expressing minimal stimulus change as a constant proportion of the reference intensity, it would have been more appropriate for him to assume the corresponding sensory change to be a constant proportion rather than a constant magnitude. To replace Fechner's law, Stevens proposed his power law—that perceived magnitude is a power function of stimulus magnitude. Instead of constructing inferred scales by summating JNDs, Stevens asks subjects for responses expressing the ratios between stimulus magnitudes and fits power functions to the resulting data.

Thurstone recognized that any response is determined by a complex of factors, and did not assume one inevitable response for every occasion of a given

19

stimulus. Rather, with the assumption of an essentially random operation of the "extraneous" variables which add their influence to that of the focal stimulus in determining responses, one may expect a Gaussian distribution of experienced intensities for a given stimulus. Thurstone termed this response distribution a discriminal dispersion, and its modal value was taken as the best indicant of the organism's experience of that stimulus. Taking as the scale unit a measure of the subjective dispersion for one member of a stimulus series, the response scale may be constructed using the method of paired comparisons which provides the proportion of choices given each stimulus over every other one. This is accomplished using the law of comparative judgment, which makes the perceived difference between any two stimuli a function of a standard measure of separation corresponding to the proportion of times one stimulus is judged greater than or less than the other, the discriminal dispersion for each stimulus, and the correlation between scale values of the responses to each stimulus. These procedures have no commitment to receptor organ neurophysiology or to univariate stimulus dimensions; such complex phenomena as attitudes may be scaled as readily as are sensory dimensions like loudness or brightness.

Ten years before the publication of Helson's landmark book (1964), Guilford (1954, p. 302) recommended AL theory as coming closest to providing a general explanatory basis for phenomena of psychophysical judgment. Helson (1964, p. 125ff) and Bevan (1965) have cogently delineated the differences in conceptual orientation which contrast the frame-of-reference approach taken by Helson to the traditional psychophysics of either Fechner or Stevens. Helson maintains that response to any stimulus depends upon its ordering within the class to which it belongs and the organism's state of adaptation to the class as a whole. It is recognized that the properties of the spatial and temporal context within which a stimulus occurs, as well as the central residue of experience, influence the behavioral effectiveness of a focal stimulus, and these influences are weighted accordingly.

In this approach, no universal psychophysical law is proposed, and accurate prediction of response from a knowledge of stimulus magnitudes alone is expected only under the rare circumstance where contextual and residual variables have zero weight in determining responsivity. Differences in the shapes of psychophysical functions are expected to accompany differences in the psychophysical methods employed and the structure of the numerical series in terms of which the data are presented. Most psychological dimensions are regarded as bipolar, varying from one quality to its complement through a transition point of neutral quality. This neutral point marks the organism's momentary and shifting state of adaptation to all relevant inputs, and it, rather than an absolute threshold value, is the appropriate referent from which to measure psychological magnitudes. In this way, a rational basis for the relativity of psychophysical judgments can be given.

As is to be expected in a discussion of frame-of-reference psychophysics, varying mathematical expressions of AL theory's working tenets bring a number of theoretical issues into focus. Those for which the theory has not yet provided solutions are as important as the issues which document its successes in indicating the potential of AL theory as a general theory of behavior. Development of this potential will depend, to a significant degree, upon the solutions offered by its proponents for the considerable range of problems addressed in the articles presented here.

Corso makes clear, in the first article of this section, the necessity for consistency between theoretical tenets and their quantitative expression. He directs our attention to the evidence that is not consistent with Helson's original definition of AL in terms of the weighted geometric mean. As Corso notes, some psychologists have found logical difficulties associated with the choice between a multiplicative and an additive correction factor in accommodating differences between perceptual dimensions and differences between experimental methodologies. Incorporating inflection points in curves reflecting anchor effectiveness under Helson's original formulation for a relationship of monotonic curvature has presented similar difficulties. It is not entirely clear whether the issues pointed out by Corso are critical to the weighted geometric mean formulation or, instead, to functions embodying AL as a parameter (such as Michels and Helson's reformulated Fechner law), which express the relation between stimuli and responses. The seriousness of the challenge for development of the theory presented by these issues should not be minimized, and Corso is correct in asserting that the quantitative virtue of AL theory depends upon the resolution of these issues.

However, as Helson, Corso, Restle, and Swets all point out, appraisal of the theory must include considerations in addition to the specifics of its mathematical expression. Both Corso and Restle recommend the general conceptual approach of AL, and while Corso criticizes the classical expressions of the theory, Restle shows, in his contribution to this section, that mathematical expressions modified from the original are satisfactory in the case of his data.

Gilinsky's use, in her contribution to this section, of AL as a quantitative index of the moon illusion also illustrates its usefulness in varying mathematical formulas. Helson (Section I) paid attention to the conceptual advances provided in Restle's treatment of size-contrast illusions and the incorporation of AL concepts in the quantitative theory of signal detectability. The point is, of course, that AL and its related functions can be given different mathematical expressions.

During the general discussion of Corso's article, Helson noted that he has not used the weighted geometric mean formula for *prediction* over the past 23 years. He observed further that no psychophysical theory has been called upon to predict psychophysical values—that Urban's method does not predict a threshold and that Stevens does not predict exponents in his power law in advance of experimentation. So, too, the weighted log mean definition has not been used except in determining the contributions of various sources of variance in a given situation *after* having determined the value of AL experimentally or by curve fitting. In his study with Masters on inflection points in anchor functions, Helson made the point that weighting coefficients were not constant. The curvilinear function that Sarris has since confirmed was observed in that study. Helson did not fit a cubic to the data of that study and give an equation for the variation in the weighting coefficients in order to avoid perpetuating the notion that one can give an equation that will hold for all situations in advance of experimentation. For this reason, Helson does not take exponents in Stevens' power law very seriously either, since it has been found that in magnitude estimation, exponents in the power law are not always the same with a given kind of material. In a summary observation, Helson expressed the belief that we do not yet have the deductive powers in psychology to derive a theory with such predictive power.

Hebert, in commenting on Swets' discussion of the equation of AL and the criterion of signal-detection theory, points out differences in orienting attitudes characteristic of the two approaches in directing research. He notes that the detection model incorporates the notion of an ideal observer relative to which the performance of actual observers is measured, while AL treats deviation from hypothesized functions as errors in measurement. Hebert suggests that the AL prediction be considered as the ideal and that one could then proceed to investigate the determinants of deviations. It seems appropriate to consider this suggestion in light of the above discussion of mathematical expressions of AL. Hebert further suggests that, as in detection theory, we investigate the possibility of shifting ALs by manipulating the costs associated with hits and false alarms, since detection criteria clearly reflect such costs. In response, Swets suggests that if the AL concept is extended from basic perceptual functions to such complex judgments as the acceptability of various good and bad acts (as in Bishop's study, referred to by Helson) we may find that AL has less lability than the criterion of detection theory.

Restle's discussion of size-contrast illusions and Gilinsky's account of the moon illusion give us a number of puzzles to work on. Restle works with the notion of different ALs for different portions of the visual field and has consistently found contrast effects of field elements upon judgments of line lengths placed in the field. His stimulus configurations and experimental methods seem well chosen for the occurrence of contrast effects. Restle uses a single-stimulus method and asks his observers for categorical responses; Swets claims that such methods permit one to see more clearly the operation of internal standards. However, we may recall Helson's statement (Section I) that AL theory can also account for assimilation effects. In her contribution Gilinsky points out the importance of assimilation as the complement of contrast.

It is also interesting to note that, although Restle employs a single-stimulus method in his studies, his test of an AL prediction versus the prediction dictated by the contour-repulsion notion depends upon a hypothesized comparative judgment of line lengths. As Restle notes, the Müller–Lyer illusion remains a puzzle for him (as it does for me). In studies discussed later in this volume, in my article with Bevan, I have asked observers for a comparative judgment of two configurations, each containing two straight lines parallel to a Müller–Lyer figure, and I have found what I interpreted to be an assimilation effect of the parallel lines upon the perceived length of the Müller–Lyer figures. Restle's work raises the question of whether the comparative judgments from my subjects directly index an AL for each configuration or, instead, reflect judgments of each configuration relative to a single internal norm. This latter possibility makes particularly meaningful Restle's questions about how individual psychophysical stimuli are processed in memory.

In her account of the moon illusion, Gilinsky incorporates the retinal and kinesthetic effects of eye position and perceived distance and presents a model to explain how adaptation to prevailing spatial frameworks varies and prompts the moon illusion. The general discussion that followed the presentations of Restle's and Gilinsky's papers at the symposium centered largely around the differences between the data from Rock and Kaufman, which Restle later emphasizes in his account of the moon illusion, and those from Holway and Boring, which Gilinsky considers crucial. Gilinsky argues that the Rock and Kaufman data show the importance of assimilation of the size of the moon's retinal image to that of large structures, like the Washington Monument. Such objects between the observer and the horizon moon result in an assimilation of the apparent distance of the moon to the perceived distance of the large nearby structure. Restle responds that, given as many conceptual tools as Gilinsky's hypotheses of many different distances, many different memories and apparent distances, a moon in front of a sky that is compared with a memory image, as well as assimilation and contrast, a perfect explanation of the moon illusion is to be expected!

Corso and Flock also respond to Gilinsky's notion of a memory moon which defines AL. Corso questions whether the influence of factors that are residues of experience and not components of a current stimulus complex do, in fact, affect anything physiologically. Gilinsky has assumed, at a basic level, a very general framework for spatial adaptation, and, in addition, specific adaptations for particular objects and the particular distances at which the objects are normally seen, both of which must be physiologically effective. According to Corso, such an image or memory may, if it is there, simply influence the observer's module for judgment.

Flock considers the problem that Restle raises having to do with possible physiological registration of empty space in his stimuli (since the extent of the gap is specified by material surfaces) as different from the physiological questions in Gilinsky's spatial adaptations. While he recognizes the importance of perceived distance in the moon illusion, Flock notes that Gilinsky's support for her notion of the normal viewing distance comes largely from Holway and Boring's data. Since the observers in that study had visual abnormalities, suggesting that the data do not reflect normal visual perception, he recommends that the study be replicated. Restle suggests that since there have been relatively few experiments on the moon illusion, and since all these may be seriously questioned, any serious argument about the moon illusion should be postponed until enough well-controlled laboratory experiments have been performed to permit tests of all the principles that both he and Gilinsky consider important.

To complement AL theory, Dinnerstein proposes her concept of multiple structures in interaction. The proposal argues that experience is intrinsically organized, and it presents an approach designed to determine the organizational factors that have a common function in structuring, within their interactions, temporally and/or spatially dispersed stimulus sequences. As Dinnerstein notes, clarification of the ways in which her approach complements the AL approach is needed. In commenting on her contribution, Well suggests that the point of most direct contact between the two approaches is the complex issue that AL theorists have referred to as the problem of relevance. Helson observed earlier (Section I) that the problem of relevance concerns the formation of classes and, in the general discussion following the presentation of Dinnerstein's paper at the symposium, Restle noted the similarity between Dinnerstein's approach and the AL approach taken by Bevan and his co-workers in seeking a quantitative account of the conditions that influence systems of intrasubjective norms. It is Dinnerstein's view that Bevan has typically worked with variables that can be measured along a single dimension and that his approach cannot handle what she terms the topological interactions between structures that her studies have demonstrated. However, we should note, among the findings of Helson, Bevan, and others, the evidence that functional grouping does not occur *only* when values are pooled along single stimulus dimensions. These investigators have also found integration of visual and auditory inputs to evolve a norm relative to which stimuli in both perceptual dimensions are judged. Similarly, structuring the "smallness" of a set of circles has been shown to be augmented by enclosing, within the circles, angles whose sizes correlated with circle sizes. Such findings appear to be consistent with Dinnerstein's goal.

What is clear from the contributions to this section is the commonness of the organismic processes underlying such diverse behaviors as psychophysical judgment, perception, memory, and cognition. While AL theory has made significant contributions to our understanding of such behaviors, a great deal of research remains to be done before the theory's full potential is realized.

REFERENCES

Bevan, W. An introduction to psychophysics. *Transactions of the Kansas Academy of Science,* 1965, **68,** 1–12.

Boring, E. G. *A history of experimental psychology.* New York: Appleton (Century), 1929.

Boring, E. G. *Sensation and perception in the history of experimental psychology.* New York: Appleton, 1942.

Guilford, J. P. *Psychometric methods.* New York: McGraw-Hill, 1954.

Helson, H. *Adaptation-level theory: An experimental and systematic approach to behavior.* New York: Harper, 1964.

Stevens, S. S. The psychophysics of sensory function. In W. A. Rosenblith (Ed.), *Sensory communication.* New York: Wiley, 1961. Pp. 1–33.

Swets, J. A., Tanner, W. P., Jr., & Birdsall, T. G. Decision processes in perception. *Psychological Review,* 1961, **68,** 301–340.

Thurstone, L. L. A law of comparative judgment. *Psychological Review,* 1927, **34,** 273–286.

ADAPTATION-LEVEL THEORY
AND PSYCHOPHYSICAL SCALING[1]

John F. Corso

INTRODUCTION

In 1938, Helson introduced the concept of adaptation level (AL) to explain the phenomena of constancy, contrast, and color conversion in the field of vision (Helson, 1938). Later, the AL concept was extended as a frame of reference for the prediction of psychophysical data in other areas of psychology (Helson, 1947). Since that time, Helson and his co-workers have performed and reported numerous studies designed to investigate the various factors that affect AL and its related functions. The comprehensive theory and supporting data were published in 1964 in a landmark book in the history of psychology: *Adaptation-level theory: An experimental and systematic approach to behavior* (Helson, 1964; see Corso, 1964). The book provides an extended treatment of AL theory as it applies quantitatively to the area of psychophysics, including both psychophysical judgments and psychophysical scaling.

In this contribution, I propose to note the current status of AL theory in psychophysics, to appraise the adequacy of its quantitative formulation, and to present some views related to the general issue of psychophysical scaling.

QUANTITATIVE DEFINITION OF ADAPTATION LEVEL

Adaptation-level theory is a quantitative extension of the classical notion of perceptual relativity which recognizes a general factor (AL) encompassing the various components in the immediate stimulus configuration, the context, previous experience, etc. The level of adaptation is defined operationally for two different judgmental situations: (*a*) In the absolute method or method of single stimuli, no standard is present and AL is defined as the physical value of the stimulus which is judged to be neutral or in the middle scale category. (*b*) In the

[1] This investigation was supported in part by a Special Research Fellowship (HD 44276) (1969–1970) from the National Institute of Child Health and Human Development, Department of Health, Education, and Welfare, U.S. Public Health Service.

comparative or relative method of judgment, a standard is presented and the comparative AL (CAL) is defined as the weighted *geometric* mean of the series AL (SAL) and the standard (*S*). Thus the theory asserts that AL will be equal to the weighted *geometric* mean of all stimuli affecting the particular judgment (Helson, 1964).

Stated more precisely, the basic equation for AL theory has the following general form:

$$A = K(\bar{S}^p B^q R^r) \tag{1}$$

or

$$\log A = \log K + (p \log \bar{S} + q \log B + r \log R), \tag{2}$$

where A is the predicted value of AL, K is an empirical constant, $\bar{S}$ is the geometric mean of the series stimuli, B is the background (standard or anchor) stimulus, R refers to residual stimuli, and p, q, and r are constant weighting coefficients (empirically determined) whose numerical sum is taken to be 1.0 (Helson, 1964, pp. 58–59).

The fundamental question one may raise concerns the adequacy of the choice of the weighted logarithmic mean in the general measurement model. The

TABLE I

Theoretical and Experimental Values of Adaptation Level for Rectangular, Skew, I-Shaped, J-Shaped, and Approximately Normal Distributions[a]

Series[b] (gm.)	Theoretical AL	Experimental limen	Error (%)
20, 25, 30, . . ., 55	31.9	29.7	+7
60, 65, 70, . . ., 100	74.7	76.3	−2
20, 25, 30, . . ., 100	50.5	48.1	+5
20, 30, 40, 50(3), 60(5)	39.2	41.2	−5
60, 70, 80, 90(3), 100(5)	80.5	75.4	+7
75(5), 80(3), 85(3), 90(2), 95, 100	78.8	77.4	+2
20(4), 25, 30, 35, 40(4)	25.0	26.8	−7
40(3), 45, 50, 55, 60, 65, 70(6)	53.0	58.3	−9
20, 30(3), 40(5), 50(3), 60	30.9	37.2	−17
40, 50(2), 60(4), 70(4), 80(2), 90	56.1	61.7	−9
Average			7.0

[a] From Johnson, D. M. Generalization of a scale of values by averaging of practice effects. *Journal of Experimental Psychology,* **34**, 1944, 425–436. Copyright 1944 by the American Psychological Association, and reproduced by permission.

[b] Numbers in parentheses following stimulus values indicate repetitions within series to give the desired distribution.

preponderance of data now indicates that Stevens' (1962) power law is more accurate than Fechner's law, even though some data (Johnson, 1944; Helson, 1964), indicate that Helson's (1938) original formulation provides an appropriate method for predicting AL (Table I). The power law implies that equal stimulus ratios correspond to equal sensation ratios, rather than equal sensation differences.

In a series of experiments, Parducci, Calfee, Marshall, and Davidson (1960) found that the mean was a good predictor of AL whenever its value was between the midpoint and median of a series of stimuli, but shifts in judgment were obtained with shifts in either the midpoint or the median of the series, even though the mean was held constant (Table II). In subsequent replications (Parducci & Marshall, 1961a, b) contradictory evidence was also obtained lending support to Stevens' (1958) position that sensory magnitudes are not logarithmically related to stimulus magnitudes following Fechner's law or its revision (Michels & Helson, 1949).

MODIFICATIONS OF THE BASIC ADAPTATION-LEVEL EQUATION AND THE ISSUE OF THE ADDITIVE CONSTANT

As indicated earlier, Helson (1947) found it necessary to modify his equation dealing with vision to account for lifted-weight data. His revised formula in logarithmic form and in Helson's notation (with changed symbols to apply more readily in terms of lifted weights) may be written

$$\log AL = \log K + \left[\frac{(k_1 \sum_1^n \log X_i/n) + k_2 \log C}{k_1 + k_2} \right], \tag{3}$$

where K is a constant, X_i refers to series stimuli, C is an anchor or comparison stimulus, and k_1 and k_2 are constants.

In order to fit lifted-weight data obtained with successive judgments by Eq. (3), Helson (1947) proceeded to weight the logarithmic mean of the series more than the comparison (standard) stimulus to account for time-order effects. For his particular data, the best value for weighting the stimulus series was found to be the same as that formerly used for the background in vision, i.e., the factor 3.

In addition, another change was required. The multiplicative constant K was replaced by an additive constant cd which was taken to be related to both the size of the step interval between series stimuli d and the order of presentation of the series stimuli V and standard (anchor) S. The time-order effects yield an empirical fractional constant c. For the order $S_1 V_2$, the best value of cd for a wide variety of data was found to be $.75d$ and, for $V_1 S_2$, the value was zero.

TABLE II

Stimulus Parameters and College Adaptation Levels[a]

Condition	N	Stimulus parameters				Adaptation levels			
		Mean	Midpoint	Median	Range	AL_p[b]	AL_o	SD	Error (%)[c]
Experiment I									
A	32	304	550	277	900	401	332	68	7.7
C	16	396	550	378	900	446	430	62	1.8
D	16	443	550	419	900	465	465	40	0
F	18	550	550	551	900	524	539	18	1.7
G	15	551	550	552	900	525	545	29	2.2
I	17	704	550	723	900	602	619	39	1.9
Experiment II									
NG	30	517	425	558	650	466	481	44	2.3
NA	30	551	425	593	650	482	494	70	1.8
GC	37	551	550	552	900	525	532	40	.8
PA	31	551	675	509	650	581	567	61	2.2
PG	28	497	675	433	650	546	553	68	1.1
PGE	30	513	675	451	650	554	536	81	2.8

Experiment III

M$_1$	33	449	550	450	900	479	494	51	1.7
M$_2$	34	444	550	350	900	434	437	91	.3
M$_3$	27	449	550	250	900	389	462	106	8.1
M$_4$	51	651	550	650	900	569	561	81	.9
M$_5$	46	654	550	750	900	614	610	92	.4
M$_6$	27	651	550	850	900	659	619	100	4.4
LL	20	500	550	500	900	501	494	38	.8
LH	21	500	550	600	900	546	548	57	.2
HL	21	600	550	500	900	501	487	44	1.6
HH	20	600	550	600	900	546	542	55	.4
PM	33	505	550	550	900	524	532	39	.9
QM	33	595	550	550	900	524	551	41	3.0
RM	33	433	550	550	900	524	527	38	.3

Experiment IV

N	30	425	425	423	650	405	419	24	2.2
P	30	674	675	677	650	656	650	55	.9
J	32	288	350	272	500	300	287	30	2.6
S	32	901	850	925	300	873	891	25	6.0

[a] From Parducci, A., Calfee, R. C., Marshall, L. M., and Davidson, L. P. Context effects in judgment: Adaptation level as a function of the mean, midpoint, and median of the stimuli. *Journal of Experimental Psychology*, **60**, 1960, 65–77. Copyright 1960 by the American Psychological Association, and reproduced by permission.

[b] Adaptation level predicted from the following regression equation: $AL_p = .547$ (midpoint) $+ .450$ (median) $- .027$ (range).

[c] Difference between obtained and predicted ALs divided by .01 (range).

Since logarithms are used, the so-called d factor is added to the left-hand side of Eq. 4, which, together with the series weighting factor, gives the following:

$$\log(AL + .75d) = \frac{(3.0\sum_1^n \log X_i/n) + \log C}{4} \qquad (4)$$

In a recent study, Sarris (1967a) tested the validity of Eq. (4) in two separate experiments. In one of these, the geometric mean of a series of weights was held equal to 291.4 gm., while the size of the step interval d was systematically varied. There were four series of weights, with the d values equal to 40, 70, 120, and 200 gm. over the four series. For the judgments, a "no-anchor" (absolute) method was used with 40 Ss randomized into four groups of 10 Ss each. Judgments were on a rating scale with nine qualitative categories.

The results of this experiment are shown in Fig. 1. Helson's predicted trend

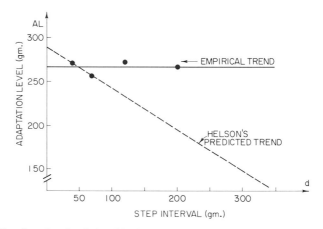

Fig. 1. The functional relationship between step interval and AL. (From Sarris, V. Adaptation-level theory: Two critical experiments on Helson's weighted-average model. *American Journal of Psychology,* **80,** 1967, 331–344. Copyright by the American Psychological Association, and reproduced by permission.)

($A = 291.4 - .75d$) is given in the dashed line; the empirical data are fitted from trend analysis by a horizontal line parallel to the abscissa. Thus, the size of the step interval does not appear to be an experimentally significant variable and the complex cd factor may be replaced, according to Sarris, by a simple empirical constant s which has no theoretical interpretation.

It should be pointed out that the introduction of the cd factor by Helson (1947, 1964) on empirical grounds (time-order error and size of step interval) has been viewed with concern by others. Johnson (1949) states that "the rationale for this constant is not quite clear to the present writer [p. 320]." Since there seems to be no significant time error in judgments of pitch, Johnson eliminates the constant with the result that Helson's basic fomula [1947, Eq. (3)] becomes identical to his own derived from a generalization theory of pitch. Parducci (1965), in reviewing Helson's (1964) book, noted that "for some data, he adds an arbitrary correction factor $(0.75d)$ which seems out of character with his theory of stimulus pooling [pp. 158–159]." Furth (1960) studied the size–weight illusion and found it necessary to use an additive factor of $.25d$ for the $S_1 V_2$ condition, but he provided no explanation for this departure from Helson's original value.

While Helson (1964) has developed a quantitative theory of time-order effects (TOE), which seems to justify an additive factor for the comparative method of determining AL, there appears to be a problem with this factor in the absolute method. In considering the data from an auditory experiment using the absolute method (Pratt, 1933), Helson (1964, pp. 151–152) was faced with the occurrence of a negative time error in judgments of loudness with one series of stimuli, and a positive time error with another series of stimuli. By using a modification of his general formula *with a correction factor* [Helson 1964, Eq. (4)], he was able to determine AL, which was found to be at a point intermediate between the two series. This was interpreted as demonstrating the effect of a remote frame of reference on judgments of loudness, with experience on one series of stimuli affecting judgments on the other.

This view, however, which apparently uses the additive factor to account for the effects of past experience, is not consistent with the position taken earlier as a justification for introducing the additive factor—that the cd factor relates to the size of the step interval and the order of presentation of stimulus materials, as in the comparative method. Furthermore, it does not seem appropriate that the size of the correction factor for lifted weights $(.75d)$ should be taken to be the same for both the absolute method and the comparative method. In the absolute method, the additive factor presumably may be included to account for residual or practice effects; in the comparative method, it must, in addition, reflect the effects which have been associated with traditional time order.

It is of interest to note that if the correction term cd is eliminated in the absolute method, the data obtained by Sarris (1967a) would be consistent with the revised prediction, that is, AL would be expected to remain constant with changes in the size of the step interval. However, the elimination of the correction factor, while apparently resolving one problem, would create another. For lifted-weight data in the comparative method, a correction factor is essential for accurately predicting AL. If the correction factor is introduced for this case, it must appear in the equation for the absolute method, since the latter is directly derived from the former. It may be concluded, therefore, that the matter of the additive factor requires further consideration, both in terms of its magnitude and the conditions under which it may be legitimately introduced in the calculation of AL.

The Problem of Adaptation-Level Inflection Points

Another issue must now be raised: this concerns the problem of inflection points in the locus of AL as a function of anchor stimuli. According to Eq. (1), inflection points are not mathematically predictable. However, a logical analysis of the experimental situation suggests that if there is no background or anchor stimulus, the background term B^q reduces to 1.0 (i.e., the stimulation of the background is zero and is weighted zero so that $0° = 1.0$). If there are no residual effects, AL is then determined entirely by the series stimuli. This means that AL will be higher with zero (no) anchor than with an anchor below the series stimuli. Consequently, anchors below series stimuli may be expected to depress AL up to a certain point beyond which AL must reverse and approach the series AL as the anchor approaches zero. The implication is that there is a critical value or region beyond which stimuli become too weak to change the AL. This deduction, however, does not follow mathematically from Eq. (1); nor is there mathematical justification for expecting an inflection point in the locus of AL with an increase in the intensity of anchors *above* series stimuli (Sarris, 1967b).

The data on this problem (Helson & Masters, 1966; Sarris, 1967a) indicate, nevertheless, that shifts in AL are obtained as a function of varying anchor size for lifted weights. The difference between the predicted trend in AL according to Helson's basic equation [Eq. (1)] and the empirical trend obtained by Sarris (1967a) (Fig. 2) is statistically significant, with two inflection points in the empirical curve. For a stimulus series of 200, 250, 300, 350, and 400 gm., the

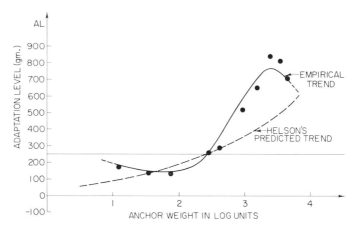

Fig. 2. Adaptation level as a function of the anchor stimulus. (From Sarris, V. Adaptation-level theory: Two critical experiments on Helson's weighted-average model. *American Journal of Psychology*, **80**, 1967, 331–344. Copyright by the American Psychological Association, and reproduced by permission.)

first inflection occurs at an anchor value of about 75 gm., where AL is lowest, and the second one occurs at an anchor value of about 2900 gm., where AL is highest. The data points do not follow the monotonic curvature mathematically implied in Helson's basic Eq. (1); but, beginning from both inflection points, the ALs seem to approach the control level (parallel to the abscissa at AL = 259.05) as the anchor assumes more extreme values. Thus, the contrast effect of an extreme-anchor relative to the stimulus series seems to disappear gradually. These data indicate that Helson's lifted-weight formula [Eq. (4)] is incorrect. The equation states that with a constant series and a variable anchor, the AL varies as the fourth root of anchor size; empirically, instead of being a monotonic function as prescribed by Eq. (4), the anchor AL function follows a cubic trend.

Since the pattern of the AL curve (Fig. 2) obtained by Sarris (1967a) closely resembles that of Helson and Masters (1966) for a slightly lighter stimulus series, the existence of inflection points in the locus of AL as a function of anchor stimuli appears to be a real phenomenon. This poses another difficulty in the basic equation [Eq. (1)]. Specifically, this indicates that the weighting coefficients for series, anchor, and residual stimuli are variable in character.

Sarris (1967a) notes that the weighting coefficient for the series stimuli varies with the size of the anchor, rather than having a constant value of 3.0 as given in Eq. (4). Sarris derived an asymmetric parabolic type of relationship between the weighting factor and the logarithm of the anchor stimulus to fit his lifted weight data (Fig. 3). When the weighting factor is taken into account, the empirical ALs

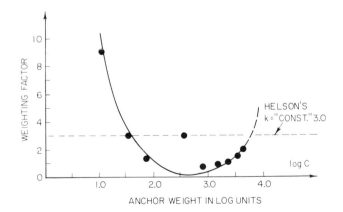

Fig. 3. The weighting factor k as a function of the anchor stimulus. (From Sarris, V. Adaptation-level theory: Two critical experiments on Helson's weighted-average model. *American Journal of Psychology,* **80,** 1967, 331–344. Copyright by the American Psychological Association, and reproduced by permission.)

become predictable (cubic curve, Fig. 2). The revision of Helson's formula for lifted weights is given in general terms by Sarris (1967a) as

$$\log(A + s) = \frac{v \log S + \log C}{v + 1},$$ (5)

where $v = f(C)$, A is AL, s is a simple empirical constant replacing the cd factor, v is a variable weighting factor, S is the geometric mean of the series stimuli, and C is the anchor stimulus. The advantages of this formulation are that (a) it takes into account the empirical findings on anchor effect; (b) it links mathematically the equations for the absolute and comparative methods of judgment; and (c) it permits a theoretical interpretation of experimentally established inflection points.

HYSTERESIS AND ADAPTATION LEVEL

This section considers the phenomenon Stevens (1957) labeled hysteresis, which is not as yet completely explained in terms of psychophysical theory. The phenomenon is found most clearly in psychophysical bisection or equipartition experiments. Given a certain range on a stimulus continuum, an S who is instructed to partition this range into equal-appearing intervals will position the variable stimuli at different locations depending upon whether the stimuli are presented in ascending or in descending order. Thus, in a bisection experiment, the midpoint will be set higher if the stimuli are presented in ascending order—lower stimulus (fixed), variable stimulus, higher stimulus (fixed)—than if the order is reversed.

Stevens (1957) has suggested that hysteresis may occur on all continua of the prothetic (intensive) class, but that it probably does not occur on metathetic (qualitative) continua. The effect has been demonstrated for brightness, loudness, and heaviness (intensive continua) (Fig. 4); there is some doubt about pitch (qualitative continuum). It may be noted in Fig. 4 that for each dimension, the ascending curve is different from the descending curve and that the midpoint of the psychological scale (50) is higher for the ascending order of presentation than for the descending order.

Stevens (1957) indicated that whenever a subject tries to equalize intervals, whether in bisection or in category rating scales, the midpoint is in error in the same direction—the point of bisection falls consistently below the point predicted by the ratio scale of subjective magnitude. In addition, a category rating scale for a prothetic continuum (obtained when a subject judges a set of stimuli in terms of a set of categories, labeled either by numbers or by adjectives) will show a shape that is concave downward when plotted against a ratio scale of subjective magnitude for the same dimension. The explanation for this nonlinearity is held to lie in the subject's sensitivity to differences (Stevens, 1957):

> Near the lower end of the scale where discrimination is good the categories tend to be narrow, and by consequence the slope of the function is steep. Near the upper end, where a given stimulus difference is less easy to detect, the categories broaden and the slope declines [p. 155].*

However, the data of Bevan, Barker, and Pritchard (1963) show that hysteresis and bowing of category scales may, at least in part, be accounted for within the framework of AL theory. In one of a series of experiments, seven weights (150–300 gm. in 25-gm. steps) were used under four conditions: (*a*)

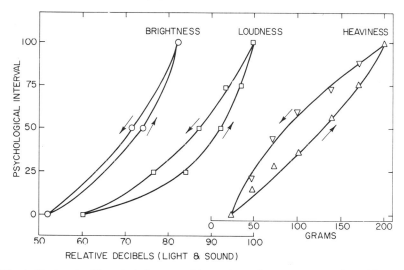

Fig. 4. Hysteresis effects in judgments of intervals on three sensory continua. The arrows indicate the order of stimulus presentation. (From Stevens, S. S. Hysteresis effects in judgments of intervals on three sensory continua. *Psychological Review,* **64,** 1957, 153–181. Copyright 1957 by the American Psychological Association, and reproduced by permission.)

light-to-heavy weights; left-to-right spatial order (L–H; L–R); (*b*) heavy-to-light weights; right-to-left spatial order (H–L; R–L); (*c*) heavy-to-light weights; left-to-right spatial order (H–L; L–R); and (*d*) light-to-heavy weights; right-to-left spatial order (L–H; R–L).

Judgments were obtained by the Newhall ratio method of scaling. For the ascending intensive order of presentation (L–H), the position of the first weight

*From Stevens, S. S. On the psychophysical law. *Psychological Review,* **64,** 1957, 153–181. Copyright by the American Psychological Association, and reproduced by permission.

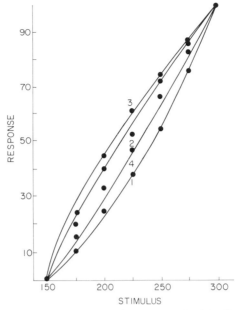

Fig. 5. Functions for the four conditions of experiment II: 1 (L–H, L–R), 2 (H–L, R–L), 3 (H–L, L–R), 4 (L–H, R–L) (from Bevan *et al.,* 1963).

was set at zero; for the descending order (H–L), it was set at 100. The results for forty *S*s (10 per group) are shown in Fig. 5. It would appear, from the curves in Fig. 5, that it is the direction of intensive change in the presentation of successive stimuli that gives rise to hysteresis. Stevens' (1957) argument that bowing of category scales is due to poorer discrimination at the upper end of the scale cannot account for these results, since it applies only for downward bowing curves.

The explanation for hysteresis offered by Bevan *et al.* (1963, p. 103) is that the "lagging behind" implied by the term hysteresis relates to AL. When the effective stimulus was taken as the difference between the variables being judged and the AL [calculated from Eq. (4) as a weighted mean of the preceding stimuli, with the immediately preceding stimulus designated as the standard], the predicted values yielded upward-bowed curves for ascending order and downward-bowed curves for descending orders. The curves for predicted and obtained values (Fig. 6) compare favorably in shape, although the slopes differ somewhat. Agreement is best near the upper end of the stimulus continuum. The average difference for all points is approximately 4%. It appears, therefore, that AL theory can account fairly well for hysteresis, despite the simplifying assumptions made by Bevan *et al.* (1963), which ignore residual effects and the recency of stimulus inputs. Furthermore, the data from additional experiments

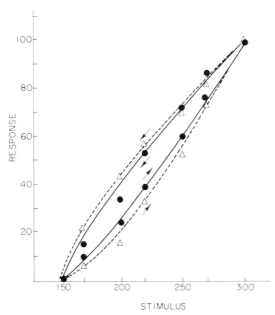

STIMULUS

Fig. 6. Data of the ascending and descending orders of experiment I are compared with corresponding functions generated from the assumption that the judged difference between stimuli of successive pairs reflects a difference between a shifting AL and the process representing the variable stimulus (second member of each pair). The solid lines indicate the empirical values; the dotted lines indicate the predicted values (from Bevan *et al.,* 1963).

in this series indicate that bowing of category scales may be related "not to ascending or descending series, but to whether or not the greater stimulus magnitude precedes or follows the lesser magnitude on individual trials (Bevan *et al.,* 1963, p. 111)." When the effects of ascending and descending series are counterbalanced by having *S* judge stimulus differences for random sequences of adjacent stimulus pairs, the bowing of the category scale is eliminated. Bowing and hysteresis, therefore, cannot be ascribed to differences in discriminability for different parts of the stimulus continuum.

In general, when the category scale is compared with other psychophysical scales, it tends to lie intermediate between a logarithmic function and a power function (Stevens, 1957), at least for prothetic continua. The category scale may, under certain circumstances, approach the logarithmic form, but ordinarily the curvature of the category scale is less than logarithmic and, therefore, does not confirm the basic assumption made by AL theory concerning Fechner's law. Nevertheless, it has been argued by Eisler (1963) that the category scale is a real Fechnerian discrimination and the deviation from the logarithmic function is caused by a corresponding deviation of the Weber function from Weber's law.

While the weight of experimental evidence for intensive continua strongly favors the power law over the logarithmic law, the issue of the psychophysical function should not be considered closed. Ross and DiLollo (1968), working with magnitude estimates of lifted weights, obtained results which failed to follow power functions and proposed a vector model based upon "assumptions about the collection of values acting as determinants of judgment of weight and the manner in which they are combined [p. 1]." The model is similar in some respects to the notion of AL, but it does not involve the assumption of an anchor or implicit reference value. A summary of the experimental evidence on the "power versus logarithmic" issue has recently been provided by Zinnes (1969).

ADAPTATION LEVEL, HYSTERESIS, AND THE PSYCHOPHYSICAL LAW

Consideration of the problem of hysteresis leads into a more fundamental matter: the psychophysical law. The psychophysical power law for intensive continua, proposed by Stevens (1957) and modified by Ekman (1958) and Luce (1959) to include an additive constant, may be written as follows (Stevens, 1961):

$$\psi = k(\phi - \phi_0)^n, \tag{6}$$

where ψ is psychological magnitude, ϕ is stimulus intensity, k is a constant scale factor depending on the choice of physical units, n is a characteristic parameter for a particular stimulus continuum, and ϕ_0 is a constant value corresponding to the "effective threshold" [p. 26]. For ranges of stimuli well above the absolute threshold, the value of ϕ_0 is usually negligible and may be omitted; however, when the scale are extended toward threshold values, the value of ϕ_0 becomes increasingly important. I have elsewhere (Corso, 1963) reviewed the historical roots of the problem and raised the question of the beginning point of sensation.

Recent findings by Eisler (1963) on the relation between magnitude and category scales have provided a model for investigating hysteresis which involves the "effective threshold" concept. According to this model, the relationship between the category rating scale K and the magnitude estimation scale ψ may be expressed as

$$K = \alpha \log(\psi - \psi_0) + \beta. \tag{7}$$

The parameter ψ_0 is the ψ intercept $(-q/k)$ of the straight line

$$\sigma = k\psi + q, \tag{8}$$

where σ is the intraindividual standard deviation of ψ. With this formulation, the hysteresis effect is predicted by different ψ intercepts $(-q/k)$ for ascending and descending series.[2]

Eisler and Ottander (1963) obtained data on subjective velocity for a luminous spot moving in a circular path by magnitude estimation and category rating (Fig. 7) that indicate the presence of hysteresis.

Since the magnitude scales (Fig. 8) for the ascending and descending series were not identical, different values were required for the "effective threshold" correction (ϕ_0) to provide a good fit to the psychophysical power law. The difference between their slopes is less than 2%, which indicates that ϕ_0 accounts completely for the difference in the subjective range that produces hysteresis.

When Eq. (7) was solved using a category scale value of "2" as the midpoint and appropriate values of α, β, and ψ_0, predicted midpoints of the ψ scale of 10.57 for ascending series and 9.57 for descending series were obtained (Fig. 9). This indicates that the hysteresis effect can be predicted from magnitude scales. Eisler and Ottander (1963) conclude that the hysteresis effect "is mostly, if not solely, due to the different 'subjective zeros' ϕ_0 in the psychophysical power function $\psi = k(\phi - \phi_0)^n$ for ascending and descending series ... Precise knowledge of the zero point would prevent hysteresis [p. 535]." Thus, ϕ_0 may well correspond to AL, but it "has not much to do with the absolute threshold ... [p. 536]."

However, Adair, Stevens, and Marks (1968) maintain that "the values of ϕ_0 computed for the numerical estimates of pain in ... four experiments are commensurate with the absolute thresholds for pain measured by various investigators using more traditional psychophysical procedures [p. 164]." Ekman and Gustafsson (1968) found that for brightness discrimination, ϕ_0 obtained from a fitted power function is remarkably close to the detection threshold for two different levels of light adaptation. Keidel and Spreng (1965), recording extracranial-evoked cortical responses to sinusoidal tones, obtained intensive power functions which yielded a fairly precise estimate of the absolute threshold curve in man. These data raise a serious question about the adequacy of the Eisler–Ottander hypothesis that ϕ_0 is unrelated to the absolute threshold.

A striking example of the need to apply the correction factor ϕ_0 was reported by Stevens and Stevens (1960) for magnitude scales of apparent warmth and apparent cold. The geometric mean of the magnitude estimates for apparent warmth are shown (Fig. 10) in log–log coordinates as a function of (a) absolute temperature in degrees Kelvin and (b) difference (in degrees Celsius) between the temperature of the stimulus and the temperature of thermal neutrality (i.e.,

---

[2] Marks (1968) has recently proposed a function in which the category scale C is a power function of stimulus intensity,

$$C + C' = k\phi^n,$$

where C' is an arbitrary constant, the value of which must be estimated.

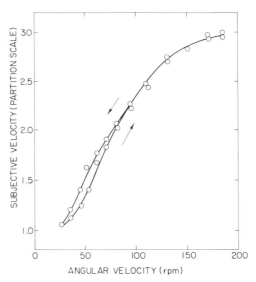

Fig. 7. Partition scale of subjective velocity as a function of angular velocity (in revolutions per minute) displaying hysteresis. (From Eisler, H., and Ottander, C. On the problem of hysteresis in psychophysics. *Journal of Experimental Psychology,* **65,** 1963, 530–536. Copyright 1963 by the American Psychological Association, and reproduced by permission.)

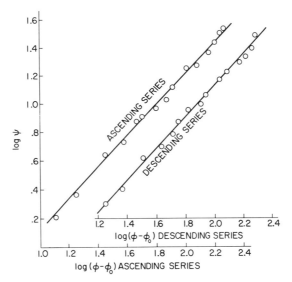

Fig. 8. Log magnitude estimations of subjective velocity as a function of the log of the difference in angular velocity (rpm) between the stimulus and the "subjective zero" (7.4 rpm for the ascending and 2.0 rpm for the descending series). The straight lines are fitted by the method of least squares. (From Eisler, H., and Ottander, C. On the problem of hysteresis in psychophysics. *Journal of Experimental Psychology,* **65,** 1963, 530–536. Copyright 1963 by the American Psychological Association, and reproduced by permission.)

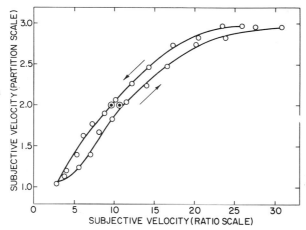

Fig. 9. Partition scale of subjective velocity as a function of the corresponding magnitude scale. The arrows indicate the order in which the stimuli were presented. The encircled dots are predicted bisection points. (From Eisler, H., and Ottander, C. On the problem of hysteresis in psychophysics. *Journal of Experimental Psychology,* **65,** 1963, 530–536. Copyright 1963 by the American Psychological Association, and reproduced by permission.)

physiological zero at approximately 32.5°C or 90.5°F). The magnitude scale is a power function (linear in log–log coordinates) only when the scale has its origin at the neutral point (32.5°C or 305.7°K). In a similar plot for the magnitude scale of apparent cold (Fig. 11), the correction for ϕ_0 is 304.2°K.

Luce (1959) has shown mathematically that apparent departures from the power law may be eliminated by subtracting a value equal to the "effective threshold" from each stimulus so as to bring the zeroes of the physical and psychological scales into coincidence. Stevens and Stevens (1960) emphasize empirically that "the large size of the threshold correction involved in the magnitude functions for warmth and cold makes especially impressive the necessity for measuring the stimulus in terms of its distance from the threshold value [p. 191]." The question, however, as raised earlier by Corso (1963), relates to the operational definition of the term "threshold."

Stevens (1961) has explicitly stated that

> ... it should probably be thought of as the "effective" threshold that obtains at the time and under the conditions of the experiment in which the magnitude scale is determined ... it becomes expedient to take as the value of ϕ_0 the constant value whose subtraction from the stimulus values succeeds in rectifying the log–log plot of the magnitude function [p. 26].

In addition to this view of ϕ_0, Stevens (1962) believes that the exponent of the power law "varies with the modality and also with such parameters as adaptation and contrast [p. 30]." These considerations and the data from

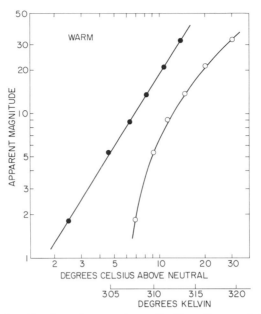

Fig. 10. Magnitude estimation of apparent warmth. (From Stevens, J. C., and Stevens, S. S. Warmth and cold: Dynamics of sensory intensity. *Journal of Experimental Psychology,* **60,** 1960, 183–192. Copyright by the American Psychological Association, and reproduced by permission.)

numerous experiments (for example, Canter & Hirsch, 1955; Michels & Doser, 1955; Helson, 1947) suggest that the "effective threshold" (ϕ_0 in terms of stimulus units) corresponds to AL. Specifying an empirically derived value of ϕ_0 permits a more valid test of the power law for intensive continua (Corso, 1963).

Irwin and Corballis (1968) recently demonstrated that a threshold parameter (ψ_0, the value of the intercept of the linear function obtained when magnitude estimates are plotted against stimulus magnitudes in log–log coordinates) can be introduced to yield a magnitude scale for softness reciprocal to the magnitude scale for loudness. To achieve the reciprocal relationship, ψ_0 was subtracted from the power function expressed in physical terms. This implies that S places the zero of his scale too high and the translation moves the scale so as to place its origin at the "true" absolute threshold. In this view, the elevated threshold may be considered to represent the AL, with the correction term applied directly in psychological rather than physical units.

When AL is introduced specifically into the power law (Helson, 1964), ϕ_0 and k may be eliminated, and the general psychophysical function becomes

$$\psi = A\phi^n \tag{9}$$

or

$$\log \psi = n \log \phi + \log A, \tag{10}$$

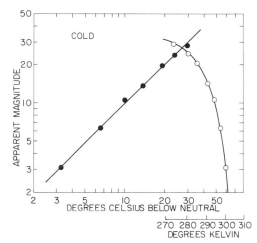

Fig. 11. Magnitude estimation of apparent cold. (From Stevens, J. C., and Stevens, S. S. Warmth and cold: Dynamics of sensory intensity. *Journal of Experimental Psychology*, **60**, 1960, 183–192. Copyright by the American Psychological Association, and reproduced by permission.)

where ψ is the subjective magnitude, ϕ is the stimulus magnitude, n is an experimentally determined value for a given sensory continuum, and A is the AL. The power law expressed in this form subsumes the influence of many variables that affect psychophysical judgments under a single parameter, AL. With the added correction ϕ_0 (or ψ_0), the Stevens' power function contains three constants. If this function is to have any special significance as a general psychophysical law, it must be shown to fit scaling data better than other functions using three constants or less. The introduction of AL in the power law provides the possibility of establishing a general function with only two constants, thereby reducing the latitude in fitting theoretical curves to experimental data in attempting to specify the psychophysical law.

Conclusions

The present status of AL theory in the area of psychophysics and psychophysical scaling has been reviewed in this contribution. It appears that a considerable amount of experimental evidence tends to support the general principle of AL, but additional research needs to be performed to permit its more precise formulation in quantitative terms. Specific reference has been made to problems associated with the geometric mean, the additive constant *cd*, and the exponential weighting factors for focal, background, and residual stimuli. From the available data, it seems likely that within the general framework of AL theory, specific quantitative functions will need to be derived for various judgmental situations.

Nevertheless, the approximations afforded by AL theory in its present form reveal the adequacy of the theory in accounting for certain psychophysical data and for particular phenomena not easily encompassed by other theoretical formulations, that is, TOE, hysteresis, and the bowing of category scales. Furthermore, the relevance of AL to the correction term required in the power law has been indicated. In general, AL theory provides a quantitative approach to a broad range of problems in psychophysics and, given a more precise definition consistent with scaling data, it may be expected that AL will enter into the statement of psychophysical laws.

REFERENCES

Adair, E. R., Stevens, J. C., & Marks, L. E. Thermally induced pain, the dol scale, and the psychophysical power law. *American Journal of Psychology,* 1968, **81,** 147–164.

Bevan, W., Barker, H., & Pritchard, J. F. The Newhall scaling method, psychophysical bowing, and adaptation level. *Journal of General Psychology,* 1963, **69,** 95–111.

Canter, R. R., & Hirsch, J. An experimental comparison of several psychological scales of weight. *American Journal of Psychology,* 1955, **68,** 645–649.

Corso, J. F. A theoretico-historical review of the threshold concept. *Psychological Bulletin,* 1963, **60,** 356–370.

Corso, J. F. Review: H. Helson, Adaptation-level theory: An experimental and systematic approach to behavior. *Choice: Books for College Libraries,* 1964, **1,** 401.

Eisler, H. Magnitude scales, category scales, and Fechnerian integration. *Psychological Review,* 1963, **70,** 243–253.

Eisler, H., & Ottander, C. On the problem of hysteresis in psychophysics. *Journal of Experimental Psychology,* 1963, **65,** 530–536.

Ekman, G. Two generalized ratio scaling methods. *Journal of Psychology,* 1958, **45,** 287–295.

Ekman, G., & Gustafsson, U. Threshold values and the psychophysical function in brightness vision. *Vision Research,* 1968, **8,** 747–758.

Furth, H. G. The effect of the size–weight illusion on adaptation level. *Journal of Experimental Psychology,* 1960, **60,** 150–154.

Helson, H. Fundamental problems in color vision: I. The principle governing changes in hue, saturation, and lightness of non-selective samples in chromatic illumination. *Journal of Experimental Psychology,* 1938, **23,** 439–476.

Helson, H. Adaptation-level as frame of reference for prediction of psychophysical data. *American Journal of Psychology,* 1947, **60,** 1–29.

Helson, H. *Adaptation-level theory: An experimental and systematic approach to behavior.* New York: Harper, 1964.

Helson, H., & Masters, H. G. A study of inflection-points in the locus of adaptation-levels as a function of anchor-stimuli. *American Journal of Psychology,* 1966, **79,** 400–408.

Irwin, R. J., & Corballis, M. C. On the general form of Stevens' law for loudness and softness. *Perception and Psychophysics,* 1968, **3,** 137–143.

Johnson, D. M. Generalization of a scale of values by averaging of practice effects. *Journal of Experimental Psychology,* 1944, **34,** 425-436.

Johnson, D. M. Generalization of a reference scale for judging pitch. *Journal of Experimental Psychology,* 1949, **39**, 316–321.

Keidel, W. D., & Spreng, M. Audiometric aspects and multisensory power-functions of electronically averaged slow evoked cortical responses in man. *Acta Oto-Laryngologica,* 1965, **59**, 201–208.

Luce, R. D. On the possible psychophysical laws. *Psychological Review,* 1959, **66**, 81–95.

Marks, L. E. Stimulus-range, number of categories, and form of the category scale. *American Journal of Psychology,* 1968, **81**, 467–479.

Michels, W. C., & Doser, B. T. Rating scale method for comparative loudness measurements. *Journal of the Acoustical Society of America,* 1955, **27**, 1173–1180.

Michels, W. C., & Helson, H. A reformulation of the Fechner law in terms of adaptation-level applied to rating scale data. *American Journal of Psychology,* 1949, **62**, 355–368.

Parducci, A. Review: H. Helson, *Adaptation-level theory.* New York: Harper, 1964. *American Journal of Psychology,* 1965, **78**, 158–159.

Parducci, A., & Marshall, L. M. Supplementary report: The effects of the mean, midpoint, and median upon adaptation level in judgment. *Journal of Experimental Psychology,* 1961, **61**, 261–262. (a)

Parducci, A., & Marshall, L. M. Context-effects in judgments of length. *American Journal of Psychology,* 1961, **74**, 576–583. (b)

Parducci, A., Calfee, R. C., Marshall, L. M., & Davidson, L. P. Context effects in judgment: Adaptation level as a function of the mean, midpoint, and median of the stimuli. *Journal of Experimental Psychology,* 1960, **60**, 65–77.

Pratt, C. C. The time-error in psychophysical judgments. *American Journal of Psychology,* 1933, **45**, 292–297.

Ross, J., & DiLollo, V. A vector model for psychophysical judgment. *Journal of Experimental Psychology,* 1968, **77**, 1–16 (Monogr. Suppl. No. 3, Part 2).

Sarris, V. Adaptation-level theory: Two critical experiments on Helson's weighted-average model. *American Journal of Psychology,* 1967, **80**, 331–344. (a)

Sarris, V. Comments on Helson and Masters' "Study of inflection-points in the locus of adaptation-levels as a function of anchor-stimuli." *American Journal of Psychology,* 1967, **80**, 304–309. (b)

Stevens, S. S. On the psychophysical law. *Psychological Review,* 1957, **64**, 153–181.

Stevens, S. S. Adaptation-level vs. the relativity of judgment. *American Journal of Psychology,* 1958, **71**, 633–646.

Stevens, S. S. The psychophysics of sensory function. In W. A. Rosenblith (Ed.), *Sensory communication.* New York: Wiley, 1961. Pp. 1–33.

Stevens, S. S. The surprising simplicity of sensory metrics. *American Psychologist,* 1962, **17**, 29–39.

Stevens, J. C., & Stevens, S. S. Warmth and cold: Dynamics of sensory intensity. *Journal of Experimental Psychology,* 1960, **60**, 183–192.

Zinnes, J. L. Scaling. *Annual Review of Psychology,* 1969, **20**, 447–478.

COMMENT: ADAPTATION-LEVEL THEORY AND SIGNAL-DETECTION THEORY AND THEIR RELATION TO VIGILANCE EXPERIMENTS

John A. Swets

I want to say how pleased I am to contribute to this volume honoring Helson. A part of my pleasure stems from a personal debt to him: He gave a favorable review to the first paper I wrote, along with Tanner, a long time ago. This was a paper that we had submitted for publication in the *Psychological Review* when we were both graduate students at Michigan, and when the editor, T. M. Newcomb, was a professor of ours. He had assured us that there was no chance of his publishing that paper (Tanner & Swets, 1954) unless someone of Helson's stature would recommend it. The gist of Helson's review was that he had never heard of these two characters, that he would not know where to begin in trying to make their paper readable, but that he was sure they were on to something significant. So, Professor Helson, at this late date, let me say that your generosity was appreciated.

There are two separate traditions in psychophysics: supraliminal scaling, on the one hand, and thresholds and the like, on the other. Corso's remarks have been largely addressed to the former, an area in which I have managed largely to remain ignorant. Rather than comment on his article, then, I have chosen to discuss, on a very general plane, some of the relationships I see between signal-detection theory (SDT) and adaptation-level (AL) theory. First, I should mention a few recent studies that relate both theories to new data. Durlach and Braida (1969) extend detection theory into the realm of scaling by adding values of d', and then they call upon the concept of AL for an explanation. Parducci and Sandusky (1970) studied recognition as opposed to detection, that is, with the standard stimulus present only in memory, and also found AL theory to be useful—more useful, in fact, than detection theory. A previous study of recognition by Tanner, Haller, and Atkinson (1967) also adduced both theories for one set of data.

49

COMPARISON OF ADAPTATION-LEVEL THEORY
AND SIGNAL-DETECTION THEORY

To illustrate some of the similarities of general concept between the two theories, I will paraphrase some comments I have extracted from Helson's writings—comments that I think apply equally well to detection theory.

Adaptation-level theory is said to provide for the interaction of inner and outer, or of personal and situational, determinants of behavior and to permit the evaluation of the relative contribution of each. At one point, Helson wrote that AL theory emphasizes the state of the organism in determining the effects of stimulation. Also, it provides a single parameter that subsumes the many variables that affect responses. Already you can see, if you're acquainted with detection theory, that Helson's ideas, along with Thurstone's and perhaps Bruner's, set the stage for the general approach of detection theory.

As an aside, I point out that AL seems in many instances to be identifiable with the concept of the decision criterion, or response criterion, in detection theory. It is a single parameter that covers a multitude of sins, and it is a null region, or null point, on the scale, as is the criterion of detection theory. However, AL includes the sensitivity parameter of detection theory along with the response or decision parameter. (Fred Kitterle, one of Helson's doctoral students, pointed this out to me in an informal conversation.)

Another aspect of AL theory that caught my eye for obvious reasons as I looked again at Helson's (1964) book is the quantitative treatment that it gives to psychophysical phenomena previously regarded as artifacts of judgment and attitudes.

It has been claimed for AL theory, as well as for detection theory, that it provides a common theoretical framework for several forms of behavior, from memory to psychopathology. In this connection, Tulving and Madigan (1970), in a chapter on memory in a recent volume of the *Annual Review of Psychology,* have accused detection theory of setting back the study of memory—about 20 years, I think it was. The chapter is beautifully done, really, despite their blindspot of concern for the use of techniques of detection theory in the area of recognition memory.

Another striking feature of AL theory is that it brings back into play the "single-stimulus," as opposed to "comparison," methods. In these methods one sees more clearly the operation of the internal standards the observer uses. I believe that detection theory has also helped to rescue the "single-stimulus," or "yes-no," method—a method that had pretty well lost its usefulness earlier, under the sway of analytical procedures inadequate to its inherent variability.

One of the differences between the two theories is that adaptation is regarded as automatic and physiological. In fact, adherents of the theory do not appreciate the suggestion that the changes involved in adaptation are only changes in the verbal response and not in perception. I would not consider that same comment a criticism when applied to detection theory. We use the term "decision criterion," connoting an intellectual process, and conceive of the observer as consciously considering values and costs and probabilities when reflecting his "perception" in a verbal response.

Probability Expectation in Vigilance Tasks

This notion of "probability expectation" brings me to some substantive remarks. A special case of AL phenomena is the probability expectation, or the probability adaptation, which is the level of probability expectation that is neutral for a given person at a given time. I will discuss some consistent changes in probability expectation as they happen in vigilance tasks. Much of this work on vigilance is reported in more detail elsewhere (see Swets & Kristofferson, 1970).

The vigilance task is interesting because the probability of a correct detection drops off very rapidly in only a half hour or so of observation. There is apparently a large decrement in performance, even though the subject is not asked to work very hard. N. H. Mackworth (1950) first demonstrated this result in an experiment in which a hand moved in jumps around a clock face at regular intervals; the signal to be detected was a double jump of the hand. Hundreds of studies in the next decade showed the same sort of decrement, with other kinds of stimuli and other sensory modalities, and at least five theories were proposed to account for the evident decrement in sensitivity.

Detection theory suggested that the probability of a correct detection, of a "hit," could decline without implying a decrement in sensitivity: If the proportion of "false alarms" also dropped, it was possible that sensitivity remained constant and that, instead, the response criterion (or AL) changed, reflecting a change in probability expectation. Indeed, the procedure in the early vigilance experiments was to show naive subjects the signal to be presented, at the rate of, say, ten per minute, and then, with no specific comments about signal frequency, begin a test with a signal-presentation rate of about two per hour. One might expect an increasingly conservative decision criterion to result from what must be a decreasing expectation of signal occurrence.

Two studies in 1963 applied the analytical techniques of detection theory to vigilance data in an attempt to determine whether or not there is a true sensitivity decrement. They were contradictory: One (Broadbent & Gregory, 1963) indicated no decrement in sensitivity, only a change in the response criterion; the other (J. F. Mackworth & Taylor, 1963) showed a decrement in sensitivity, that is, in the detection-theory parameter d'. A quickly formed hypothesis was that the results were modality-dependent, because the former study used an auditory signal whereas the latter used a visual signal. However, several studies by others (see Swets & Kristofferson, 1970) then confirmed the result of Broadbent and Gregory—no sensitivity decrement—with different senses. The sensitivity index d' remained relatively constant, while the response index β changed in the predicted manner.

Still, Jane Mackworth continued, in three or four more studies (1964a, b; 1965a, c) to find a decline in d'. She used, in every case, a signal consisting of a brief pause in the otherwise continuous movement of a hand about a clock face. It then occurred to her that this "continuous-clock" test might differ from other tests in use—in which signals could occur only at regular and obvious intervals—by requiring a relatively high "rate of observing." The subject exposed to a "jump-clock" test, for example, could regularly rest a bit between jumps, but her subjects' attention could not safely wane at all. Because of this, she conducted a study in which the required rate of observing was varied. The background event, on which the signal was superimposed when it occurred, was presented at a rate of 200/min. in one condition and 40/min. in another. The higher rate led to a decrement in sensitivity and the lower rate did not (J. F. Mackworth, 1965b). She then compared the two clock tests and again found a sensitivity decrement in the continuous-clock test, but none in the jump-clock test, that is, none in the test originally used by her husband to start all of this (J. F. Mackworth, 1968).

Another study, by Loeb and Binford (1968), contributed to an explanation of why a sensitivity decrement is found in some tests and not in others. They pursued the notion of "task coupling": A task is loosely coupled (to the observer) if he can avoid the signal altogether, for example, by looking away from a visual display, and closely coupled if he cannot avoid the signal, as is the case with an auditory signal presented in earphones. One might expect sensitivity decrements because of increasingly frequent lapses of attention in the former case, and only criterion changes in the latter case. An experiment presenting visual and auditory signals at different required rates of observing confirmed this hypothesis: Sensitivity decrements occurred in the visual test, larger as the rate of observing increased, and sensitivity remained constant over time in the auditory test, at all the rates of observing examined.

I submit that now the traditional variables in vigilance experiments—work-rest cycle, intersignal interval, irrelevant stimulation, incentives, drugs, age, sex, and the like—are of interest for only a limited set of displays. With any kind of display, however, there is a behavior change over time: a change in the AL or decision criterion. A challenge now is to try to train the observer to hold a constant criterion, so that his reports of signal presence or absence will mean the same thing no matter how long he has been at the task.

REFERENCES

Broadbent, D. E., & Gregory, M. Vigilance considered as a statistical decision. *British Journal of Psychology,* 1963, **54,** 309–323.

Durlach, N. I., & Braida, L. D. Intensity perception. I. Preliminary theory of intensity resolution. *Journal of the Acoustical Society of America,* 1969, **46,** 372–383.

Helson, H. *Adaptation-level theory: An experimental and systematic approach to behavior.* New York: Harper, 1964.

Loeb, M., & Binford, J. R. Variation in performance on auditory and visual monitoring tasks as a function of signal and stimulus frequencies. *Perception and Psychophysics,* 1968, **4,** 361–367.

Mackworth, J. F. The effect of true and false knowledge of results on the detectability of signals in a vigilance task. *Canadian Journal of Psychology,* 1964, **18,** 106–117.   (a)

Mackworth, J. F. Performance decrement in vigilance, threshold, and high-speed perceptual motor tasks. *Canadian Journal of Psychology,* 1964, **18,** 209–223.   (b)

Mackworth, J. F. Decision interval and signal detectability in a vigilance task. *Canadian Journal of Psychology,* 1965, **19,** 111–117.   (a)

Mackworth, J. F. Deterioration of signal detectability during a vigilance task as a function of background event rate. *Psychonomic Science,* 1965, **3,** 421–422.   (b)

Mackworth, J. F. Effect of amphetamine on the detectability of signals in a vigilance task. *Canadian Journal of Psychology,* 1965, **19,** 104–110.   (c)

Mackworth, J. F. The effect of signal rate on performance in two kinds of vigilance task. *Human Factors,* 1968, **10,** 11–18.

Mackworth, J. F., & Taylor, M. M. The *d'* measure of signal detectability in vigilance-like situations. *Canadian Journal of Psychology,* 1963, **17,** 302–325.

Mackworth, N. H. *Researches on the measurement of human performance.* Medical Research Council Special Report Series No. 268. London: H. M. Stationery Office, 1950.

Parducci, A., & Sandusky, A. J. Limits on the applicability of signal detection theories. *Perception and Psychophysics,* 1970, **7,** 63–64.

Swets, J. A., & Kristofferson, A. B. Attention. *Annual Review of Psychology,* 1970, **21,** 339–366.

Tanner, W. P., Jr., & Swets, J. A. A decision-making theory of visual detection. *Psychological Review,* 1954, **61,** 401–409.

Tanner, T. A., Jr., Haller, R. W., & Atkinson, R. C. Signal recognition as influenced by presentation schedules. *Perception and Psychophysics,* 1967, **2,** 349–358.

Tulving, E., & Madigan, S. A. Memory and verbal learning. *Annual Review of Psychology,* 1970, **21,** 437–484.

VISUAL ILLUSIONS[1]

Frank Restle

This contribution consists of three main parts: (*a*) a set of propositions regarding the role of frame of reference in the visual illusions—assertions directed at fellow AL theorists and assertions directed at the general psychological public; (*b*) a sketch of some complications that we have uncovered in our laboratory work; and (*c*) two questions I cannot answer, problems that others may be able to solve.

THEORETICAL PROPOSITIONS

One characteristic of simple visual illusions is that the subject judges the lengths of various lines. It is perfectly clear to everyone, subjects included, what it means for one line to be twice as long as another, and the judgment of line length is relatively accurate. When Ss make magnitude estimates of line length, they obtain powers near 1.00, indicating that the judgments are simply proportional to the line lengths. Therefore, there is somewhat less uncertainty about response "scaling" in these experiments than is the case in weight lifting, brightness or loudness judgments, and other psychophysical tasks.

Propositions within Frame-of-Reference Theory

The formulas I shall use are those that have served in the analysis of our experiments on judgment of line length:

$$J(X) = X/A_x. \tag{1}$$

Let X be the length of the test line x; then let A_x be the AL for line x; and let $J(X)$ be the judgment of the test line. Note that Eq. (1) differs from that derived by Michels and Helson (1954), for they put the judgment equal to $\log X/A$, and

[1] This research was supported by Public Health Service Grant MH 16817.

did not specifically put a subscript on the AL to show that it belongs to the test object.

Suppose that the field being judged contains not only the test line, but other lines, boxes, spaces, etc., as well, having magnitudes B_1 and B_2. Then

$$A_x = B_1^{b_1} B_2^{b_2} K^{1-b_1-b_2}, \qquad (2)$$

the usual geometric mean. However, because of the constant term K, Eqs. (1) and (2) do not necessarily imply that A_x will be at the middle of the response scale. The value K is the suitable weighted average of such things as the width and height of the room, the dimensions of the screen upon which stimuli are projected, Ss nose, and the traces of past stimuli. Of course, the memory trace system is not constant, but in our experiments the stimuli are presented in random order, so the mean of recent traces is a random variable which has a stationary distribution.

The role of the constant K is to produce the veridical component of judgments. To the extent that A_x is controlled by the constant K, the judgments are based upon a constant AL. To that degree, $J(X)$ will be proportional to X.

There is an adaptation level A_x for any test line x chosen for judgment. Two different lines shown in the same field may have different ALs. We shall see in detail how this works in the theory. The coefficients b_1 and b_2 in Eq. (2) refer both to the background stimuli of magnitudes B_1 and B_2 and to the test line. Thus, it would be more explicit to write

$$A_x = B_1^{b_1,x} B_2^{b_2,x} K^{1-b_1,x-b_2,x},$$

thereby showing that the weighting coefficients b measure the effect of the inducing stimulus B on the test object x. In particular, these weights for given B will vary depending upon the location of stimulus x, since objects will have a stronger influence upon nearby stimuli and a weaker influence on things farther away. Each location in the field will have a different AL, and we should think of A_x, not as a constant, but as a field function defined over all the possible places a test stimulus can be placed.

My third point with respect to the theory is the interpretation of the parameters b_1, b_2, and $1-b_1-b_2$. The third of these is the weight of the constant factor; hence it is a veridical factor. I believe that the other weights b_1, b_2 represent a distribution of attention. When S is instructed to judge the length of x, his first natural question must be, "with respect to what?" A relativistic theory of perception assumes that any judgment must be relative to something. Instructions are somewhat unclear, however, so the result is that S (or, on the average, the group of Ss) places some attention on the background object 1, some attention on object 2, and so forth. That is, Ss tend to compare x with these various objects, and there is a probability or relative weight for each subject object.

To illustrate this point, I can describe a study we have just completed (Restle, 1970a). A group of Ss were shown stimuli similar to those in Fig. 1. We varied the length of the horizontal test line X, the lengths of the vertical lines at the ends (which were equal to one another but were of variable length E), and the length of the vertical line crossing the center of the test line (which was of length C). Seven times in seven random permutations every S saw the set of $3 \times 3 \times 3 = 27$ slides and gave a judgment of the horizontal test line.

Fig. 1. Typical figure used to study the effects of instructions on a visual illusion.

We should expect that the judgment $J(X)$ would decrease with longer end lines, for the end lines clearly establish a frame of reference for x. Similarly, the longer the center line C, the smaller should be the judgment $J(X)$ of the test line. The relative weights of the end and center lines can be evaluated merely by determining the slope of the function relating $\log J(X)$ to $\log E$ or $\log C$.

In our experiment, Ss received two different instructions. In Condition 1, they were instructed, "Pay attention to the vertical lines at the ends of the test line, and use them as a frame of reference to help you in your judgments." The Ss were also told, "Try to disregard the center vertical line." The weight of the end lines was estimated at .17, and the center line at .07. In Condition 2, Ss were told to try to disregard the end lines and use the center line as a frame of reference. They gave a weight of .19 to the center line, and only .02 to the end lines. From this it can be concluded that the weight of a given part of the field on a test line depends not only upon the particular arrangement of the field, but also upon instructions given S, that is, upon cognitive and intentional factors. This seems to me to be direct support for the proposition that the parameters b_1 and b_2 in Eq. (2) represent the probabilities that various factors in the field will be used as the frame of reference for the test line.

The above theoretical propositions are related to AL theory itself. The particular formula for judgments is a mild deviation from that usually employed. The various factors in adaptation level A_x are interpreted somewhat differently from the usual interpretation, in that more emphasis is placed upon the constant factor K that leads to veridical judgments. Finally, the weights of various factors, b_1, b_2, are interpreted in a probabilistic fashion; and it is shown that instructions telling S to use one or another frame of reference have corresponding effects on the weights b.

Propositions about Illusory Figures

The second set of propositions is not directed at AL theory, but instead relates to the interpretation of various illusions. My basic position is that the usual visual illusions are not "distortions of perception," but instead relate to changes and inhomogeneities in the frames of reference.

First, I must admit that the position I take is not sufficient to handle all illusions. In particular, it does not handle that most famous and puzzling of illusions, the Müller–Lyer arrowhead illusion. Still, there are quite a number of illusions that can be interpreted as "size-contrast" illusions, in which a given line is judged shorter when it is surrounded by large things than when it is surrounded by small things. This class of illusions is the one I have been studying, and I shall try to show how the frame-of-reference interpretation is enough to handle the results in considerable detail.

Restle and Merryman (1969) varied the length of a test line of length L (4, 6, 8, 10, 12, or 14 cm.), and also varied the height B of boxes at the ends of the line. The two boxes were square and of the same height (4, 6, 8, 10, 12, or 14 cm. high). All $6 \times 6 = 36$ possible slides were made and judged by each S. Figure 2 shows a typical stimulus, and the data from this experiment are given in

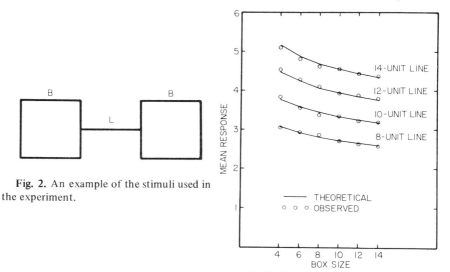

Fig. 2. An example of the stimuli used in the experiment.

Fig. 3. Observed and predicted responses for the longest four lines.

Fig. 3. One may notice that as the box becomes larger, the judgment of line length decreases regularly.

Our interpretation is that the perception of the length of the line is not distorted in this experiment, but that the nearby boxes serve an important role in the frame of reference. We estimated the weight of the boxes variously from

.093 to .138, depending upon how we handled the data. Remember that Ss cannot easily judge the length of the line relative to the screen (which is 130 cm. square and therefore relatively remote from the line) or other parts of the room (which are even more remote). Furthermore, memories of past lines must be relatively faded and unsure. It seems natural that even though the boxes are obviously varying in size, and hence do not make a stable frame of reference, Ss tend to use them anyway as perhaps .10 of their total distribution of attention.

Therefore, according to this approach, what happens is that a given test length L is placed in different fields with different adaptation levels A, and as a result it is judged differently.

In the earlier discussion, we argued that A_x was a function of the field and would take various values in various parts of a given field. Other things being equal, a given background figure should have its greatest influence on test lines near it, and less influence on test lines farther away. This "distance effect" was examined in another study by Restle and Merryman (1969).

The experiment was very like the previous one, again involving a test line and boxes at each end. However, this time we separated the boxes from the ends of the test line by a gap of width D (a typical stimulus display is shown in Fig. 4).

Fig. 4. Typical display showing the test line of length L, boxes of height B, and a distance between line and box of length D. (The screen was 130 cm. square.)

Again, we varied the length of the test line (13, 16, and 19 cm.) and the heights of the boxes (6.4, 13, and 19 cm.), and we also independently varied the distance between the ends of the line and the box (0, 1.6, 3.2, 6.4, and 13 cm.). This produced 3 x 3 x 5 = 45 displays, which were shown an average of 65 times to nine experienced undergraduate students.

Again, the judgments increased very regularly with the length of the test line, and decreased regularly with the size of the box. We expected that the slope relating log J to log B would decrease with a greater distance between box and line, for a larger distance should result in the decreased influence of the box. In fact, the slopes obtained were .089, .052, .055, .043, and .032 for the five increasing distances.

One other effect that was surprising at first, but later turned out to be helpful, appeared in this experiment. As the distance D between the box and line was increased, the test line appeared shorter and shorter on the average. We had expected the judgment of the test line to become gradually independent of the box size, but had not anticipated that it would also show a constant tendency toward minification.

The theoretical answer to this finding is that the gap between box and line (or, perhaps, the space between the two boxes) is itself a factor in the frame of reference. This simply means that such a gap has length, just as does a line, and the two kinds of length (or extent) influence one another.

When this hypothesis was introduced into the analysis of the data, it was found that the distance from end of line to box would be given a weight of approximately .026, a small value, but enough to produce a considerable effect in the overall data. With this theoretical correction, the frame-of-reference theory fits all details of the data as closely as might be expected.

This finding has two applications in the study of visual contrast illusions. One is as an answer to the puzzling problem of the "control" line. In several preliminary experiments, we employed lines with boxes and then introduced a few test lines without boxes at the ends. These were "control lines" and it was thought that they would provide a baseline so that we could determine whether the boxes produced positive, negative, or mixed illusions relative to a no-box control. It turned out that the control lines did not help very much, because judgments of them were quite variable; and the control line would appear to be of different lengths relative to given boxes, changing its relative position from one experiment to the next.

In an experiment of this type the control line actually is surrounded by a relatively large extent, the precise size depending upon the relative size of the field, the strength of contours at the edges of the field, and whether the line is drawn on a piece of paper or projected on a screen. Generally speaking, a control line all alone in a field has very large background factors—the wide extents to the edge of the field; but these extents, being mere empty gaps, may have a relatively low weight (.03 vs. .09 for boxes nearby). Depending upon Ss instructions and hypotheses, and upon the total field shown with the control line, it is possible to obtain a rather wide variety of judgments to a control line. In our more recent work, we have dispensed with this control line and evaluate the magnitude of an illusion produced by B as the slope of the function relating log J to log B; we no longer attempt to find out whether the illusion is positive or negative relative to a control line.

A second application of our findings relative to a gap is in the analysis of the moon illusion (Restle, 1970b). A mathematical and theoretical analysis of the Rock–Kaufman (1962) data on the moon illusion showed that their findings would agree with the following hypothesis: The size of the moon is judged larger near horizon because there is a relatively small gap from the moon to the horizon in that field. When the moon is overhead, the frame of reference includes a very wide gap from moon to horizon, and therefore the zenith moon is judged smaller.

COMPLICATIONS

A quantitative formula to fit the data of a very simple experiment is good to have, but it has little importance in itself. The results of the above experiments have a very simple structure, and it is not terribly difficult to find equations that will agree in good detail with such simple tables of data. Therefore, it is necessary to apply the theoretical approach to somewhat more complicated situations and see if it is possible to carry through a complete analysis. In this way the theory is put under a great strain, so that its weaknesses can be seen; at the same time the logical and combinatorial properties of the theory are exploited and thereby developed.

The two experiments to be discussed next were devised by Merryman and reported by Merryman and Restle (1970). The discussion begins with the idea that the results of our earlier experiments can be explained not only through frame-of-reference theory, but also from the point of view of contour repulsion. This theory assumes that illusions are really distortions of perception and attempts to describe how one part of a display modifies the image of other parts.

In general terms, this theory usually says that one contour, edge, or other distinguishing local stimulation tends to produce near it a field of some sort of satiation, refractoriness, or inhibition. This in turn inhibits the formation of another contour in the same region. If the apparent location of a contour depends upon the locus of the maximum of a distribution of excitation, then it is possible that when there is a field of inhibition at one side of a potential contour, the point of maximum stimulation will actually be shifted somewhat in the opposite direction. For this reason, contours will appear to repel one another.

Now suppose that the two squares in Fig. 2 set up a surrounding field of inhibition. The intensity and spread of this field could very well depend upon the size of the squares, being greatest when the squares are large. If so, then the test line lies within a field of inhibition, and the inhibition is most intense when the squares are large. If the line appears smaller when in a field of inhibition, or if the ends of the line are driven inward by contour repulsion, the result will be that the test line will look shorter as the end squares are increased in size. This is exactly the illusion found in our study.

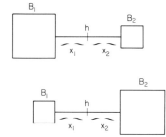

Fig. 5. An example of the stimuli used in the experiment on the Baldwin figure.

The contour-repulsion theory can be tested by using a version of the Baldwin figure (Fig. 5), where hash mark h divides the X into two equal segments, X_1 and X_2 (top). According to the frame-of-reference theory, both the larger square box of height (B_1) and the smaller box (B_2) should influence the apparent lengths of both X_1 and X_2. But I have stated above that the closer a box is to a line, the more influence it has on that line (Restle & Merryman, 1969). Therefore, X_1 (being closer to B_1) should be affected more by B_1 and should appear shorter than X_2 (which is affected more by B_2). If X_1 is seen as shorter than X_2, then the hash mark h should be judged closer to B_1 than to B_2.

A simple interpretation of the contour-repulsion concept would say that B_1, being larger, produces a greater field of inhibition than B_2. The greater inhibition should repel the nearby contour (the hash mark, h) making it appear farther from the larger box and closer to the smaller box. This conclusion is opposite to that derived from the frame-of-reference theory.

To do the experiment we used an 11-cm. line on which the hash mark could be located 4, 5, 6, or 7 cm. from the left end. Boxes of differing sizes were placed at the two ends of the line (8 cm. vs. 4 cm., 12 vs. 4, 16 vs. 4, 12 vs. 8, 16 vs. 8, and 16 vs. 12), and the left–right positions of the boxes were varied. This produced $4 \times 6 \times 2 = 48$ slides, which were shown in random order four times, the last three constituting the data.

It was consistently found that the hash mark was judged as if it were displaced toward the larger box. Furthermore, the amount of discrepancy of judgments was quite consistently related to the ratio of the two box sizes. Thus, the results appear to be in good general agreement with AL theory.

However, good general qualitative agreement may serve as a cloak covering serious theoretical inconsistencies.

The Ss in this experiment were judging the location of the hash mark h, and this is somewhat different from judging a quantity such as a single length. Judging the location of h on a constant 11-cm. line is equivalent to comparing the judged lengths of the two-line segments X_1 and X_2 of Fig. 5. Therefore, this judgment of location should depend upon $J(X_1)$ and $J(X_2)$. The theory given above does not permit us to combine two judgments this way, so a theoretical extension is required.

The following hypothesis was found to fit the data in detail. Assume that S compares X_1 and X_2 by a mental manipulation of moving one of the lines on top of the other and observing the difference or overhang. The process of comparing and judging should produce an overhang of judged magnitude $J(X_1) - J(X_2)$, taking a negative value when the hash mark appears to the left of the center (that is, when X_2 appears to be longer than X_1). However, since the judgment is relative, this difference is compared with some suitable basis. It could be compared with the constant line of 11 cm., or with the sum of the two judgments $J_1 + J_2$. Or it could be compared with the judgment of one of the two segments, $J(X_1)$ or $J(X_2)$. If so, the question would be, which part?

If the difference is compared with the judgment of the whole line, then responses should be essentially a linear function of the actual location of the hash mark. If the judgment of the difference is compared with the shorter of the two segments, then the curve relating the response to actual placement should rise most rapidly when the hash mark is at the most extreme locations of 4 and 7 cm., and should rise more slowly near the middle. If the judgment of the difference is compared with the longer of the two segments in every case, then it would rise slowly near locations of 4 and 7 cm., and more rapidly near the center at locations of 5 and 6 cm. The data show a slight but unmistakable form in general agreement with the last of these three hypotheses, namely, that the judgment of difference is compared with the larger of the two judged segments.

Our interpretation of this tendency is illustrated in Fig. 6, which is a pictorial

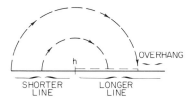

Fig. 6. An illustration of the process of mental manipulation by which S is assumed to compare the two line segments.

representation of how S might judge the relative position of hash mark h, which is off-center on a line. He would transport the shorter part of the line so as to compare it directly with the longer part, thereby isolating the difference or "overhang." This overhang, since it is part of and lies upon the longer line, would then be compared with the longer line.

The formula giving the judged location of h is

$$J(h) = \frac{J(X_1) - J(X_2)}{\max[J(X_1), J(X_2)]}, \tag{3}$$

where the expression $\max(a, b)$ refers either to a or to b, whichever is larger. The actual response made by an S depends upon the responses available and upon his tendency to use all the response alternatives. We write the response itself as

$$R(h) = c \cdot J(h) + R_0, \tag{4}$$

where R_0 corresponds to the response made when the stimulus is judged to be in the center. In our six-choice apparatus, this would be response 3.5.

Detailed analysis begins with Eq. (4), into which we insert the detailed expression for $J(h)$ found in Eq. (3). This, in turn, contains $J(X_1)$ and $J(X_2)$, judgments of the two line segments on either side of the hash mark in the Baldwin figure. These expressions can be developed using Eqs. (1) and (2), that is,

$$J(X_1) = X_1/A_1 \qquad \text{and} \qquad J(X_2) = X_2/A_2.$$

Here, of course, X_1 and X_2 are the lengths of the two segments on the screen (for example, 4 and 7 cm. if the hash mark is appearing in the position farthest to the left). The illusion is produced by discrepancies in the adaptation levels A_1

and A_2. We ignore the effects of X_1 and X_2 themselves upon the AL and concentrate on the influences of the boxes.

Suppose that a small box B_1 is at the left end of the figure and a larger box B_2 is at the right end. Then A_1 (the AL for the length of the left line segment) is strongly influenced by B_1 and more weakly influenced by B_2. In fact, using the data reported earlier for boxes placed at various distances from a line, one would expect that an adjacent box might have weight .089 and a box 4–7 cm. away would have a weight of approximately .044.

The adjacent box has weight .089, and the more distant box has weight .044. All other factors are constant and must have weight $1-.089-.044 = .867$. Therefore,

$$A_1 = B_1^{.089} B_2^{.044} K^{.867} \qquad \text{and} \qquad A_2 = B_1^{.044} B_2^{.089} K^{.867}.$$

When the above values are introduced into Eq. (1), one obtains

$$J(X_1) = X_1 B_1^{-.089} B_2^{-.044} K^{-.867},$$

$$J(X_2) = X_2 B_1^{-.044} B_2^{-.089} K^{-.867},$$

and these can be substituted into Eq. (3) to get a value for the judgment of the hash mark $J(h)$. First, take the case in which $J(X_1)$ is greater than $J(X_2)$. Equation (3) turns into

$$J(h) = [J(X_1)-J(X_2)]/J(X_1).$$

If we substitute the above values for $J(X_1)$ and $J(X_2)$, the result is

$$J(h) = \frac{X_1 B_1^{-.089} B_2^{-.044} K^{-.867} - X_2 B_1^{-.044} B_2^{-.089} K^{-.867}}{X_1 B_1^{-.089} B_2^{-.044} K^{-.867}}.$$

This expression can be simplified by canceling the common factor $K^{-.867}$ and then dividing through by the remainder of the denominator, producing

$$J(h) = 1 - (X_2/X_1) \frac{B_1^{-.044} B_2^{-.089}}{B_1^{-.089} B_2^{-.044}}.$$

The last fraction simplifies into

$$J(h) = 1 - (X_2/X_1)(B_1/B_2)^{.045}. \tag{5}$$

Equation (5) holds, provided X_1 is judged greater than X_2. If $J(X_2)$ is greater, then the same argument yields

$$J(h) = -1 + (X_1/X_2)(B_2/B_1)^{.045}. \tag{6}$$

Equations (5) and (6) are transformed into predicted responses by applying Eq. (4) above, that is, by multiplying by the single arbitrary scale constant so as to spread responses across the response scale the way Ss do and then adding 3.5 to move the zero judgment up to the middle of the response scale. The resulting formulas provide a prediction for every response to every placement of the hash mark (X_1/X_2) for every pair of box sizes (B_1/B_2).

The calculated predictions are shown in Fig. 7 along with the mean observations from 46 Ss. The experimental results were extremely consistent from S to S and, as can be seen in Fig. 7, the predicted values almost exactly mirror the data observed. This is true despite the fact that the main parameter,

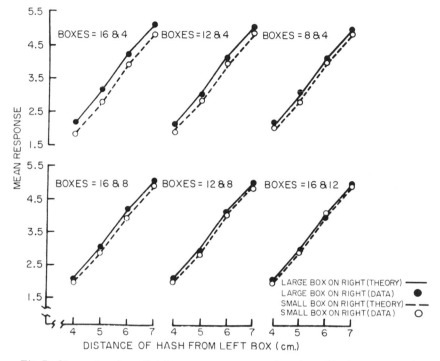

Fig. 7. Observed and predicted mean responses as a function of hash location and sizes of the end boxes.

representing the effect of the boxes on the two parts of the line, was obtained not from these data, but from the results of a previous experiment using different figures.

The calculation provides a demonstration that this quantitative theory not only can handle relatively simple size-contrast illusions and extend to such separate facts of the moon illusion, but it can also be carried through carefully and systematically to yield a close analysis of a different and more complicated judgment in a slightly more complicated field. This still leaves us a long way from a general and complete account of judgments of length of line within simple fields, and we still have only a partial account of one class of illusion.

Nevertheless, the small accomplishment reported above may help in the development of a more powerful and useful theory.

QUERIES

Despite having a feeling of some accomplishment in the experiments and calculations described above, I must admit to having some serious difficulties in working with AL theory. The fact that the above calculations are successful is not itself a blessing unless one can understand the theory underlying the calculations. Otherwise, each success of the model must lead to deeper and deeper theoretical perplexity.

My first difficulty arises from the finding that one can compute ALs based upon the lengths of lines. An adaptation for brightness or for a given component of hue makes a considerable amount of psychophysical and physiological sense; and it is natural that AL theory should have roots in color vision. I can understand that the visual system might adapt itself to the overall level of energy. However, a long line and a short line do not necessarily represent different amounts of energy. In fact, it was argued above that in the AL for length, an empty space acts just like a length. However, the empty space has no energy in it, and in fact represents a part of the retina that is receiving no energy, forming no contours, and generally just resting. For this to be commensurate with the length of a narrow luminous line on the same screen is peculiar, to say the least.

One interpretation of such findings is to assume that they are tied to physiological facts. The fact that there is an AL for length must mean that there are, somewhere within the brain, "length receptors" which somehow respond differentially to lengths in the visual field. The two edges of an empty space might single out and stimulate the appropriate length receptor tied to the particular separation between contours, and the two ends of a luminous line of the same length would presumably stimulate the same length receptor. Then the system of length receptors would be presumed to operate on some "opponent-processes" basis that produces judgments similar to those found in the present studies. If this is the correct interpretation, it has exciting consequences, for it means that this kind of simple psychophysical study of complex fields may give us detailed information about the operation of hidden and otherwise unknown neurons in the brain.

However, I am afraid that if we were to ask the subjects for judgments of other stimulus properties, they would all show the same sort of AL phenomena. This, if true, would mean that there are neurons for each such dimension of stimulation. There are so many neurons in the brain that it is conceivable that there is one for every possible definable stimulus dimension that S can judge. There may be different neurons for "beauty" and "loveliness," but I should rather leave that sort of conclusion for physiological investigation and not generate such neurons from a series of psychophysical experiments, each bolstered by an unsupported assumption.

If AL theory is thought of as a mathematical or logical model, then analysis of Eqs. (1) and (2) reveals another sharp and serious constraint. Equation (2), when studied in detail, suggests the following possibility: If all the factors in the equation are measured in centimeters, then A_x is in centimeters. If all the factors in the equation are in grams, then A_x is also in grams. Now, if the test object is measured in grams and A_x is also in grams, then $J(X)$ is a dimensionless number, for it is the ratio of two numbers expressed in the same units. Generally, if all the factors in the AL are commensurate (in the same measurement units) and if the test object is measured in the same units, then $J(X)$ is a pure, dimensionless number.

Such a result is necessary for the theory to make sense. Suppose that $J(X)$ were not a dimensionless number; suppose instead that X is measured in grams, but A_x comes out to be measured in both grams and centimeters, $\text{gm.}^{.9}\ \text{cm.}^{.1}$ then writing just in terms of units of measurement,

$$J(X) = X/A_x = \text{gm.}/[\text{gm.}^{.9}\ \text{cm.}^{.1}] = \text{gm.}^{.1}/\text{cm.}^{.1}$$

Now suppose that we changed the unit of measurement of weight from grams to milligrams. This increases all the numbers measuring weight by a factor of 1000, and the result is that it changes $J(X)$ by a factor of $1000^{.1} = 1.58$. However, this is nonsense, for there is no reason why a change in measurement units, which cannot be sensed by the subject, could change his judgment.

This means that there must be an AL for any dimension judged by S, and that all factors in the AL should be measured in the same units as the test stimulus. This is quite a different restriction from the assumption of a certain neuron in the head, and I must admit that this is as deep as I have penetrated into the question. Basically, the theory seems to say that any measurable, sensible dimension can be judged, and that there is an AL for that dimension. There is no obvious way to decide what dimensions are measurable and sensible, and what, if any, are not.

My second query is probably related, and has to do with the use of memory in psychophysics. One possibility is that actual stimulus traces from the past remain over time and enter into the AL. A line 10 cm. long is shown and then turned off. Ten sec. later, when a line of 12 cm. is shown, the earlier line is present, and enters into the AL just as would a 10-cm. line immediately present, though perhaps with different weight. I find myself in some difficulty to believe that the sensory register can keep such information in its raw form for any length of time.

The second possibility is that the stimulus information from the first line is "encoded," and this message is stored in short- or long-term memory. Then, when the second stimulus is shown, the coded form of the first stimulus can be retrieved, with a certain probability, and the new stimulus compared with the decoded form of the first one.

This sort of memory theory suggests that the encoding of stimulus quantities is of great importance in psychophysics, and the coding of a stimulus should correspond closely to the judgment it elicits. If a stimulus S_1 is shown in conjunction with adaptation level A_1, and then that stimulus enters into a later adaptation level A_2, is it the stimulus S_1 or the judgment S_1/A_1 that is remembered? It makes a great deal of difference, for in the first case other stimuli that accompanied S_1 on its first appearance would have no influence on A_2, whereas in the second case, a large stimulus accompanying S_1 would make J_1 smaller, hence would make A_2 smaller, and in that way would have a paradoxical effect on the later judgments. This result has been observed by Bevan and Turner (1965), but they do not expand on the theoretical complications that may arise. My second query is, "memory of what?"

Conclusions

I have reviewed here a few experimental studies of visual illusions, and have offered a detailed and quantitative theoretical account of the results. This should eventually lead to improvements of AL theory. It has already called the logarithmic relationship into question, and has shown clearly that the AL is not necessarily a constant, but may be a field function.

Certainly, I believe that this kind of theory of visual illusions has something to contribute to the study of such visual phenomena. The recent review of explanations of geometrical illusions by Over (1968) contains no reference to simple size-contrast effects or to anything closely resembling AL theory, though his criticisms of other theories, and particularly his emphasis on the existence of such effects in haptic space, suggest that an AL theory would find some success. However, the complications of this total experimental area are such as to make it very unlikely that a simple quantitative theory can handle all the relevant facts.

One advantage of work in the field of visual illusions, and the study of length and distance, is that it takes away one of the major excuses psychologists use for failures of exact prediction—namely, the supposed loose coupling between physical measurements and perceived or psychological quantities. The fact is that people judge lengths of lines in a given, fixed frame of reference without any noticeable systematic distortion and with only a modest variable or random error. Therefore, one is inclined to expect judgments to reflect perception and thus to give credence and serious attention to any consistent discrepancies between theoretical prediction and experimental result. This confidence then provides the motivation for the kind of exact theoretical calculation and careful experimental manipulations that might eventually provide a satisfactory account of visual illusion.

REFERENCES

Bevan, W., & Turner, E. D. The potency of a lightness-anchor as a function of the reflectance of its background. *American Journal of Psychology,* 1965, 78, 645–650.

Merryman, C. T., & Restle, F. Perceptual displacement of a test mark toward the larger of two visual objects. *Journal of Experimental Psychology,* 1970, 84, 311–318.

Michels, W. C., & Helson, H. A reconciliation of the *Veg* scale with Fechner's law. *American Journal of Psychology,* 1954, 67, 677-683.

Over, R. Explanations of geometrical illusions. *Psychological Bulletin,* 1968, 70, 545–562.

Restle, F. Instructions and the magnitude of an illusion: Cognitive factors in the frame of reference. *Perception and Psychophysics,* 1970a.

Restle, F. Moon Illusion explained on the basis of relative size. *Science,* 1970b, 167, 1092–1096.

Restle, F., & Merryman, C. T. An adaptation-level theory account of a relative-size illusion. *Psychonomic Science,* 1968, 12, 229–230.

Restle, F., & Merryman, C. T. Distance and an illusion of length of line. *Journal of Experimental Psychology,* 1969, 81, 297–302.

Rock, I., & Kaufman, L. The moon illusion. Part II. *Science,* 1962, 136, 1023–1031.

COMMENT: ADAPTATION LEVEL, CONTRAST, AND THE MOON ILLUSION[1]

Alberta Steinman Gilinsky

Helson's (1964) contribution to our understanding of visual illusions has been underestimated by Restle (1970). Restle's formulation, although clever, does not explain illusions, and fails to show how neatly AL theory removes the mystery from that most astonishing and perplexing of all natural phenomena—the moon illusion. The moon illusion can be explained by the very concepts and relations that Restle discards.

In common with other recent investigators (Kaufman & Rock, 1962; Rock & Kaufman, 1962), Restle overlooks the classic experiments of Holway and Boring (1940) that showed the full extent of the moon illusion (a ratio of 2 to 1). These experiments showed that the moon illusion strikingly illustrates two fundamental principles of perception: (*a*) that the perceived size of an object depends essentially upon the perceived distance of the object; and (*b*) that perceived size depends upon the angle of regard.

Two sets of factors are involved. One set consists of the oculomotor adjustments associated with the changes in the elevation of the eyes from the primary position (Hermans, 1954). The other set reflects the many cues to depth—perspective, texture gradient, interposition, and motion parallax—available on the ground but missing from empty space (Gilinsky, 1951, 1955). As Ptolemy realized, a filled extent is perceived as greater than the same extent of empty space. Therefore the horizon ought to look farther away than the zenith; the sky is a flattened bowl or dome.

This observation led to the most commonly held explanation of the moon illusion, the apparent-distance hypothesis. According to the usual interpretation of this hypothesis, the horizon moon looks big because it appears to be farther away. Since the visual angle remains constant, the moon must appear farther away in order to seem larger. Boring (1943) rejected this argument for the "simple reason that the moon in elevation looks farther away than the moon on

[1] The work on which this paper is based was supported in part by Research Grant GB-6067 from the National Science Foundation.

71

the horizon [p. 56] ." The horizon moon rising behind buildings and landmarks not only looks enormous—it appears *nearer*. A paradox? If the moon appears nearer at the horizon, it ought to look smaller—as its visual angle dictates. But it looks bigger—and its perceived size cannot be simultaneously both the consequence and the cause of its perceived distance. Restle, too, finds that the relatively great apparent distance of the horizon is useless or confusing as a factor producing the moon illusion. I will try to show that the paradox can be resolved and that this ancient idea of Ptolemy's, when combined with the AL theory, has considerable power to explain many puzzling phenomena of space perception.

Resolution of the Apparent-Distance Paradox

The paradox can be resolved first, by making a clear distinction between the apparent distance of the *sky* and the apparent distance of the *moon*; and second, by relating the concepts of AL theory with the concepts of a mathematical model previously formulated for visual space (Gilinsky, 1951) and applying them to the moon illusion.

The traditional view based on apparent distance assumes that the retinal image of the moon, like the afterimage, is projected outward to the sky. Since the sky–ground changes its apparent distance from the observer, coming closer at the zenith, it will produce a diminishing size image of the moon. The argument implies that the perceived moon is simply proportional to the projected size of the constant retinal image and therefore it is proportional to the distance of the surface of the background.

This argument is wrong. The moon is not its retinal image; the moon is an object in three-dimensional space. Even a photograph does not show the moon as a retinal image pasted on the sky—a flat circle cut into the surface of the sky—but as an object that stands out in front of the sky.

Boring and his co-observers (Holway & Boring, 1940) gave size matches to the moon that were much larger than the retinal image of the moon would require. The moon, 240,000 miles away, subtends a visual angle of about $.5°$. The equivalent stimuli, 3.5 meters away, subtend angles that vary from $2.0°$ to $6.8°$—i.e., their retinal images are linearly from 4 to 12 times as large as the images for the moon. The artificial moon at the Hayden Planetarium (in New York) projects a $1°$ image to the dome. Although this is twice the visual angle of the moon, the director of the planetarium told me, "Many people are disappointed, being of the opinion that it appears too small."

They are right. The retinal image is not the sole determinant of the perceived size of the moon. There is no doubt that the perceived size of any object, even the moon, depends upon more than the size of the retinal image; it takes into account the perceived distance of the object. Even at astronomical distances, the perception of distance is a fact and must be considered. But that does not mean the physical distance of the object, and it does not mean the registered distance of the background or sky. What is perceived is the perceived distance of the object fixated and that depends upon the *level of adaptation to the prevailing spatial framework.*

Now, however, Restle (1970) proposes to explain the moon illusion as a result of contrast. The zenith moon is small, he says, "because it is in a uniquely large empty visual extent, being surrounded by the large $(90°)$ space to the horizon ... The horizon moon is large because it is compared with the small $(1°)$ space to the horizon [p. 1096]."

This explanation lacks sense. Even if the observer, with head thrown back, could examine the moon when it is $90°$ above, his eyes would be in the same position as the supine observer. As Holway and Boring's studies showed, from this supine position, the observer, looking straight ahead at the zenith moon, requires a large matching disk. To the supine observer, the moon, even though surrounded by the large, empty sky, does *not* look small; the illusion, under these conditions, is reversed. Actually, the eyes can be elevated (with head fixed) only about $40°$, and the full amount of variation of perceived size is reached in that span. Moreover, reducing the amount of visible surround, by a reduction tube, does not make the moon expand in size. Both the horizon moon and the zenith moon shrink when viewed through a tube or pinched between the thumb and forefinger. Eliminating the surrounding space or gap does not make the moon look large; its presence does not always make the moon look small. Thus, contrast between the moon and the gap of sky surrounding it is not the correct solution of the moon illusion.

Undoubtedly, contrast is important, but not in the way Restle suggests. Restle rejects years of careful research and the accumulated evidence of Pozdena (1909), Schur (1925), and Holway and Boring (1940a, b) when he denies the effect of eye position and apparent distance as determinants of size perception— and emphasizes contrast solely. Yet there is no necessary incompatibility of the various explanations, and the thesis of this discussion is that, properly interpreted, the several determinants may be combined and related to a theory of visual space adaptation that is essential to a complete understanding of the moon illusion.

Helson (1964) recognized that spatial characteristics of objects interact no less than other features, and showed that "illusions of length, size, direction, and perspective all attest to the potency of spatial pooling [p. 75]." Important interactions occur not only within the field of vision but also across modalities, so that sight, sound, touch, and kinesthesis exert mutual influences to determine the effective AL.

ADAPTATION TO VISUAL SPACE

Woodworth (1938) spoke of "registering" the distance as well as the general illumination in a given situation so as not to imply in all cases an explicit perception of them. The initial response to each field of view must be a registering of the general scale; an adjustment not only to the prevailing illumination, but also to the prevailing structure of spatial relations. The resulting level of adaptation to visual space serves to establish the subjective scales for both the perceived distance and the perceived size of objects.

Our adaptation to visual space depends primarily upon three factors: (a) the availability of cues to distance; (b) the direction of regard in all dimensions (there is the well-known vertical–horizontal illusion as well as the zenith–horizon illusion); and, most surprisingly, (c) the total depth or distance range. (See Gilinsky, 1951, 1955.)

Our visual space expands or contracts as we move from one physical space to another. The total distance range is an important determinant of visual space. The observer acts as though his visual space adjusted its scale up or down in adaptation to the prevailing level of spatial excitation. This adjustment is analogous to the adjustment of brightness and color adaptation to the prevailing illumination and has parallel biological significance for the organism.

THE UPPER LIMIT OF PERCEIVED DISTANCE

The dependence of the AL governing space perception upon stimulus variables of distance and direction may be expressed quantitatively (Gilinsky, 1951). The basic concept is A, the maximum perceived distance. Although physical space is infinite, visual space is finite. The observer acts as though his visual space had an upper limit—a ceiling or maximal depth of field set by the horizon. This subjective horizon is relatively close; the limit A is of the order of .5–300 ft., depending upon the individual and the situation.

Perceived size depends upon two factors: the size of the retinal image and the perceived distance. The retinal image φ multiplied by the perceived distance d gives the perceived size s.

$$s = \varphi \cdot d \qquad (1)$$

is the basic relation between perceived size and perceived distance. As perceived distance d approaches A—the upper limit or threshold value of perceived distance d—objects become more nearly completely dependent on the retinal image factor alone. The sun and the moon appear nearly the same size, although the sun is 407 times as big as the moon, because their retinal images are nearly the same size.

Still, the moon illusion is a striking example of the general principle that perceived size depends on something more than the retinal image; that it depends also on both distance and direction.

DETERMINANTS OF A

Children have smaller A values than adults (Gilinsky, 1960; Harway, 1963; Leibowitz & Hartman, 1959). As the child grows and becomes progressively mobile, his world expands, and A increases. The value of A varies with the availability of cues to distance; as cues are added, A goes up; when the cues are reduced, A is also reduced. The limit A is also a function of the viewing angle of elevation, or direction in which an object recedes from the observer. You see the sky as a flattened bowl, because A has a lower value for empty-space perception (elevated vision without foreground) and a higher value for horizontal vision (with foreground) due to differences in the prevailing spatial stimulation.

The data of Holway and Boring (1940) on the moon illusion provide a striking demonstration of the dependence of A on the *elevation of the eyes; A* is thus a measure of the moon illusion.

The data for the two Os who served under both the erect and the supine posture conditions are shown in Fig. 1. The plots show A—the upper limit of perceived distance—as a function of elevation. The pair of curves for each O show how the illusion is reversed by eye position. The point at which the curves cross may be taken as the nodal point, indeed, the null point of the illusion.

With the aid of two concepts, the normal viewing distance and the normal viewing elevation, these data show how we can account for the moon illusion on the basis of AL theory.

The Normal Viewing Distance

In order to determine the relative perceived sizes of different objects, and also the relative perceived sizes of the same object at different distances, we need to select one of these viewing distances as "the normal viewing distance" δ, and we can call the corresponding perceived size of the object the "true size" S. The normal distance at which O forms a concept of "true size" of an object may vary widely, depending on the object, whether it is a printed page, a person, a house, a mountain, or the moon. As James (1890) noted, "this is the distance at which we hold anything we are examining. Farther than this we see it too small, nearer too large [p. 179]." Your hand held close up to your face looms enormous—it is both larger and nearer than you are accustomed to seeing it.

The Normal Viewing Angle

In addition to the normal viewing distance, we need to establish the normal viewing angle for a given object. Thus, we normally see faces as right side

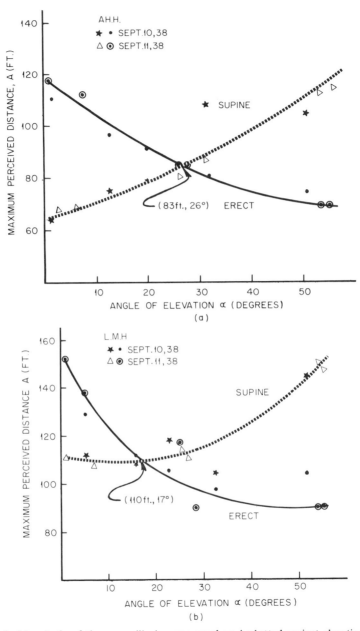

Fig. 1. Magnitude of the moon illusion expressed as A plotted against elevation for the erect and supine positions; (*a*) observer A.H.H, (*b*) observer L.M.H. Compare the nodal points where the two curves cross for each observer. [Values calculated from Eq. (1) based on data from Holway and Boring (1940).]

up—and the moon—neither straight ahead at $0°$ or up overhead at $90°$. Rather, we form a gnostic unit (Konorski, 1967) or "memory moon" at its most frequent and convenient angle of regard—about $20°$ above the ground. This "memory moon" need not consciously be held in mind during any particular observation. It provides the internal baseline or standard referent, the AL from which deviations in either direction are noted.

The reason for the paradoxical shifts in the perceived distance of the moon now becomes clear. The range effect, the maximum limit of perceived distance A in our formulas, is governed by the apparent remoteness of the sky, not the apparent remoteness of the moon. There is a locus at which sky and moon meet, and the two perceived distances coincide. This is the point given by the normal viewing angle at which $\delta = A = d$, the normal viewing distance is equal to the maximum perceived distance, and the two limits converge to yield the perceived distance of the moon. Nearer than δ, the moon is too large, farther than δ, the moon is too small. Only at $d = \delta$ does the "inconstant" moon appear "true."

Adaptation-Level Theory and the Moon Illusion

In order to apply AL theory to the moon illusion, we must first establish the reference point or standard at which the moon is her normal "true" size. Departures from this standard constitute the illusion.

Holway and Boring's observers have such a moon and a set of gnostic units that preserve it in memory. This implicit standard is given by the exact locus in space at which the normal viewing distance and the normal viewing elevation coincide for the particular observer. We may discover the precise coordinates of that point by noting where the two curves (for the erect and supine positions) actually cross. For A.H.H, the nodal point gives A as 83 ft. and the angle α as $26°$; for L.M.H the corresponding values at the crosspoint are A as 110 ft., and the angle α as $17°$. The individual differences are striking and consistent over a period of three years of experimentation. The observer L.M.H always matched the moon to larger comparison stimuli than the other observers and thus must always have seen the sky as farther away. The consistently higher values of A for this observer express an expanded visual world with a wider or farther horizon.

For a given observer, the higher the value of A, the more nearly objects will appear their true size, "regress" towards size constancy, and the more nearly perceived distances will resist foreshortening and correspond to true physical distance. The lower the value of A, the further the reduction of object size to retinal size, and the more compressed or limited will be the visual distance scale.

Accordingly, we have two moon illusions, not one. Neither the physical size nor the physical distance of the moon varies with the angle of elevation. But visual space depends upon the calibration of the organism, expressed by A, and

A is controlled by the registration of the closeness or remoteness of the visible ceiling or sky. As the angle of regard changes from the elevated position of the eyes to straight ahead, the value of A increases, and the visual distance scale expands outward in the direction of the increasing value of the anchoring agent A.

Since the scale remains anchored at the end near the observer, and extends outward in the direction of the upper limit A, the scale "moves past" the stimuli that lie at the top of the stimulus range (McGarvey, 1943). The result is that a celestial object, the sun or the moon, will now be perceived as *closer* to the observer than before the shift in the scale took place.

The effect of changes in elevation will be greatest on objects that are most distant from the observer and scarcely noted at near distances. Adaptation results in a greater change in the perceived distance of far objects than of near objects. But an alteration of registered distance A causes two effects. In addition to the strong effect on perceived distance, there will be a remarkable effect on the perceived size of the distant object. The moon will appear both *nearer* and *larger*. The perceived size that depends on the expanded AL will be enlarged in proportion to the adaptive displacement of the visual space scale, that is, in proportion to the increase in the value of A.

SUMMARY AND CONCLUSION

An explanation of the moon illusion has been offered that is based on the adaptation theory of visual space. This theory assumes that the perceived size and the perceived distance of an object both depend on the adaptation to the total distance range. Note that the perceived distance of the moon is not the same as the perceived or registered distance of the sky. The two psychological magnitudes are related, however, by their mutual dependence on the absolute space value of the total field of view—the absolute level of spatial adaptation.

To provide for the fact that the visual space appears larger or smaller and that objects within it expand or contract in magnitude as the AL changes in adjustment to changes in the spatial excitation, the model contains a basic parameter A, defined as the upper limit of registered distance. Thus, A provides a measure of the AL to visual space. Since A varies systematically as the moon changes its altitude from horizon to zenith, A is a measure of the moon illusion.

REFERENCES

Boring, E. G. The moon illusion. *American Journal of Physics,* 1943, **11**, 55–60.
Gilinsky, A. S. Perceived size and distance in visual space. *Psychological Review,* 1951, **58**, 460–482.

Gilinsky, A. S. The effect of attitude upon the perception of size. *American Journal of Psychology*, 1955, **68**, 173–192.

Gilinsky, A. S. The effect of growth on the perception of visual space. Paper presented at the meeting of the Eastern Psychological Association, New York, April 1960.

Harway, N. I. Judgment of distance in children and adults. *Journal of Experimental Psychology*, 1963, **65**, 385–390.

Helson, H. *Adaptation-level theory: An experimental and systematic approach to behavior.* New York: Harper, 1964.

Hermans, T. G. The relationship of convergence and elevation changes to judgments of size. *Journal of Experimental Psychology*, 1954, **48**, 204–208.

Holway, A. H., & Boring, E. G. The moon illusion and the angle of regard. *American Journal of Psychology*, 1940a, **53**, 109–116.

Holway, A. H., & Boring, E. G. The apparent size of the moon as a function of the angle of regard: Further experiments. *American Journal of Psychology*, 1940b, **53**, 537–553.

James, W. *The principles of psychology.* New York: Holt, 1890.

Kaufman, L., & Rock, I. The moon illusion, I. *Science*, 1962, **136**, 953–961.

Konorski, J. *Integrative activity of the brain.* Chicago: University of Chicago Press, 1967.

Leibowitz, H., & Hartman, T. Magnitude of the moon illusion as a function of the age of the observer. *Science*, 1959, **130**, 569–570.

McGarvey, H. R. Anchoring effects in the absolute judgment of verbal materials. *Archives of Psychology*, 1943, No. 281.

Pozdena, R. F. Eine Methode zur experimentellen und konstruktiven Bestimmung der Form des Firmamentes. *Zeitschrift für Psychologie*, 1909, **51**, 240–246.

Restle, F. Moon illusion explained on the basis of relative size. *Science*, 1970, **167**, 1092–1096.

Rock, I., & Kaufman, L. The moon illusion, II. *Science*, 1962, **136**, 1023–1031.

Schur, E. Mondtäuschung und Sehgrosskonstanz. *Psychologische Forschung*, 1925, **7**, 44–80.

Woodworth, R. S. *Experimental psychology.* New York: Holt, 1938.

ADAPTATION LEVEL AND STRUCTURAL INTERACTION

ALTERNATE OR COMPLEMENTARY CONCEPTS?

Dorothy Dinnerstein

Twenty-five years ago, when Helson was at Bryn Mawr, I spent a year as a visitor in AL territory. It was one of those visits that turn out to be much more deeply memorable than can possibly be foreseen at the time. Since then, I have studied a number of different ways in which the wider context can affect the character of some local piece of what we experience as reality. Some of these context effects have seemed to me quite easy to conceive of in AL terms. Others have not. In the latter case, it has seemed necessary to take into account structural, grouping, or configurational considerations. To deal with such considerations, I have been thinking in what might be described as a neo-Gestalt way: This way of thinking moves beyond the relatively global classic Gestalt concept of structure; it rests on the more differentiated concept of *multiple structures in interaction.* My purpose here is to try to sketch the relation between this neo-Gestalt approach and the AL approach: The two are, I now believe, complementary, rather than alternative, ways of studying perceptual–cognitive events.

About ten years ago, a paper of Stevens (1958) provoked me into doing a study of discrimination among hefted weights (Dinnerstein, 1965a). This study was designed to support an observation of Helson's which had always made sense to me, and which Stevens had challenged on methodological grounds: that a perceiver's capacity for fine discrimination is flexibly focused at the center of the currently attended-to range of stimuli, and that, therefore, a shift occurs in the zone of maximal discriminative sensitivity within a given series of judged items when one introduces into the situation a nonjudged "anchor" item of greater or lesser intensity. What my study showed was that this kind of shift is not (as Stevens had suggested it might be) just a semantic artifact of the method of single stimuli. The same shift in zone of maximal discriminative sensitivity occurs when one uses the method of constant stimuli: one asks a subject to make a series of successive comparisons between standard and variable weights, introducing as the anchor another (nonjudged) weight, which the subject simultaneously lifts in his left hand each time he lifts one of the comparison pair in his right; under these conditions, the point in the series at which the most errors occur varies with the heaviness or lightness of the anchor.

As I pointed out in discussing that finding, a shift of this kind can be seen not only in AL terms, but also as an instance of a more general Gestalt principle: that the field is most detailed and internally differentiated at its phenomenal center. Köhler and Adams (1958), for example, had expressed this classic principle in some experiments in which they showed that attention affects the discriminability of rows or columns in a weakly structured dot matrix: When the center of the phenomenal field is shifted by making the matrix a background for a figure that a subject has to judge, the matrix becomes internally less differentiated; that is, its subunits (rows or columns) are less distinct. It seemed to me that one difference distinguishing the AL type of anchor-induced shifts in the zone of maximal sensitivity from other instances of this principle, like Köhler's, was that anchor experiments change the center of the phenomenal field by varying some single perceptual dimension like brightness, size, hue, or weight. Such variation is not the only way in which the structure of a field, and the location of its phenomenal center, can be changed, although, since unidimensional variables are relatively simple to measure, it is, methodologically, an especially interesting way. To me, however, the main virtue of the AL approach lies, not in its methodological convenience, but in its conceptual emphasis on the *flexible responsiveness of the nervous system to the available stimulus array, a responsiveness which enables the perceiver to extract the optimal amount of experience, of exercise for his perceptual capacities, and of useful information, out of each situation in which he finds himself.*

Shortly afterward I thought of a way of using the method of constant stimuli to show that what Helson had said about anchor effect on weight judgment can be confirmed, not just for shifts in the zone of maximal discriminability, but also for shifts in apparent heaviness itself. I have used this technique in a number of experiments with student collaborators. It involves the use of nonjudged items that vary from trial to trial, or even within a trial, instead of staying constant for a long period. Since the term "anchor" cannot apply to such unstable stimuli, we call them context items instead. In all these experiments, the subject makes a short series of paired comparisons between a standard (s) and a set of 5 or 7 variable (v) items. In each such comparison, one contrasting (for example, lighter or smaller) nonjudged context item is presented with or just before the standard, and a different contrasting (for example, heavier or larger) nonjudged context item is presented with or just before the variable.

In one study (Dinnerstein, Curcio, & Chinsky, 1966), S was asked to compare two medium weights (s and v), which he lifted successively in one hand, one accompanied by a heavy (H) and the other by a light (L) context weight in the other hand (see Table I).

TABLE I

Constant-Stimuli Weight-Judgment Task with Accompanying Intermanual Context Weights (s–v Pair Successive, Intramanual)[a]

	Condition A		Condition B	
	Left hand	Right hand	Left hand	Right hand
First lift	H	s	L	s
Second lift	L	v	H	v

[a] Here, s = 80 gm.; v = 65–95 gm. The S compares s with each v,
in random order. Every v in the series is more often judged heavier than
s in condition A [where the 320-gm. context weight (H) accompanies
s and the 20-gm. context weight (L) accompanies v] than in
condition B, where H and L are reversed.

TABLE II

Constant-Stimuli Weight-Judgment Task with Preceding Intramanual
Context Weights (s–v Pair Simultaneous, Intermanual)[a]

	Condition A		Condition B	
	Left hand	Right hand	Left hand	Right hand
First lift	H	L	L	H
Second lift	s	v	s	v

[a] Here, s, v, H, and L are as in Table I, except that the v series was
extended from 50 to 110 to embrace the greater magnitude of the
context effect in this situation. Results for conditions A and B differed
as in the situation sketched in Table I, but about 10 times as strongly.

In another study (Dinnerstein, Gerstein, & Michel, 1967), the subject was
asked to compare two medium weights which he lifted simultaneously in both
hands, one preceded by a heavy, and the other by a light, context weight in the
same hand (see Table II).

The same technique has also been used (Dinnerstein, Michel, & Byrwa, 1968)
to study context effects on kinesthetic breadth. The conditions here were
exactly like those just described, except that s and v are now medium breadths,
grasped between the fingers, and H and L are instead W and N, wide and narrow
context breadths.

In all these situations, the same effect appears: Every v item is judged heavier
(or wider) than s more often in condition A than in condition B, and the point
of subjective equality (PSE), of course, correspondingly shifts. The apparent
weight (or breadth) of a judged item hefted (or grasped) in one hand changes

when the context item simultaneously hefted (or grasped) in the other hand is changed. It also changes—much more strongly—when the context item just previously hefted (or grasped) in the same hand is changed.

This work has raised a number of interesting questions. The kinesthetic breadth experiments, to mention just one such question, could clearly be followed up to explore the relation between figural aftereffects and AL effects. My central point here, however, is the relation between the AL approach and my own structural interaction approach.

Adaptation-level theory fits both the weight and the breadth findings, provided that we conceive of an AL which can shift up and down from one heft or grasp to the next and which can be different for the right hand than for the left hand. Helson (1966) sees no difficulty in this notion. On the other hand, while this work was going on, I was also doing some work in visual form perception and in memory, work of a kind that springs from—and I believe requires—a more structural approach. The ideas that I had been developing for this work seemed also to fit the psychophysical material described above. They fitted it neither better nor worse than AL theory does, but rather in a different way. Adaptation-level theory has the advantage of providing a quantitative way of answering some of the questions that this material raised. The other ideas have the advantage of unifying the psychophysical data with a kind of data in which the problem of structure—a problem which, as I shall show, is also implicit in the weight and breadth studies I have just described—is more focal and explicit. The two approaches thus appear to me not as alternatives, but rather—in some way that needs further clarification—as complementary.

The approach that I have been developing extends classic Gestalt theory in a direction that I believe could open a way out of some of that theory's dead ends. Let me illustrate it with one example from form perception, one from memory, and one that bridges these two fields, before showing how it fits the studies of context effects on weight and breadth that I have just described.

Consider Fig. 1, which I shall call area X. When groups of assembled college students are asked to describe this figure in writing, virtually nobody fails to describe it as an unequivocal el. In an old study (Dinnerstein & Wertheimer, 1957), it was established that, under the conditions of Fig. 2, this same area X is an unequivocal square, while under the conditions of Fig. 3, it is an el for about half the Ss. Now there are many ways in which you can think about this simple finding. My way is to note that in Fig. 2, area X is a member of a group consisting of a pair of squares, while in Fig. 3, it is a member of two groups—actually of two *potential* groups, a square pair and a symmetrical constellation of els—which cannot, phenomenally, exist simultaneously. Area X can belong either to one or to the other at any given moment. (For some people, it remains stably in one of these organizations. For others, it switches back and forth.) If this conception of competing groups is tenable, then weakening one of the competitors should make the other more effective; and, indeed, this is just what happens. When the el constellation is made more diffuse or less cohesive (Dinnerstein, 1965b), the square pair regains its dominance. In Fig. 2, area X is described as an el by 4% of the Ss; in Fig. 3, it is described as an el by 53%; and in Fig. 4 it is described as an el by only 12%.

Now, one central point of the interacting-structures conception of a finding like this lies, for me, in its way of handling the issue of effects of previous experience. Many psychologists still think of the intrinsic structure of the field, on the one hand, and the effects of memory, set, and so forth, on the other hand, as dichotomous concepts providing alternate explanations for a given phenomenal outcome. They would suggest, for instance, that maybe area Xs tendency to look el-shaped in Fig. 1, square in Fig. 2, and more el-shaped again in Fig. 3 need not be traced to the classic perceptual factors of simplicity, symmetry, coherence, similarity, and proximity which seem to me relevant for this outcome. Perhaps, they would say, the outcome depends essentially on the fact that the subject knows certain things from experience: He knows that an irregular-looking shape just at the edge of a regular one is more likely to be, in fact, a regular shape that is partly hidden; he knows that similar items often

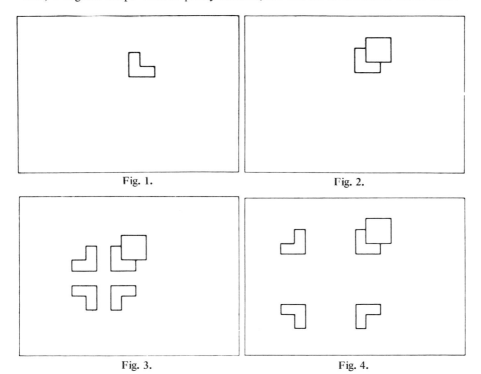

Fig. 1.   Fig. 2.

Fig. 3.   Fig. 4.

occur together; he knows that bilaterally symmetrical, economical, and stable forms occur frequently in nature; and so on. From a structural interaction viewpoint, however, the fact that preceding experience exerts effects provides not an *alternative* to the notion of intrinsic perceptual structuring, but rather an *example* of the intrinsically organized character of experience.

Items occurring across time form groups or structures; these interact with spatial groups or structures formed out of mutually concurrent items, just as spatial structures (like the square pair and el constellation in Fig. 3) interact with each other. Suppose, for example, that the weak el constellation in Fig. 4 were embedded in a temporally extended group of constellations, just as in Fig. 3 a potential el was embedded in a spatial group or constellation of els. Could a temporal group of constellations increase the constellation quality of the potential constellation in Fig. 4, just as a spatial group of els increased the el quality of the potential el in Fig. 3? To test this possibility (Dinnerstein, 1965a), Fig. 4 was preceded, for one group of Ss, by the neutral series depicted in Fig. 5 and, for another group, by the series depicted in Fig. 6. Area X in Fig. 4 was described as el-shaped by 12% of the Ss who had previously seen the Fig. 5 series and by 42% of those who had previously seen the Fig. 6 series.

To give another example from the same set of experiments, Figs. 7 and 8, when shown *separately* to two groups of Ss, are described as a cube and a

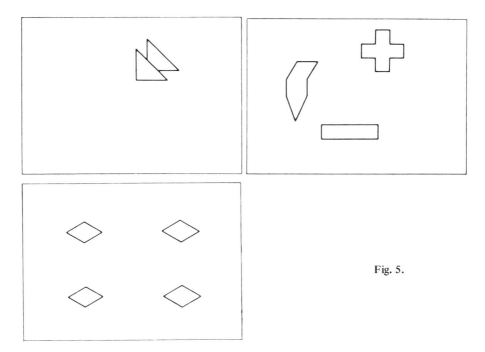

Fig. 5.

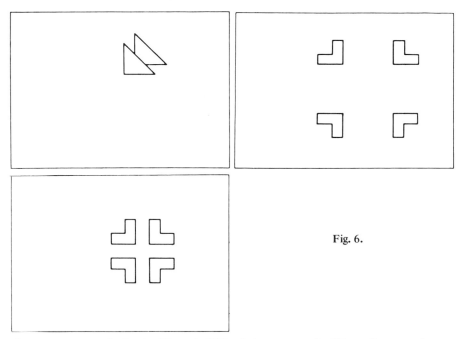

Fig. 6.

hexagon, respectively, in 72 and 79% of the protocols. When they are shown simultaneously (that is, when the constitute a *spatial pair* of potentially similar forms) the two dimensionality of Fig. 7 goes up from 26 to 48%. A corresponding, but stronger, effect occurs when the two appear as a *temporal pair*: Preceded by Fig. 8, the two-dimensionality of Fig. 7 goes up from 26 to 58%; and preceded by Fig. 7, the three dimensionality of Fig. 8 (which the spatial pairing left unaffected) goes up from 21 to 53%. This finding both confirms the functional similarities between spatial and temporal groupings and points up differences between them, which, once we have recognized the similarities, we are in a position to consider more lucidly than was possible before.

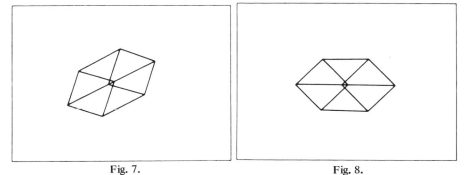

Fig. 7.   Fig. 8.

Let me turn now to a small experiment in rote memory (Dinnerstein & Egeth, 1962) which illustrates this same general principle. (It was oriented also to a more transient issue, which need not concern us here.) In this experiment we presented the subject, just once, with the list of item pairs shown in Fig. 9. Then we showed him the left-hand member of each pair and asked for recall of the right-hand member. We then analyzed his intraserial errors. What emerged was that, proportionately, wrong answers involving confusion between two highly similar items (for example, JULY instead of JUNE, or the upright instead of the inverted triangle) were over 2.5 times as likely as wrong answers involving moderately similar items (for example, JULY and FIVE, or a triangle and a rectangle). And they were over 4.5 times as likely as errors involving the least similar items (for example, a triangle instead of JULY). Now, this finding can, of course, be viewed as a banal instance of a familiar principle specific to rote learning, the principle of intraserial interference. If instead we view it as an illustration of the more general principle of structural interaction, it comes to bear an interesting resemblance to the findings of the form experiments discussed above. Thus, FIVE is a member of a group with DAK; this grouping is based on spatial proximity, and on the subject's intention to try to remember because of the instructions. But by similarity (and similarity, as Wertheimer said, can be conceived of as proximity of quality), FIVE is a member of a group with FOUR (and, to a lesser degree, with JUNE and JULY); this grouping happens across time and despite the subject's intentions. The group constituted by FIVE and FOUR is competing with the group constituted by FIVE and DAK, just as the square pair and the el constellation competed in the experiment previously

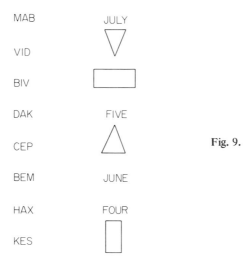

Fig. 9.

described. In both cases the internal coherence of a given subgroup within the larger array is a function of the nature of the other subgroups that are present. The fate of an item belonging to any one subgroup depends upon the relations among all the subgroups or substructures, spatial and temporal, of which this item is a part.

Another example bridges, I think, perception and memory. Asch (1962) has shown that a color and a form presented together are more likely to be correctly matched with each other in a later memory test if they originally appear as in Fig. 10 (a relation which he calls perceptually "unitary"), than if they appear as in Fig. 11 ("nonunitary"). A recent study (Dinnerstein & May, 1968) has made it clear that the internal coherence of the "unitary" color–form pair—reflected in the probability of correct matching in a later test of memory—is not, in fact, purely a local matter of spatial coincidence between these two items; it also depends on the larger structure in which this pair is embedded. A remote context of the same color as the form (Fig. 12) can work to dismember this pair, perceptually and mnemonically. The subjects shown a series of different color–form pairs arranged as in Fig. 12 when compared with the subjects shown a control series in which the remote context is black (see Fig. 13), are less likely to say that the central area always consisted of a colored form lying on top of the surrounding surface (10% as compared with 55%). They also make significantly fewer (two-tailed, $p < .02$) correct color–form matches on a later recall test. The subject's perception of color–form pairs, and also his success at recalling which color went with which form, are thus a function of the interaction between the local area at which color and form coincide and the larger figure of which this area is a part: In the situation shown in Fig. 12, there is competition between the potential existence of a stable color–form pair and the potential existence of a stable, continuous, homogeneous, colored surface, part of which is visible through a hole in the white circle.

Both this study and the one previously described can profitably be seen in terms of the concept, which I regard as central to AL theory, that cognitive energy is distributed over the parts of a stimulus field according to the characteristics of that field. In these experiments, however, the field characteristics studied are grouping or configurational characteristics.

The concept of structures and substructures is, of course, not new to Gestalt theory, or to any other organically oriented approach. What is new is to think in a detailed and systematic way about *interactions* among the different structures of which a given item is part.[1] Any given item is part of a number of different structures, which may overlap or be organized hierarchically, and which may work in the same direction or in opposite directions on the phenomenal quality

---

[1] I believe that this way of thinking is extremely relevant to Restle's and Gilinsky's discussions of apparent size.

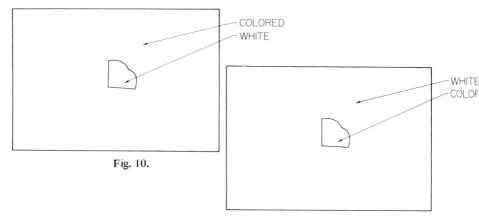

Fig. 10.

Fig. 11.

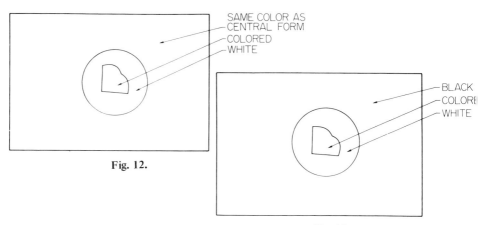

Fig. 12.

Fig. 13.

of this item which is a part of each of them. Their relative strengths can determine the item's phenomenal shape, its distinctness, its size, the intensity of its interaction with a neighboring item in perception, or its cohesiveness with that item in memory. Considered in this way, the sharp distinction between perception and memory dissolves, as it did in Köhler's thought, and does, of course, in Helson's, and, recently, also in Gibson's (1966). The present approach, however, not only rejects the memory–perception distinction, but also permits a systematic analysis of the *interplay* between what is traditionally called perception (the organization of a contemporary stimulus array) and what is traditionally called memory (the organization of the temporally more extended sequence of which the contemporary array is part). This interplay is an instance of the operation of a single set of rules whose nature must be explored, rules that apply in the same way both to interaction between a spatial and a temporal structure and to interaction between two spatial structures, or between two temporal structures.

To return, now, to the weight and breadth studies with which I began: From the structural-interaction viewpoint, these studies show that a given judged weight or breadth in the experimental situation described (see Tables I and II) is a member of two conflicting pairs.[2] One is the pair it forms with the other judged weight or breadth with which it is being compared. The other is the pair it forms with the nonjudged context item which appears simultaneously in the other hand or previously in the same hand. The stronger its interaction with the context item, the more the comparison with the other judged item will be deflected from veridicality. An intermanual pair is, of course, weaker than an intramanual pair. When, therefore, the pair our item forms with the other judged item is intermanual and the pair it forms with the context item is intramanual, the context effect should be stronger, and the judgments deflected further from veridicality, than when these relations are reversed. This, as I have said above, is just what does happen.

In these experiments, the conflicting pairs are simultaneous and temporally extended, respectively. A *simultaneous* pair relation (judged item and context item presented together, one to each hand) can deflect comparison between the members of a *temporally extended* pair (*s* and *v* presented successively to same hand); conversely, a *temporally extended* pair relation (judged item and context item presented successively to same hand) can deflect comparison between the members of a *simultaneous* pair (*s* and *v* presented together, one to each hand). It happens in these experiments that the latter effect is stronger than the former. This is not, however, because temporal pairing *per se* is more powerful, but rather because the temporal pair in this case happens to be the intramanual one. We (Dinnerstein, Byrwa, & Walsh, 1969) have repeated the weight studies using a procedure in which both pairs were temporally extended (see Tables III and IV), and found both intra- and intermanual context effects of the same order of magnitude as those previously reported. This experiment shows that interaction between *two temporal groupings* is functionally similar to interaction between *a spatial and a temporal grouping*. This point complements one made earlier in connection with visual form: that interaction between *two spatial groupings* bears a functional resemblance to interaction between a *spatial and a temporal grouping*.

I said earlier that AL theory and the approach just described seem to me to be complementary. Let me sketch very briefly how. The factors that go into the present kind of AL formula always have a kind of informal face validity.

[2] Actually, it is a member of many other structures, too, but we will consider just those two pairs.

TABLE III

Constant-Stimuli Weight-Judgment Task with Preceding Intermanual Context Weights (*s–v* Pair Successive, Intramanual)[a]

	Condition A		Condition B	
	Left hand	Right hand	Left hand	Right hand
First lift	H		L	
Second lift		*s*		*s*
Third lift	L		H	
Fourth lift		*v*		*v*

[a] Here, *s, v,* H, and L are as in Table I. Results (i.e., more "heavier" judgments for every *v* in the series in condition A than in condition B) were similar to those obtained in the situation sketched in Table I.

TABLE IV

Constant-Stimuli Weight-Judgment Task with Preceding Intramanual Context Weights (*s–v* Pair Successive, Intermanual)[a]

	Condition A		Condition B	
	Left hand	Right hand	Left hand	Right hand
First lift	H		L	
Second lift		L		H
Third lift	*s*		*s*	
Fourth lift		*v*		*v*

[a] Here, *s, v,* H, and L are as in Table I. Results were similar to those obtained in the situation sketched in Table II.

Usually it is intuitively clear beforehand what these factors will be, although their precise weights must, of course, be established empirically in each situation; sometimes[3] important factors can be neglected because of their very self-evidence. It seems to me that the concept of structures in interaction which I have tried to outline here might make it possible to designate in a more formal way what factors ought to be relevant in a particular situation, and what relations among them make this so. Initial analysis in terms of such a concept

[3] This was pointed up, for example, by Brown's experiment (see Section V) on the previously overlooked importance of meaning in determining the effect of anchor weights on judged weights.

could provide an explicit systematic background (instead of an implicit commonsense background) for the decision about what to measure in an AL experiment. An AL approach modified to encompass configurational considerations would explore *in their structural setting* the shifts in intensity, discriminability, etc., that Helson has shown us how to measure. At the same time, a configurational approach modified to encompass the AL concept would be reoriented to appreciate the *active, flexible responsiveness of the perceiver.*

What I am arguing for, most centrally, is an atmosphere for our work in which certain family connections could be experienced more vividly and used more articulately: family connections not only between AL theory and classic Gestalt theory, but also among AL theory and some of Gestalt theory's other living relatives.

REFERENCES

Asch, S. E. A problem in the theory of associations. *Psychologische Beiträge,* 1962, **6,** 553–563.
Dinnerstein, D. Intermanual effects of anchors on zones of maximal sensitivity in weight-discrimination. *American Journal of Psychology,* 1965, 78, 66–74. (a)
Dinnerstein, D. Previous and concurrent visual experience as determinants of phenomenal shape. *American Journal of Psychology,* 1965, 78, 235–242. (b)
Dinnerstein, D., & Egeth, H. On the development of associations. *Psychologische Beiträge,* 1962, 6, 544–552.
Dinnerstein, D., & May, R. Internal coherence of an entity, perceptual and mnemonic, as a function of wider context. Unpublished manuscript, 1968.
Dinnerstein, D., & Wertheimer, M. Some determinants of phenomenal overlapping. *American Journal of Psychology,* 1957, 70, 21–37.
Dinnerstein, D., Curcio, F., & Chinsky, J. Contextual determination of apparent weight as demonstrated by the method of constant stimuli. *Psychonomic Science,* 1966, **5,** 251–252.
Dinnerstein, D., Gerstein, I., & Michel, G. Interaction of simultaneous and successive stimulus groupings in determining apparent weight. *Journal of Experimental Psychology,* 1967, 73, 298–302.
Dinnerstein, D., Michel, G., & Byrwa, D. Inter- and intramanual context effects on kinaesthetically perceived breadth. Unpublished manuscript, 1968.
Dinnerstein, D., Byrwa, D., & Walsh, W. Interaction between two temporally extended pairs in the contextual determination of perceived heaviness. Unpublished manuscript, 1969.
Gibson, J. J. *The senses considered as perceptual systems.* Boston: Houghton, 1966.
Helson, H. Private communication, 1966.
Köhler, W. & Adams, P. A. Perception and attention. *American Journal of Psychology,* 1958, 71, 489–503.
Stevens, S. S. Adaptation-level vs. the relativity of judgment. *American Journal of Psychology,* 1958, 71, 633–646.

COMMENT

Arnold Well

Dinnerstein suggests that the concept of structure or configuration (as found in Gestalt psychology) be extended to a concept of multiple structures in interaction. At the simplest level it is suggested that contextual effects can occur on the basis of stimulation presented concurrently with, or prior to, the item to be judged or described. It is further suggested that it may be fruitful to consider these antecedent and concurrent contextual influences within a common conceptual framework. Hopefully, then, it may be possible to find a single set of rules—sort of an extended set of Gestalt principles—that apply in some way to interactions between spatial and temporal structures as well as to those between different temporal structures and between different spatial structures.

The weight and breadth studies mentioned by Dinnerstein do seem to show that a simultaneous-pair relation can influence comparisons between members of a temporally extended pair and also that a temporally extended relation can have a similar effect on a simultaneous pair. The work cited on visual form again shows a kind of functional similarity between the effects of concurrent and antecedent context. Perhaps then, as suggested, a common set of rules can be found underlying both kinds of contextual effects. It is, however, difficult to reconcile rules of this sort with the fact that it is possible for the very same contextual item to have very different influences on the perception of a stimulus item, depending upon whether stimulus and context are presented simultaneously or successively. If, for instance, two concentric circles are presented simultaneously, the smaller circle will be seen as larger than it would have been in the absence of the larger circle. It is also well known (Cooper & Weintraub, 1970) that if the circles are presented successively with the larger circle presented first, then the smaller circle will be seen as smaller than it would have been in isolation. Very likely, some real conceptual distinction will have to be maintained between temporal and spatial groupings.

It may be of some interest to note that the above result is consistent with AL theory if one is willing to consider that the "relevant" contextual item for the smaller circle is the diameter of the larger circle when they are presented successively, and the width of the annulus formed by the two circles when they are presented simultaneously. There seem, however, to be no very compelling reasons to think that this should be the case. Unfortunately, those factors determining which stimulus aspects serve as effective contextual influences on the perception of other stimuli are not well understood. In the absence of any clear understanding of this concept of relevance, discussion tends to become somewhat circular. That is, if a stimulus modifies the perception of another stimulus, we call it relevant, and if a stimulus is relevant, then it should modify perception.

If I understand Dinnerstein's approach correctly, it is directed at this type of problem. Perhaps thinking in terms of multiple structures in interaction will make it possible to determine some of the factors underlying the concept of relevance. If this approach meets with success in generating rules for determining what kinds of things constitute structures, what structures interact with other structures, and possibly what the nature of these interactions might be, then a valuable step forward will have been taken. The problem is to avoid the kind of circularity encountered in dealing with the concept of relevance in the ultimate definition of terms like structure, multiple structures, and interaction.

REFERENCE

Cooper, L. A., & Weintraub, D. J. Delboeuf-type circle illusions: Interactions among luminance, temporal characteristics, and inducing-figure variations. *Journal of Experimental Psychology*, 1970, 85, 75–82.

Perception and Reaction (Vigilance)

INTRODUCTION

John A. Hebert

The excellence of the contributions to this section convinces one of the richness and continuing vitality of AL theory. Reading Flock's article and the subsequent discussion by Judd, one finds oneself the victim of a recency effect: At the conclusion of Flock's article one is quite convinced that the "half-life" of the Adams–Cobb–Judd–Helson formula for lightness is just about finished; then Judd convinces one that for "the range [of luminance] of distinct but comfortable vision" the lightness formula is very adequate. One can have no doubt that the swing back and forth on the reader's part could go on indefinitely if we continued alternating these two persuasive scientists. Hopefully, however, the swings would gradually decrease in magnitude, until one finally reached a stable opinion on the matter. Adaptation-level theory would predict, of course, that the final position on the matter would be in the middle of the two judgments. In any case, Flock has clearly demonstrated the limitations of the lightness formula and has offered some substitute quantifications, while Judd clearly demonstrates the practical value of the formula for the human visual apparatus.

In a sense, Judd talks about relevance, that is, for all practical purposes luminance level is not a necessary ingredient in the calculation of AL—except at extreme levels (for example, very dim or very bright). This topic is explored in some depth by the Avant–Bevan contribution and is certainly talked about in Trumbull's ensuing discussion. The experimental investigation of relevance is perhaps the most interesting aspect of the Avant–Bevan article. Until the limiting influence of certain classes of stimuli—say anchors on weight judgments—is firmly established experimentally, it may not be possible to know the scope of applicability of AL theory to all specific situations. We must be prepared to accept the fact that individuals may differ widely on what they consider to be relevant, and so one might never achieve a general statement for determining relevance.

It is interesting that most of the disagreements about AL matters revolve around problems of quantification. The fact that a given empirical formula for the calculation of AL may be an inadequate approximation in some instances is disturbing, but this does not necessarily reflect badly on the theory itself. Helson (1964) has pointed this out, as Flock does here. Many critics of AL theory, unfortunately, fail to make this distinction.

Adaptation level is a theoretical construct which is defined in many ways. Starting with the general statement that $AL = f(S)$, where S is stimuli, we have a first definition. To be useful, this definition has to be expanded, as, for example, in the form

$$AL = S^p B^q R^r,$$

where S are focal stimuli, B are background stimuli, R are residual stimuli or past experience, and p, q, and r are the relative weights given to those three classes of stimuli. Even at this point, however, relatively lttle testing of the formulation is possible, since any of the weighting coefficients could equal zero, eliminating that class of stimuli in the calculation of AL, or it could be shown that a fourth class of stimuli needs to be included, and so forth.

When a more specific model, such as

$$\log(AL + .75d) = (\log X_i)/n + 3 \log C$$

is offered, more detailed questions can be raised (and experimental verification sought). For instance, does the size of the interval between stimuli (d) affect judgment? Should the anchor be weighted by a factor of 3? Questions such as these lend themselves to the impression that a "no" answer is a critical blow to AL. This is simply not the case, however. The fact that a given empirical mathematical model is inappropriate in a particular situation simply suggests that revision of that model may be in order, not that AL is an invalid concept. Nevertheless, this does not mean that AL is beyond disproof. In our efforts to find good quantitative formulas for rather precise prediction, we tend to forget that AL theory often makes some rather precise *ordinal* predictions based on some theoretical statements about AL. It is relatively rare to find gross errors in ordinal predictions with AL theory. One should recall that correctly predicting the order of mean response level to, say, five stimuli is something of the order of less than one chance in a hundred by guessing. This is not to disparage the attempt to seek further refinement by quantitative methods, but when that attempt at refinement falls short of its goal, one should not assume that the theory is to blame. If, however, ordinal predictions fall short of the mark, one should seriously question the validity of such formulations.

The theoretical power of AL does not derive from any specific quantification, but from its implicit definition as an internal reference point by which the subject judges stimuli. The power of the notion lies in the simple chain of inference that if the subject judges stimuli with reference to AL, and if AL changes by virtue of experimental manipulation, a concomitant shift in the subject's judgment *must* occur. What is needed at this point is some method for predicting when AL will shift and in which direction, as well, perhaps, as a redefinition of AL in new operational terms. Helson defined AL operationally as that stimulus which is rated neutral with respect to some dimension (for example, light–heavy), on a category rating scale. This definition followed fairly directly from one of a set of statements implicitly defining AL—the neutral or null-point notion. Once AL was defined operationally, it was possible to develop an empirical model by plugging in the variables that seem to affect the value of AL. The model could then be used to predict in new situations.

One does not need a terribly accurate empirical model to make simple ordinal predictions. For example, if one is dealing with a set of weights whose midpoint is around, say, 500 gm. and is asking for ratings from subjects on a rating scale, introducing a value above the midpoint is likely to pull the AL upward, while introducing a value below the midpoint is liable to bias AL downward. The advantage of a more precise model, however, is the foreknowledge that the perceived midpoint will be decentered below the arithmetic mean. Lest I be accused of having rather lax criteria for acceptable prediction, let me say that I have in mind the application of AL in areas such as learning and social psychology, where exact quantitative methods are only beginning to be successfully applied. As a final note, let it be said that the full power of AL is only starting to be realized. Defining AL in new operational terms—such as the group norm, the category boundary line for human decision making, the stored referent in single-stimulus training—will lead to new applications of this rich construct. Indeed, thinking of AL in different operational terms can lead to a construct validation (see the Appendix).

REFERENCE

Helson, H. *Adaptation-level theory: An experimental and systematic approach to behavior.* New York: Harper, 1964.

ADAPTATION LEVEL AND VISUAL SPACE PERCEPTION[1]

Lloyd L. Avant and William Bevan

Our purpose here is rather straightforward and uncomplicated: to demonstrate the influence of AL in the perception of the several aspects of visual space. Essentially, AL theory has contributed to our understanding of space perception by refining a widely employed concept—the notion of context or frame of reference—and by providing a psychophysical model which integrates the contributions of both focal and contextual stimuli in the generation of perceptions.

Illustrations of the importance of context to an understanding of visual perception—regardless of one's theoretical persuasion—are readily available in the historical literature. Hering's local sign for height at each retinal point required the associated signs for breadth and depth in order to be effective. Wundt's explanation of visual localization required the integration of experienced eye and body movement. For Mach and Schumann four lines at right angles became either square or diamond depending upon their orientation—the context afforded by the horizontal and vertical axes of the figure. A *new* perception required the presence of at least one prior image for Titchener, and adjustive behavior rendered the context for *old* perceptions obvious. Wertheimer showed that the conditions of presentation of two alternately flashing lights determined what would be seen: an apparently shifting single light, two stationary lights, or stationary succession.

In the AL approach the contributions of context to perception take on a significance in formal theory which has not been previously accorded them. The AL model describes the interaction of three broad classes of perceptual determinants. Two of the classes are explicitly contextual, and all three are given quantitative definition: $AL = S^p B^q R^r$, where S represents the focal stimulus, B

[1] Preparation of this paper was supported, in part, by Contract N00014-67-A-0163-0001 between the Physiological Psychology Branch, Office of Naval Research and the Johns Hopkins University. Two of the experiments reported herein were performed while the first author was Visiting Professor at the Behavioral Research Laboratory, U.S. Army Human Engineering Laboratories, Aberdeen Proving Ground, Maryland.

its immediate surround, and R the inputs the perceiver brings to the viewing situation with him. The exponents p, q, and r indicate the contribution of each class of variable to the AL. This model allows for the definition of stimuli in terms of behavioral effectiveness rather than in simple physical terms, and it assumes a process of organismic integration whose logical properties relate the contributions of separate classes of variable, irrespective of their substantive nature, to specific behavioral results.

Almost from its beginning, the AL concept has been viewed by its proponents as the basis of a general theory of perception (Bevan, 1958). At the same time, the development of the theory in its most explicit form has most frequently involved experimentation with sensory dimensions or dimensions that are essentially sensory in character, such as time. If the goals of general theory making are to be served, it is now important that the AL paradigm be more frequently applied to settings which are peculiarly representative of the tradition of perceptual psychology, and no problem so characterizes that tradition as the effort to understand the perception of solid objects dispersed in three-dimensional space. To demonstrate the contribution of AL theory to such an understanding, we will review various data, drawn for the most part from the writers' laboratories, which we think address these fundamental issues of space perception: the necessary presence of context for even the most primitive sensing of space; the analysis of perceptual space in terms of its fundamental characteristics; the notions of veridical and illusory space perception; and the organism's estimation of space parameters when stimulus input is minimal.

The Essential Character of Context or Surround

Under most circumstances visual space is so impressively stable that it is easy to conceive of it in static and absolute terms; thus the ancient assumption that perception is a pictorial copy of the physical world. Attempts to account for the stability of perceived space brought the lively *nature–nurture* debate of an earlier century, and although Helmholtz convincingly demonstrated the limitation of Hering's doctrine of retinal local signs (see Hochberg, 1962, pp. 284–287), recognition of the importance of retinal registration continues to be seen in the modern experimental emphasis on controlled visual angle. That the perception of visual space is, however, more than the passive reception of sensory patterns is clearly evidenced by, for example, the geometrical illusions, the Gestalt studies of perceptual organization, and the clinical observations of persons who gain sight in adulthood. For present purposes, the importance of context in perceptual organization can be quickly demonstrated by a recent study on metacontrast suppression by Bevan, Jonides, and Collyer (1970). We have selected it because it permits illustration of the interplay of spatial, temporal, and chromatic properties of briefly presented stimuli in the generation of a simple perceptual response.

The experiment employed the Werner (1935) ring–disk paradigm. The Ss were presented with disks followed by rings in all combinations of four colors—red, yellow, green, and blue—and at 10 different interstimulus intervals varying, in 7-msec. steps, from 5 through 68 msec. Lightness and saturation for all stimuli were Munsell value 6 and chroma 10, respectively. Disk duration was fixed at 18 msec., while ring duration was 100 msec. Within a significant portion of the range of intersignal intervals used (12–40 msec.), color combinations indeed proved to be a determinant of masking effectiveness. Total masking of the disk occurred least frequently (18.1%, on the average) when the disk and annulus were of complementary colors, and most frequently (30.8%, on the average) when both were of the same color. When disk and annulus were of different but noncomplementary colors, an intermediate frequency of masking (an average of 26.6%) was observed. Table I presents the relative frequency of masking under these three conditions at each of the intersignal intervals employed in the experiment.

TABLE I

Percent Trials on Which S Failed to Detect the Disk, When Disk and Ring Pairs Were (A) Identical in Hue, (B) Different but Not Complementary, and (C) Complementary[a]

Interstimulus interval (ISI)	Ring-disk chromatic relations		
	A	B	C
5	66.3	70.6	63.8
12	63.8	53.8	37.5
19	35.0	37.5	23.8
26	31.3	22.5	16.3
33	15.0	11.9	11.3
40	8.8	7.5	2.5
47	2.5	3.1	1.3
54	1.3	1.3	0
61	0	0	0
68	1.3	0	0
Overall $\bar{X}$:	22.5	20.8	15.6

[a] From Bevan, W., Jonides, J., and Collyer, S. C. Chromatic relationships in metacontrast suppression. *Psychonomic Science*, 1970, **19**, 367-368, p. 367. Copyright 1970 by Psychonomic Journals, Inc., and reproduced by permission.

Bevan *et al.* (1970) account for these results as follows: When presented for a sufficiently long duration, the ring tends to tinge the region near its inside boundary with its complementary color. This irradiated color, in turn, interacts with the emerging contour of the briefly flashed disk. When the induced color is the same as that of the emerging contour, emergence is enhanced, and the probability of masking is accordingly reduced. On the other hand, when the two colors are complementary, the irradiated color desaturates that of the emerging contour, and the probability of masking is maximal. When the colors are noncomplementary the effect is partial desaturation, and an intermediate level of masking results. However, irrespective of particular interpretation, the data clearly indicate that whether a briefly presented disk is perceived at all depends upon the spatiotemporal properties, as well as the color, of its surround.

ADAPTATION LEVEL AND THE BASIC PROPERTIES OF VISUAL SPACE

Early in his book on the perception of the visual world, Gibson (1950) pointed out (pp. 12–23) that classical accounts of space perception had been attempts to determine the mind's contribution to sensory input, and that four categories of analysis marked this earlier discourse. These categories are (a) *extensity,* the character of being spread out in two dimensions; (b) *shape* or form; (c) *location,* a property which has to do with the identification of position through coordinates; and (d) *depth* or distance, which involves the third dimension. Based on the contributions of Gestalt psychology, one may add a fifth category: (e) *spatial organization,* that is, the relationships that obtain among discrete forms arranged in space. The distinction between sensations and the mind's contribution to perception has largely vanished as a result of the modern recognition that sensation and perception cannot be empirically separated (see Corso, 1967, p. 187; Helson, 1967, p. 313), but the analytical categories remain and are of broader significance because of their freedom from the metaphysical constraints of earlier thought. Approaching the understanding of space perception through each of these categories, our strategy has been to show that the perceptual response is sensitive to shifts in a *perceptual norm* which, in turn, reflects the interaction between a focal stimulus and those stimuli which form its context. Let us illustrate by reviewing some representative data from our laboratories that are relevant to each of these five analytical categories.

Extensity

Several years ago Helson and Bevan (1964) reported a series of experiments on the judgment of relative area, one of which is particularly instructive at this point. In this experiment the subjects were asked to estimate, by percentage, the proportion of the total area of a rectangular white card taken up at its center by a black rectangle of the same shape. For each of three experimental conditions there was a seven-member stimulus series in which the white cards varied in size from 1.5 x 2.0 to 10.5 x 14.0 inches, with each card being 1.5 inches wider and 2.0 inches longer than the preceding member of the series. For each experimental group the size of the black rectangle was a *constant* proportion of the total area. For one group of Ss this proportion was 21%, for a second 53%, and for a third 81%. Figure 1 presents the results of this experiment. There was, first of all, a marked error of overestimation in all groups which we need not consider in the present discussion. More importantly, the amount of overestimation varied with

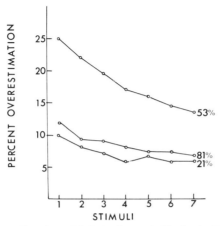

Fig. 1. Error of overestimation with judged area held physically constant and size of background varied. Background size was increased from stimulus 1 to stimulus 7. The parameters indicate relative size of the area judged. (From Helson, H., and Bevan, W. An investigation of variables in judgments of relative area. *Journal of Experimental Psychology*, 1964, **67**, 335–341, p. 340. Copyright 1964 by the American Psychological Association and reproduced by permission.)

the relative size of the area judged. It was largest for the intermediate-sized black area (53%) and approximately equal when relative size was either larger (81%) or smaller (21%).[2] Finally, apparent size was found to be related inversely to overall fixed size, being clearly greater for the smaller than for the larger white cards in each stimulus sequence. In summary, perceived extensity was found to depend upon both the relative size of the focal stimulus and the overall size of its background. Two things are important to emphasize about the method employed to obtain these results. They were obtained with an absolute response language (namely, discrete percentages, not category labels such as "greater than" vs. "smaller than," or "small," "very small," and the like, vs. "large," "very large," and so forth) and the focal stimuli were of *fixed* relative area.

[2] It is worth noting that in order for overall field size to influence perception of the centered black squares predictably, field size had to *vary* within each S's experience. In an earlier experiment in this same series, card size remained constant while size of square changed, and no influence of background upon judgment was demonstrated.

Shape

The role of AL in the judgment of shape is readily illustrated by some data reported by Bevan and Pritchard. These investigators conducted a series of experiments concerned with determining the limits within which anchoring stimuli exerted influence upon the judgment of shape. The question of limits, of course, identifies the general problem of relevance, a matter to which we shall return later. Meanwhile, an experiment early in the series (Bevan & Pritchard, 1963b) will serve to illustrate that perceived shape—a metathetic domain— reflects pooling no less than do such prothetic dimensions as loudness and lightness.

The subjects received a four-item series consisting of a square (5 x 5 cm.) and three rectangles (4.8 x 5.2 cm.; 4.6 x 5.4 cm.; 4.4 x 5.6 cm.), and judged these shapes for their departure from squareness, using an open-ended scale with categories proceeding from "square" and "square but slightly rectangular" to "more rectangular than square" and "rectangular." Stimuli were black rectangles on a white background and were presented in a Harvard tachistoscope. Two groups were tested: One judged only the series members; one also judged an additional rectangle (4.0 x 6.0 cm.) after every third trial with the series members. In half the trials, the rectangles were presented in the horizontal orientation, and in the other half, in the vertical. The results (summarized in Fig. 2) show, first, that the introduction of the additional stimulus prompted a shift in the series judgments in the direction of squareness. Second, none of the figures, including the geometric square, appeared perfectly square. Third, it is clear that orientation of the rectangles made a difference in appearance, the figures generally being judged more rectangular when vertically oriented. This last finding, of course, merely identifies the horizontal–vertical illusion. However, it is of particular interest here that the interaction between stimulus shape and orientation was reliable; that is, the more rectangular the shape, the greater is the illusory effect. Finally, the effects of anchor (the additional stimulus) and of orientation were discrete functions, for when the figures were in the vertical orientation, anchor and orientation tended to work against each other, while for the horizontal orientation they tended to reinforce each other, yielding impressions which most frequently were expressed as squareness. Perceived shape, then, like extensity, reflects the integration of varying stimulus inputs.

Like many of the early experiments generated by the AL approach, this one required the subjects to categorize particular stimuli by discrete labels. Such experiments have been subjected to the criticism that the data reveal simple changes in the use of category labels rather than perceptual shifts (Stevens, 1957, 1958). However, the probability that genuine perceptual changes are indeed involved is indicated by the significant anchor x orientation interaction

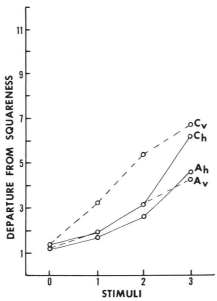

Fig. 2. The influence of a rectangular anchor upon the judged departure from squareness of rectangular figures when the stimuli were presented in horizontal (h) and vertical (v) orientations. The values on the abscissa represent the series stimuli ordered from the 5 x 5-cm. square (0) to the 4.4 x 5.6-cm. rectangle (3). The anchor position is designated A. C and A labels on the curves refer to control and anchor groups, respectively. (From Bevan, W., and Pritchard, Joan F. The anchor effect and the problem of relevance in the judgment of shape. *Journal of General Psychology*, 1963, **69**, 147–161, p. 151. Copyright 1963 by the Journal Press and reproduced by permission.)

and by the failure of these subjects to respond to the geometric square with the label "square."

Location

Data from an unpublished experiment by Bevan and Bell on the effects of systematic stimulus impoverishment illustrate the operation of AL in the estimation of spatial location. Members of the stimulus series were colored photographs of a model terrain consisting of a uniformly painted green felt surface containing a painted roadway (two solid white side lines and a dotted white center line) receding into the distance and a yellow model automobile facing the observer in the right lane. The series consisted of seven such stimuli selected from a larger set of 27 photographs taken with the camera a constant physical distance from the car but at angular subtenses varying from 0° (at the surface of the display) to 90° (directly above the car). Series members covered a

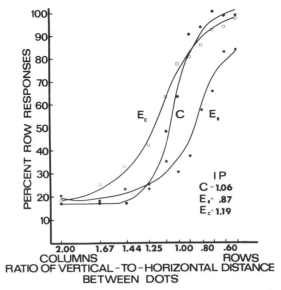

Fig. 3. Relative frequency with which a matrix of dots was perceived to consist of a set of rows when the ratio of vertical-to-horizontal distances between pairs of adjacent dots varied from .50 to 2. (Data are for control C, and column and row anchor, E_C and E_R, conditions.) (From Bell, R. A., and Bevan, W. Influence of anchors upon the operation of certain Gestalt organizing principles. *Journal of Experimental Psychology,* 1968, 78, 670–678, p. 672. Copyright 1968 by the American Psychological Association and reproduced by permission.)

show clear contrast shifts. The Ss in the row anchor group more frequently reported series members as column arrangements, the IP shifting to an array in which the vertical separation was 22% greater than the horizontal. Though less pronounced, a clear shift in the opposite direction occurred in the column anchor group, the IP being identified with an arrangement in which the vertical distance between dots was only 87% of the horizontal distance. So impressive were these anchor effects that, in some cases, they prompted a response opposite to that expected on the basis of the physical pattern obtaining in the series member. These findings were interpreted as support for Helson's (1966) conclusion that "there are spatial adaptations, no less than chromatic adaptations, which are responsible for the way spatial patterns are formed [p. 173]."

These data, like certain of those discussed earlier, answer the charge (Stevens, 1958) that AL shifts simply reflect the readjustment of category labels when the stimulus range is extended by the introduction of the anchor. More recently, Sekuler and Erlebacher (1971) have criticized these results on still other grounds as artifacts of the category method. These writers reason, from reports by

Parducci and Haugen (1967) and Tune (1964) that the subjects tend to use all available psychophysical categories with equal frequency, approximately as follows: Because an anchor is clearly separated from the stimulus series, it will, on practically all its presentations, produce its characteristic response (for example, row), thus reducing the probability for assignment of that response to more ambiguous stimuli near the middle of the stimulus series. As a consequence, a shift in the IP toward the opposite end of the stimulus series must accompany the corresponding increase in the probability that other responses will be made to series members. Such a shift thus is mistaken for an anchor-produced shift in AL.

This argument obviously overlooks several relevant considerations. It neglects the report of Michels and Helson (1954) that judges are unable to distinguish order of presentation when standard and variable stimuli are of the same magnitude although time-order effects (TOE) do systematically occur. It also ignores the finding (Bevan & Pritchard, 1963a) that subthreshold—and therefore uncategorized—tones systematically alter loudness judgments of supraliminal tones. The argument is likewise denied by every instance in which inflection points in the effectiveness of anchors are observed (see, for example, Helson, 1967, pp. 338–339) and by the fact that the same predictable anchor shifts occur when experimenters employ stronger forms of scaling than the category method [see, for example Egeth, Avant, and Bevan (1968), and the following section of this contribution]. At any rate, while we appreciate the limitations inherent in the category method, we are compelled by numerous data to conclude that pooling results in genuine changes in perception.

ADAPTATION LEVEL AND ILLUSORY SPACE PERCEPTION

The phrase, "illusory space perception," is a misleading one. As Boring (1942) has correctly observed, "Strictly speaking, the concept of illusion has no place in psychology because no experience actually copies 'reality' [p. 238] ." Indeed, perceptual experience may be conceived as varying along a continuum marked, at one extreme, by those perceptions which are determined essentially by the physics of the visual input and, at the other, by those perceptions which are determined predominantly by intrasubjective variables. A major virtue of AL theory is that its formal model allows the experimenter to work logically unimpeded at any region along this continuum.

Boring (1942, p. 268) dates the beginning of interest in the illusions with Necker's cube; we might begin ours with a report of the influence of AL on its perceived orientation (Turner & Bevan, 1964). While it is not properly identified as an illusory figure, the reversible character of the Necker cube reflects the operation of intrasubjective factors no less than do geometrical illusions. Indeed, it is possible, with a two-field mixing tachistoscope, to create cubes which vary in their susceptibility to reversal. With this in mind, Turner and Bevan arranged a psychophysical series that varied from a cube in an unambiguously left orientation through the completely ambiguous Necker cube to a cube that was always seen as oriented toward the right (see Fig. 4). Three experiments were performed, all with the same experimental rationale. This involved an adaptation series during which one or another of several procedures was employed to generate an orientation norm favoring *either* the left *or* the right orientation,

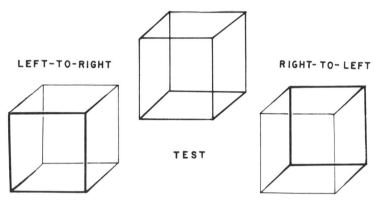

LEFT-TO-RIGHT   **RIGHT-TO-LEFT**

TEST

Fig. 4. The stimulus figures. The figure on the left side is the left-oriented figure; that on the right, the right-oriented. The center figure is the balanced (ambiguous) cube. Not shown is the soft shading on the "near surface" (that bounded by the heavy contours) used to enhance the impression of left or right orientation. (From Turner, E. D., and Bevan, W. Patterns of experience and the perceived orientation of the Necker Cube. *Journal of General Psychology,* 1964, **70,** 345–352, p. 347. Copyright 1964 by the Journal Press and reproduced by permission.)

after which Ss were presented with the ambiguous (Necker) cube on a short series of three test trials. The expectation that the ambiguous cube would be perceived with preponderant frequency in the orientation opposite to that of the adaptation series was clearly confirmed in all three experiments. To illustrate, on 28 of the 30 test trials of experiment I (10 Ss x 3 test trials), Ss reported the ambiguous cube to be in the orientation opposite to that favored during adaptation. The intention in these experiments was to study the evolution of *locational* norms, and as such they form part of the background of understanding for the experiments on veridical perception of location and distance described above.

The approach taken by Avant and his students has employed traditionally identified illusory figures (Avant & Kent, 1970; Wagner & Avant, 1970; Avant, Wagner, & Kent, 1970). Their rationale considered the illusions to involve perceptual dimensions of varying complexity. Thus the research strategy has involved applying the anchor paradigm of AL theory to the study of an illusion of *linear extent* (the simplest dimension), one of *areal extent,* and one of *confluence* (the most complex dimension). Accordingly, the Müller–Lyer illusion, Titchener's circles, and a variant of Zöllner's illusion were the figures selected for study.

In the first experiment, Ss were presented with two Müller–Lyer figures, centered in the right and the left halves of one field of a Harvard tachistoscope. These horizontally oriented illusory figures were either 1.5, 2, or 2.5 inches long, and were bordered above and below by simple straight horizontal lines which were either 1 or 3 inches long. The Müller–Lyer figures were considered by the experimenters to be focal stimuli, and the bordering lines to be anchors. The three stimulus lengths, two anchor lengths, and the inward versus outward orientation of the Müller–Lyer obliques· were combined to generate a 12-member stimulus series which was presented for judgment by the method of pair comparisons. The presentation interval was .50 sec., and Ss were asked to report the longer of the two Müller-Lyer figures in each comparison. Each S's judgments were converted, by Woodworth and Schlosberg's procedure (1954, pp. 252–254), to z' scores for each configuration, and these scores were then evaluated by analysis of variance. The data are summarized in Fig. 5. In this graph, the two members of each successive pair of stimuli are, except for the length of the anchors, exactly the same. In each pair, the left member contained the short anchor, and the right member contained the long anchor. Each of the figures anchored by short lines appeared shorter than its companion which was anchored by long lines. Without anchors, the members of each pair would have been identical, and could have been represented by only a single z' score which would have been reasonably expected to fall between those shown in Fig. 5. The main effects of stimulus length, anchor length, and stimulus obliques were significant, and there were no interactions. It thus appears that perceived length of these focal stimuli depended upon the pooling of all spatial magnitudes within each configuration. It is reasonable to recommend the same interpretation of the perceptual result when only the Müller–Lyer figure is judged.

The outcome of the first experiment was confirmed and extended in a second experiment employing the same rationale and procedure. Here, stimulus configurations were presented as in experiment I, but simple straight lines were the centered focal stimuli, and the bordering anchoring lengths consisted of Müller–Lyer figures. Four stimulus lengths and two anchoring lengths were employed, and these, combined with inward vs. outward obliques on the Müller–Lyer figures, served to constitute a 16-member series for pair comparisons. Again, Ss reported the longer of the two focal–stimulus lines, and data were handled as in experiment I. The data are summarized in Fig. 6 in which the significant three-way interaction among stimulus length, anchor length, and anchor obliques is plotted. The left panel presents judgments of

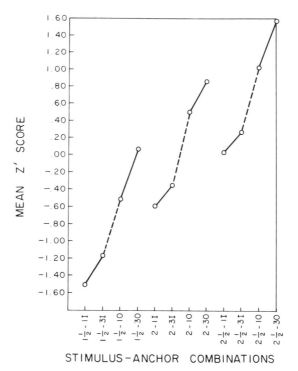

MEAN Z' SCORE

STIMULUS–ANCHOR COMBINATIONS

Fig. 5. Average *z'* scores for each of the 12 illusion–anchor combinations of experiment I. Stimulus configurations are identified on the abscissa by first, focal stimulus length, second, anchor length, and third, inward versus outward obliques on the Müller–Lyer figure (from Avant & Kent, 1970).

configurations containing the short anchors and the right panel presents judgments of configurations containing the long anchors. The plotted parameter is the influence of anchor obliques across stimulus lengths. One may notice in the left panel that when the anchor and stimulus length were both short, the influence of inward obliques was to make the focal stimulus appear shorter, while outward obliques made it appear longer; with the short anchor and the longest stimulus length, this effect of obliques was reversed. The same effects appear in the right panel; the stimulus length which most nearly approximated the length of the anchor was made to appear shorter by inward obliques and longer by outward obliques, and as stimulus length deviated from anchor length, this effect of obliques was reversed. Thus, both an assimilation and a contrast effect were observed, and whether inward Müller–Lyer obliques prompt an apparent shortening or lengthening of stimulus lines depends on the pooling of other spatial magnitudes within the stimulus array. These data are reminiscent of those of Helson and his colleagues (Helson, 1963; Helson & Rohles, 1959;

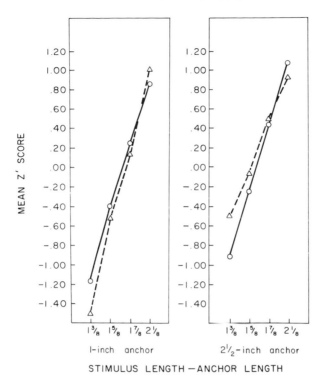

Fig. 6. Average z' score for each of the 16 stimulus configurations of experiment II: (– – –) inward obliques; (———) outward obliques (from Avant, Wagner, & Kent, 1970).

Helson & Joy, 1962) that reveal the full range of pooling from assimilation to contrast in the perception of lightness.

The third experiment employed Titchener's illusion of areal extent. The series for judgment consisted of 11 figures in which the ratio between surrounding and center circle diameters varied, in .05 steps, from .75 to 1.25. A control group judged whether the center circles were larger than surrounding circles in each member of the series five times. Members of one experimental group were presented with series stimuli the same number of times alternated with presentations of an anchoring configuration in which the ratio between surrounding and center circle diameters was .20; for a second experimental group the anchoring configuration ratio was 1.80. A summary of the results of experiment III is presented in Fig. 7. They prompt the same conclusions as those drawn from the experiments with the Müller–Lyer figure. The AL (IP) for the control group was found to be at a surrounding-to-center ratio of approximately 1.05, reflecting the greater contribution of the single central area to judgment. For the group judging the .20 anchoring ratio, the IP shifted to about .95, and the IP shift in the 1.80 anchor group was to about 1.18. These shifted IPs

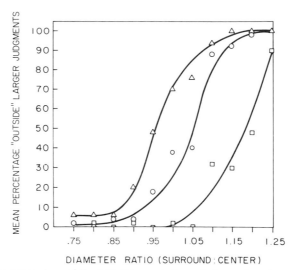

Fig. 7. Mean percentage of "outside" larger judgments for each series configuration by the control and the two experimental groups of experiment III: (○) control group (*C*); (△) group which received an anchoring configuration with a ratio of .20 ($E_{.20}$); (□) group for which the anchoring ratio was 1.80 ($E_{1.80}$) (from Wagner & Avant, 1970).

differed reliably from that of the control, and judgments of individual members of the stimulus series showed the expected effects of different loci for ALs for areal extent.

The same experimental paradigm was also employed in an investigation of one variant of the Zöllner illusion, a 3-inch square in which parallel diagonal lines generally appear *not* to be parallel because of short transverse lines crossing the main diagonals. For this experiment a seven-member stimulus series was constructed in terms of the acute angle between the major diagonals and the short transverse lines. For series stimuli, these angles were 22.5, 30.0, 37.5, 45.0, 52.5, 60.0, and 67.5°, and for each configuration, the control group judged whether or not the diagonals appeared parallel. An experimental group similarly judged the series stimuli along with an equal number of randomly interspersed judgments of an anchoring configuration in which the angle separating diagonals and transversals was 90°. Figure 8 presents the mean percentage of "not parallel" judgments for the series stimuli for these two groups. For the control group, diagonals tended toward the appearance of being not parallel as the diagonal–transversal angle decreased, the effect maximizing at an angle of 30°. Expected increases in frequency of "not parallel" judgments for all stimuli occurred in the experimental group, and the effect of the anchoring configuration was, as anticipated, greater on those configurations in which the diagonal–transversal angle more nearly approximated that of the anchor.

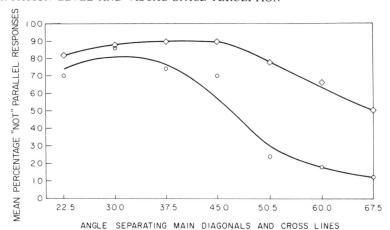

Fig. 8. Mean percentage of "not parallel" responses to each stimulus configuration by the control and experimental groups of experiment IV: (○) control; (◇) experimental (from Avant, Wagner, & Kent, 1970).

While the last two experiments may be viewed in terms of the limitations of the category method, the method of pair comparisons employed in the studies of the Müller–Lyer figure is immune to such suspicion. The consistency of these findings, irrespective of experimental procedure, support the conviction that spatial adaptation is a major determinant of pattern perception. Meanwhile, work is continuing with experimental paradigms which avoid the criticisms just mentioned.

The Conditions for Pooling

At various times (for example, Bevan, 1968; Avant & Helson, 1972) the inquiry into the conditions under which pooling occurs has been referred to as the problem of relevance. Not all physical events to which an organism is subject influence his perceptions and judgments. Nor for those that do is their effect a simple matter of magnitude or frequency of occurrence. Thus, an understanding of the conditions under which stimuli do influence the system of intrasubjective norms becomes an important prerequisite to a full understanding of the potential of AL theory. While some relatively clear conclusions have resulted from laboratory studies, we have, at best, only a partial understanding of this problem.

It appears, first of all, that some minimal amount of stimulus information must be provided the individual in order for pooling to occur. Earlier in our discussion we referred to an unpublished study by Bevan and Bell involving shifts in judgments of angular orientation under the influence of an angular perspective anchor. The stimulus series in this experiment consisted of the previously described photographs of a simple terrain model with a yellow car facing the observer in the right lane of a roadway. One aspect of this study involved systematically removing information from the display so that the relationship of stimulus impoverishment to pooling could be more clearly understood. A sequence of impoverished displays was arranged as follows:

1. The colored photographs were replaced by black-and-white tracings which included the horizon, the side lines of the roadway, the dotted center line, and the car in outline.

2. The same display as in 1 except that the outline of the car was replaced by a relatively small solid black dot.

3. The horizon line and the dotted center line were removed, leaving the dot in place of the car along with the two side lines.

4. The horizon line and the two side lines were removed, leaving the dot and the dotted center line.

5. The same display as in 4 except that the dotted center line was replaced by a solid center line.

6. All structure was removed except the dot and the side line adjacent to it.

Two groups of Ss, a control and a 90°-anchor group, were tested under each of the conditions described above. While the data have not yet been completely analyzed, several interesting conclusions appear to emerge from them. First of all, the tendency to overestimate angular perspective is preserved throughout the several conditions of impoverishment. Indeed, it appears to have been enhanced as the extent of impoverishment was increased. With the original colored photographic display, there was an average error of overestimation of about 14°. When this was replaced by the black-and-white contour display, overestimation increased to 17°, and as elements of the outline drawing were successively removed, the average errors were 24, 23, 26, 25, and 31°, respectively. Furthermore, as one might expect, a decrease in systematic judgments appears to accompany enhancement of the level of impoverishment. Even so, when the display was limited to one side line and the target dot (6), judgment was not totally devoid of order, and Ss could still clearly discriminate between the flat and steep angles of inclination. Finally, pooling occurred *only* when the contour of the car was present to guide judgments. This appears reasonable, since the vehicular contour is clearly the part of the display in which the greatest amount of information resides. Gibson (1950, 1966) has made this point clear in stressing the importance in perception of the varyingly complex energy gradients provided at the proximal surface by distal stimuli. With the loss of the automobile contour, further impoverishment of the display represented relatively little additional loss in information.

It is obvious that, in seeking the limits of pooling in terms of the characteristics of the stimulus configuration, the approach has been that of traditional experimental psychology. That approach is not, in any sense, to be denigrated. At the same time, we are obliged to think that a full understanding of pooling is going to require that we devote increasingly greater attention to intrasubjective mechanisms and the role of pooling as a cognitive strategy.

The results from a number of our studies incline us to put strong emphasis upon the assumptions made by the observer about the task which confronts him and about the interrelationships among the elements of the display in the task situation. One class of assumptions relates to the criteria by which stimuli are classed together in thought. We earlier referred to a study by Bevan and Pritchard (1963b) on the judgment of shape. In this study, Ss were asked to judge four-sided figures for their departure from squareness. It was found that judgments could be altered by the presentation of a clearly elongated rectangular figure. However, pooling in this situation appeared to involve more than the simple shape requirement of four-sidedness, for when either the size or the color of the anchor was changed from that of the stimulus series, its effectiveness as an anchor ceased. In a subsequent study, these investigators (Pritchard & Bevan, 1966) further found that an anchor rectangle exerted its influence as long as it was not less than one-fourth the size of series members or did not exceed four times that size. A threshold for relevance also has been reported in studies of latency of response to tones (Bevan, Bell, & Taylor, 1966). Anchor pitches deviant from those of the experimental series increased their effectiveness in influencing response latency—up to a point; once the pitch of the test tone differed too greatly from those of the adaptation series, they ceased to function as anchors.

But the matter of pooling, and the assumptions made about the experimental task by the observer, are not as simple a matter as these findings might be taken to indicate. Black and Bevan (1960), as well as Bevan and Pritchard (1963a), have reported that pooling is not limited by the absolute threshold as it is conventionally defined. And while Behar and Bevan (1961), studying the judgment of visual and auditory time intervals, found that anchors exerted greater influence within the same sensory mode, they also reported that the influence of visual stimuli on audition was significant, as was the influence of auditory stimuli on visual judgments. On the other hand, Turner and Bevan (1962) have described the induction of multiple, independent anchor shifts when Ss were asked to make judgments of shape, size, and lightness with figures differing in these properties. Helson and Kozaki (cited in Avant & Helson, 1972) have shown that when observers judged the size of overlapping (orange or green) series of squares, the judgment of the square included in both series depended upon the color of the series in which that square had been seen. Finally, Helson, Bevan, and Masters (1966) found that experience with a set of small circles had greater influence on subsequent size judgments of larger circles when the small circles contained angles whose sizes correlated with circle sizes than when the angles were missing. Apparently, the angles accentuated "smallness" in the adapting circles.

The extent to which the matter of the influence of cognitive strategies upon the limits of pooling merits investigation is suggested by Avant and Helson's recent (1972) conclusion that anything that directs attention to, or focalizes, or lends greater relative weight to stimuli, regardless of such factors as physical similarity or nearness, tends to magnify their role in pooling to modify subjective norms. As Bevan has recently pointed out (1968), we need to look beyond a literal view of the physical nature of stimuli and responses and their correlation, and ask what they represent of function within the individual's perceptual, cognitive, and motivational systems.

REFERENCES

Avant, L. L., & Helson, H. Theories of perception. In B. B. Wolman (Ed.), *Handbook of General Psychology*. Englewood Cliffs, New Jersey: Prentice-Hall, 1972, in press.
Avant, L. L., & Kent, M. Anchoring lines and the Mueller–Lyer illusion. Paper presented at the meeting of the Midwestern Psychological Association, Cincinnati, May, 1970.
Avant, L. L., Wagner, K., & Kent, M. Helson's pooling model and the geometrical illusions in vision. Unpublished manuscript, 1970.
Bell, R. A., & Bevan, W. The influence of anchors upon the operation of certain Gestalt organizing principles. *Journal of Experimental Psychology*, 1968, 78, 670–678.
Behar, I., & Bevan, W. The perceived duration of auditory and visual intervals: Cross-modal comparison and interaction. *American Journal of Psychology*, 1961, 74, 17–26.
Bevan, W. Perception: Evolution of a concept. *Psychological Review*, 1958, 65, 34–55.
Bevan, W. The contextual basis of behavior. *American Psychologist*, 1968, 23, 701–714.
Bevan, W., & Pritchard, J. F. Effect of "subliminal" tones upon the judgment of loudness. *Journal of Experimental Psychology*, 1963, 6, 23–29.   (a)
Bevan, W., & Pritchard, J. F. The anchor effect and the problem of relevance in the judgment of shape. *Journal of General Psychology*, 1963, 69, 147–161.   (b)
Bevan, W., Bell, R. A., & Taylor, C. Changes in response latency following shifts in the pitch of a signal. *Journal of Experimental Psychology*, 1966, 72, 864–868.
Bevan, W., Jonides, J., & Collyer, S. C. Chromatic relations in metacontrast suppression. *Psychonomic Science*, 1970, 19, 367–368.
Black, R. W., & Bevan, W. The effect of subliminal shock upon the judged intensity of weak shock. *American Journal of Psychology*, 1960, 73, 262–267.
Boring, E. G. *Sensation and perception in the history of experimental psychology*. New York: Appleton-Century, 1942.
Corso, J. F. *The experimental psychology of sensory behavior*. New York: Holt, 1967.
Egeth, H., Avant, L. L., & Bevan, W. Does context influence the shape of a perceptual scale? *Perception and Psychophysics*, 1968, 4, 54–56.
Gibson, J. J. *The perception of the visual world*. Boston: Houghton, 1950.
Gibson, J. J. *The senses considered as perceptual systems*. Boston: Houghton, 1966.
Helson, H. Studies of anomalous contrast and assimilation. *Journal of the Optical Society of America*, 1963, 53, 179–184.

Helson, H. Some problems in motivation from the point of view of the theory of Adaptation Level. In D. Levine (Ed.). Nebraska Symposium on Motivation, 1966. Lincoln: University of Nebraska, 1966.

Helson, H. Perception. In H. Helson & W. Bevan (Eds.), *Contemporary approaches to psychology*. Princeton, New Jersey: Van Nostrand, 1967. Pp. 311–343.

Helson, H., & Bevan, W. An investigation of variables in judgments of relative area. *Journal of Experimental Psychology*, 1964, **67**, 335–341.

Helson, H., & Joy, V. L. Domains of lightness assimilation and contrast. *Psychologische Beiträge*, 1962, **6**, 405–415.

Helson, H., & Rohles, F. H., Jr. A quantitative study of reversal of classical lightness-contrast. *American Journal of Psychology*, 1959, **72**, 530–538.

Helson, H., Bevan, W., & Masters, H. G. A quantitative study of relevance in the formation of adaptation levels. *Perceptual and Motor Skills*, 1966, **22**, 743–749.

Hochberg, J. E. Nativism and empiricism in perception. In L. Postman (Ed.), *Psychology in the making*. New York: Knopf, 1962. Pp. 255–330.

Michels, W. C., & Helson, H. A quantitative theory of time-order effects. *American Journal of Psychology*, 1954, **67**, 327–334.

Mowrer, O. H. Preparatory set (expectancy)–some methods of measurement. *Psychological Monographs*, 1940, **52** (Whole No. 233).

Parducci, A., & Haugen, R. The frequency principle for comparative judgments. *Perception and Psychophysics*, 1967, **2**, 81–82.

Pritchard, J. F., & Bevan, W. Anchor effectiveness as a function of stimulus variation on an incidental dimension. *Journal of General Psychology*, 1966, **74**, 245–251.

Sekuler, R., & Erlebacher, A. The invalidity of "Invalid results from the method of constant stimuli": A common artifact in the methods of psychophysics. *Perception and Psychophysics*, 1971, **9**, 309-311.

Stevens, S. S. On the psychophysical law. *Psychological Review*, 1957, **64**, 153–181.

Stevens, S. S. Adaptation-level vs. the relativity of judgment. *American Journal of Psychology*, 1958, **71**, 633–646.

Tune, G. S. Response preference: A review of some relevant literature. *Psychological Bulletin*, 1964, **61**, 286–302.

Turner, E. D., & Bevan, W. Simultaneous induction of multiple anchor effects in the judgment of form. *Journal of Experimental Psychology*, 1962, **64**, 589–592.

Turner, E. D., & Bevan, W. Patterns of experience and the perceived orientation of the Necker Cube. *Journal of General Psychology*, 1964, **70**, 345–352.

Wagner, K., & Avant, L. L. Anchoring stimuli and Titchener's illusion. Paper presented at the meeting of the Midwestern Psychological Association, Cincinnati, May, 1970.

Werner, H. Studies in contour. I. Qualitative analyses. *American Journal of Psychology*, 1935, **47**, 40–64.

Woodworth, R. S., & Schlosberg, H. *Experimental Psychology*. (Rev. ed.) New York: Holt, 1954.

COMMENT

Richard Trumbull

What must be done to assure realization of the full potential of AL theory? Avant and Bevan begin by suggesting that it is important to apply the AL paradigm more frequently in settings peculiarly representative of the tradition of perceptual psychology. But as Helson has noted, there will be changes in AL, and we must explore a broader world than traditional perceptual psychology for its full understanding and utilization. As attractive as it tends to be, we cannot become absorbed in a researching of all of perceptual psychology history. We already know that AL is capable of encompassing the factors that contribute to the disparity between the real and the perceived—from the limitations in simple sensory input to the complex contributions of personality. It is time AL was considered less as a new means for analysis and more as a basis for synthesis.

The major new item added by Avant and Bevan is an analysis of the relationship of stimulus impoverishment to pooling. Among the findings reported, we note an emphasis upon "intrasubjective mechanisms and the role of pooling as a cognitive strategy." We recognize, again, the assumptions made by the subject of the task before him. Their closing word on interactions between contributions of both the perceived and the perceiver is a long way from the seeming retreat to traditional perceptual psychology of their opening remarks.

The research reported by Avant and Bevan (1967) provides one more datum for demonstrating the capability of AL theory to serve as that intervening variable which provides the primary unifying principle underlying an otherwise apparently divergent set of psychological studies. Over the years, previous research by others has been interpreted and new research undertaken to establish the pervasive nature of this theory.

Adaptation-Level Theory as a Framework

One of the intriguing aspects of a theory such as AL is that it provides a framework for a review of a major portion of psychology. It is like a new microscope—or the extension of any technique—which allows, even demands, a review of the old, and equally important, provides the stimulus to look at the new. While one might believe that in the beginning Helson was merely looking at the simple psychometrics, today he is concerned with the total spectrum of sensation, perception, concept formulation, and memory, with all their attendant determinants of selective sensing, selective processing, bias, and inhibition. Even dealing with but one sensory modality, the method of recall, whether by verbal statement, comparison or contrast measurement, or a simple check-off list of attributes or patterns, raises a number of methodological questions. One must reduce these variables to a minimum in the experimental design, or he is faced with a *post facto* delineation of determinants and anchors which recapitulate the past and recent history of the individual and of the involved sensory system as well as the present environment in which the experiment is undertaken. Further, one must deal with objective measures versus semantics and methods of recording as well as the influence of the experimenter upon the subject. Indeed, the proponents of AL even indicate the potential influence of the future or anticipated future (Helson, 1966).

I have personally made a number of abortive efforts to structure this theory and found it to be an irritating tease. One has the feeling that it must be simple, that nearly all the appropriate things have been stated to allow this to be, but it keeps eluding one. There are indications that this also is the experience of Helson and Bevan as they both recognize its potential for extension and then come face to face with the constraints and the information needed for its application to studies of motivation, personality, vigilance, attention, and other former monolithic strongholds of psychological specialists.

SENSORY CAPABILITY

Let us begin our discussion of this theory with clarification of the sensory capability. Of all the stimuli available to man, his own system, even where he is adequately "attentive" or "motivated," has its limitations for sensing that environment. This is true whether we are talking about hearing deficits, limits to visual fields, wavelength sensitivities, or muscular tone. We cannot think of all men as being equally capable as receptors even under the most ideal situations, even if we control their worlds of sensation. There is evidence of those with much richer "frames of reference" or "perceptual masses" against which any present stimulus will be measured. These are the contributors to variances in studies of such capabilities. While we can combine them and talk about means for easier expression of research findings, in the final analysis we must understand these individual variances in capability.

There also is the question about the past selective processes involved and the nature of that "composite of previous experience" that we use as a referent, just as we must concern ourselves with the present selective processes involved and the nature of the perceived present as derived from all the stimuli impinging upon one at a given moment.

Is there a consistency in selective perception? Some researchers imply that there is and have associated it with a number of other variables, including set, attenuation and various factors of personality. Helson talks about an ever-changing AL. Can we accept that concept with the understanding that it varies within some range which is determined by capabilities and experience? We note a beginning for our understanding of this in the finding that AL varies as the midpoint or median, but *not* with the mean of a series of stimuli. This should invite further definition.

As the child grows and interacts with his environment, physiological and biochemical processes come into being, bringing new parts of the spectrum into his sensible world, and, finally, become degraded as he arrives at the stage "sans teeth, sans eyes, sans taste, sans everything." This is a dynamic thing. The psychogenic nature of dark adaptation (Trumbull, 1941), peaking of eidetic imagery, and results of sensory deprivation indicate some optimum periods for establishment of the experimental base for AL. Piaget's observation of active children's interest in increasing sensory inputs, and Hunt's (1966) work related to the lack of such drive in orphanage-reared children may be noted.

This dynamic process associated with AL has been recognized further by the declaration that every stimulus pulls the AL towards itself. Whatever the sources of these types of response to stimuli, it must be recognized that we are not just matching what might be called a passive receiver reacting selectively to present stimuli against some earlier, established frame of reference. Differentially, whether determined by inherent tendencies, the nature of the stimulus, the present environment, or a host of other variables, man can range from such a passive system to one that is an extremely active seeker of input (Notterman & Trumbull, 1959). We believe that this activity can be augmented by periods of sensory deprivation, up to a point. Earlier, Henry Murray would have attributed some of it to "needs." Avant and Bevan discuss this difference in relation to "motivation."

Passive versus Active Reception

Another aspect of this same question requires further refinement as we differentiate between discrimination by touch when the stimuli are applied to a passive receiver as opposed to when the finger and muscles are allowed actively to seek and move across the stimuli. Similarly, the eye that is presented a variety of stimuli in sequence for judgment, choice, or discrimination, is not the same receptor system as one seeking out a match from among a variety of alternatives presented *en masse*.

The interaction of sensory systems is nicely demonstrated by an earlier example of comparative judgments of weights when one reference is a fountain pen and the other is a baseball bat. A major determinant here is the visual appreciation that we are talking about a pen or a bat. We can eliminate the visual support or augmentation of kinesthetic sense and have the same weight in objects of the indicated size. Thus, the feeling of appropriateness relates to size alone and proprioceptive and kinesthetic feedback are expected to be consistent with previous experience. This explains the usual first response to balsa wood where, even blindfolded, the concept of gross size–weight relationships is violated.

What can we say about the influence of such factors as set, attention, and predisposition? For one, we must determine how the subject is asked to respond to the stimuli. Clearly, our verbal instructions play a role. So does the nature, sequence, and placement of our anchors. Thus, we find that anchors within or near a series produce "assimilation" where the shift is toward the anchor, while those anchors more distant can produce contrast effects where the shift is away. Sherif and Hovland (1961) attempted to explain this influence of anchor relevance: "assimilation implies perceived similarity between related aspects of the stimulus situation, while contrast implies perceived difference [pp. 48–58]."

Here we find an aspect of anchor proximity dominating other determinants of the perceptual frame of reference. Avant and Bevan express concern about this—with the spatial aspect emphasized—in pattern perception. Here the recurring anchor results in perceptual organization. If the anchor is temporary and shifting (due to presently unquantified influences), the repetition of anchor in appropriate spatial patterning might serve only as a reminder or reorganizer of the perceptual world. What happens if, over trials, the subject is reminded verbally "Remember, you are to . . ."?

POOLING

There have been a number of papers on pooling and the properties of the variables that determine their relevance for pooling. Helson calls this an affective, cognitive, and attitudinal process. Avant and Bevan indicate that there is a subliminal aspect, if we accept present physiological measures of reaction to shock as an adequate and valid measure of system disturbance. Judgment is found to be a more sensitive indicator of the influence of the shock. Finally, AL theory provides for pooling *across* as well as within sense modalities and among sensory, affective and cognitive processes. Further, there is the potential for interaction between sensory and emotional processes. Relevance for pooling assumes a new dimension in this extrapolation. Helson (1966) recognizes this in his statement that "the more we learn about environmental influences . . . the more important it becomes to envisage outer and inner determinants of behavior within a single conceptual frame of reference [p. 139] ."

It is clear that these considerations take us far beyond the realm of single sensory modalities and the environment provided for a given experiment. We are in that area where Avant and Bevan, in relation to vigilance, state that "it would appear that whether or not stimulus load and false signals influence vigilance depends upon how the subject defines the task for himself and the way in which the objective structure of the task influences that definition." This is where that which S brings to the situation, not the controlled introduction of anchors, is critical.

One of the problems in the recall criterion for attention is proving to be this determination of that which the subject brings to the situation. There can be no doubt but that instructions immediately preceding training and total stimulus composition can influence the recall of various selected stimuli or attributes of certain stimuli. There have been reports of subjects "still seeing" the stimuli in a visual pattern, and it must be assumed that some subjects would have a counterpart to eidetic imagery in sound or touch perception as well. To what extent have these "natural" capabilities been recognized or even encouraged by instructions to "try to visualize" along with other guidance to recall? Lumping a total population together for a study and obtaining means is not very informative, unless we know the degree to which different subjects tend to augment recall by this method, especially if they have a natural capability not shared by others.

SEQUENCE OF RECALL

A further item of this nature has been recognized, but one sees little attention paid to it in research. If sequence of recall is part of the task, the degree to which this imposed sequence varies from either the "natural" encoding or recall system is important. If one tells a subject that the following three aspects are going to be elicited after exposure, it is true that one has imposed some structure to the ordering of his recall, but one could venture the guess that deviations still would be present. There are steps, then, that should be taken (short, perhaps, of completely ambiguous situations) to ascertain any natural tendency for recall in any given sequence. Ascertaining this base before a study is an important step away from the current practice which assumes that all subjects are equal in characteristics that might be quite relevant and varied, just because we do not presently know how to measure them. One cannot argue about the contribution that the concept of residuals has for AL theory, but this should never be accepted as the "unknown" part of the equation. There should be constant effort to reduce this to a minimum, especially in respect to motivational and other inner factors that the subject may bring to the experimental situation.

INDIVIDUAL DIFFERENCES

As Helson and Bevan (1967) acknowledge, "Individual differences in vigilance are in evidence in a large number of studies but data are largely unsystematic and provide little in the way of a clear picture of the dimensions of these phenomena [p. 407]." The appearance of research on personality and other factors determining self-definition of tasks has been very late. It is a shame that more is not known here for those interested in utilizing or optimizing capabilities. Many discussions of theories of vigilance founder when transitioning from controllable, objective features of the task into the personality or internal factors. To deny the relevance of a theory on inconsistency cannot be done on averaged research results. The individual differences must be more than acknowledged in an off-hand way as we report the usual means and standard deviations. The means can well be the products of self-canceling personality factors in the subjects as much as of any other variable.

The study by Helson, Blake, and Mouton (1958) of a petition-signing exercise with "planted" respondents inducing variance in AL allowed a correlation with personality variables from the Allport–Allport A–S reaction study. This sociopsychological application of AL theory demonstrates a type of verification of the reference. There is a long history of this personality–perception relationship that must be considered anew. It can provide a basis for prediction of AL shifting or anchoring in this realm. The problems of finding the point of interaction between factors are many. The role of perceptual organization is now being explored and appears to be one promising avenue. It will take the experimenter far afield from his "settings peculiarly representative of the tradition of perceptual psychology." He will need the help of specialists in the other areas involved. The gathering of such talents in this volume augurs well for the interpretation, extrapolation, and determination of a viable AL theory.

REFERENCES

Helson, H. Some problems in motivation from the point of view of the theory of adaptation level. In D. Levine (Ed.), *Nebraska symposium on motivation, 1966.* Lincoln: University of Nebraska Press, 1966. Pp. 137–182.
Helson, H., & Bevan, W. *Contemporary approaches to psychology.* Princeton, New Jersey: Van Nostrand, 1967.
Helson, H., Blake, R. R., & Mouton, J. S. Petition-signing as adjustment to situational and personal factors. *Journal of Social Psychology,* 1958, **48**, 3–10.
Hunt, J. McV. The epigenesis of intrinsic motivation and early cognitive learning. In R. N. Haber (Ed.), *Current research in motivation.* New York: Holt, 1966. Pp. 355–370.
Notterman, J. M., & Trumbull, R. Note on self-regulating systems and stress. *Behavioral Science,* 1959, **4**, 324–327.
Sherif, M., & Hovland, C. I. *Social judgment.* New Haven, Connecticut: Yale University Press, 1961.
Trumbull, R. A psychogenic study of dark-adaptation. *Journal of General Psychology,* 1941, **24**, 259–271.

TOWARD A THEORY OF BRIGHTNESS CONTRAST

Howard R. Flock

Adaptation-level theory began nearly 40˙ years ago as a formulation for the relativity of chromatic and achromatic color phenomena. In the intervening years, it has expanded into and influenced problem areas far removed from its sources in the domain of color. But what has become of AL theory in the field of color, where it started? Have inevitable afterthoughts, new theories, refurbished data, or reformulations diminished it? To assess this, I propose to consider one of the content areas with which AL theory was first identified, that of the relation between brightness contrast on the one hand, and achromatic color responses or, preferably, lightness responses on the other hand.

In 1932, and certainly before, Helson (Helson & Judd, 1932) became preoccupied with the effects of changing adaptation on lightness responses, or on what are called black, gray, and white responses.[1] After a period of incubation and a preliminary report (Helson & Judd, 1936), in 1938 Helson published his empirical findings and the quantitative expression, Eq. (1) (Table I). The equation should probably be called the Adams–Cobb–Judd–Helson formula. Adams and Cobb first germinated it around 1922. Judd gave the expression its present form. It was Helson, however, who used it to seed an extended theoretical domain. The most general form of the expression, Eq. (2), was given by Judd (1940, 1941).

The purpose of Eqs. (1) and (2) was to predict the "lightness (i.e., whether a sample of paper was black, dark gray, mid gray, light gray, or white) of any sample on any background" (Helson, 1938, p. 453). In other words, the equation would predict the effect of all changes in contrast between, for example, a piece of gray paper and its background. A piece of gray paper on a black background appears light; on a white background it appears darker. The change in lightness of the gray paper is correlated to the change in brightness contrast between the gray paper and its background. The fact of that change in lightness and its amount (L) were predictable from these equations. Even when the background of a

---

[1] Helson was interested in the relation between adaptation and both chromatic and achromatic responses. The chromatic part of the story, dating to 1926, has been entirely omitted from this contribution.

TABLE I

Theoretical Expressions of Adaptation-Level Theory

$$L = \frac{10}{(10-0.3)} \cdot \frac{(10A-0.3)}{(AL+A)} (AL+1), \tag{1}$$

(Helson, 1938)

$$\log AL = \frac{3 \log A_{bg} + (\log A_i + \cdots + \log A_s)/s}{4}, \tag{1a}$$

(Helson, 1938)

$$AL = (k)AL', \qquad AL = AL' \mid k, \tag{1b}$$

(Helson, 1938)

$$L = \frac{(A-A_n)(AL+A_x)}{(A_x-A_n)(AL+A)}, \tag{2}$$

where $AL > O$, $O < A_x \leqslant 1$, $A_n < kA_x$; probably $.01 < k < .1$; A_x is the region of highest reflectance; and A_n is the region of lowest reflectance (Judd, 1941).

$$AL = \frac{A_{bg} + (A_i + \cdots + A_s)/s}{2}, \tag{2a}$$

(Judd, 1940)

$$AL = \frac{nA + A_{bg} + (A_i + \cdots + A_s)/s}{n+2}, \tag{2b}$$

(Judd, 1940)

$$P = k \cdot \frac{X_i - A}{X_i + [(1+b)/(1-b)] A}, \tag{3}$$

where P is the response to stimulus X_i, k is the value assigned to the topmost rating in the category scale; and b is the y intercept of Eq. (3), when changed to linear form (Helson, 1948; and 1970, personal communication).

$$L = \frac{10(1-AL/A)}{[1+R(AL/A)]} + 5, \tag{3a}[a]$$

$$J = C + k \log(X/A) \tag{4}$$

where $k = -[\log(1.0 - N^{-1.0})]^{-1.0}$; $\log A = p \log X + q \log X_{bg} + r \log X_r$; and $p + q + r = 1.0$ and are weighting constants (Michels & Helson, 1949).

$$L = 5.0 + 10.0 \log (A/AL), \tag{4a}[b]$$

$$k = \frac{(\log L_{bg(e)} - \log L_{\overline{tf}(e)})^2}{(\log L_{h(e)} - \log L_{l(e)})}, \tag{5}$$

where $\log L_{\overline{tf}(e)} = (\log L_i + \cdots + \log L_n)/n$; $L_{bg(e)}$ is the luminance of background at illuminance e and is the region being judged; L_i is the luminance of any region other than the region being judged, at illuminance e, and n is the number of these regions; $L_{h(e)}$ is the highest luminance at illuminance e; and $L_{l(e)}$ is the lowest luminance at illuminance e (Flock & Noguchi, 1970b).

TABLE I (*continued*)

$$L = k_1 (B_S - B') \frac{(B_S + 1)}{(B' + 1)} + k_2 \frac{B_S B'}{(B' + k_3 B_S)} + 1.0, \qquad (6)$$

$$B' = (B_0^a \bar{B}^b)/(a + b),$$

where B_S is the luminance of object fixated, B' is the adaptation luminance, B_0 is the luminance of background, a is the area of background, $\log \bar{B}$ is the mean log luminance of all other objects in the field, b is the area of all other objects in the field, L_a is the adaptive level of the eye, which is the sum of the last two terms in Eq. (6), and k_1, k_2, k_3 are scale factors (Helson, 1970, personal communication).

---

[a] In Eq. (3), substitute L, A, and AL for P, X_i, and A, respectively, to give the same notation as in Eq. (1). Since k is the top value of whatever numerical scale is used, then for the scale of $0-10$ used in Eq. (1), $k = 10$. In deriving L, the constant $.5k$ must be added to Eq. (3) (Helson, 1948, pp. 303–306, and particularly Table 3). These changes and insertions in Eq. (3) will yield Eq. (3a) if, in addition, the numerator and denominator of Eq. (3) are divided by X_i, and the constant $(1 + b)/(1 - b)$ is designated as R.

[b] In Eq. (4), substitute L, A, and AL for J, X, and A, respectively, to give the same notation as in Eq. (1). For some numerical scale, there will be $2N + 1$ categories. Hence, for a $0-10$ scale, there are eleven categories and $N = 5$. Substituting $N = 5$, gives $k = 10$. Finally, ". . . when the judgment scale is represented by the integers $0, 1, 2, \ldots 2N$, we have $C = N \ldots$" (Michels & Helson, 1949, p. 359). Hence, for $N = 5$, $C = 5$. These insertions in Eq. (4) give Eq. (4a).

sample paper was heterogeneous (as in Fig. 1), the change in lightness of the sample would be predictable. These various conditions involved a change in the brightness contrast (or luminance ratio) between the brightness (or luminance) of a sample and the average weighted brightness (or luminance) of its background. Since the equations predicted the perceptual effects of this change in contrast, Eqs. (1) and (2) set forth a general theory of brightness (or luminance) contrast.[2]

The conceptual principle from which AL theory was to take its name is the term AL in Eqs. (1) and (2). It was defined by Eqs. (1a), (2a), and (2b) in Table I. In these equations AL corresponds to the weighted average of all the various surface reflectances in a scene. The weighting refers to the fact that surfaces laterally removed from a fixated area are weighted less; closer surfaces are weighted more. Smaller surfaces are weighted less; larger surfaces are weighted more. This requirement that everything in the scene should be measured, appropriately weighted, and entered was and is the *sine qua non* of AL theory. Parenthetically, this requirement is also inconvenient. It means, for

---

[2] The appropriate meaning of brightness, as it is being used here, is given, I believe, by the term luminance, which is indicated in parentheses.

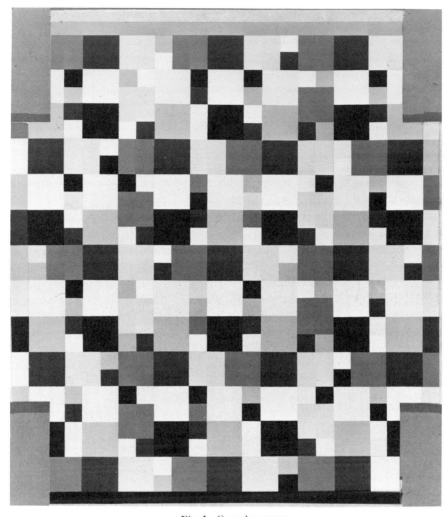

Fig. 1. Complex scene.

example, that any bright highlight or reflection in a viewing tube should be measured, weighted, and entered.

Operational Definitions of Adaptation Level

In the early years AL was quantified in a variety of ways. Helson (Helson, 1938; Helson & Jeffers, 1940) often preferred Eq. (1a), in Table I. The A s in Eq. (1a) refer to the proportion of light reflected by perfectly diffusing samples of paper and, therefore, to the reflectances of the various regions in the scene. A_{bg} is another such region, but, because it is usually much larger, it is called the background and is given a weight of 3, whereas the other regions together are given a weight of only one. The number of samples or regions in the scene that are the same size is indicated by s.

Judd (1940) preferred a somewhat different expression for AL [Table I, Eq. (2a)], substituting an arithmetic average for Helson's geometric average. Moreover, because an observer (O) is likely to fixate the target region longer than other regions, Judd believed that AL should take that fixation time into account. Hence, he introduced n as a weighting factor for the time that O fixates target region A [Table I, Eq. (2b)].

Both Helson (1938, 1947) and Judd (1940) also introduced other weighting factors. Expressions like Eqs. (1a) and (2a) were sometimes designated as AL', so that AL was equal to the product or to the sum of a constant k and AL', where k was associated with residual factors specific to the individual perceiver or to the experimental arrangements [Table I, Eq. (1b)].

Helson and Judd tended to be pragmatic in the matter of weights and transformations, using what gave a best fit to the data. This pragmatism was inescapable. Given the requirement that everything must be measured, weighted, and entered, the rules for transforming and for weighting appropriately within and between experimental situations could not be immediately evident. Only through the processing of a vast amount of experimental data would it be possible to discover general rules.

The weighted average of the surface reflectances defined AL on the stimulus side. On the response side AL was defined by its correspondence to the midvalue of a judgmental scale. For example, on a 0–10 scale applied to the lightness of gray samples, AL was specified by the sample judged as 5. Hence, the weighted average of surface reflectances would specify an AL for the organism, and that AL would be indicated by the middle of a judgmental scale.

In the years before 1947, the problem of lightness responses was a central topic in Helson's papers. After 1947, this interest seemed to be replaced by a general application of AL theory to psychophysics. By 1964, when *Adaptation-Level Theory* appeared, the early prominence of lightness as a topic in AL theory had faded. One measure of this eclipse was the relatively small space given to it in the book. A second was the citation in the book of Eq. (1), which had been developed in 1938, as the only quantitative expression for lightness responses.

The loss of interest resulted, I believe, from two reasons: the conceptual status of early AL with regard to lightness, and the near absence of data on the relation between lightness responses and illumination.

Consider again Eqs. (1) and (2). The terms A and AL refer to surface reflectances and to the average of surface reflectances. But the reflectance of a surface is a property of a surface. It is not light, although it does determine the proportion of incident light that will be transmitted to an eye. Moreover, luminance terms for light cannot be appropriately substituted into Eqs. (1) and (2). When the substitution is attempted, the equations predict that lightness increases at approximately the same rate as illumination is increased.[3] Since lightness can only take values from 0 to 10 in Eq. (1) and from 0 to 1.0 in Eq. (2), the substitution yields inappropriate outputs from the equations.

Equations (1) and (2) specify what should be called a distal psychophysics. On the one hand are surface properties A and AL, which are not adequate stimuli for vision, and on the other hand are lightness responses. Between these two is a correlation specified by Eqs. (1) and (2). Since light, rather than distal objects, is the effective stimulus for vision, what then is the relation between light and lightness, and between light and reflectances?

There is, moreover, a disquieting omission from Eqs. (1) and (2). Except for Judd's (1941, p. 289) statement that the equations applied only to photopic vision, there was no other reference to levels of illumination. Presumably we are to believe that the equations will succeed under any conditions of photopic illumination. That would mean that, for any level of illumination on a scene, the lightness of all the samples in the scene would remain unchanged. Much later, Helson (1964) may have referred to the problem, when he said that Eq. (1) will yield "excellent predictions of reports of lightness by trained observers under a wide variety of conditions provided illuminance is held constant [p. 277]." But this does not say at what level illuminance should be held constant.[4]

The implied claim of Eqs. (1) and (2) that the lightness of samples would be unchanged by a general increase in illumination is, in fact, paradoxical. Judd (1941) alluded to the paradox, saying that although "the average brightness of the scene is not mentioned explicitly [in Eq. (2)] . . . it is measured by the average luminous apparent reflectance of the field . . . [p. 289]." In other words, AL indicated the average brightness of the field. Judd could have had in

---

[3] In Eq. (1), if A and AL are not allowed to take values less than 7, the equation reduces approximately to

$$L = [10/(10 - 0.3)] [10A/(AL + A)] (AL).$$

This is equivalent to

$$L = 10.3(AL)/[1 + (AL/A)].$$

For a change in illumination F, then,

$$L' = 10.3(F)(AL)/[1 + (AL/A)] = F(L).$$

[4] In a personal communication Helson has written that he and Judd envisaged their lightness formulation as applying only to a uniform illuminance and within "normal" limits of seeing, which is neither very, very bright nor very, very dark. Nevertheless, even this restriction does not manage the problem, as will be shown by the data cited below, all of which lie within those limits.

mind that when a white background is substituted for a black one, AL from Eqs. (1a) or (2a) will necessarily increase, as will the average brightness (and the luminance). That substitution of background is equivalent to the introduction of a hidden light source that is perfectly registered to the black background. When the hidden source is turned on, the black background appears white, just as if it were, in fact, a surface of high, instead of low, reflectance. Under these conditions the increase in the average luminance would be correlated to the upward shift in AL (and to the downward shift in lightness judgments). But if AL (and therefore lightness judgments) is correlated to the average luminance under these conditions, why is this not the case when the *general* level of illumination of the scene is increased? Judd deflected this issue by stating that the use of Eqs. (1) and (2) held only if the scene were uniformly illuminated *and were perceived as uniformly illuminated* (Judd, 1941, pp. 289–290). That statement simply obscured the issue of the relation between AL and the average luminance (and brightness) of the scene. If AL were an indicator of the average luminance, how could it both *be that,* as when a hidden source did and did not illuminate a black background, and *not be that,* as when the total illumination of the scene was changed?

Judd's requirement that the scene be perceived as uniformly illuminated was not endorsed by Helson (1938), who said that it was unnecessary "to invoke a 'noticing of the illumination' in the sense of Katz" or "to assume a 'discounting of the illumination' as Jaensch has done . . . [p. 450]." Helson, thereby, took a strong stand against the then current neo-Helmholtzian views. But he avoided the necessary step: He failed to deal with the problem of levels of illumination; and thereby he also failed to bring luminance into a quantitative relationship with lightness responses. As a result, he never transformed the distal psychophysics of lightness responses into a proximal psychophysics.

After 1947, new quantitative expressions defining AL theory were forthcoming (Helson, 1948; Helson & Himelstein, 1955; Helson, Michels, & Sturgeon, 1954; Michels & Helson, 1949, 1954), and were implicitly or explicitly understood to apply to lightness. In one case Michels and Helson (1949, pp. 362–364) used one of these new expressions to predict lightness judgments [Eq. (4), Table I]. Again, surface reflectances, not luminances, were entered as the stimuli. Two of these later expressions [Eqs. (3) and (4)], have been modified to give Eqs. (3a) and (4a), where the notation and numerical scales are the same as in Eq. (1). If luminances are substituted for reflectances A and AL in Eq. (3a), then the equation will predict no change in lightness when illumination is increased over a scene. Correspondingly, if Eq. (4) is modified to make the residual term X_r a constant weighting factor (its apparent function in the earlier instances of AL theory), then Eq. (4a) also predicts no change in lightness when luminances are substituted and illuminance is increased. It should be remembered, however, that these substitutions are not necessarily licensed by the equations. In fact, I can find no instance in the published work of Helson or his associates where luminances are used quantitatively to predict lightness judgments.[5]

With reference to Eq. (1), Helson (1938) wrote that "the relation of sample reflectance to adaptation reflectance explains all of the facts ... [p. 450]." But in 1947, citing Eq. (1a), he described A_{bg} as the brightness (luminance?) of the background and the As as the brightnesses[6] of the samples on the background (Helson, 1947, p. 3). As I have indicated above, the terms in those equations were not luminances, and luminances could not be substituted into them. But if his 1947 statement is taken as evidence that he saw the need to restate the problem of lightness in luminance terms, why did he not do so? Why, after 1947, did lightness virtually disappear as a topic for quantitative treatment in Helson's papers?

ILLUMINATION AND LIGHTNESS JUDGMENTS: DEFINING DATA

The development of AL theory may have bypassed the topic of lightness after 1947, because the level of empirical information and inquiry were inadequate to the requirements of AL theory. If theoretical equations are to describe accurately how lightness is related to distributions of luminances, then data that relate these and measurements that accurately describe the luminances are required. I want to suggest that this information was not available in 1947, and that perhaps it is still not available.

It would seem that Eqs. (1)–(4) require lightness to remain unchanged when the general illumination of a scene is increased. What is the empirical support for this prediction? First, Helson (1938) reports that over a change in intensity of 96:1, "large changes in intensity of illumination have comparatively little effect ... on the lightnesses of the samples [although] a slight tendency is evident for lightness ... to drop about one step at the lowest intensity [p. 461]." The statement that decreasing illumination by 96:1 or by two log units drops a lightness judgment by one step means a 10% drop on the 0–10 scale. It may be true that "mere change of background reflectance has greater effect" (Helson, 1938, p. 462), but the effect of changing illumination is not unappreciable.

A similar effect of illumination was implied by Helson in a paper in 1943. "White and black also behave differently in high and low illuminations ... the former gaining in pronouncedness in strong light, the latter losing under the

---

[5] For a possible exception, see Helson (1964, p. 186). But insufficient information is given there to evaluate the implications.

[6] Since A_{bg} and the As are reflectances, brightness as a substitute for them may here mean luminance or a subjective indicator of luminance.

same conditions" (Helson, 1943, p. 249; see also, Helson, 1968, for approximately the same view). The cited changes in pronouncedness mean that as illumination is increased, a white becomes whiter and a black becomes a less deep black. Parenthetically, perhaps a dark gray becomes less dark. However, does not this say that as illumination is changed upward, all the grays from black to white become lighter?

There were, however, other data with different fluctuations. In 1964, Helson cited the following as evidence for AL theory: (a) Jameson and Hurvich's 1961 data, that had been cited by those authors as refuting AL theory; (b) Marimont's (1962) model of brightness and lightness, that depended on Jameson and Hurvich's data configuration; and (c) Bornemeier's data (Helson, 1943, pp. 251–256), that can be shown to be like Jameson and Hurvich's data configuration. In Jameson and Hurvich's experiment, a display similar to the cross in Fig. 2, but with five instead of seven squares, was presented at three levels of illumination over 1.1 log units. The Ss adjusted the luminance of a comparison square to a match, where the comparison square was surrounded by a large bright field.

The subjects' match judgments to a square in the cross for the three levels of illuminance are shown in Fig. 3. Straight lines have been fitted to the mean data points. (The curved lines are Jameson and Hurvich's.) The lowest line, corresponding to the blackest square, was negative, indicating that as illumination was increased the black square became blacker. The top line, corresponding to the whitest square, was positive, indicating that as illumination was increased the white square became whiter. The second line from the bottom, corresponding to the dark gray square, was horizontal, indicating that lightness remained constant as illumination was increased. These results are opposed to the belief cited earlier that the black became less pronounced as illumination was increased. Nevertheless, in the sense that one of the grays remained unchanged in lightness these results could fit a hypothesis of AL theory that AL, as a neutral point or indifference point, will remain unchanged by changes in illumination.

Bornemeier's data (Helson, 1943, 1964) also support the finding that there is an indifference point (horizontal line) below which regions become darker and above which regions become lighter as illumination is increased. In his experiment, the Ss adjusted the black and white mix on a color wheel under constant high illumination to match each of six standard (ST) disks presented at three different levels of illumination. The ST disks, which appeared as blacks, grays, and whites, were presented against black, gray, and white backgrounds.

His data replotted with match responses on the ordinate and illuminance on the abscissa are shown in Fig. 4. For the gray and white backgrounds, as illumination was increased, the blackest ST disk required a lower match response and produced negative curves corresponding to the one plotted by Jameson and Hurvich.

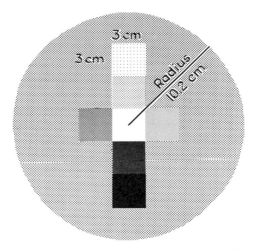

Fig. 2. Scene composed of eight regions with various reflectances.

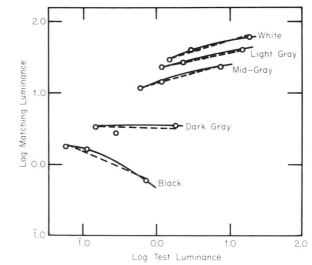

Fig. 3. Jameson and Hurvich's (1961) experimental data replotted. The dashed lines show the linear trend of their mean data points for the five presumed objective colors of their test fields. The curved lines are Jameson and Hurvich's.

There may be one important similarity between the experimental conditions governing these data and those in the experiment by Jameson and Hurvich. In both cases, it may be that the Ss were allowed to look back and forth from the brightly illuminated match region to the very dimly illuminated test region. If that were the case, then the eyes would always be light-adapted to a relatively high level when they observed the darkest test disks under very dim illumination.

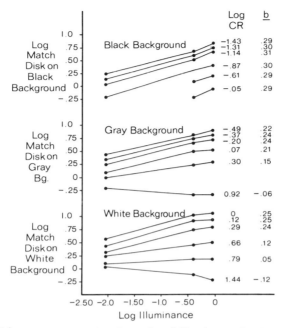

Fig. 4. Match responses over two log units of illuminance for black, gray, and white backgrounds (after Helson, 1943, Table 2).

That kind of explanation for the negative lines would clearly require an AL explanation in terms of the matching as well as the test field.

At least three different current theories of lightness and brightness responses are based on data configurations similar to those of Jameson and Hurvich (1961) and Helson (1943): the theories of Marimont (1962); Jameson and Hurvich (1964); and Stevens and Stevens (1960), Stevens (1961). None of the three theories implied that the data configuration might depend on the extreme variations in adaptation levels, as in looking back and forth from a brightly illuminated match disk to a dimly illuminated test disk. Rather, they assumed that the cited data configuration was general to what happens when illumination is raised on an array of samples.[7]

ILLUMINATION AND LIGHTNESS JUDGMENTS: SOME RECENT DATA

Even if the class of explanation that I have proposed for these data is incorrect, I will dare to say, nevertheless, that the negative lines found in these experiments are not general to what occurs when illumination is raised on an

[7] For a discussion of this class of theory, see Flock (1970a).

array of mat samples. With respect to the question of how illumination affects lightness judgments, some recent data (Flock, 1969) may be relevant. The cross in Fig. 2, on either a black, gray, or white background, was presented to the right eye. The illumination of the cross was varied over three log units in seven steps. Before each judgment, the S was light-adapted for approximately 42 sec. to the luminance level of the display. The S judged each of the seven squares in the cross as well as the background—a total of eight regions. Since there were seven illuminances, three backgrounds, and eight regions, there was a total of 168 conditions. The experimental conditions were presented in random order. The experiment was replicated on the S on the second day. Ten Ss participated.

The task of the S was to look at a square designated by its position and to say at once whether it was black, gray, or white. He was then required to assign a number to it, indicating its degree of grayness. He was told to apply the following criteria in assigning numbers: If the square appeared to lie exactly between a black and a gray, as might happen with either a very dark gray or a very light black, then he was to assign to it the number 10. If the square appeared to lie exactly between a gray and a white, he was to assign to it the number 20. Zero was to be assigned only if a square corresponded to the blackest black imaginable. Thirty was to be assigned only if a square corresponded to the whitest white imaginable. In this experiment, therefore, there were three scales: one for black between 0 and 10; one for grays between 10 and 20; and one for whites between 20 and 30. In fact, no S ever used the numbers 0 and 30. Also, an S's immediate color response—indicating that a square was either black, gray, or white—always corresponded to his subsequent choice of scale. For example, every S who said a square was black also used the scale from 0 to 10.

In Fig. 5 are shown the lightness responses for the seven squares on the three backgrounds over change in illumination. For any one of the three backgrounds, the lowest line corresponded to the darkest square, the next lowest to the next darkest square, and so on. As the illumination was altered by a ratio from 1 to 1000, one line had a slope of zero and all of the other slopes were positive.[8] There were no negative slopes.

The one line that had a slope of zero corresponded to the midgray square on a white background. Moreover, the mean of the data points specifying that line was 14.8, which was very close to the mid-value, 15, of the scale. Furthermore, the same gray patch on gray and black backgrounds yielded almost flat slopes, which were also located near the mid-value, but above it. These findings also support the hypothesis that the middle of a scale, corresponding to the AL, will be unaffected by changes in illumination.

The remaining lines give a different picture, however. For a particular background, moving from the middle of the scale toward the whites or the

_____

[8] These results are similar to those obtained when a brightness task is substituted for a lightness task. (See, for example, Flock & Noguchi, 1970a, b).

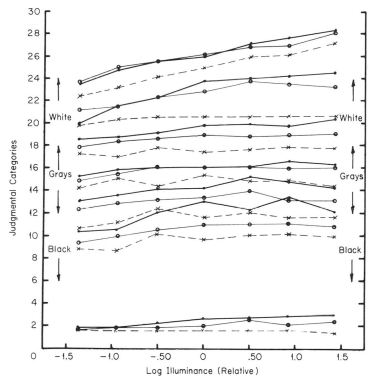

Fig. 5. Mean data points for seven test field squares on black (———); gray (– – –); and white (- - - - -) backgrounds plotted against illuminance (after Flock, 1969).

blacks, the slopes of the lines become steeper. That was true, at least, for all but the blackest square, where again the slopes of the lines are relatively flat.

It should be noted that as illumination was increased, some squares shifted over from gray to white and some from black to gray. Within the gray family, there was a tendency for all the grays to become lighter. In the language of Katz, there was a change in pronouncedness over the entire black-to-white dimension, the change being greater, the greater the distance from the middle of the scale.

The point of this excursion into the data on illumination and lightness responses was to put this question: Do we now know how changes in illumination generally affect lightness responses? Earlier, I speculated that AL theory did not develop in the lightness area for lack of a broad spectrum of data. Without that data, it was simply impossible to think theoretically about the problems of lightness.

The need for data was complemented by a need for good and complete measurements of all the impinging light. You will recall that AL theory requires that everything within the visible scene be measured, weighted, and pooled. Thinking theoretically about the problem of lightness required, therefore,

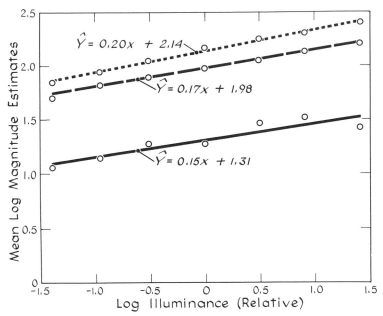

Fig. 6. Predicted functions for the judgments of three backgrounds and mean data points, plotted against illuminance: background color: white (- - - - -); gray (− − −); black (────) (from Flock & Noguchi, 1970b).

accurate specification of the stimuli. An example of this requirement is neatly illustrated by an attempt to explain (Flock & Noguchi, 1970b) the relation between brightness responses and luminance relationships. The experiment was similar to the one described above on lightness, except that magnitude estimates of brightness replaced lightness judgments. Some kind of theoretical statement to explain the data was desired. At the very least, the intention was to write an equation that described the data but used luminance terms and avoided arbitrary constants. At the end of the first day, an equation had been produced for which the lines in Fig. 6 paralleled the data points but did not go through them. By the end of the fourth day, the first day's equation still fit the data best. But the constant error in the location of the lines was baffling; and the resolve not to insert an arbitrary constant continued to be strong. At that point, a critical footnote was remembered. The tabled luminances for the backgrounds, given in the article, had been footnoted in an earlier article, where the same arrangements had been used. In that footnote it said that the background luminances in the table were all too high by an average of .09 foot-Lamberts.[9] When these

[9] Background luminance had been measured at the center of the display. Because the center was covered by elements of the cross (see Fig. 2), the actual visible background, in the region around the edges of the cross, was, on the average, .09 foot-Lamberts lower than the center.

corrected background values were inserted into the first day's equation, the fit of theoretical lines to data was that shown in Fig. 6.

The part of the equation that predicted the separation of the lines is Eq. (5) in Table I. The term in the numerator is the ratio of the log luminance of the judged region to the average log luminance of the other regions. The term in the denominator is the log ratio of the highest to the lowest luminance. The terms describe what was visible in the display and include nearly all that was visible. The expression for k is clearly a statement in the manner of AL theory. But this suggestive theoretical result must have inevitably failed or have been discouraged with incorrect or with incomplete measurements.

For a theory of lightness, 1947 was a turning point. Since then, there has been little progress toward a theory of brightness contrast. It is true that Wallach (1948) updated Kardos' (1935) and Gelb's (1929) theory of luminance ratios, but his theory seems not to fit the facts. Recently, there has been some renewed interest in Koffka's (1935) pairing of luminance ratios with ideas of spatial organization (Coren, 1969; Flock, 1971; Freedberg & Flock, 1967; Gogel & Mershon, 1969; Mershon & Gogel, 1970), but Koffka's ideas seem to lead back to notions like accounting for the illumination. All the neo-Helmholtzian ideas, with their requirements for the perception of and compensating for illumination, seem to have little empirical basis (see, for example, Flock, 1970b, 1971). Recent theories by Stevens and Stevens (1960) and Stevens (1961), Jameson and Hurvich (1964), and Marimont (1962) are defined by data that may refute the theories, if we consider the conditions under which the data were collected. Some theorists now hope that the current neurophysiology may be the source of new insights. Perhaps that will be the case.

It would be incorrect to suggest that Helson has wholly abandoned the domain of lightness, which was one of the major sources of his inspiration. His continuing work on assimilation and contrast (Helson, 1943, 1963; Helson & Joy, 1962; Helson & Rohles, 1959)—problems that no general theory of lightness can ignore—is just one measure of his continuing interest. (For a review of this work, see Steger, 1968.) Nor has Helson completely abandoned the theoretical pursuit of AL and lightness. Equation (6) (Table I) is an unpublished formulation in which luminances replace reflectances.

Conclusions

Although little progress has been made toward a quantitative formulation of lightness responses, the empirical evidence cited previously has been suggestive of AL theory. Even as data were cited to prove the limitations of Helson's quantitative formulations, emergent in these same data were configurations consonant with the theory itself, if not with various attempts to quantify the theory. Lightness judgments do not do, necessarily, what the Adams–Cobb–Judd–Helson formulation would have them do. But the middle of a judgmental scale, where AL is specified, does seem to have something special about it, as was indicated by the flat lines near the scalar value of 15 in my data and by the steepening of the lines as they were increasingly removed from the mid-value (Fig. 5). Perhaps, also, no known AL quantitative statement will describe Flock and Noguchi's (1970b) brightness data (Fig. 6). But only when everything that was visible was correctly measured, entered, and averaged, could the separations between the lines be quantitatively described. The expression that emerged was an embodiment of AL theory [Eq. (5), Table 1].

The negative lines that are found in a number of different data configurations (Figs. 3 and 4) may have little generality beyond the class of conditions under which they were observed. But the class of explanation that I proposed to rationalize them invoked Helson's dictum: *Everything* in the visible scene must be entered and pooled. "Everything" includes the very bright match field as well as the dimly illuminated test field.

Important theories in psychology do not necessarily rise and fall over the seemingly inevitable half-life of the quantifications that are attempted in their name. Rather, they flourish because they use fertile constructs out of which future theory can grow. Adaptation-level theory seems to have that promise.

REFERENCES

Adams, E. Q. A comparison of the Fechner and Munsell scales of luminous sensation value. *Journal of the Optical Society of America*, 1922, 6, 932–939.
Adams, E. Q., & Cobb, P. W. The effect on foveal vision of bright (and dark) surroundings. V. *Journal of Experimental Psychology*, 1922, 5, 39–45.
Coren, S. Brightness contrast as a function of figure-ground relations. *Journal of Experimental Psychology*, 1969, 80, 517–524.
Flock, H. R. Lightness changes in a complex field with changing illumination and background. Paper presented at the meeting of the Eastern Psychological Association, Philadelphia, April 1969.
Flock, H. R. Jameson and Hurvich's theory of brightness contrast. *Perception and Psychophysics*, 1970, 8, 118–124. (a)
Flock, H. R. Lightness, embeddedness, and contrast. *Technical Report FPL-2*, 1970, York University. (b)
Flock, H. R. Achromatic surface color and the direction of illumination. *Perception and Psychophysics*, 1971, 9, 187–192.
Flock, H. R., & Noguchi, K. An experimental test of Jameson and Hurvich's theory of brightness contrast. *Perception and Psychophysics*, 1970, 8, 129–136. (a)
Flock, H. R., & Noguchi, K. Brightness functions for a complex field with changing illumination and background. *Technical Report FPL-3*, 1970, York University. (b)
Freedberg, E., & Flock, H. R. Perceived angle of incidence and achromatic surface color. Paper presented at the meeting of the Eastern Psychological Association, Boston, 1967.

Gelb, A. Die "Farbenkonstanz" der Sehdinge. In A. Bethe (Ed.), *Handbuch der normalen und pathologischen Physiologie. Receptionsorgane II. Photoreceptoren I.* Vol. XII. Berlin: 1929. Pp. 594–678.

Gogel, W. C., & Mershon, D. H. Depth adjacency and simultaneous contrast. *Perception and Psychophysics,* 1969, 5, 13–17.

Helson, H. Fundamental problems in color vision. I. The principle governing changes in hue, saturation, and lightness of non-selective samples in chromatic illumination. *Journal of Experimental Psychology,* 1938, 23, 439–476.

Helson, H. Some factors and implications of color constancy. *Journal of the Optical Society of America,* 1943, 33, 555–567.

Helson, H. Adaptation-level as frame of reference for prediction of psychophysical data. *American Journal of Psychology,* 1947, 60, 1–29.

Helson, H. Adaptation-level as a basis for a quantitative theory of frames of reference. *Psychological Review,* 1948, 55, 297–313.

Helson, H. Studies of anomalous contrast and assimilation. *Journal of the Optical Society of America,* 1963, 53, 179–184.

Helson, H. *Adaptation-level theory: An experimental and systematic approach to behavior.* New York: Harper, 1964.

Helson, H. Perceptual constancy. In D. L. Sills (Ed.), *International encyclopedia of the social sciences.* Vol. XI. New York: MacMillan and Free Press, 1968. Pp. 544–546.

Helson, H., & Himelstein, P. A short method for calculating the adaptation-level for absolute and comparative rating judgments. *American Journal of Psychology,* 1955, 68, 631–637.

Helson, H., & Jeffers, V. B. Fundamental problems in color vision. II. Hue, lightness, and saturation of selective samples in chromatic illumination. *Journal of Experimental Psychology,* 1940, 26, 1–27.

Helson, H., & Joy, V. L. Domains of lightness assimilation and contrast. *Psychologische Beiträge,* 1962, 6, 405–415.

Helson, H., & Judd, D. B. A study in photopic adaptation. *Journal of Experimental Psychology,* 1932, 15, 380–398.

Helson, H., & Judd, D. B. An experimental and theoretical study of changes in surface colors under changing illuminations. *Psychological Bulletin,* 1936, 33, 740–741.

Helson, H., & Rohles, F. H., Jr. A quantitative study of reversal of classical lightness-contrast. *American Journal of Psychology,* 1959, 72, 530–538.

Helson, H., Michels, W. C., & Sturgeon, A. The use of comparative rating scales for the evaluation of psychophysical data. *American Journal of Psychology,* 1954, 67, 321–326.

Jameson, D., & Hurvich, L. M. Complexities of perceived brightness. *Science,* 1961, 133, 174–179.

Jameson, D., & Hurvich, L. M. Theory of brightness and color contrast in human vision. *Vision Research,* 1964, 4, 135–154.

Judd, D. B. Hue saturation and lightness of surface colors with chromatic illumination. *Journal of the Optical Society of America,* 1940, 30, 2–32.

Judd, D. B. The definition of black and white. *American Journal of Psychology,* 1941, 54, 289–294.

Kardos, L. Versuch einer mathematischen Analyse von Gesetzen des Farbensehens. Nähere Bestimmung des funktionalen Verhältnisses zwischen Farbenerlebnis und Reizgesamtheit. *Zeitschrift für Psychologie und Physiologie der Sinnesorgane.* Part 2: *Zeitschrift für Sinnesorgane,* 1935, 66, 182–212.

Koffka, K. *Principles of Gestalt psychology.* New York: Harcourt, 1935.

Marimont, R. B. Model for visual response to contrast. *Journal of the Optical Society of America,* 1962, 52, 800–806.

Mershon, D. H., & Gogel, W. C. Effect of stereoscopic cues on perceived whiteness. *American Journal of Psychology,* 1970, **83,** 55–67.

Michels, W. C., & Helson, H. A reformulation of the Fechner law in terms of adaptation-level applied to rating scale data. *American Journal of Psychology,* 1949, **62,** 355–368.

Michels, W. C., & Helson, H. A quantitative theory of time-order effects. *American Journal of Psychology,* 1954, **67,** 327–334.

Steger, J. A. Reversal of simultaneous lightness-contrast. *Psychological Bulletin,* 1968, **70,** 774–781.

Stevens, S. S. To honor Fechner and repeal his law. *Science,* 1961, **133,** 80–86.

Stevens, S. S., & Stevens, J. C. Brightness function: Parametric effects of adaptation and contrast. *Journal of the Optical Society of America,* 1960, **50,** 1139.

Wallach, H. Brightness constancy and the nature of achromatic colors. *Journal of Experimental Psychology,* 1948, **38,** 310–324.

COMMENT

Deane B. Judd

Flock has made a number of valid points regarding the limitations of the Adams–Cobb–Judd–Helson formula for predicting lightness, and I hasten to acknowledge them.

NEGLECT OF LUMINANCE EXTREMES

First, it is true that this formula for lightness involves reflectance only, not luminance. Second, this formula does indeed imply that variations in illuminance can be neglected; and this is so obviously wrong that it perhaps does not even need pointing out. Without doing any experiments at all, we know that if the illuminance is zero, there will be no visual object to which a lightness estimate may be attached. The experiments by Jameson and Hurvich (1961, 1964) suggest that as illuminance approaches zero, lightness approaches dark gray (see Flock's Fig. 3, p. 138); those by Bornemeier (reported by Helson, 1943) likewise suggest dark gray (see Flock's Fig. 4, p.139); those by Flock (1969) suggest that as illuminance decreases, whites and light grays become middle gray, and dark grays become black (see Flock's Fig. 5, p.141). All three studies suggest that, with more light to see by, the observer sees the lightest of his perceived grays increasingly different from the darkest of them. Yet we know without doing the experiment that if the illuminance is made so high that the luminances of all parts of the scene exceed that of the sun's disk, that, too, renders impossible the perception of objects in the scene. One may speculate that for illuminances considerably higher than those shown on Flock's Figs. 3, 4, and 5, the lightness range will again decrease and approach a quality between middle gray and white before perception of objects is prevented by the observer becoming temporarily, if not permanently, blinded by glare. The Adams–Cobb–Judd–Helson lightness formula describes none of these inabilities of the human observer to discriminate objects either with too little or too much light. In the sense that any theoretical treatment of color that pretends to be complete must deal with the dependence of lightness perception on illuminance, the Adams–Cobb–Judd–Helson formula is quite inadequate.

However, I regard the Adams–Cobb–Judd–Helson formula as a valid way to obtain a first approximation to the lightnesses perceived to belong to objects in scenes that are sufficiently illuminated to fall within the range of distinct but comfortable vision. It is not true that interest in this formulation has died out.

The Helson–Judd formulation for the hue, lightness, and saturation of object colors perceived in any well-lighted scene has been recently verified for an extensive range of colors by Pearson, Rubinstein, and Spivack (1969), and this formulation has been used with some satisfaction at Bell Telephone Laboratories in studies of choice of color primaries for television and videophone pictures. The Adams–Cobb–Judd–Helson lightness formula is a basic part of this formulation. It was tested in the form of Eq. (2) in Flock's Table I (p. 130) for conformity to the lightness judgments of five observers. The colors judged were square elements chosen by a stochastic process that together made up what was called a "quilt"; so the background of each color had a pattern bearing some resemblance to the complex scene shown in Flock's Fig. 1 (p. 132). The adaptation level was evaluated as the simple arithmetical mean of the colors of all elements in the quilt. The numbers of trials in four sets of 100 each in which the prediction fell among the lightnesses estimated by five observers varied from 65 to 85.

A theoretical attempt to generalize the Adams–Cobb–Judd–Helson formula to apply to lightness perceived to belong to objects of any angular size illuminated to any degree has been made by Kaneko (1964). Instead of defining adaptation level (AL) as some kind of weighted mean of the reflectances of objects as in Eqs. (1a), (1b), and (2a) of Flock's Table I, he defined it as an area-weighted mean of the object lightness L and the background lightness L_{bg}:

$$\text{AL} = pqL + (1-p)qL_{bg}, \tag{7}$$

where the fraction p of the visual field occupied by the object ranges between 0 and 1, and q is inversely proportional to the illuminance of the scene; hence, it is always greater than zero. From Eq. (7), we discover that the perceived lightness of the background may be expressed as

$$L_{bg} = (\text{AL} - pqL)/(1-p)q,$$

but

$$L = A/(A + \text{AL}) \qquad \text{and} \qquad L_{bg} = A_{bg}/(A_{bg} + \text{AL}),$$

so

$$L = \frac{(\text{AL})^2 + A_{bg}\,\text{AL} - (1-p)qA_{bg}}{pq(A_{bg} + \text{AL})}. \tag{7a}$$

Equation (7a) and its implied definition, Eq. (7), of AL, may thus be added to the six formulas for lightness shown in Flock's Table I.

It may easily be shown that Eq. (7a) implies that for a dark background ($A_{bg} = 0$) the lightness perceived to belong to a nominally white object ($A = 1$) approaches zero as the illuminance approaches zero in agreement with Bornemeier's observations summarized in Flock's Fig. 5. By setting $A_{bg} = 0$ in Eq. (7a), we obtain $L = AL/pq$; if we substitute the resultant AL into the equation $L = A/(A + AL)$, we find both

$$A = pqL^2/(1-L)$$

and

$$L = [(A^2 + 4pqA)^{1/2} - A]/2pq, \tag{8}$$

where $A_{bg} = 0$. For a nominally black object, A approaching 0, Eq. (8) obviously indicates that the prediction of perceived lightness also approaches zero; that is, the Kaneko (1964) extension of the Adams–Cobb formula states that regardless of the illuminance (inversely specified by q), as directional reflectance A of the object approaches zero, the perception of the object on a black surround itself approaches black.

For a nominally white object, A approaching 1, viewed on a black surround, $A_{bg} = 0$, Eq. (8) reduces to the expression $L = [(1 + 4pq)^{1/2} - 1]/2pq$, and we have to inquire into the values of L for q (the inverse measure of illuminance) approaching first zero (infinite illuminance) and second infinity (zero illuminance). Although at these limits, the expression for L becomes indeterminate, it is easy to show (for example, by insertion of numerical values) that for high illuminances, q approaching 0, the predicted lightness ($A = 1$, $A_{bg} = 0$) may be made as close to unity (perception of perfect white) as is desired, and that for illuminances approaching zero, q approaching infinity, the predicted lightness also approaches zero (perception of perfect black).

CRISPENING

I have been fortunate to have two gifted colleagues, Drs. Takasaki and Semmelroth, to work on lightness perception under my direction during the last five years. Their studies have indicated that the Adams–Cobb–Judd–Helson formula can be importantly improved upon in a respect unrelated to extremes in luminance.

Takasaki (1966) used a lightness-match method to evaluate lightness experimentally as a function of reflectance of object and background. If we have identical dark grays, one on a white background, the other on a black, all observers find that the white-surrounded gray appears irresistibly darker. The observer is then instructed to choose a lighter gray that has the same lightness surrounded by white that the original gray has surrounded by black. Then a different gray is placed on the black background, and the process is repeated. In the upper left half of Fig. 1, the Munsell value of the white-surrounded gray (ordinate, V_2) is plotted against that of the black-surrounded gray (abscissa, V_1) that was found to make a lightness match. The points obtained by two observers are shown as crosses, circles, or dots, and the curves fitted to them come from

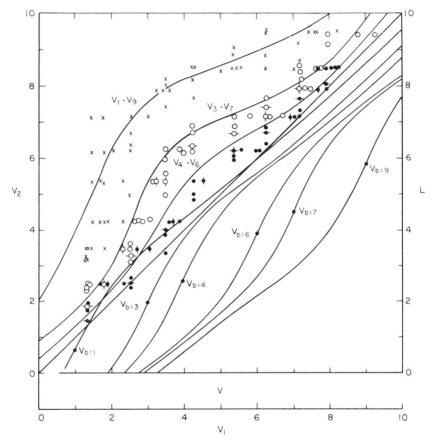

Fig. 1. Empirical simulation of the pooled observations of observers H and T, for background pairs of the same average Munsell value. The lightness-prediction formula is

$$L_i = V_i - 0.35 V_{bi} + 0.5 \bar{V}_b [(V_i - V_{bi})/1.5] \exp -|V_i - V_{bi}|/1.5 \, ,$$

where $i = 1,2$; and $\bar{V}_b = (V_{b1} + V_{b2})/2$. Lightness is plotted against Munsell value V under the 45° line on the figure. The curves above the 45° line are a plot of V_2 against V_1 which have the same L value. A pair of coincident data points is indicated by a vertical or horizontal line through the dot, and a trio of coincident points is indicated by an additional cross on the dot (from Takasaki, 1966).

the empirical formula given in the caption. The crosses refer to backgrounds of Munsell values $V_b = 1$ and 9; the circles, to 3 and 7; and the dots, to 4 and 6. Curves expressing lightness as functions of Munsell value V of target, V_b of its background, and $\bar{V}_b$ of the average of backgrounds of the two targets, are plotted below the 45° line. Note that each such function has the maximum slope for $V = V_b$ arising from the third terms of the empirical formula, and that the increases in slope for Munsell value of an object near that of its background are required to fit the lightness-matching data. Takasaki gave the name "crispening" to this increased slope. Small changes in the Munsell value of an object near that of its background produce larger changes in lightness than equal increments elsewhere. In Fig. 2 similar data are shown for the same two

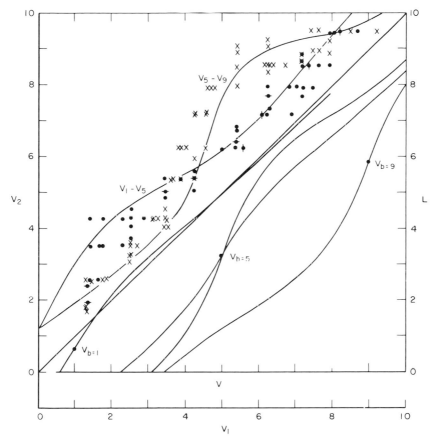

Fig. 2. See caption for Fig. 1, but the background pairs do not average to the same value. Note that the average background value $\bar{V}_b$ is different for the background pair of N1–N5 and N5–N9; so there are two L-vs.-V curves for the N5 background, one applying for the background pair N1–N5 and the other for N5–N9 (from Takasaki, 1966).

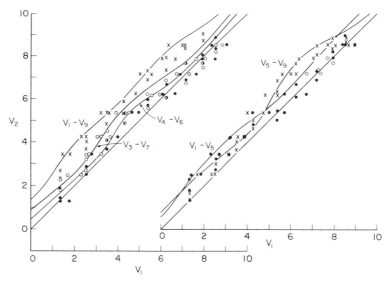

Fig. 3. Empirical simulation of the observations of observer Y. The lightness-prediction formula is

$$L_i = V_i - 0.20 V_{bi} + 0.15[(V_i - V_{bi})/0.8] \ \exp(-|V_i - V_{bi}|0.8)$$

(from Takasaki, 1966).

observers for a background of 5 (middle gray) combined with 9 (white); and for 1 (black) combined with 5 (middle gray). Similar data are given in Fig. 3 for another observer, who shows less crispening. The Adams–Cobb–Judd–Helson formula fails to predict any crispening. On this account, its predictions are far from optimum at any average scene luminance—even those within the range of comfortable vision. Kaneko's (1964) modified formula likewise shows little if any crispening. As soon as the significance of Takasaki's experimental results was appreciated, Kaneko's experimental determinations of the lightness scale for various background reflectances were reexamined. It was found that these data, too, indicate crispening, though to a lesser degree than that found by Takasaki's observers under the somewhat different experimental conditions of having only two objects and backgrounds in the field of view instead of the 11 objects on one background seen by Kaneko's observers.

Semmelroth (1970) has explored the relative conformity of experimental determinations of lightness to the predictions of formulas of the following type:

$$L = (EA)^m + K[E(A - A_{bg})]^n, \qquad \text{where} \quad A \geqslant A_{bg};$$
$$L = (EA)^m - K[E(A_{bg} - A)]^n, \qquad \text{where} \quad A \leqslant A_{bg};$$

(9)

where E is illuminance, and K, m, and n are constants to be adjusted to fit the data. The idea of these formulas is that the luminance EA of the object makes a contribution to the perceived lightness in accord with the luminance raised to a power less than one, and the absolute value of the luminance difference between object and background contributes similarly, either as an increment or decrement.

Semmelroth found that his formula fitted Takasaki's data as well as or better than Takasaki's own, more complicated, empirical formula (see Fig. 4). The lightness functions generating these predictions of lightness matches are shown in Fig. 5.

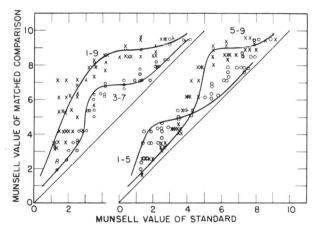

Fig. 4. Simulation of the data shown in Figs. 1 and 2 by means of the special case of Eq. (9) obtained by setting $m = n - K = 0.2$ (from Semmelroth, 1970).

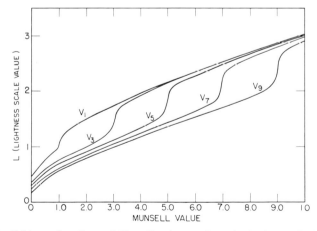

Fig. 5. The lightness functions of Munsell value used to obtain the predictions shown in Fig. 4 (from Semmelroth, 1970).

Finally, Semmelroth shows (Fig. 6) that his own formula, though not successful either, fails in a strikingly simple way to account for the Bornemeier observations. The lightness computed by his formula for the strongly illuminated comparison disk is uniformly higher than that computed for the shadowed, dimly illuminated standard (note change of scale from abscissa to ordinate by a factor of 5). If seeing the screen shadowing the standard caused the observer to

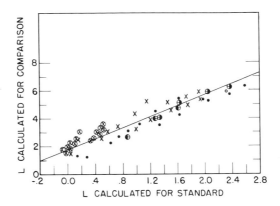

Fig. 6. Demonstration that the Semmelroth formula [Eq. (9)] when applied to Bornemeier's standards, yields a high linear correlation with the results of the same formula applied to the comparison stimuli judged to be equally light. Note, however, that the lightnesses calculated for the comparison disk seen by the observer to be strongly illuminated compared to the shadowed standard is consistently higher than that calculated for the standard (from Semmelroth, 1970).

perceive the lightness of the standard at a regularly higher level, one might say that these data indicate that the observers were perceiving the reduction in illuminance and discounting it. Perhaps no better explanation of these experimental results exists.

IS ADAPTATION LEVEL FOR LIGHTNESS PREDICTION DIFFERENT FROM THAT FOR HUE AND SATURATION PREDICTION?

The success of the Semmelroth formula [Eq. (9)] for lightness prediction suggests that for such predictions AL is the same as the reflectance A_{bg} of the background. Takasaki crispening refers to the reflectance of that part of the background seen contiguous to the object, and not to any average of the elements that go to make up a variegated background. Lightness difference perceived per unit difference in object reflectance seems to reach a relative maximum precisely as A approaches A_{bg}; therefore, A_{bg} is obviously the natural value of AL from which to count lightness difference. The formula

$$\text{AL (for lightness prediction)} = A_{bg} \qquad\qquad (9a)$$

might thus be added to Flock's Table I.

For predicting color perceptions, the AL is quite different from the reflectance A_{bg} of the immediate background or any weighted mean of the elements making up a variegated background such as described in Eqs. (1a), (2a), (2b), or (4a) of Flock's Table I, or by the Kaneko proposal [Eq. (7)]. It is definitely and necessarily less than such averages [see Eq. (1b) of Flock's Table I, stating that AL $= (k)$AL$'$].

The term AL$'$ should be read "adaptation level for the purpose of predicting the chromatic aspect of a color perception"; and k is a constant < 1 taken by Helson (1938) as $^4/_5$, and by Judd (1940) as $^3/_7$. The necessity of assigning to k a value less than unity may be understood in terms of the Troland (1917) dimming effect. He found that if an observer becomes locally adapted to the color of an object and then projects the negative afterimage of this color onto a field of the same chromaticity but of different luminance, the afterimage is seen to have either the hue perceived to belong to the object, no hue at all, or the complementary hue, depending upon how much the luminance of the field is dimmed below that of the object. This result is consistent with the report by Helson and Judd (1932), who found that if they adapted to a chromatic field, the saturation perceived to belong to it approaches, but does not reach, zero. The result was corroborated by the extensive study on the effect of chromatic adaptation on achromaticity by Helson and Michels (1948), who found that for an object of any chromaticity viewed against a background of closely the same chromaticity, there exists a luminance of background greater than that of the object for which the object is perceived as having no hue. Therefore, an object of the same chromaticity as the average of the background will look gray only if it is dimmer than the average background color, that is, for k of Eq. (1b) < 1. If you count as AL the field to which the observer is adapted, then $\overline{\text{AL}}$ can be a weighted mean $\overline{A}$ of the elements making up the scene, as in Eqs. (2b) and (4a); but if you count as AL the reflectance that a nonselective object must have in order to appear gray, then AL must be some fraction of that weighted mean, thus:

$$\text{AL (for hue and saturation prediction)} = (k)\overline{A}, \qquad k < 1. \qquad (9b)$$

Equation (9b) is equivalent to Eqs. (1b) and (2b) taken together.

The answer to the question, "Is adaptation level for lightness prediction different from that for hue and saturation prediction?" is thus, "Yes, it is always higher."

REFERENCES

Flock, H. R. Lightness changes in a complex field with changing illumination and background. Paper presented at the meeting of the Eastern Psychological Association, Philadelphia, April 1969.

Helson, H. Fundamental problems in color vision. I. The principle governing changes in hue, saturation, and lightness of non-selective samples in chromatic illumination. *Journal of Experimental Psychology,* 1938, **23,** 439–476.

Helson, H. Some factors and implications of color constancy. *Journal of the Optical Society of America,* 1943, **33,** 555–567.

Helson, H., & Judd, D. B. A study in photopic adaptation. *Journal of Experimental Psychology,* 1932, **15,** 380–398.

Helson, H., & Michels, W. C. The effect of chromatic adaptation on achromaticity. *Journal of the Optical Society of America,* 1948, **38,** 1025–1032.

Jameson, D., & Hurvich, L. M. Complexities of perceived brightness. *Science,* 1961, **133,** 174–179.

Jameson, D., & Hurvich, L. M. Theory of brightness and color contrast in human vision. *Vision Research,* 1964, **4,** 135–154.

Judd, D. B. Hue saturation and lightness of surface colors with chromatic illumination. *Journal of the Optical Society of America,* 1940, **30,** 2–32.

Kaneko, T. A reconsideration of the Cobb–Judd lightness function. *Acta Chromatica,* 1964, **1,** 103–110.

Pearson, D. E., Rubinstein, C. B., & Spivack, G. J. Comparison of perceived color in two-primary computer-generated artificial images with predictions based on the Helson–Judd formulation. *Journal of the Optical Society of America,* 1969, **59,** 644–658.

Semmelroth, C. C. Prediction of lightness and brightness on different backgrounds. *Journal of the Optical Society of America,* 1970, **60,** 1685–1689.

Takasaki, H. Lightness change of grays induced by change in reflectance of gray background. *Journal of the Optical Society of America,* 1966, **56,** 504–509.

Troland, L. T. Preliminary' note: The influence of changes of illumination upon after-images. *American Journal of Psychology,* 1917, **28,** 497.

Learning and Motivation

INTRODUCTION

Francis W. Irwin

Of the two contributions to this section, Adamson's applies AL theory to problems of "reinforcement" and Bower's uses AL theory as a starting-point toward solving an important problem of verbal learning. Taken together, these two articles make evident the fact that whether one is dealing with objects with such seemingly disparate functions as, on the one hand, that of altering the probability of the occurrence of acts upon which occurrence of the object is contingent or, on the other hand, acting as members of a set of objects of cognition, their motivational or cognitive values are determined in part by their magnitudes relative to other objects that have had the same function in the history of the organism. This means that AL theory can be brought to bear upon questions that initially appear to have nothing in common.

Adamson focuses upon those properties of reinforcers as stimuli that permit pooling effects and positive and negative contrast effects to be subjected to analysis by AL theory. To the extent that this is possible, he suggests that nothing beyond AL theory is necessary to account for many striking phenomena for which accounts in the languages of frustration theory, cognitive dissonance theory, and the theory of latent learning are otherwise brought forward. Wilson raises the question of whether such a line of argument adequately takes into account the *reinforcing* properties of reinforcers. Thus, even if AL theory throws light upon both psychophysical and motivational functions of the events that are experienced by an organism, it may still be necessary to have distinct theories of psychophysical and motivational aspects of behavior.

Bower presents a theory of the serial position curve that is based upon the pooling of stimulus-generalization effects. He then proceeds to the notion of a higher-order "conceptual relational coding" in order to deal with transfers between linear continua and "transposition" within a single dimension; the importance of this development is stressed in Holtzman's discussion. Because AL theory is sometimes presented as if the role of an organism in its own behavior were little more than the passive reception of information and the calculation of a few elementary statistics upon it, it is refreshing to see Bower taking a few steps beyond this. One would like to see how he, or others who were so disposed, would attack such generally neglected problems of organization as are pointed to by the work of Brown (1953) on the differential effects of an "anchor" in psychophysical judgments depending upon whether or not it was perceived as a member of the series upon which judgments were to be made, and that of Wishner, Shipley, and Hurvich (1957) on serial position curves for lists of nonsense syllables presented as single lists or as composed of two, or three, distinct sublists.

References

Brown, D. R. Stimulus-similarity and the anchoring of subjective scales. *American Journal of Psychology,* 1953, **66,** 199–214.
Wishner, J., Shipley, T. E., Jr., & Hurvich, M. S. The serial-position curve as a function of organization. *American Journal of Psychology,* 1957, **70,** 258–262.

CONTRAST EFFECTS AND REINFORCEMENT[1]

Robert Adamson

This article relates to three primary areas having to do with the phenomenon of contrast. One concerns the effects of manipulating reinforcement in certain ways; another is an attempt to extend the exploration in connection with other learning variables; and the third is an effort, quite tentative at this point, to try to establish limits in range for those stimuli that induce contrast.

There is, of course, nothing new in the phenomenon. Probably at some distant time, a caveman broke his club and had to resort to a lesser cudgel, leaving his mate pleasantly surprised at his newfound tenderness. In which case, he would have been one of the earliest experimenters in contrast effects and reinforcement.

Apparently, though, serendipity did not take, and the effect, insofar as it related to learning, did not become subject to psychological investigation until fairly recently (probably in the 1940s), and then in a variety of guises.

My own interest in contrast developed slightly over ten years ago, when Bevan suggested that he and I adopt a position derived from frame-of-reference psychophysics—more specifically, from AL theory—and do some rethinking about traditional views of reinforcement. A bias of this sort emphasizes among other things, that recurrent, unvarying stimulus inputs do little more than establish a steady state for the organism. Historically, rewards have been given in such a fashion, but then current learning theory had not satisfactorily come to grips with the effects elicited by variations in amount of reward or those occasioned by changes in the schedule of reward presentation.

We were led to emphasize the importance of discrepant stimulation as an agent of behavioral change. Accordingly, we viewed reinforcers as stimuli to be pooled by the organism into an internal average or norm; each new administration of a reinforcer would provide a value to be related to this average. If the discrepancy between the new stimulus value—the new reinforcer—and the

[1] This research has been supported by the Air Force Office of Scientific Research, Grants 1163-66 and 69-1823.

159

norm were marked in either direction, radical alterations in behavior could be expected (see Bevan & Adamson, 1960, 1961).

One set of experimental results provided an important impetus to this viewpoint: Crespi's findings (1942) of positive and negative contrast with shifts in reward magnitude. Thus, if animals were moved from a regimen of low-magnitude reward to one of high magnitude, their resulting performance exceeded that of controls which had been on high magnitude throughout. The converse condition led to negative contrast.

The Crespi paradigm has characterized a considerable body of work since that time. However, for this discussion, I shall use the term "contrast" in a somewhat broader sense, related to other experimental approaches as well. I shall also extend its application to effects unrelated to reinforcement per se.

CONTRAST IN LEARNING

Without attempting a formal definition of contrast in learning, I would like to mention one of its characteristics, namely, that the behavioral effect belies the stimulus history of the organism when the latter is considered in an absolute sense. Thus, in positive contrast, it is the animal with the least amount of reward in its history that provides the greatest measure of response strength. Several experimental phenomena tend to demonstrate this characteristic.

For example, differential preadaptation to stimuli on the same dimension as the reinforcing stimulus tends to enhance or degrade response measures to a common reinforcer. Bevan and Adamson (1960) found the effect with human subjects, and with Black (Black, Adamson, & Bevan, 1961) we found that the same procedure was effective with rats. More recently, Murray and Kohfeld (1965) reported similar findings in a reaction time study using a common 70-dB. tone as a response signal after preadapting subjects to tones of different, lesser intensities.

With the pooling, or averaging, assumption, one may construe as contrast the relative elevation of response rates following interpolation of extinction trials. The argument used by Adamson, Bevan, and Maier (1961) was that extinction trials had the effect of lowering the AL for reinforcement, hence, increasing the discrepancy between the AL and the reinforcer at the time the latter was reintroduced. Essentially the same argument applied to partial reward effects in that nonreinforced trials were viewed as reducing the reinforcement AL.

In any event, a relativist view of reinforcement strongly implies the prediction of contrast effects whenever there is a pronounced change from an established history of reinforcement, and it is probably unnecessary to appeal to higher-order constructs—such as frustration or cognitive dissonance—to account for them.

CONTRAST EFFECTS AND SECONDARY REINFORCEMENT

Most of the work in this area has utilized what is typically called "primary reinforcement" and has involved changing the amount of food, water, etc. given to animals during an experiment. One question that occurs is whether analogous effects would obtain with conventionally defined secondary reinforcers. If these have other than a pure cue function, one would expect their manipulation to show effects similar to those associated with the manipulation of primary reinforcers.

To test this notion, Adamson and Henke (1970) argued that responses to a secondary reinforcer (common to all subjects) would vary depending upon preadaptation to other stimuli on the cue dimension: specifically, that preadaptation to differentially illuminated stimuli would affect response measures to a common illumination value which had been associated with food reinforcement.

Our procedure was as follows: First we conditioned 24 rats to bar-press in the presence of a positive cue consisting of a clear 2 x 2-inch patch of 237 apparent foot candles as opposed to a negative patch of the same illumination which was distinguished by a cross pattern. Criterion for the discrimination was a ratio of 10 : 1 between correct and incorrect responses. Following attainment of criterion, Ss were placed in four groups matched for mean response rate at asymptote. The groups were then placed on a regimen of 10 min. of differential preadaptation followed by 50 min. of reinforced responding in the presence of the test patch.

The preadaptation values were as follows: The control group was preadapted at the test value of 237 foot candles, the same as the cue value; the other three groups were preadapted, respectively, at 77, 23, and 1.3 foot candles. During the 10 min. of preadaptation, the animals were in the Skinner box but with the bar withdrawn. They were maintained on this schedule for 14 days after which they were placed on an extinction schedule for 6 days. During extinction, conditions were as before except for the withdrawal of the food reward.

The effects of differential preadaptation were manifest in the extinction trials, as we expected, not during the reinforced trials. I think the reason for this was twofold: First, the animals were asymptotic in terms of response rate before they were placed on preadaptation; second, the food reward was present throughout and would tend to minimize differences deriving from secondary reinforcement.

The extinction differences were, on the other hand, pronounced and orderly (Fig. 1). They suggest that secondary reinforcers are subject to relational emphasis, in the same sense that primary reinforcers are. Beyond that, the data are somewhat puzzling. The greater the discrepancy between the preadaptation value and the test value, the more rapid was extinction. One possible explanation

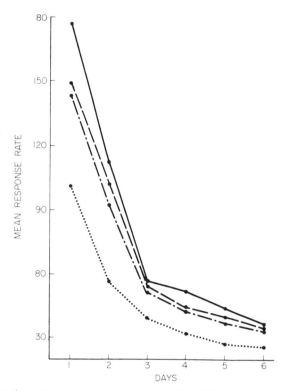

Fig. 1. Extinction rates to a common cue with differential preadaptation: (———) control; (– –) group I; (– - –) group II; (· · · ·) group III (from Adamson & Henke, 1961).

is that relatively bright light constituted aversive stimulation for the rats. Another explanation, somewhat more labored, suggests a reversal in role for the cue when primary reinforcement is withdrawn. That is, if it is possible to order cue magnitude on the basis of the discrepancy between pre- and postadaptation, in extinction one would wind up with a group of secondary reinforcers on the same dimension but differing in effectiveness, since they were now being associated with a lack of primary reinforcement. The question is, would the more effective cue become a more effective conditioned inhibitor?

While explanations of the order effects must be cautious, one may still conclude that the subjects responded to the relative magnitudes of the secondary reinforcer during extinction, and that the effectiveness of the preadaptive value increased as the discrepancy between it and the test magnitude increased.

CONTRAST EFFECTS AND EFFORT

It began to appear that contrast effects had a certain ubiquity. Our next step was to try to see whether such effects would show up in connection with other variables assumed to be important in learning. Probably the major such variable, other than reinforcement, is work. Adamson and Gunn (1969) hypothesized that controlled shifts in the effort expended in responding might demonstrate contrast; that is, a shift from a history of responses requiring quite a bit of effort to relatively effortless responses, each effective in producing reward, should show positive contrast, and the converse should also be true.

We used an approach similar to Crespi's, randomly assigning rats to four main groups, again in a bar-press situation. The animals were on a continuous reinforcement schedule, the only difference between the groups being the amount of counterweight on the bar, hence the amount of effort needed to activate the feeder switch. The counterweights were either 16 or 33 gm. To test for positive contrast, a light-weight control was opposed to the group that started with the heavy counterweight and was then switched to the light weight. To test for negative contrast, the conditions were reversed for the other two groups.

The heavy–light (H–L) and light–heavy (L–H) groups ran for 10 days with their initial counterweight and then were shifted for an additional 10 days, whereas the controls ran for 20 days with either a light or heavy counterweight. Following this, all animals were extinguished for 6 days.

The results for the H–L group (see Fig. 2) indicated that positive contrast was obtained, but the shape of the curve suggested that it might be transient. However, analysis of simple main effects supported the observation of positive contrast throughout. Apparently, the elevated performance level of the H–L group could be attributed to the counterweight shift, and was significantly above the performance of the light-weight control group. This difference was maintained throughout the 20 trials, and it was impossible to conclude that the effect was transitory within the temporal limits of the experiment.

The appearance of negative contrast was also confirmed in terms of a comparison between the L–H group and the heavy counterweight control group (see Fig. 3), although the difference could possibly be attributed to an increase in rate for the control. In any event, the shift resulted in significantly lower rates for the L–H group as compared with the control group, whereas no difference had existed between group means prior to the shift.

In this study, we felt that we were dealing with shifts in proprioceptive stimulation derived from responding to different work demands. It is reasonable to assume that the same sort of mechanism operated as that reported in the reinforcement studies; that is, that animals integrate such feedback as they do any other sort of stimulation, and that major response changes are associated with deviations from the norm.

The study also indicates that the total work history of the subjects leads to the paradoxical results I mentioned earlier as a characteristic of contrast, since those animals that expended the greater absolute amount of effort overall performed at the higher rate, and those who expended less effort performed at

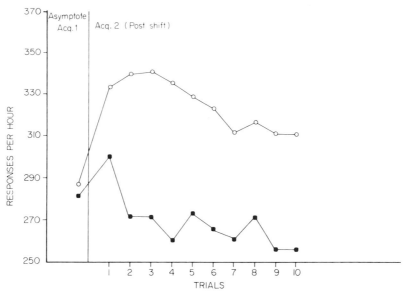

Fig. 2. Positive contrast with a shift from a heavy to a light work load: (o) H–L group; (■) light-weight control group.

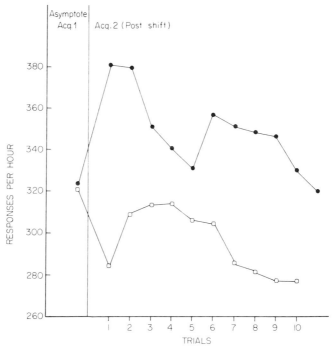

Fig. 3. Negative contrast with a shift from a light to a heavy work load: (□) L–H group; (o) heavy-weight control group.

164

the lower rate. This finding would appear to raise questions for any theory involving response-induced inhibition—unless "other things being equal" is a broader phrase than I think it is.

Contrast Effects across Blocks of Learning Trials

I would now like to report some results from a study that is only partly complete. The purpose of the study was to ascertain whether the phenomenon of contrast would operate across blocks of trials in a typical learning situation and whether the shape of the learning curve would be materially affected if it did. One would be tempted to predict a quantal curve of performance change with successive shifts in reinforcement.

In the study, I conditioned two groups of four rats each to an escape–avoidance response in a modified Miller–Mowrer box. The rats jumped a 3-inch fence to a buzzer–shock combination, with a 3-sec. conditioned stimulus (CS) interval. Reinforcement consisted of four different shock intensities: 0.1, 0.13, 0.16, and 0.2 mA, the only difference between conditions being the order in which the different intensities were delivered. One group, a control, received them in random order over 48 trials. The other group received the four intensities in order from lowest to highest for blocks of 12 trials at each level.

My supposition was that the important factor in performance would be the order effect, since it implied successive shifts from one adaptive value to a more intense value, each such change possibly eliciting contrast.

The results for this part of the experiment are shown in Fig. 4. While the control curve, barring a hump or two, is fairly typical in depicting latency change over trials, the data for the group that received an orderly progression of shocks suggests some possible surprises.

It is unquestionably quantal, and the general hypothesis of contrast operating over trials appears to have been supported. The two groups were significantly different in terms of overall mean performance and in terms of mean performance for 12-trial blocks $(F > 1, 24 = 27, p < .01)$.

Beyond this finding, I would like to point to two aspects of the experimental group's performance: First, there is no apparent slope within each block of trials at a given shock level; second, just about all the performance increment appears to be coincident with the first shift in reinforcement. The lack of slope is emphasized by the horizontal lines shown for each block of trials which represent mean performance for the block.

Both these characteristics tempt me to the conjecture that possibly we are seeing much the same thing that Blodgett (1929) and Tolman and Honzik (1930) saw in their experiments on latent learning. In each case, there was a marked change in behavior associated with a single increment in reinforcement.

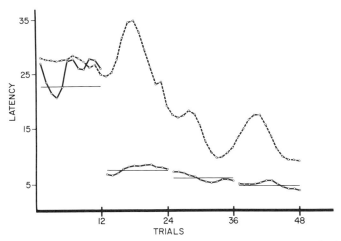

Fig. 4. Avoidance performance with ordered shock increments over 12-trial blocks: (- - - - -) random; (———) ordered (curves were smoothed by successive averaging).

The major difference between the studies appears to be in the assumed reinforcement base line.

I am suggesting that the AL construct may be able to account for latent learning as a form of contrast. In this connection, I think it interesting that, with the introduction of reinforcement, both the Blodgett and the Tolman–Honzik experimental groups showed a drop in errors that went below the control error level. The conjecture is strengthened if one is able to assume that some reinforcement was operating in the latent learning situation, an assumption that many have willingly made on the basis of the minor but consistent drop in errors shown by the test animals.

This explanation affords an alternative to one that emphasizes "signs" in the latent learning situation. A further assumption would also have to be made about these studies: that is, whatever reinforcement was operating during the early trials was somehow relevant to the identifiable reinforcer (food) used in the later trials and throughout the control situation. I shall consider that question in my conclusions.

In any event, I have started to replicate the foregoing study using positive reinforcer shifts in one case and shifts in deprivation in another. In the latter case, a study by Hillman, Hunter, and Kimble (1953) suggests that both positive and negative contrast operates with deprivation shifts. In a maze-learning task, they switched rats from 2 to 22 hr., and from 22 to 2 hr., of deprivation, respectively. For both groups, there was a small overshoot of the control function.

How Much Discrepancy Is Effective?

If—in accord with the foregoing—we do assume that the organism reacts to discrepancies from a norm, however constituted, we must then ask another question. How much discrepancy is effective? We have evidence (Adamson, 1967; Sarris, 1967, 1969) of the decline in effectiveness of anchor stimuli past some point of maximum influence, and it is reasonable to ask whether an analogous situation exists with respect to reinforcement. For this reason, and for others, I decided, along with Henke and O'Donovan (Adamson Henke, & O'Donovan, 1969), to attempt to extend the findings of Black and Bevan (1960) and Bevan and Pritchard (1963)—which dealt with subliminal effects of anchor stimuli in human subjects—to lower animals.

In this study, we initially tried to find thresholds for reaction to shock by rats, looking at data on crossings from a shocked to a nonshocked side of a grid and on defecation. In this preliminary testing, we used values of .004, .008, and .02 mA, and no shock. We found no signs of behavior change for the .004- and .008-mA groups. The .02-mA shock was, on the other hand, clearly aversive.

We then proceeded to condition four groups to an avoidance response—fence jumping to a buzzer—following differential preadaptation to the foregoing values.

The unconditioned stimulus (US) was .03 mA for all groups, and the preadapting shock was delivered for 10 sec. prior to each trial. In summary, conditions were identical for all groups except for the magnitude of shock during preadaptation.

The results were unequivocal in showing the effects of preadaptation. The no-shock control required a mean of 50.5 trials to a criterion of 12 correct responses out of the terminal 15 trials. Next in order was the group that had been preadapted to .02 mA, clearly a suprathreshold value. This group required a mean of 37 trials to criterion. The .004-mA group required a mean of 22.5 trials, and the .008-mA group 22 trials. An analysis of variance by ranks yielded an H of 16.32 $(p < .01)$.

Additionally, the results would seem to extend the findings of Bevan and his co-workers, which had dealt with human subjects, to lower animals as well.[2]

While our results in this study were, unfortunately, somewhat ambiguous, and we currently are attempting other approaches, the main question we attempted to attack was that of relevance. There is a growing amount of data, from studies already cited, from the work of Bevan and Pritchard (1963), and from ongoing

---

[2] These results as well as those of Bevan and co-workers seem to me to counter the supposition of Sarris that extreme stimulus effects are a function of "attention." The concept appears somewhat overextended if it is to include the reactivity of a rat to a current of .004 mA. It appears that the effects of minute physical energies are subtle and automatic to an extent that refutes awareness, much less attention.

work in our laboratory, which indicates that stimulus relevance is basic to the construction of effective dimensions, whether they be in psychophysics, in learning, or in other areas. The evidence appears to suggest that such relevance extends across both modalities and attributive stimulus dimensions. However, pursuing this subject would take us well beyond a consideration of contrast. That phenomenon appears to be well established, affording strong support to the more general principle of psychological relativity expressed in AL theory (Helson, 1964).

REFERENCES

Adamson, R. Anchor effect limits. *Psychonomic Science,* 1967, **9,** 179–180.

Adamson, R., & Gunn, D. Contrast effects with a shift in work load. *Psychonomic Science,* 1969, **14,** 11–12.

Adamson, R. E., & Henke, P. G. Cue effectiveness as a function of differential preadaptation. *Journal of General Psychology,* 1970, **82,** 207–214.

Adamson, R., Bevan, W., & Maier, B. Shifts in bar pressing as a function of alternating extinction and reinforcement. *Journal of General Psychology,* 1961, **64,** 147–152.

Adamson, R., Henke, P., & O'Donovan, D. Avoidance conditioning following preadaptation to weak shock. *Psychonomic Science,* 1969, **14,** 119, 121.

Bevan, W., & Adamson, R. Reinforcers and reinforcement: Their relation to maze performance. *Journal of Experimental Psychology,* 1960, **59,** 226–232.

Bevan, W., & Adamson, R. Internal referents and the concept of reinforcement. In *Interdisciplinary Research Conference, University of New Mexico.* Vol. II: N. F. Washburn (Ed.), *Decisions, values, and groups.* Oxford: Pergamon, 1961.

Bevan, W., & Pritchard, J. F. The anchor effect and the problem of relevance in the judgment of shape. *Journal of General Psychology,* 1963, **69,** 147–161.

Black, R. W., & Bevan, W. The effect of subliminal shock upon the judged intensity of weak shock. *American Journal of Psychology,* 1960, **73,** 262–267.

Black, R., Adamson, R., & Bevan, W. Runway behavior as a function of apparent intensity of shock. *Journal of Comparative and Physiological Psychology,* 1961, **54,** 270–274.

Blodgett, H. C. The effect of the introduction of reward upon the maze performance of rats. *University of California Publications in Psychology,* 1929, **4,** 113–134.

Crespi, L. P. Quantitative variation of incentive and performance in the white rat. *American Journal of Psychology,* 1942, **55,** 467–517.

Helson, H. *Adaptation-level theory: An experimental and systematic approach to behavior.* New York: Harper, 1964.

Hillman, B., Hunter, W. S., & Kimble, G. A. The effect of drive level on the maze performance of the white rat. *Journal of Comparative and Physiological Psychology,* 1953, **46,** 87–89.

Murray, H. G., & Kohfeld, D. L. Role of adaptation level in stimulus intensity dynamism. *Psychonomic Science,* 1965, **3,** 439–440.

Sarris, V. Adaptation-level theory: Two critical experiments on Helson's weighted-average model. *American Journal of Psychology,* 1967, **80,** 331–344.

Sarris, V. Anchor-effects in psychophysics: Tests on the adaptation-level model. Paper presented at 19th International Congress of Psychology, London, 1969.

Tolman, E. C., & Honzik, C. H. Introduction and removal of reward, and maze performance in rats. *University of California Publications in Psychology,* 1930, **4,** 257–275.

COMMENT

Martha Wilson

For some reason, 1968 was a good year for considering contrast effects in reinforcement. Beside the article by Bevan (1968), which discussed reinforcement in terms of general contextual effects, there were several attempts to make some sense out of the literature in this area (Black, 1968; Dunham, 1968). These reviews made it clear that, at the time they were written, traditional Hullian–Spencian kinds of views of the relationship between incentive-motivation and performance continued to be invoked as explanations of contrast effects. This literature can evoke dismay, since so few experiments seem to be useful tests of the assumptions mentioned above, and yet purport to be critical tests of alternative theories. A later review (Bitterman & Schoel, 1970) acknowledged the need for some principle of hedonic averaging in order to encompass the results of varying the magnitude, delay, and probability of reinforcement, but the authors do not mention AL theory as a possibility.

Adamson has clearly stated the background for the experiments he has described; namely, the assumptions that reinforcers are stimuli and, like other kinds of stimuli, they are averaged over time by the organism, so that some AL results. Stimuli that depart from the prevailing level are potential sources of behavioral change. The Bevan–Adamson model has often been characterized as a perceptual–motivational rather than an emotional–motivational approach, and it is said that its validity depends upon the demonstration of positive as well as negative contrast effects. The other approaches, on the other hand, do not predict positive contrast, and cannot easily explain such effects, since some form of a frustration variable or generalization decrement is usually invoked.

A common response to this theoretical difficulty by critics of an AL approach is to deny that positive contrast effects occur—or to maintain that they are very rare or very small. However, in Adamson's experiment using the amount of effort as a variable, positive as well as negative effects occurred. Since early work (Crespi, 1942; Zeaman, 1949) had suggested effects in both directions, the failure to obtain evidence for positive contrast could be viewed as confirming the null hypothesis, a procedure generally treated with caution.

It is certainly true, however, that positive contrast has been a much more difficult phenomenon to demonstrate than negative contrast. It has been suggested that this may result from ceiling effects on performance measures, or, as Bower (1961) suggested, from physiological effects inherent in these measures. Perhaps, in many of the experiments that have failed to demonstrate positive contrast, it should not have been expected. The psychophysics of reinforcement variables has not always been considered, and a rat may not be elated even though the experimenter thinks he has arranged for such a condition.

This specific point leads to a general complaint about many experiments designed to evaluate effects such as these. One of the major attributes of a quantitative theory is precisely that it *is* quantitative—and yet much of the work in the literature does not exploit the possible elegance of design and potential for prediction available in AL theory. The algebra of inequalities is often the limit of mathematical power that the experimenter is willing to use. This may be the result of quasi-quantitative formulations from old-time learning theory. It is clear that Bevan and Adamson are notable exceptions.

One study (Crandall, 1963) that was very successful in terms of showing the effects of previous reinforcement history did not use quantitative variables and yet produced extremely clear-cut results. The lesson to be drawn from this is that it is often easier to intuit good procedure in human studies than in animal studies. In this experiment, it was hypothesized that zero reinforcement or silence on the part of an adult would have different reinforcement value for children, depending upon whether the child had previously experienced positively or negatively reinforcing comments in the same situation. This was clearly shown: silence proved reinforcing when negative comments had been the rule, but was disappointing when praise was expected. In addition to the situational variable, a residual effect attributable to the past history of the child was demonstrated, and this reminds us that the effects of remote standards cannot be ignored in animal studies just because they have been controlled for.

REINFORCEMENT VERSUS STIMULUS ASPECTS OF REINFORCEMENTS

Now, given the Bevan–Adamson model, one puzzling question has been whether one can distinguish reinforcement and stimulus aspects of reinforcements. The model asserts that reinforcements are stimuli that behave like other kinds of stimuli, but that they are reinforcements, after all. While their effectiveness depends upon the prevailing level, the effectiveness of a reinforcer may change as the motivational state of the organism changes. This is a different point, obviously, than the assertion that differences in drive level will affect acquisition or performance. In experiments on contrast effects, such differences are considered as sources of variance to be controlled. But if it is assumed that the stimulus characteristics of a reinforcer may vary with tension level, is it sensible to ask whether reinforcing characteristics also vary? The parameter of drive level has not been explored as thoroughly as some of the other variables in contrast effects, so it is good to know that Adamson is planning to manipulate drive level as well as level of reinforcement.

The question of whether the Bevan–Adamson approach allows a distinction between reinforcement as a stimulus and reinforcement as a reinforcer suggests a possible source of confusion. It is not clear whether those who describe the model as a perceptual model are thinking of how the organism perceives the size or goodness of the reinforcement. If a reinforcement is a stimulus, it should be perceived in the same manner that any stimulus is, which may or may not be relational. But this says nothing about how reinforcement acts as a reinforcement. W. A. Wilson (1959) clarified the stimulus and reward aspects of reinforcement by showing that monkeys' choices between two quantities of food pellets were a function of the perceptual distinctiveness of various ratios, not of the reward value of those ratios. But is this preconsummatory stimulation the sense in which reinforcers are said to be stimuli? The issue is not one of perceptual–motivational versus emotional–motivational theories, but rather between a relational view and an absolutist view, of the mechanisms of reinforcement.

The Adamson–Henke results on secondary reinforcers, described in the preceding contribution by Adamson, in which groups were preadapted to different intensities of illumination, are puzzling for the same reasons. It can be asked if this experiment deals with secondary reinforcers in the conventional sense. One could view these results as a straightforward demonstration of a change in the effective value of the stimulus, with the response to that stimulus most changed by previous experience being the most affected in extinction. Were there really shifts in the reinforcing values of the stimuli? Having raised the question of whether critics of AL theory have confused perceptual and motivational properties of stimulation, it is also possible to ask whether Adamson's experiment has not confused motivational with perceptual properties of stimulation. A third possibility, which is that I am confused about perceptual and motivational properties of reinforcement, cannot be discounted.

The notion that reinforcing stimuli are reinforcing in a relational way is supported in a recent paper by Menzel (1969), using chimpanzees. This reminds us that depression effect was first described by Tinklepaugh in 1928, when he observed that monkeys got angry when they found a piece of lettuce under a plaque instead of the banana tidbit that they had seen previously, even though lettuce under other circumstances was quite acceptable. In the experiments by Menzel, chimpanzees could choose one of three objects, presented two at a time. Both learning trials and transfer problems were presented. All responses yielded a banana reward, but the rewards differed in size. The medium-size piece was visible under a transparent shield and served as one of the three objects, while the larger and smaller pieces were hidden by junk objects. It was found, among other things, that the chimpanzees learned to choose the object associated with the larger reward, whether it was an object or a banana; that the medium-size piece of banana served reversibly as a positive or negative object; and that a new object without a visible reward was chosen over the visible medium reward. His tests for transitive ordering of choices on transfer problems also showed that chimpanzees learned whether a cue was positive or negative, but the positive and negative could be defined only in terms of some internal standard.

Menzel (1969) introduced these studies by stating,

> Psychologists have been impressed at the extent to which reinforcing agents such as food behave like psycho-physical stimuli. . . . Nevertheless, the psychophysics of bananas and classical psychophysics continue to be treated as independent topics. Perhaps this is simply because reinforcement theorists have staked their claims and grounded their principles on one class of objects and psychophysicists have concentrated on other classes of objects [p. 484].

Menzel went on to state that all his evidence suggests that the subjects' ordering of objects and rewards were relativistic rather than absolute, and were reversible, labile, and subject to learning. He concluded, "It is possible that a theory such as Bevan and Adamson's, or Helson's, which emphasizes such factors, could have predicted all of the present findings [p. 489]."

And I will conclude by saying that I think this represents progress.

REFERENCES

Bevan, W. The contextual basis of behavior. *American Psychologist,* 1968, **23,** 701–714.
Bitterman, M. E., & Schoel, W. M. Instrumental learning in animals: Parameters of reinforcement. *Annual Review of Psychology,* 1970, **21,** 367–436.
Black, R. W. Shifts in magnitude of reward and contrast effects in instrumental and selective learning: A reinterpretation. *Psychological Bulletin,* 1968, **75,** 114–126.
Bower, G. H. A contrast effect in differential conditioning. *Journal of Experimental Psychology,* 1961, **62,** 196–199.
Crandall, V. C. Reinforcement effects of adult reactions and nonreactions on children's achievement expectations. *Child Development,* 1963, **34,** 335–354.
Crespi, L. P. Quantitative variation in incentive and performance in the white rat. *American Journal of Psychology,* 1942, **55,** 467–517.
Dunham, P. J. Contrasted conditions of reinforcement: A selective critique. *Psychological Bulletin,* 1968, **69,** 295–315.
Menzel, E. W., Jr. Responsiveness to food and signs of food in chimpanzee discrimination learning. *Journal of Comparative and Physiological Psychology,* 1969, **68,** 484–489.
Tinklepaugh, O. An experimental study of representative factors in monkeys. *Journal of Comparative Psychology,* 1928, **8,** 197–236.

Wilson, W. A., Jr. The role of learning, perception and reward in monkeys' choice of food. *American Journal of Psychology,* 1959, 72, 560–565.

Zeaman, D. Response latency as a function of the amount of reinforcement. *Journal of Experimental Psychology,* 1949, 39, 466–483.

ADAPTATION-LEVEL CODING OF STIMULI AND SERIAL POSITION EFFECTS[1]

Gordon H. Bower

Traditionally, AL theory had its origins and main data base in describing people's judgments of unidimensional stimuli. Accepting the notion that a potential stimulus becomes transformed into an effective stimulus by virtue of an *encoding process,* AL theory provides a hypothetical (and quantitative) description of this encoding—that the functional stimulus is the deviation of the physical stimulus from an internal norm, the AL. This characterization of the functional stimulus has many implications and applications which Helson has systematically pursued and reviewed in his book, *Adaptation-Level Theory* (Helson, 1964).

I wish to apply the theory to a phenomenon which occurs universally whenever subjects learn identifying responses to multiple stimuli that differ from one another along one dimension or in one attribute. The universal phenomenon is the "serial position effect" (SPE). Except for a brief allusion in his book to Murdock's (1960) theory of stimulus distinctiveness, Helson does not discuss SPEs in relation to AL theory, and I hope to show more firmly the relation between the phenomenon and the theory. The plan of this contribution is as follows: First, a few experiments will be reviewed to indicate the ubiquity of the SPE; second, considering theories for the SPE, I shall describe Murdock's (1960) theory, describe a new experiment testing it, then criticize that theory; third, an alternative theory of the SPE will be briefly proposed that is more compatible with AL concepts; and fourth, the major failing of these theories will be brought out in experiments implying that human adults also map (encode) stimuli along various sensory dimensions onto a common conceptual domain composed of abstract elements arrayed in a linear order.

[1] The research reported in this article was supported by Grant MH-13950, from the National Institute of Mental Health.

SERIAL-POSITION EFFECTS IN ASSOCIATIVE LEARNING

It is well to begin by citing a few examples of the phenomenon that commands our attention. It arises when subjects learn to associate "identifying responses" to stimuli which are values of a unidimensional physical variable. In the jargon of verbal learning, this is paired-associate learning. The stimuli may be on either substitutive or intensity dimensions. Examples would be tones varying in pitch, loudness, or duration, gray squares varying in size, brightness, or spatial position, lines varying in length, and so on.

The experiments involve selecting several values along one of these dimensions, assigning some unrelated identifying responses to the stimuli, then training human subjects on a paired-associate (PA) procedure until they learn the stimulus–response (S–R) assignments. The procedures differ from the psychophysical method of absolute judgments in that the PA responses are unordered with respect to the stimuli, whereas the responses in absolute-judgment experiments are always ordered numerically or verbally (for example, from "very low" to "very high") and assigned to the stimuli with a perfect correlation. Also in the PA procedure, there is an experimentally defined "correct response" to each stimulus and the subject receives feedback regarding this after each guess. These procedural aspects are missing in the absolute-judgment experiments.

Experiments of this sort have been done many times and quite a few have been published. In every one of the published experiments there is a large SPE in learning. The subjects make the fewest errors on the stimulus values at the end of the range, whereas they make the most errors on stimuli in the middle of the range. A bowed curve is obtained when some measure of performance (for example, correct responses or errors) is plotted against the value of the stimulus on the physical dimension.[2]

The basic phenomena to be explained are illustrated in Figs. 1 and 2. Figure 1 shows the relative SP error curve from an experiment by Ebenholtz (1963). The stimuli were 10 locations of a 1-inch red patch; the 10 cells were arrayed in a vertical column 10.3 inches high. The responses were 10 pronounceable nonsense syllables assigned randomly to the spatial locations. Training was done by the method of anticipation to a criterion of one perfect trial. The spatial stimuli were presented each trial in a different random temporal order. The chief

---

[2] Many of the curves to be shown will be "percentage-normalized" curves, the errors or correct responses at each position being expressed as a percentage of the total errors or total correct responses made, summing over all positions. This description of SP curves cancels out the absolute numbers of errors or corrects, and inspects only the relative numbers at the several positions. This procedure follows in the tradition of McCrary and Hunter (1953), who found that relative SP error curves for rote serial learning were remarkably constant even though total errors varied considerably with manipulations of meaningfulness, pacing rate, intertrial interval, and similar variables.

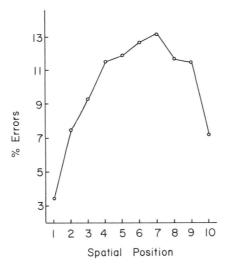

Fig. 1. Percentage of total errors contributed by each positional stimulus during paired-associate learning. Data are conditions D–T and I combined, as reported by Ebenholtz (1963).

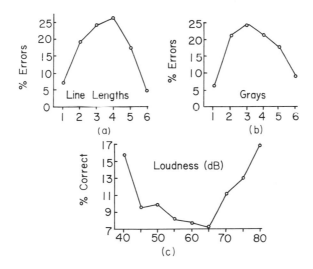

Fig. 2. Relative percentage error curves from the author's experiments using as stimuli (*a*) lines varying in length, and (*b*) gray squares varying redundantly in size and brightness. Part (*c*), from Murdock (1960), is relative percentage correct curves for tones varying in loudness.

thing to notice about Fig. 1 is the bowed shape, the fact that fewest errors occurred on the extreme stimuli. Jensen (1962) reported similar SP curves.

Figure 2 shows similar bowed-shape curves this time for the stimulus dimensions of length of a line, of brightness, and size of a gray patch (from our experiments), and of the loudness of a 1000-Hz tone (from Murdock, 1960). The Murdock data are relative correct SP curves (inverted from the relative error SP curves of the other data).

Serial-position curves such as those illustrated above have been found several times for these dimensions as well as for heaviness, pitch of a tone, temporal durations, and areas of a square or a circle. So the claim is that an SPE results any time a subject learns identifying responses to specific stimuli arranged along a one-dimensional continuum.

MURDOCK'S THEORY ON STIMULUS DISTINCTIVENESS

Murdock (1960) collated several SP curves like those above, and offered a theory to predict the shape of these curves. He noted the similarity of his theory to AL theory; Helson subsequently (1964) reviewed Murdock's paper with approval, considering it to be a good application of AL concepts. A critical reexamination of Murdock's theory seems warranted.

Murdock's concern was to devise a measure of the relative distinctiveness of a stimulus within a given set of stimuli, and to relate this measure to the relative accuracy of performance when the subjects were giving absolute judgments or learning PA responses to these stimuli. First, using the Weber–Fechner law, he assumed that the effective stimulus would be the logarithm of the physical stimulus. Second, the distinctiveness of a given stimulus within a set was defined to be proportional to the sum of the distances between it and each of the other stimuli in the set. Table I illustrates the method of computation for a set of five

TABLE I

Computation of PD Measures for Five Logarithmically Spaced Stimuli[a]

Stimuli	Sum of distances (d)[b]	% distinctiveness (PD)
1	1+2+3+4 = 10	10/40 = .250
2	1+1+2+3 = 7	7/40 = .175
3	1+1+2+2 = 6	6/40 = .150
4	1+1+2+3 = 7	7/40 = .175
5	1+2+3+4 = 10	10/40 = .250

[a] According to Murdock's (1960) hypothesis.
[b] Sum of all distances = 40.

logarithmically spaced stimuli, denoted simply as 1, 2, 3, 4, and 5. The distances from each stimulus to every other stimulus in the set are indicated in the second column. The distinctiveness of each stimulus relative to that of all other stimuli is shown in the third column. Murdock assumed that the percentage-distinctiveness (PD) measure would be predictive of the *relative* degrees of accuracy in performance to these stimuli. This amounts to assuming that whatever the overall level of correct performance to the stimuli (provided it is not perfect nor at chance), the ratio of correct-response probability for stimulus i to that for stimulus j should be the same as the ratio of the two distinctiveness measures. Therefore, the relative percentage correct curve should be identical to the theoretical PD curve; in other words, relative SP curves (for correct responses—but, by implication, for errors too) should be predictable from simply knowing the stimuli involved in the learning task. Murdock compared the predicted PD numbers with several observed SP gradients and found neither significant nor systematic discrepancies. He thus concluded that this PD measure gave an adequate account of relative SP curves. By implication, the frame-of-reference or AL concepts used in Murdock's hypothesis received further confirmation.

Anchor Stimuli in Learning

Inherent in AL theory and Murdock's hypothesis are many implications about learning with unidimensional stimuli. One set of implications, which my student, Peter Arnold, and I have tested, concerns the effect of anchor stimuli on the SP curve obtained during PA learning. The experimental procedure and theoretical predictions may be illustrated by reference to Table II. The stimuli 1–9 are nine horizontal line lengths logarithmically spaced from 1 inch long up

TABLE II

Schematic Procedure for PA Learning to Middle Stimuli 3, 4, 5, 6, 7 with or without Anchors at the Low or High End[a]

| | Log stimulus | | | | | | | | |
Condition	1	2	3	4	5	6	7	8	9
No anchors	p	p	R_1	R_2	R_3	R_4	R_5	p	p
Low anchors	+	+	R_1	R_2	R_3	R_4	R_5	p	p
High anchors	p	p	R_1	R_2	R_3	R_4	R_6	+	+
Both anchors	+	+	R_1	R_2	R_3	R_4	R_5	+	+

[a] The $R_1, \ldots, R_5$ are nonsense-syllable response terms; + denotes that the stimulus was presented; and p denotes that the stimulus was replaced by a neutral picture.

to 9.81 inches long (Weber fraction of $\frac{1}{3}$). These were shown one to a flash card; the subject looked at each and either responded or did not respond. All subjects learned to pair the five middle stimuli S_3–S_7 with five unrelated nonsense syllables–JUL, KAW, TES, NEY, and DIZ. The subjects were trained by the conventional anticipation method at a 3:3-sec. rate. During presentation cycles of these five items, four other stimuli were also presented, mixed in randomly with the critical stimuli. These four extra stimuli required no response—in fact, a checkmark on the card informed the subject of this—that he was merely to look at the stimulus.

Four experimental conditions were formed differing in the four extra stimuli. For the no-anchor group, the extra stimuli were colored pictures (advertisements) taken from *Life* magazine. These were intended to be so unlike the line stimuli that they would not be pooled into the AL for judging the critical lines, and the pictures should not influence the learning of responses to the lines. For the low-anchor condition, two of the pictures were replaced by cards displaying the shortest two lines (1.00 and 1.333 inches, respectively). These were shown printed on cards but with a checkmark, so the subject knew that no response was required to such stimuli. For the high-anchor group, the two longest lines (8 and 9) replaced the same two pictures. For the both-anchors group, all four pictures were replaced by the two shortest lines (1,2) and by the two longest lines (8,9). Each subject was tested ten trials, or to a criterion of three consecutive errorless cycles on the five critical stimuli, whichever occurred first.

We shall focus upon the SP curve for stimuli S_3–S_7 for the four experimental groups. What are the expectations of Murdock's hypothesis regarding these SP curves? The theoretical calculations are summarized in Table III and the percentage-distinctiveness measures are shown in graph form (Fig. 3). In following through the calculations of the PD measures, one should be reminded that responses are being collected only to stimuli S_3–S_7, and therefore the PD measures for these stimuli must sum to unity.

In Fig. 3a the SP curves predicted for the no-anchor and both-anchors conditions are compared. The AL, midpoint, and minimum of the symmetric SP curves are predicted to be the same in these two conditions, but the flatness of the two gradients should differ. In particular, the presence of low- and high-anchor stimuli should reduce the former distinctiveness of the end points of the critical stimuli, S_3 and S_7, and therefore performance to these end stimuli should not be much better than that to the middle stimulus. Incidentally, intuition would also suggest that the both-anchors condition should have poorer absolute performance than the no-anchors condition, as well as a flatter relative gradient. In Fig. 3b the relative SP curves predicted for the low- and high-anchor conditions are compared. Performance on end stimuli near the anchors should be depressed relative to the midpoint of the series, and the PD of the stimulus at the opposite end should be enhanced.

TABLE III

Theoretical Calculations of PD Measures for Four Experimental Conditions[a]

Condition	Measure	Stimulus								
		S_1	S_2	S_3	S_4	S_5	S_6	S_7	S_8	S_9
No anchors	d	—	—	10	7	6	7	10	—	—
	PD	—	—	.250	.175	.150	.175	.250	—	—
Low anchors	d	21	16	13	12	13	16	21	—	—
	PD	—	—	.173	.160	.173	.214	.280	—	—
High anchors	d	—	—	21	16	13	12	13	16	21
	PD	—	—	.280	.214	.173	.160	.173	—	—
Both anchors	d	36	29	24	21	20	21	24	29	36
	PD	—	—	.218	.192	.182	.192	.218	—	—

[a] Line d gives the summed distance measures from that stimulus to every presented stimulus, and the PD measure is d divided by the sum of d measures for stimuli S_3–S_7.

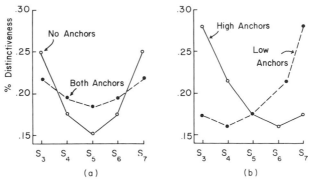

Fig. 3. Percentage-distinctiveness curves for groups with high or low anchors (b) or both high and low anchors or neither (a) graphed from values in Table III.

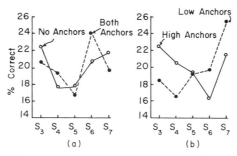

Fig. 4. Observed relative percentage correct curves for the four experimental conditions. The results are to be compared to theoretical predictions shown in Fig. 3: (a) the no-anchors and both-anchors groups; (b) the low- and high-anchors groups.

Those are the predictions. The actual results of the experiment are shown in Fig. 4, which gives the relative percentage correct curves, after pooling data from two different replications of this experiment (a total of approximately 20 Ss per condition). The no-anchors and both-anchors conditions on the left side do not compare too favorably to the theoretical expectations in Fig. 3. The both-anchors condition was supposed to yield a flatter SP curve; instead it produced an irregular SP curve, with the point at stimulus S_6 simply out of line according to any sensible interpretation. The end points on the both-anchors SP curve are lower than for the no-anchors curve, as expected, but the middle stimulus is also lower. The prediction that both-anchors Ss would make more errors than the no-anchors Ss was confirmed in both replications of the experiment. So one is left without any clear theoretical decision in this case, presumably because the effects are small relative to the sampling variability of the mean errors at each point.

In Fig. 4b SP curves for the high- and low-anchor groups are given, and these compare favorably with the expectations in Fig. 3. With the low-anchors group, the minimum point of correct responding is shifted down toward the anchors and the gradient is raised at the upper end; with the high anchors group, the minimum is shifted to the right (in other words, to longer line lengths).

To summarize, then, the anchor experiment has given only equivocal support to Murdock's theory. The results with asymmetrical anchors came out as expected, whereas those with both anchors were not entirely as predicted.

Critique of Murdock's Theory

Although Murdock's theory delivers some accurate predictions, I think it can be shown to be wrong. First, it is a simple matter to concoct "*Gedanken* experiments" in which the theory's predictions must be false; second, as will be shown later, most of the theory's predictions of SP curves do not differentiate it from a large class of simple, alternative theories. That means, of course, that the SP data that have been fit by Murdock's theory are not particularly critical or discriminating.

First, a *Gedanken* experiment for which the theory's prediction about percentage correct responses must surely be false. Consider an absolute-judgment experiment or PA learning experiment arranged as follows: Beginning with three widely spaced stimuli, say, tones of 5, 45, and 85 dB. above the threshold, we then add very many new tones that differ by less than a just noticeable difference (JND) from the low and high tones. For example, by adding two low and two high tones, the new set for discrimination might be 3.9, 4.0, 4.1, 45, 84.9, 85.0, and 85.1 dB. Murdock's PD measure implies that the end stimuli, 3.9 and 85.1 dB., will be the most distinctive and will have the most correct responses, whereas the middle stimulus, 45 dB., will be the least distinctive and will have the fewest correct responses. One need not run this experiment to know that the prediction must be wrong; in such an experiment, the middle stimulus would surely have the most correct responses, because it stands out from the clumps of confusing tones at the high and low ends of the range. Along the same vein, Murdock's hypothesis implies that the relative percentage correct curve for three equally log-spaced stimuli will be the same, independent of their physical spacing. Thus, relative performance in discriminating tones of 5, 45, and 85 dB. is predicted to be the same as that in discriminating 44.9, 45.0, and 45.1 dB. But clearly, by manipulating the spacing one can create sets of three tones for which absolute judgments are either random (PDs = .33), intermediate (PDs = .38, .25, .38), or perfect (PDs = .33) in accuracy. The point is that Murdock's relativistic hypothesis does not take proper account of the spacing between the physical stimuli, nor does it address the question of how indistinguishable stimuli can be predicted by the theory to differ in relative discriminability.

A further point is that Murdock's theory provides no clear way to incorporate the effect on the SP curve of wide variations in differential frequencies of presenting the series stimuli. For example, if, in the no-anchors condition, the longer stimuli (S_6 and S_7) had been presented three times as frequently as the shorter stimuli (S_3–S_5) the AL should shift upwards and have an effect on the SPE similar to that observed in the high-anchors condition. Such relative frequency effects are seen in the shapes of generalization gradients (see, for example, Capehart, Tempone, & Hebert, 1969) and would doubtless occur in relative SP curves, yet it is not clear how Murdock's hypothesis can be addressed to such matters.

Perhaps a more serious criticism of Murdock's approach is that it proposes an *ad hoc* descriptive measure of PD, but it provides no mechanistic explanation whatsoever for why that measure ought to be correlated with performance. It tells us nothing about how learning occurs, what kinds of errors are likely and how they are overcome, how responses are eventually differentiated to nondistinctive stimuli, and so on. It gives no account of generalization errors, and there can be no doubt about such errors. For example, in Fig. 5 (for our line-length experiment) a pooled gradient of remote intrusion errors, expressing the relative frequency with which an error was the response actually appropriate to a stimulus one, two, three, or four steps away is given. The precise shape of the gradient is not as important as the fact that it decreases monotonically. Such intrusion-error gradients are the most elementary manifestations of stimulus

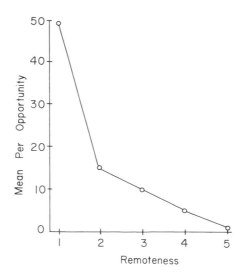

Fig. 5. Gradient of remote intrusion errors in the line-length experiment. Data are pooled over serial positions, with correction for differential logical opportunity for errors of different degrees of remoteness.

generalization, of giving responses R_3 or R_5 to S_4 because S_4 is "close to" S_3 and S_5.

One would like to have some "mechanism" theory of the learning and generalization process. In the next section it will be shown that the most elementary learning-and-generalization model derived from AL theory can deliver predictions of SP curves that are practically indistinguishable from those implied by Murdock's measure.

A STIMULUS-GENERALIZATION MODEL

This model uses simple notions of associative learning and stimulus generalization, but the effective stimulus is the discrepancy of the physical stimulus from the AL. The evidence for this latter view has been marshalled effectively in a paper by Capehart *et al.* (1969). Along with the usual weighted-log definition of the AL, we define the effective code, C_i, for physical stimulus S_i as the algebraic difference between $\log S_i$ and $\log$ AL, all of which is equivalent to the log of the ratio of S_i to the AL. The substantive assumptions are that learning and generalization of responses occurs in the standard "Spencian" manner but with respect to the C_i measures. That is, reinforcement of response R_i in the presence of specific stimulus S_i causes R_i to become associated maximally to C_i; but the response generalizes to other stimuli accordingly as their codes are close to C_i. For illustrative purposes here, let us assume that the stimulus-generalization gradient is linear when habit is plotted on the C scale, namely, against the logarithm of the physical stimulus. In particular, for stimuli spaced by steps of one log unit, the illustrative generalization gradient for response R_i to stimulus S_x will be

$$_xH_i = \begin{cases} {}_iH_i[1 - \frac{1}{3}|C_i - C_x|] & \text{for } |C_i - C_x| \leqslant 3 \\ 0 & \text{otherwise,} \end{cases}$$

where ${}_iH_i$ is the habit strength of R_i to coded stimulus C_i. Since $C_i = \log S_i - \log$ AL, the absolute difference between the Cs is expressible simply as $\log S_i/S_x$.

To perform computations with this model, consider the habit profile existing after one training cycle through a list of five pairs. Suppose $S_1 - S_5$ denote the stimuli as equally spaced on a log scale. If the stimuli are presented equally often, then the AL will be at S_3 and the coded stimuli will have values $-2, -1, 0, +1$, and $+2$ for $S_1 - S_5$, respectively. The calculations of performance are given in Table IV, where sequential effects are ignored but it is assumed that training has brought the correct habit to a strength of three at each stimulus. The entries in Table IV are habit strengths of the column response to the row stimulus, and the $(3, 2, 1)$ generalization gradient has been used here. Across any row of Table IV, say that for S_1, the strengths of the several response tendencies to that

TABLE IV

Computations of Habit Strengths for Generalization Model

Stimuli	Coded cues	Responses					Correct/sum	Relative PD
		R_1	R_2	R_3	R_4	R_5		
S_1	−2	3	2	1	0	0	3/6	.240
S_2	−1	2	3	2	1	0	3/8	.180
S_3	0	1	2	3	2	1	3/9	.160
S_4	+1	0	1	2	3	2	3/8	.180
S_5	+2	0	0	1	2	3	3/6	.240

stimulus can be seen. It is presumably these remote response tendencies that are manifested in gradients of remote intrusion errors to each stimulus.

A "response axiom" is needed for deciding how the hypothetical S should respond. A simple one to use for the moment is Luce's (1959) choice rule which supposes that the probability of R_i to an eliciting stimulus is the ratio of the strength of R_i to that stimulus divided by the summed strengths of all responses to that stimulus. The probability of a correct response, calculated according to this ratio rule, is shown in the next-to-last column of Table IV. In order to compare this model with Murdock's, these correct response probabilities have to be normalized by dividng them by the sum of the correct-response probabilities to all stimuli (which is in fact the expected total number of correct responses if the items $S_1 - S_5$ were to be tested now). This division is shown in the final column PD, and this is the theoretical measure which is to be compared to actual data as well as to the PD predictions from Murdock's hypothesis.

The first point to notice about the numbers in Table IV is that a symmetric SP curve is predicted (see the last column), with the fewest errors on the end stimuli and the most errors on the middle stimulus. Second, by reading across any row we obtain an impression of the source of errors. In particular, the probability of an error of n steps remoteness should decrease with n, in a regular gradient of remote intrusions, as shown in Fig. 5.

The next inquiry is whether and how well this generalization model can mimic the PD predictions of Murdock's earlier measure. The PD predictions for the generalization model (G) and for Murdock's measure (M) were calculated for sets of 4, 5, 6, or 7 equally log-spaced stimuli. These calculated values are displayed for comparison in Table V. The most remarkable feature of Table V is the closeness of the G and M measures in every case. The largest absolute discrepancy is around .015, which is too small a difference to detect, given the sampling error of the usual points in an SP curve. We may therefore conclude that the stimulus-generalization theory mimics Murdock's PD measures for stimuli equally spaced on a logarithmic scale. For that reason, it will fit all those

TABLE V

Comparison of Generalization (G) and Murdock (M) Theories on PD Measures for Training on Sets of 4, 5, 6, or 7 Stimuli Equally Spaced on a Logarithmic Scale

| | Number of pairs | | | | | | | |
| | 4 | | 5 | | 6 | | 7 | |
Stimulus	G	M	G	M	G	M	G	M
S_1	.285	.300	.240	.250	.207	.213	.182	.187
S_2	.214	.200	.180	.175	.155	.159	.136	.143
S_3	.214	.200	.160	.150	.138	.127	.121	.116
S_4	.285	.300	.180	.175	.138	.127	.121	.107
S_5			.240	.250	.155	.159	.121	.116
S_6					.207	.213	.136	.143
S_7							.182	.187

PD curves based on equally log-spaced stimuli which Murdock fit and offered as evidence for his theory.

The generalization theory also handles the effects of anchor stimuli if it is assumed that certain neutral or "inhibitory" responses come to be associated to the anchor stimuli, and that these inhibitory tendencies generalize to neighboring stimuli just as do active response tendencies. The effect of low anchors (S_1, S_2) on the response tendencies to the active stimuli S_3–S_7 is illustrated in Table VI, where R_1 and R_2 denote "inhibitory responses" in this context. These inhibitory responses may occur to stimuli S_3–S_7, probably causing omissions and thus lowering the probabilities of correct responses to

TABLE VI

Generalization Theory Applied to the Low-Anchor Condition[a]

Stimuli	R_1	R_2	R_3	R_4	R_5	R_6	R_7	Correct/sum	PD
S_1	3	2	1						
S_2	2	3	2	1					
S_3	1	2	3	2	1			3/9	.178
S_4		1	2	3	2	1		3/9	.178
S_5			1	2	3	2	1	3/9	.178
S_6				1	2	3	2	3/8	.200
S_7					1	2	3	3/6	.267

[a] Here, R_1 and R_2 denote "inhibitory responses," whereas R_3–R_7 are relevant experimental responses.

stimuli near the low end of the scale. The PD measure shown in the last column of Table VI may be compared to the PD numbers in Table V (for 5 stimuli with no anchors) and to Murdock's prediction for the low-anchor condition in Table III (also in Fig. 3b). The predictions for the high-anchors condition would be symmetrical to those for the low-anchors condition. The main point to note is that the expected PD gradient for the low-anchor condition for the generalization theory is virtually indistinguishable from that predicted by Murdock's hypothesis. So, insofar as Murdock's hypothesis fits the gradients from the anchor study, to that extent the generalization theory is also supported. It should be noted that the generalization theory could accommodate the anchor results in this instance only by assuming that "inhibitory" or neutral responses become conditioned to the anchor stimuli. It does not suffice to merely assume that anchors alter the AL in this experiment, since that factor consistently cancels out of the relative generalization gradients.

This is all I wish to say comparing the generalization model to Murdock's PD hypothesis. I have emphasized the similarities of their predictions of SP curves for stimuli that are equally spaced on a logarithmic scale. The two theories could probably be differentiated in a number of ways. For example, the generalization theory explains the deleterious effects on performance of subliminal spacing of stimuli, which was a criticism of Murdock's hypothesis raised earlier. Also, the theories may differ in their predictions of relative accuracy of performance with unequally spaced stimuli, but it would appear that the relevant differentiating experiments have not been done. In any comparative tests of the competing theories, it must be kept in mind that the height and slope of the generalization gradient are parameters to be selected in the one theory. My selection of a height of 3 and slope of $1/3$ was purely fortuitous and casual, and no special significance is to be read into this choice of parameters.[3]

CONCEPTUAL DIMENSIONS

Both Murdock's theory and the generalization theory outlined above are incomplete because they do not give adequate recognition to several "cognitive" aspects of learning responses to linear orders. First, some evidence will be reviewed showing that the SPE occurs with words located symbolically along a

[3] With the learning rules as stated (that is, linear increments in the advantage of the correct response), Luce's response rule will not predict eventual perfect learning of responses to a small set of stimuli. An alternative response rule that predicts nearly 100% correct responding (for a small stimulus set) is Hull's (1943), where the habit strengths of different responses to each stimulus are normal random variables, and the choice is to that response with the highest momentary strength. This rule is quite similar to Luce's axiom (see Suppes & Zinnes, 1963) except at the extreme values which are of concern in this footnote.

semantic or conceptual continuum. Second, other evidence will be reviewed showing transfer of arbitrary "response scales" both within and between sensory dimensions in such a manner as to force one to a belief in an abstract, conceptual linear ordering of cognitive elements which has multiple sensory inputs. These two points, along with an important counterargument to the first, will be taken up in turn.

Symbolically Ordered Stimuli

When stimuli vary in physical characteristics like brightness or heaviness or linear extent, there would appear to be a physiological effect of such stimuli which varies monotonically as the stimulus varies. That is, one can practically see, in the functioning of the peripheral nervous system, the grounds for assuming distinct physiological "dimensions" in these cases. But SPEs appear just as strongly with derived dimensions or with symbolic, "conceptual" dimensions where there is no possibility of an elementary correspondence to a physical stimulus.

One example of a "derived" dimension is elapsed time, a dimension for which there is no physical stimulus. When PA responses are learned to a series of time intervals used as separate stimuli, SPEs arise, as Murdock (1960) has shown. The most well-known SPE occurs, of course, when the subjects learn to produce a temporal series of items, by the method of rote serial anticipation. Of the multiple cues possible for the responses in rote serial learning, a plausible one is the time interval elapsed since the beginning of the list; if the time per item is t, then an elapsed-time interval of nt would be the cue for the $(n+1)$th response item. Murdock's data implies that the learning of associations to a randomly presented set of regular time intervals would itself produce an SPE.

Another plausible cue for the response in rote serial learning is the *number of events* elapsed since the start of the trial, so that something like a subjective count of items might be kept by the subject. Associating responses to variations in number of events *qua* stimuli would also probably produce our ubiquitous SP curve. With a constant rate of item presentations, elapsed time and number of events are confounded, but they could easily be unconfounded in special experiments. The point of these remarks is that elapsed-time intervals and number of events elapsed are cues implicit in the rote serial-learning procedure and that these acting alone produce an SPE in PA procedures; therefore, they may be considered as likely contributors to the total SPE observed in the rote serial procedure.

Serial-position effects with symbolic dimensions have been found for numerals and for conceptual (semantic) dimensions. Examples of the first type are experiments by Ebenholtz (1966), who used the first 8–10 integers as stimuli to be associated to 10 unrelated nouns as response terms (in his Experiment 1) or to 8 nonsense-syllable responses (in his Experiment 2), and Pollio and Draper (1966), who used the integers 1–5 as responses to be associated with nonsense-syllable stimuli. The SP curves are shown in Fig. 6. The Ebenholtz data (Fig. 6a) are relative error percentages with digit stimuli; the Pollio and Draper data (Fig. 6b) are mean trials to criterion for pairs with digit responses of one to five, but the relative percentage error curve should have a similar shape. It is clear that high and low numbers are learned the fastest whether they serve as stimuli or as responses for the other element of the pair. This is not simply a

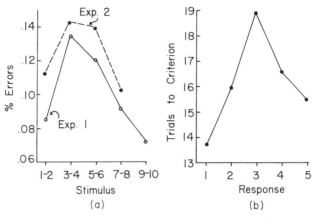

Fig. 6. Relative-error gradients to digits used (*a*) as stimuli (results taken from Ebenholtz, 1966); or (*b*) as responses in PA learning (results taken from Pollio & Draper, 1966).

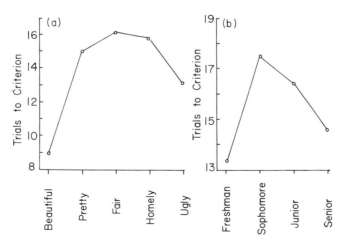

Fig. 7. Trials to criterion for pairs with the response terms arrayed on a semantic continuum: (*a*) data from Pollio and Deitchman (1964) (*b*) data from DeSoto and Bosley (1962).

function of the "meaningfulness" or association value of these digits (as scaled by Battig & Spera, 1962) since, for example, 3, 4, 5, and 6 have higher-rated association values than do 7 and 8, but the former are learned slower (as Fig. 6a shows).

Serial-position curves to words arrayed along an implicit semantic dimension have been studied by DeSoto and Bosley (1962) and by Pollio and Deitchman (1964). Examples of the obtained SP curves are shown in Fig. 7. Pollio and Deitchman (Fig. 7a) had their subjects learn to associate an adjective response (beautiful, pretty, fair, homely, ugly) to 15 girls' names, each adjective being assigned as a response to three names. DeSoto and Bosley (Fig. 7b) had their Ss learn to associate a school class (freshman, sophomore, junior, senior) to 16 male names, four in each class. The significant fact in both cases is that response words at the extreme ends of the semantic scale are more easily learned. This suggests that the internal representation of the meanings of the words are ordered in proximity as though they were points along a one-dimensional continuum.

Induced Linear Orderings

In the experiments previously reviewed, it could be said that the stimuli existed in a linear order for the subject before he came into the experiment, this prior ordering revealing itself in SPEs when the person learns to associate any responses to stimuli lying along that dimension. However, a simple principle exists for creating linear order among any new set of stimuli which previously were unordered. To induce a linear ordering onto a new set of unrelated elements, one simply associates them one to one with a second set of elements that were previously linearly ordered, perhaps on a "primary sensory" basis. To be more explicit, the principle is this: If elements $a_1, a_2, \ldots, a_n$ are linearly ordered in some primitive sense, and if we take any unrelated elements whatever, $b_1, b_2, \ldots, b_n$ and associate the two series in pairs (a_i, b_i), then the set $b_1, b_2, \ldots, b_n$ will acquire a derivative linear ordering. The critical implication of this derivative linear ordering is that stimulus generalization among the b_is will now vary (in more or less degree) according to the proximities of the associated as. That is, the proximity structure of the a set has been induced onto the b set, which were formerly unrelated elements.

A corollary of these proximity relations is that an SP curve will arise if we now try to use elements from the b set as stimuli for PA learning. This is obviously an important principle, because it provides a possible way to think about how symbolic or conceptual linear orderings might have arisen from a history of analogical association to perceptually primitive orderings.

An experiment illustrating this principle was done by Phillips (1958), when she had her subjects associate six Turkish words (effectively, nonsense) with six shades of gray varying from black to white. Thereafter, one of the Turkish words was paired with electric shock so that a GSR was conditioned to that word. Finally, the other Turkish words were presented in order to observe the amount of GSR generalizing to them. The findings were that the GSR generalization between two Turkish words was higher when the gray patches associated to those two words were closer together. That is, the proximity metric of the gray patches had been induced onto the previously unordered set of nonsense words.

An experiment on an induced SPE was done successfully by Ebenholtz (1966). His subjects first learned a rote serial list of ten unrelated nonsense

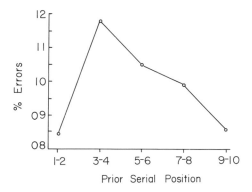

Fig. 8. Relative-error gradient during PA learning with syllable stimuli that formerly had occupied serial positions in a serial list learned before the PA task. (From Ebenholtz, S. M. Serial position effects of ordered stimulus dimensions in paired-associate learning. *Journal of Experimental Psychology,* **71,** 1966, 132-137. Copyright 1966 by the American Psychological Association, and reproduced by permission.)

syllables. After the serial list was well learned, the ten syllables were then paired arbitrarily with ten unrelated nouns, and the person learned the list of ten syllable–noun pairs by the usual PA procedure. The inquiry centered upon the difficulty in learning a particular PA depending upon the SP that the stimulus syllable had occupied in the prior serial list. The results in this respect are shown in Fig. 8 in terms of the percentage error gradient, and again the SPE is evident. Syllables formerly at the initial and final ends of the serial list now serve as the more distinctive stimuli so that fewest PA errors are committed on them. This is an example of an SPE produced by an induced linear ordering: the SPs are the primary stimuli $a_1, a_2, \ldots, a_{10}$, while the nonsense syllables learned in serial order served as the secondary stimuli $b_1, b_2, \ldots, b_{10}$. The induced ordering of the b_i is then inferred by the SPE when they are later associated to the set of unrelated nouns $c_1, c_2, \ldots, c_{10}$.

One might suppose that most cases of symbolic dimensions (of numbers or word meanings) have the behavioral characteristics of linear orderings because they have acquired their connotative meanings by association to concrete analogs of physical continua. For example, our vocabulary for locating events in egocentric time is thoroughly infused with spatial analogs—the future lies *ahead*, and one's past is *behind* one. As a second example, most people's subjective interpretation of numbers is as analog magnitudes—as heights, sizes, intensities, or distances along a line (the "real line"). These properties characterize the common, concrete exemplars used in teaching numerical concepts to children. We even use size adjectives in talking about "big" and "small" numbers, and speak of one number being "far" from another. Restle (1970) reported that the snap judgments which people make about numbers appear to be based on their initial fast interpretation in terms of analog magnitudes. Also, something like this analog correlation is relied upon in the psychophysical method of "magnitude estimation" in which the subject assigns a numeral representing the subjective intensity or quantity of some attribute of a stimulus.

One may recognize this principle of derivative linear orders, and its probable implication in the establishment of some conceptual dimensions, without believing this to be the complete story for all conceptual dimensions. Although the corresponding physical variables are clear for semantic continua like heavy to light, black to white, and cold to hot, it is not at all obvious what are the physical, analogical dimensions for semantic continua such as beautiful to ugly, love to hate, freedom to oppression, or many other contrastive oppositions in our language.

Perhaps the insufficiencies of the "derivative-ordering" principle will become apparent if we examine it more closely. The principle itself is a "low-level descriptive" law; it describes one procedure for inducing a given proximity structure upon a set of unrelated elements, namely, the association of elements of one set with elements of the other, in pairs (a_i, b_i). The principle states nothing about underlying mechanisms or representations which mediate these effects.

In this respect, there would appear to be two general classes of theories regarding the induced linear ordering; the two views may be illustrated by their differing interpretations of Phillips' experiment on Turkish words and gray squares. According to one interpretation, the Turkish word becomes directly conditioned to a "sensory response" or mental image corresponding to a fractional part of the perception of the associated gray patch. Staats (1968), for example, explicitly favors this alternative, with the presumption that such "sensory responses" are the intermediaries causing the Turkish words and gray squares to have the same proximity metric. An alternative interpretation is that the transfer of the metric to the Turkish word is mediated not by a mental image of the specific referent (the gray patch), but rather by a more abstract conceptual representative referring to the *relative position* of each stimulus in the range presented or, in Phillips' experiment, perhaps to just a verbal description or name for the physical stimulus. In the following I will develop this notion of an abstract linear order more fully and present some facts that I think are relevant.

A Cognitive Structure for Linear Orderings

The viewpoint to be espoused is that people either have innately or develop (learn) the general concept of a linear ordering of stimuli, with its primitive relations of comparison, progression, and betweenness with respect to a focused attribute. In early development, the concept is exemplified by physical attributes like brightness, size, distance, heaviness, and heat, but the concept becomes extended to include the more symbolic, semantic dimensions. In other words, the generalized internal representation of linear ordering is a cognitive structure or scaffold that is applied to the arrangement of a number of stimulus domains. These statements give explicit recognition to the communalities among various linear orderings of stimuli; it is these communalities which permit a type of interdimensional transfer which "mental images of specific referents" could never explain.

The hypothesis is that when response R_i is reinforced to stimulus S_i, it becomes associated not only to the coded version $C_i = \log(S_i/AL)$, but also to an implicit conceptual representative corresponding to C_i's relative position in the series, such as "first," "middle," or "last." The latter are relational concepts exemplified in a number of physical and semantic dimensions, and they are quite independent of the specific ranges or even the specific dimensions involved. That is, "position within a linearly ordered series" is a transsituational concept. It refers to a set of *intradimensional* invariants—the notions of "middle and end" stimuli always apply, regardless of the specific range of values involved. It also refers to a set of *cross-dimensional* invariants—the same notions apply regardless of the specific dimensions being discussed.

I will cite evidence of two kinds to support the view that responses become associated to these conceptual, relational stimulus codes. One kind concerns positive transfer of linear-ordered response scales between different ranges of values along one dimension; this is the traditional problem of "relational transposition" and it exemplifies my point about intradimensional invariance. The second kind of evidence involves transfer of linear orderings between two different dimensions, and this is addressed to my point about cross-dimensional invariance.

Transposition

Transposition studies examine transfer of relational responding to sets of stimuli *within* one and the same dimension. The usual transposition experiments (see Reese, 1968) have been done with animals or children, typically with simultaneous presentation of two or three stimuli, the subject being rewarded for selecting a specific one out of the array. The following experiment[4] violates all these procedural strictures. We used adults learning PAs; in technical jargon, they were learning multiple "successive discriminations" with verbal responses. The change in procedure itself is a novelty in the literature on transposition.

The design of this experiment can be seen by referring to Table VII. Paired-associate learning was carried out originally for all subjects (college students) with the six low-valued stimuli paired with unrelated nonsense-syllable responses. (In one experiment, the stimuli were nine horizontal lines of varying lengths; in the other, they were eight squares varying redundantly in brightness and size.) After 12 initial trials, the subject was told that he would be learning another set of pairs involving the same responses but a new range of stimuli, and he was exposed to one presentation cycle of the six longest stimuli, S_4–S_9, to familiarize him with the new range. (No response information was given at this time.) On the next cycle, the subject was permitted to respond if he wished, and he was informed of the new correct responses. Twelve transfer training trials then followed. Three conditions were formed that differed according to the new pairings between the old responses $(R_1 - R_6)$ and the new stimuli $(S_4$–$S_9)$.

TABLE VII

Stimulus-Response Assignments during Original Learning and Transfer for the Relational, Absolute, or Random Conditions[a]

	Stimulus								
Conditon:	S_1	S_2	S_3	S_4	S_5	S_6	S_7	S_8	S_9
Original learning:	R_1	R_2	R_3	R_4	R_5	R_6			
Relational				R_1	R_2	R_3	R_4	R_5	R_6
Absolute				R_4	R_5	R_6	R_2	R_1	R_3
Random				R_3	R_6	R_1	R_2	R_5	R_4

[a] Here, S_1–S_9 denote stimuli along a continuum; R_1–R_6 denote nonsense-syllable responses; entries denote S–R assignments; blanks denote nonpresented stimuli.

In the relational condition, the entire "response scale" was shifted up the stimulus scale, so that absolute stimuli S_4–S_6 had their responses altered. In the absolute condition, these three stimuli retained their former responses, while the three new values S_7–S_9 had responses R_1–R_3 assigned randomly to them. In the

[4] The experiment was conceived by David Tieman and the author, and was conducted at Stanford University by Lynn Carter and James Antognini.

random condition, responses were assigned to the six stimuli so that neither a relational nor an absolute basis for transfer was available.[5]

Comparison of the relational versus absolute groups in transfer is as follows: if Ss have associated the responses $R_1 - R_6$ to conceptual stimuli reflecting *relational* codes (like "first, middle, last"), then transfer to the relational response assignments should be relatively easy, whereas the absolute response assignments, which destroy the former relational order of the responses, should appear as difficult to learn in transfer as the random assignments. On the other hand, if stimuli are mainly reacted to on an *absolute* basis, the positive transfer should appear for the absolute assignments [which preserve three out of the six prior stimulus–response (S–R) assignments] but not for the relational assignments (which alter all specific S–R assignments). On this basis, one would predict that the relational and random groups should show similar poor transfer performance with the absolute condition showing best transfer.

TABLE VIII

Median Total Errors for Three Transfer Conditions Using Line-Length Stimuli or Squares Varying in Size and Brightness

Experiment	Relational	Absolute	Random
Line lengths	7.0	14.0	14.5
Gray squares	8.0	13.5	15.5

The results of the two replications of the experiment are shown in Table VIII in terms of the median total errors (summing over all six pairs) during the transfer trials for the three conditions. Both experiments show the same outcome pattern, namely, substantial positive transfer for learning the relational assignments, but virtually no transfer for the absolute assignments compared to the random control condition. The indicated differences are statistically significant at a suitable level in each experiment.

It appears as though the subjects were encoding the stimuli relationally—that is, relative to the end points and range in use—and associating syllables to these coded cues. The chief question to be raised with a strict relational interpretation of these data is why there were any errors at all in the relational condition. Various reasons might be given for the failure of perfect transfer, but most

___

[5] For convenience, I have described the design as starting everyone at the low end of the stimulus scale and shifting to the high end. In fact, only half the subjects were tested in this way, while the remainder transferred from the high to the low end of the scale. This counterbalancing in direction of shift is of no theoretical importance; the patterns of results were the same shifting in either direction, so this factor will not be mentioned further.

would require reference to specific or absolute characterizations of the stimuli.

The results in Table VIII exemplify *intra*dimensional transfer of a response scale. Now, that is the kind of transfer that is handled well by AL theory. In fact, the generalization theory outlined earlier, with the assumption that responses become associated to the code $C_i = \log(S_i/\text{AL})$, explains the transposition results very neatly (see also James, 1953). During initial training with the set S_1-S_6, the AL is at 3.5 (recall, it is a log scale); therefore $C_1 = -2.5$, and this C value was formerly associated to R_1, which is currently the correct response. Transfer is less than perfect, according to this theory, because the AL does not shift immediately to the center of the new stimulus range; rather, it lags because of "residuals" from the training series. This hypothetical story implies particular details regarding the shift of error profiles for the different groups over the course of the transfer trials as the AL adjusts to the new stimulus series, but those details will not be pursued here.

I began this section by offering transposition as evidence for abstract conceptual elements arrayed in linear orders that mediate transfer. It does constitute such evidence; unfortunately, however, transposition of the type shown here is also explicable in terms of AL coding of stimuli. So the data are compatible with both hypotheses. I believe that both hypotheses are true, that both factors operate in· a complementary fashion to promote transfer in this particular case, and that more ingenious experiments are required to unconfound them. A variety of intradimensional shift experiments might be tried. Discriminating ones would be those which study transfer when (*a*) the S–R assignments during transfer are simply the reverse ordering of those used in training, with or without a new stimulus set, or (*b*) the transfer stimulus set is an expansion (or contraction) of the stimulus range, centered around the training AL, with responses assigned according to their original relative scale position. In such cases, the abstract-mediation theory expects positive transfer, whereas a strict AL theory would predict little if any transfer. Until such experiments are done, the best evidence for the abstract-mediation theory comes from the studies on *cross*-dimensional transfer and intermodal interactions.

Cross-Dimensional Transfer of Response Scales

The most ingenious experiments of this type have been done by Ebenholtz. In one of these (Ebenholtz, 1965), students were first trained to associate eight nonsense syllables to eight lines varying in length from shortest to longest. They were then transferred to learning these same eight syllables as responses assigned to eight gray squares that varied in brightness. For one group of subjects, the ordering of the eight syllable responses assigned to the eight gray squares was the same as the ordering of responses that had been assigned to the short-to-long line lengths. That is, the response R_1 that had formerly been assigned to the shortest line was now assigned to the lightest gray; succeeding responses were also ordered, the response assigned to the darkest gray being that formerly learned to the longest line. The response assignments may be characterized by saying that the indices or ordinal positions of the two sets of stimuli assigned successively to the set of responses were perfectly correlated. The subjects learning these correlated response assignments were compared to others learning a random reshuffling of the eight syllable responses over the eight new gray-patch stimuli. Half of the subjects in the experiment were transferred from lines to grays, and half in the opposite direction.

The simple result was that the experimental subjects learned the correlated transfer pairs very much faster than the control subjects learned the random transfer pairs. This positive transfer would appear to be due to the learning of a "transdimensional" ordering of the responses—a response scale—which transcends specific sensory dimensions. Thus, by pairing the syllable MIB with the shortest line, it becomes partially associated to "least (or first) element in the series"; this is also the position occupied by the lightest gray patch, which is also paired with MIB, thus causing positive transfer. In this case the positive transfer cannot be accounted for by generalization of responses around specific dimensionalized stimuli. Nor does it seem helpful to assume that MIB comes to evoke a mental image of a specific line length, because that is not in the same mode as the gray squares to which transfer is being tested. In short, the results call for a set of *dimensionless* mediating elements such as "first, middle, last" in the series.[6]

Further research relevant to transdimensional transfer will be reviewed very briefly. In another study Ebenholtz (1963) showed high positive transfer, in either direction, between learning the *spatial positions* of nonsense syllables (top to bottom in a column) and learning their temporal position within a serial list (from beginning to end of the temporal list). Spatial and temporal locations are particularly susceptible to cross-talk or interaction with one another. In some of our experiments we have investigated these interactions by having the subjects learn to order items according to one stipulated dimension (say, their temporal order), while coincidentally the items also vary in a second dimension (their spatial position when presented).

In one of our designs, the subject learns a temporal series of nine letters, such as M Z L B X T Q K R, by the method of rote serial anticipation. But when each

---

[6] The coded stimuli $C_i = \log S_i/AL$ are dimensionless numbers (the dimensions cancel in the ratio), but will not fill the desired bill of particulars. First, the C_i have a particular directional orientation, whereas the results probably do not depend on whether, say, the shortest line is mapped onto the lightest gray or the darkest gray. Second, the C_i vary greatly according to the spacing of the two sets of stimuli, whereas the transfer of response scales would probably be evident for any discriminable spacing of the stimuli. However, these are empirical matters which cannot be prejudged with any certainty.

letter is presented visually, it occurs coincidentally in one of nine circles laid out in a row, so that that letter event has both temporal and spatial coordinates or index numbers. In one condition, the time and space indices are perfectly correlated—the first temporal element occurs in the spatial location farthest left, and succeeding elements in the time series march successively across the spatial array. In another condition, the two indices are uncorrelated, so that the first letter in the temporal series may appear in the fifth spatial location, the second in time may appear in the third location, and so on, in either constant or variable locations over trials. As the important result, relative to a "one-location" control group (the usual memory-drum slot), the temporal series is learned more rapidly when space is correlated with time, and more slowly when the two dimensions are uncorrelated. A similar difference between correlated and uncorrelated presentation occurs in the converse experiment, when the subjects are supposed to recall elements by their spatial location regardless of their temporal position in a presentation series. Many different conditions have been studied, checking out alternative explanations; a plausible explanation, however, is that of redundancy versus conflict of dual codes for the ordinal location of the elements. If time and space mapped onto totally distinct continua, and the person could attend selectively to either dimension according to how he is to order his recall, then there would be no confusion or interference in the uncorrelated presentation condition. However, to the extent that temporal position and spatial location map onto the same conceptual elements for "position in series," then learning the position in which an item is to be recalled is helped by time–space coordinates which coincide, but is hindered when they conflict. So, in this case, the cross-talk or interaction between two dimensions is explained by the idea that both project partially to a set of relative-position concepts which mediate the interaction.

Thus far I have reviewed evidence from learning and transfer experiments to support the idea of abstract concepts of relative position that are "aroused" by multiple sensory and semantic continua. But the transfer data may be indirect, and perhaps the most convincing evidence is the simplest, namely, cross-modality matching in psychophysical judgments. The subject can set a tone subjectively as loud as a light appears bright, or as loud as a weight feels heavy, and so on. Given any two linear continua, I suppose that the subjects could perform such cross-modality matchings reliably, especially if they are given a standard for each dimension ("call this loudness 10, and this brightness 10"). I am not concerned here with the form of the psychophysical relationship; for example, if Stevens (1957) is right, the logs of the matching physical variables will plot as straight lines. I am instead interested in our interpretation of how the performance can be done at all—how is it possible to compare the loudness of a tone to the brightness of a light? The only reasonable way anyone has imagined to do this is to transform each stimulus into a *dimensionless* scale, for example, a number expressing the ratio of the subjective magnitude of the current test stimulus to one's memory of the standard referent (the loudness called 10). This ratio is computed (or "immediately sensed") and the number assigned for both stimuli, and when the two numbers are equal, the person reports a "cross-modal match." So far as my argument goes, the important point is the conversion to a common "numerical magnitude" scale, since that qualifies as the abstract concept of linear order to which I have referred. The claim I am making for all such cases is essentially similar to that made by some linguists (see Shank, 1969), that an interlingual base of semantic and syntactic (universal) concepts exists into which all languages can be translated, and that it serves as the cognitive base for doing translations, say from English text into German or Swahili or Mandarin.

VERBAL MEDIATION?

To reiterate, the transfer results require the notion of conceptual or cognitive elements that are linearly ordered, implicit elements or concepts that are transsituational or transdimensional. For human adults, the most likely candidates are words or "verbal responses." These could be verbal labels for stimuli along the continua, "shortest" to "medium" to "longest," or implicit, numerical category scales, "first, second, . . . , nth, . . . , last" in the series exposed to the subject. These are relational concepts, of course. According to this view, transposition within a dimension or between two different dimensions would be interpreted as being verbally mediated by implicit numerical labels that the subject applies to the training and testing stimuli. Were this "verbal mediation" theory the correct interpretation, then animals or preverbal children should not demonstrate transdimensional transfer of the sort Ebenholtz found with adult humans. On the other hand, it is possible to argue, somewhat as Piaget might, that linearly ordered stimulus domains exist in the world, that children acquire general cognitive mappings or representations of such linear orderings, and that perceptual notions of succession, progression, interposition, and ordering come into play long before the child learns the words required in counting or in describing linear order. In this interpretation, because linearly ordered stimulus domains exist in the world, the basic perceptual–conceptual scaffold is acquired preverbally; it is only later that numerical labels become attached to these perceptual–conceptual elements. I wish neither to elaborate upon nor to argue for either of these interpretations at the moment. But they do provide some of the larger context in which the present research may be placed.

REFERENCES

Battig, W. F., & Spera, A. J. Rated association values of numbers from 0-100. *Journal of Verbal Learning and Verbal Behavior*, 1962, **1**, 200–202.

Capehart, J., Tempone, V. J., & Hebert, J. A theory of stimulus equivalence. *Psychological Review*, 1969, **76**, 405–418.

DeSoto, C. B., & Bosley, J. G. The cognitive structure of a social structure. *Journal of Abnormal and Social Psychology*, 1962, **64**, 303–307.

Ebenholtz, S. M. Position mediated transfer between serial learning and a spatial discrimination task. *Journal of Experimental Psychology*, 1963, **65**, 603–608.

Ebenholtz, S. M. Positional cues as mediators in discrimination learning. *Journal of Experimental Psychology*, 1965, **70**, 176–181.

Ebenholtz, S. M. Serial-position effects of ordered stimulus dimensions in paired-associate learning. *Journal of Experimental Psychology*, 1966, **71**, 132–137.

Helson, H. *Adaptation-level theory: An experimental and systematic approach to behavior.* New York: Harper, 1964.

Hull, C. L. *Principles of behavior.* New York: Appleton, 1943.

James, H. An application of Helson's theory of adaptation level to the problem of transposition. *Psychological Review*, 1953, **60**, 345–352.

Jensen, A. R. Temporal and spatial effects of serial position. *American Journal of Psychology*, 1962, **75**, 390–400.

Luce, R. D. *Individual choice behavior.* New York: Wiley, 1959.

McCrary, J. W., Jr., & Hunter, W. S. Serial position curves in verbal learning. *Science*, 1953, **117**, 131–134.

Murdock, B. B., Jr. The distinctiveness of stimuli. *Psychological Review*, 1960, **67**, 16–31.

Phillips, L. W. Mediated verbal similarity as a determinant of the generalization of a conditioned GSR. *Journal of Experimental Psychology*, 1958, **55**, 56–62.

Pollio, H. R., & Deitchman, R. The activational characteristics of a serial cognitive structure having oppositional end points. Mimeographed manuscript, University of Tennessee, 1964.

Pollio, H. R., & Diaper, D. O. The effect of a serial structure on paired-associate learning. *Journal of Verbal Learning and Verbal Behavior*, 1966, **5**, 301–308.

Reese, H. W. *The perception of stimulus relations.* New York: Academic Press, 1968.

Restle, F. Speed of adding and comparing numbers. *Journal of Experimental Psychology*, 1970, **83**, 274–278.

Shank, R. C. A conceptual dependency representation for a computer-oriented semantics. Technical Report CS 130, Computer Science Department, Stanford University, 1969.

Staats, A. W. *Learning, language, and cognition.* New York: Holt, 1968.

Stevens, S. S. On the psychophysical law. *Psychological Review*, 1957, **64**, 153–181.

Suppes, P., & Zinnes, J. L. Basic measurement theory. In R. D. Luce, R. R. Bush, & E. Galanter (Eds.) *Handbook of mathematical psychology.* Vol. I. New York: Wiley, 1963. Pp. 1–76.

COMMENT

Wayne H. Holtzman

Over the past 30 years Helson's adaptation-level theory has proved to be sufficiently flexible and general to cover an amazing array of significant topics. The number of individuals reporting on current research related to AL theory in this volume is testimony to the vigorous work growing out of Helson's theoretical contributions. My personal experience with AL theory goes back to the early 1950s when Helson was at the University of Texas and we did a series of experiments on contextual factors in the personal judgment of personality traits. This work is adequately summarized in Helson's book, *Adaptation-Level Theory* (1964) and needs no further comment here.

One of the attractive features of AL theory is the way in which investigators in fields far removed from Helson's original research on color perception have been stimulated and challenged by his theoretical formulations. Bower's most recent work on the distinctiveness and coding of stimuli in relation to serial position effects (SPEs) in paired-associate (PA) learning is an excellent example of how theoretical advances can grow out of equivocal empirical findings in experiments designed to test earlier formulations. He starts with the universal phenomenon of the SPE in which stimuli at either end of a recognized dimension have a distinctiveness that makes associative learning of specific responses to these stimuli much easier than to stimuli in the mid-range of the dimension. Regardless of the stimuli employed, a bow-shaped curve results when number of errors (or number of correct responses) is plotted against serial position (SP) on the stimulus dimension in question.

This phenomenon led Murdock (1960) to develop a first approximation to a quantitative theory for explaining the bow-shaped curve in SPEs which was quite similar to AL theory in its emphasis upon distinctiveness and pooling. Murdock's work suggested that the relative distinctiveness of a stimulus in PA learning could be measured by summing the distances between each stimulus and all other members of the set, and then computing the percentage distinctiveness (PD) for each stimulus relative to the total pool in question. If the stimuli are conveniently arranged on a log scale with respect to the primary physical dimension on which they are ordered, the Weber–Fechner law provides an easy basis for the computation. Murdock stopped short of testing his theory against other alternatives, being content with demonstrating a rough goodness of fit between the theoretical PD curve and the empirically obtained relative percentage correct curve for several examples.

Bower has gone one step further, conducting an experiment designed to test Murdock's concept by studying the effects of strong anchors at the ends of the stimulus dimension. He reasoned that high and low anchors would produce greater distinctiveness at the low and high ends, respectively, of the stimulus dimension, while the presence of both anchors in the same series would flatten out the SPE. The obtained results were highly equivocal, leading Bower to examine more critically the underlying assumptions of Murdock's concept of relative PD. Quite rightly, Bower points out that Murdock would be unable to handle mid-range stimuli that are widely separated from adjacent clusters of stimuli in the extremes of the dimension, since Murdock's hypothesis does not take into account the spacing between the physical stimuli. He also criticizes Murdock's theory for failing to provide any means of incorporating the effect of wide variations in differential frequencies of presenting the series stimuli. Bower's last criticism of Murdock's approach is that the PD measure is only of *ad hoc* descriptive value, providing no explanatory mechanism to account for why the phenomenon occurs. Bower then convincingly shows how an elementary learning-and-generalization model derived from AL theory can predict SP curves that are practically indistinguishable from those resulting from Murdock's PD measure. The stimulus-generalization model does indeed mimic Murdock's measures while also handling the predicted effects of anchor stimuli in a more effective manner. The problems of goodness of fit to the empirical findings and discrimination among alternative hypotheses in Bower's experiment still remain, however.

Of greater theoretical interest, in my opinion, is the last section of Bower's contribution, in which he builds a case for conceiving of a generalized internal representation of linear ordering as a cognitive structure or scaffold that provides for recognition of communalities among various linear orderings of stimuli. When a specific response is reinforced to a specific stimulus, as in PA learning, it becomes associated not only with the coded version based on AL theory but also with an implicit conceptual representative of this coded version corresponding to its relative position in the series. He cites a number of ingenious studies to support this point of view, some dealing with positive transfer between different ranges of values along one dimension and others involving the transfer of linear orderings from one dimension to a completely different one. The mediating cognitive elements may be verbal labels of a relational type, or individuals may acquire representations of such orderings from early experience without any verbal mediation. In either case, the important point is the resulting internalization of linear orderings and its pervasive influence.

In this sense, Bower's hypotheses are not far removed from Helson's earlier concepts of bipolarity, pooling, and distinctiveness. As Helson (1964) has pointed out in his discussion of seven basic characteristics of behavior, categorizing and scaling is implicit in all behavior. If bipolarity, essential to linear ordering, is not inherent in the physical dimension, an individual will try to impose it upon a set of stimuli. Pooling, as Helson uses it, is a concept similar to stimulus generalization, and distinctiveness concerns the effectiveness of a stimulus as a function of its distance from the AL. Although incomplete in important respects, Bower's integration of work on stimulus coding in PA learning with Helson's AL theory is a significant step forward that should stimulate additional experimental research and theoretical refinement along the lines he has suggested.

References

Helson, H. *Adaptation-level theory: An experimental and systematic approach to behavior.* New York: Harper, 1964.
Murdock, B. B., Jr. The distinctiveness of stimuli. *Psychological Review,* 1960, **67,** 16–31.

Social Psychology and Personality

INTRODUCTION

Ross Stagner

I am happy to have this opportunity to join in paying my respects to Harry Helson. I have not known him as long as some of the other participants, but I was stimulated by his work long before I met him personally. My interest in AL theory derives mainly from my long-term concern with the psychology of personality. The theory offers an approach to the quantification of some aspects of personality research which generally have been treated in a qualitative way, or at best with ordinal scaling techniques. I believe that AL theory offers conceptual tools for precise, parametric research on personality variables.

Years ago I became interested in a paper by Lewin (1935) in which he proposed, as an important attribute of personality, a characteristic which he called "flexibility."[1] It is fairly easy to obtain impressionistic ratings of people as regards this attribute, but quantitative measures of the extent to which people yield to or resist inputs designed to change some percept or attitude have been difficult to design. I believe that AL theory shows us how this job can be done; and the contributions to this section illustrate the results to be expected.

Brown and Reich describe some of their research on individual differences in flexibility, using as stimulus materials both lifted weights and verbal stimuli. Manis continues and amplifies the Brown–Reich article, since he uses verbal stimuli, but in a context of communication. Obviously the psychophysical experiment, as the format used by Brown–Reich, is a highly stylized form of communication between the experimenter and the subject; hence, the Manis

[1] Lewin also used such terms as "fluidity," "dynamical firmness of boundaries," and "rigidity" as descriptions of this attribute of personality which may in varying degrees resist the coercive effect of environmental input on perceptual norms (see Lewin, 1935, Chapters 2 and 7).

studies should be interpreted as a more complex (and slightly more realistic) variation on the kinds of investigation which have provided most of the empirical data described in the preceding sections.

Since I have long felt that AL theory had relevance for research on personality and social judgment, I am pleased to have this relevance documented and demonstrated. Helson is to be congratulated on having propounded a set of theoretical concepts which emphasizes the essential unity of psychology, tying together the laboratory research in psychophysics with investigations oriented more toward clinical and social problems.

There is only one cautionary note I would like to emphasize: AL theory, if taken superficially, might suggest that the organism is a passive victim of a series of environmental events. It is important to remember that psychological processes are modified by the nature of the organism; that behavior is often active, not merely reactive.

The array of experimental evidence presented in this volume so far may lead us to overestimate the extent to which experience is purely a function of stimulus input. I would like to reassert the role of the organism in processing incoming data.

We should recall, for example, the experiments of Klein (1951), Witkin *et al.* (1954), Solley and Murphy (1960), and others who have shown that individuals differ substantially in the way they respond to changing arrays of stimuli. If the AL effect were the only phenomenon to be considered, Klein could never have identified his "levelers" and "sharpeners." People simply do not react in a completely uniform and predictable way to the weighted average of the stimulus inputs.

This is not contradictory to Helson's theory. In Chapter 5 of *Adaptation-Level Theory* (1964) he allows for individual differences in stimulus processing (notably in Eq. 4, p. 267). As far as I can see, the theory has built-in flexibility adequate to handle such phenomena. However, enthusiasts in this tradition have often ignored the implications of this equation. There is a strong tendency—which I noted in some of the preceding contributions to this volume—to introduce correction factors and to assume that the theory must give accurate predictions—that deviations are due to experimental artifacts, and so forth.

I would like to endorse strongly the position taken by Hebert earlier when he suggested that we treat the AL equation as the hypothetical "ideal observer," and, when empirical observations do not conform perfectly, that we ask: What are the conditions which lead to specified kinds of deviations? In other words, he was suggesting (if I interpreted him correctly) that we stop treating all deviation from predicted performance as error. These deviations may be quite systematic, and they may be significant for the areas of psychology which interest me. For example, if one subject takes a very cautious stance in the laboratory, he may give quite a different set of judgments from one who habitually takes risks; or, if the subject interprets the instructions of the experimenter as calling for exact repetition of a judgment when the physically identical stimulus reappears, he will give results varying from one who accepts the task as one of continuous comparison.

There are other cautions which we need to keep in mind when we use AL theory, either in psychophysics or in social psychology. Helson's writings, quite properly, seek to define stimulus inputs in objective terms. But it has become clear, from the contributions to this volume as well as those in the literature, that the organism *categorizes* stimuli, and the weighted-average formula holds only for those stimuli perceived as fitting into a certain category.

This is particularly important in relation to the *exclusion* effect. Sometimes the person excludes some members of the stimulus series, thereby producing a weighted average (AL) which would not have been predicted by an experimenter who assumed that all stimuli were equally effective. This is confirmed by the lifted-weight and adjective data presented by Brown and Reich; but I would like to give you an example that is even more relevant to the topic of this section. Baron and Bass (1969) were experimenting with inner-city youths on effects of praise as reinforcement. In their study, they encountered the puzzling finding that 25% reinforcement was sometimes more effective than 75% reinforcement. Interviews indicated that several of the young men who received praise for 75% of their trials simply rejected the praise as insincere; they felt that the experimenter could not possibly mean what he said, so they excluded these rewarding remarks as irrelevant. The objective stimuli, then, were not the subjectively significant stimuli.

We observe the same phenomenon in Festinger's dissonance experiments. Festinger reported (see Festinger & Carlsmith, 1959) that inducing a person to behave contrary to his attitudes had a different effect according to reward magnitude, with very large rewards producing virtually no attitude change. He "explained" this by saying that the person felt "overwhelmed" by the magnitude of the reward, that he felt "coerced" into behaving in a certain fashion and hence did not revise his personal attitude. This explanation has of course been challenged by others (see Rosenberg, 1965). My own interpretation is that the subjects simply defined for themselves what was a "reward" for behaving in a certain fashion, and excluded from this category the very large payments offered (but apparently not paid in some instances).

Finally, let me note that the exclusion phenomenon applies to the Osgood–Tannenbaum congruity model. These authors found that, when they applied a source–message combination with an extreme discrepancy on the evaluative factor (for example, Eisenhower, +3, endorses communism, −3), the recipient did not show an extreme attitudinal shift; rather, he disregarded the message.

The active role of the subject in interpreting the demands of the experimental situation is also pointed up by Egeth in his comments on the contribution by Brown and Reich. Egeth actually raises two questions, both important:

1. To what extent does the apparent "flexibility" of the subject depend on how he interprets the demands imposed by the experimenter?

2. Is "flexibility" to be ascribed to changing the subjective point of neutrality, or to a change in the frequency of use of parts of the rating scale?

Inasmuch as these questions are relevant for much contemporary research on personality, I would like to comment on both.

1. S rarely comes to a psychophysical experiment in a truly naive state. He generates hypotheses as to the experimenter's intentions, and may try to cooperate with—or resist—them. Thus, if he becomes aware that the experimenter is changing the stimulus series, he may react by deciding either to go along with the shift, or to hold to his subjective midpoint. It should be possible, with more intensive postexperimental quizzing, to establish the frequency and determinants of such artifacts.

2. The terms "flexibility" and "rigidity" are commonly used, but the operational measures often correlate poorly with one another. I would like to propose that the term "rigidity" be applied when the evidence indicates that the subject has given heavier weight to items occurring *early* in the stimulus series, and "flexibility" used for cases in which the later-occurring items have more effect on AL. Without an extensive review of the literature I cannot document this notion, but I believe that such a definition might bring more harmony into the rather discrepant findings on this problem. I would suggest, for example, that a "rigid" child is one who clings to his early image of his parents in the face of changed parental behavior; and a "flexible" child is one who judges them solely on current actions, disregarding perhaps a preponderance of past behavior of a different type.

Individual differences are also important when AL concepts are applied to social psychology. The input series may be affected by family and cultural factors (biased loading leading to a deviant neutrality point), or it may be distorted by the active exclusion of certain inputs (refusal to include them in the stimulus series.) Eagly, in her comments on Manis' article, uses the example of the young man who is perceived by a conservative as a "cowardly draft dodger" and by a liberal as a "hero committed to higher principles." I am sure that, if we could examine the data series of the conservative, he too would have a category for a "hero committed to higher principles," but he would either have lived in a family where such a label was never applied to persons resisting governmental policy, or would have excluded all such cases from his own phenomenal classification with this label. The definition of a stimulus series thus must become, at least with respect to social stimuli, personal and subjective rather than objective.

The familiar data on positive correlations of children's social attitudes with those of their parents suggest that much of this defining process is cultural in character. However, there may also be a place for biological qualities of the organism, and for accidents of the individual biography, in providing anchor stimuli for such series. There is a great need for longitudinal studies of children within an AL frame of reference.[2] Some developmental data indicate that the "range of acceptability" of instances of a certain concept will increase with age up to a certain point, then begin to narrow again. This may, of course, be a function of other parallel developmental sequences, notably the ability to differentiate and to abstract symbolic similarities. Certainly the process is so complex that the diversities of individual personalities can be plausibly accounted for within an AL kind of approach.

From this concern with social stimuli and judgments of social objects let me turn back to the problem of biology. I noted earlier that I wanted to remind AL enthusiasts that adaptation occurs within an active organism. The human mind is not a *tabula rasa* at birth, and the central nervous system is far more than a simple-minded computer determining weighted means for series of stimuli. This is clear from the Goldstone–Lhamon data and in Steger's speculation that the consistent differences between the auditory and visual modalities result from the earlier development of auditory AL. It would be fruitful for them to recall that the cochlea is a marvelous instrument for wave analysis, and that time differences in microseconds can be discriminated for inputs to the two ears. The retina, on the other hand, is almost useless as a wave analyzer (try identifying component colors in a mixture!) but does extraordinarily well at spatial analysis. I would suggest therefore, that biological properties of the organism may well account for the major findings in the Goldstone–Lhamon experiments.

This is not to deny the importance of the cognitive processing which they stress. Indeed, it has long been obvious that cross-modality information processing offers significant clues to the impairment of higher mental processes.[3] All I really want to say is that, while pursuing the problem of how AL predictions help us to understand cross-modality information processing, we should not lose sight of individual differences in data-processing equipment. One inference from the brain-damage studies described by Goldstone and Lhamon

---

[2] It is interesting, for example, that Chodorkoff (1960) found an apparent shift in preferred auditory inputs in newborn infants over a period of about 1 month. Some babies who seemed disturbed by noisy radio or television inputs when first seen at home had changed in 4 weeks, to an apparent liking for this volume of sound. We interpret this as evidence of a shift in auditory AL.

[3] Note the value of tactual identification of three-dimensional objects in the diagnosis of brain damage.

may be that there are also innate differences in cross-modality competence (some children behave early in life as if they suffered a block between the auditory input system and the kinesthetic–proprioceptive controls for spoken speech output, to use a single example). Personality differences are not due *solely* to variations in AL induced by accidents of the environment which imposed variations in series inputs. They may arise also from differences in biological endowment which are essential to the processing of these inputs.

I want also to reemphasize a point that Brown made in an earlier personal communication and that might otherwise get lost. This is that different kinds of stimulus materials have different salience and differing memory values for individual subjects. A college sophomore who is asked to judge lifted weights has little reason to try to recall exactly what rating he assigned to a specific item, if he is given a second run through the series. On the other hand, if the stimuli are photographs of beautiful women, or statements by U.S. Senators, or other meaningful material, he may both wish and be able to recall just what rating he had previously given. Honestly, I think Helson should be amazed that his predictions, derived from low-meaning stimuli such as tones, weights, and colors, hold even fairly well for the complex kinds of data reported by Brown and Reich, Manis, and Bower. Perhaps it is also a tribute to the unity of the human personality, that basic models of information processing, which the infant must necessarily develop long before his social environment has much meaning for him, continue to operate and determine how he will handle series of religious, economic, political, erotic, and other stimuli. I would like to mention a specific example of this kind. Rudin and I (1958) have shown that the Witkin phenomena (field dependence in a physical perception task; see Witkin *et al.*, 1954) are significantly correlated with parallel phenomena in a social perception task. Persons were asked to rate themselves as to "self-image" in a variety of imagined environments. Those who showed greatest variation (modification of perceived self-attributes according to social context) were those who showed greatest field dependence in the rod-and-frame task. Thus, the person tends to use his physical information-processing model to handle inputs from his social environment (people evaluating him) and from his phenomenal field (his evaluation of himself). Of course, the original sponsors of the symposium assumed that this extrapolation of AL theory was justified, or they would not have organized these discussions of social and personality phenomena. I believe that researchers in social–personality areas will find the conceptual and methodological tools derived from AL theory of great value and significance.

References

Baron, R. M., & Bass, A. R. The role of social reinforcement parameters in improving trainee task performance and self-concept. Final Report, U.S. Department of Labor, Office of Manpower Evaluation and Research. Washington, D.C.: U.S. Govt. Printing Office 1969.

Chodorkoff, J. Infant development as a function of mother-child interaction. Unpublished doctoral dissertation, Wayne State University, 1960.

Festinger, L., & Carlsmith, J. M. Cognitive consequences of forced compliance. *Journal of Abnormal and Social Psychology,* 1959, **58,** 203–210.

Helson, H. *Adaptation-level theory: An experimental and systematic approach to behavior.* New York: Harper, 1964.

Klein, G. S. The personal world through perception. In R. R. Blake & G. V. Ramsey (Eds.), *Perception: An approach to personality.* New York: Ronald Press, 1951.

Lewin, K. *A dynamic theory of personality.* (translators, D. K. Adams & K. E. Zener.) New York: McGraw-Hill, 1935.

Rosenberg, M. J. When dissonance fails: On eliminating evaluation apprehension from attitude measurement. *Journal of Personality and Social Psychology,* 1965, **1,** 28–42.

Rudin, S. A., & Stagner, R. Figure-ground phenomena in the perception of physical and social stimuli. *Journal of Psychology,* 1958, **45,** 213–225.

Solley, C. M., & Murphy, G. *Development of the perceptual world.* New York: Basic Books, 1960.

Witkin, H. A., Lewis, H. B., Hertzman, M., Machover, K., Meissner, P. B., & Wapner, S. *Personality through perception.* New York: Harper, 1954.

INDIVIDUAL DIFFERENCES
AND ADAPTATION-LEVEL THEORY [1]

Donald R. Brown and Carol M. Reich

Starting with Klein and Krech (1951) and continuing through Bruner (1957), Berkowitz (1960), and White (1959), many writers have declared their increased interest in and dependence on processes generally referred to as cognitive in providing a model of the social world of humans. This return to the world of experience as a proper subject matter of psychology has had far-reaching effects on all areas of psychological theory. Recent changes in psychoanalytic theory, as expressed in the writings of Rappaport (1959), are typical. The general results in personality theory have been summarized by Sanford (1963) as placing more emphasis on the "higher" potentials of humans, on the greater degree of directed, active behavior as contrasted to the previously stressed passivity, and on current conscious processes rather than past and unconscious processes. MacLeod (1947), Krech and Crutchfield (1948), and Asch (1952), among others, have documented the implications for social psychology.

These developments have a long history, starting with the phenomenological movement in European psychology and moving through the Gestalt school and the work of Lewin (1947).

The recognition of cognition as an internal mediational process has not been without methodological pitfalls, however. The charge of subjectivity has been raised early and frequently, and as a consequence attempts have been made to center investigation on a specific aspect of cognition, namely judgment, in order to bring subjective decision into the laboratory. Indeed, subjective scales were commonly referred to as "absolute scales."

The early work of Helson (1948) in the Bryn Mawr laboratory in formulating AL theory was a major step in making the study of experience acceptable, objective, and one with the long tradition of psychophysical investigation.

[1] This work was in part supported by the Language Development Program Grant 5 PO1 HD 01368-04.

INDIVIDUAL DETERMINANTS OF STIMULUS CATEGORIZATION

As useful as Helson's model is in explaining effects commonly referred to as anchoring [and more recently by Perloe (1961), Hovland and Sherif (1952), and Berkowitz (1960) as assimilation and contrast, or by Klein (1956) as leveling and sharpening], it tended in its early formulation to assume the absolute specification of the physical and/or social stimuli that constituted the range being attended to by the subject. Brown (1953) published results that demonstrated the necessity of determining which properties of stimuli will cause subjects to categorize them in groups relevant to the judgment task called for by the experimenter.[2]

Briefly, these studies were designed to test the generality of any theory of judgment that ignored the individual categorization scheme of the subject and to explore the general dimension of functional similarity of stimuli. The underlying theory was based on the assumption that the making of a judgment—whether relating to some physical attribute of a stimulus or to a value statement pertaining to some more tangible social configuration—always involved reference to an intact system in the brain field of the individual making the judgment. A system is an organization of traces developed through past experience with a series of stimulus complexes possessing functional similarity (for example, seen as the same by the subject). At any given moment there exists a point of indifference or a *level of adaptation* (AL) located at the weighted mean of the series of experienced stimuli, and judgment involves a comparison of the present stimulus to the present AL. The weighting involved may be relatively simple—a geometric mean—if the stimuli vary along a single dimension, or impossibly complex if the stimuli vary in numerous interacting aspects. The nature of the system operating at the moment of judgment, and hence the prevailing AL, depends on the total situation—instructions given to the person making the judgments and the procedure or conditions under which the judgments are made—as well as the nature of the objects being judged. The system operating, then, is the neural correlate of set and is responsive to all aspects of the situation; the characteristics of the system that is operating and any changes that it undergoes will be reflected in the AL and changes in that level.

The properties of the system operating will be influenced by manipulation of such factors as the properties of the objects being judged and the use made of the objects by the subject. Only those objects that are perceived by the subject as relating to the system then operating will be judged with reference to the AL and will affect that AL—even though the judgment being made is of the same order. Experience with objects perceived as unrelated to a given system will form

---

[2] Since then Helson and his co-workers have given considerable attention to these phenomena, as other contributions to this volume attest.

a separate system with its own AL. Between the extremes of identity and complete separation of systems exists a whole realm of organizations involving the interaction of two or more systems, each possessing its own AL. In concert, however, these systems provide a subordinate AL governing judgments of objects having some common property, though they are heterogeneous as to other properties. In the formation of systems, then, a given situation allows for a wide range of adjustment varying from extreme generality to extreme specificity in the differentiation of systems.

It is just such generality and specificity of systems together with the factors involved in their formation that may be what we mean by "personality structure" in cognitive terms.

A typical such study, involving weight judgments, reported by Brown (1953), involved three independent variables: (a) similarity of an anchor to a stimulus series; (b) the subjects' response to the anchor (judging or not judging); and (c) weight of the anchor. The first variable was tested by two types of anchor: a tray dissimilar to a series of weights, and a weight identical to the series of weights. The second variable was dealt with by having the subject either judge or not judge the anchor, and the third variable was represented by having three physical values of anchors.

Seventy-two Ss were randomly split into 12 groups of 6 each. Every group was run in one of 12 experimental conditions in which all possible combinations of the three variables were included. The Ss judged a series of 120 weights by the method of single stimuli, using a five-category scale running from "very light" to "very heavy."

It was hypothesized that the degree of shift in the subjective scale of the judgment would be a function of the three experimental variables and would go from greatest shift to least shift in this order: weight anchors farthest from the series judged, weight anchors farthest from the series not judged, tray anchors farthest from the series judged, and no effect with tray anchors not judged. All these hypotheses were confirmed. Davidon (1962), using size of rectangular figures, replicated these findings. Parducci (1959), in a long series of experiments following the one described above, has explored several parameters of anchoring effects in psychophysical judgments, whereas Hovland and Sherif (1952), Levy (1961), Perloe (1961), Fillenbaum (1961), Berkowitz (1960), and Tajfel (1959) have applied similar methods to social stimuli. Gleitman and Hay (1964) have extended these findings to the interpretation of time error in successive comparisons using weights as stimuli, and Kind and Brown (1966) have confirmed these findings for the visual modality. Brown and Bass (1962) have also generalized the method to verbal stimuli and demonstrated differential indifference points to statements regarding voluntary sterilization as a function of level of information, previous commitment, and intensity of attitude.

Toward a Structural Model of Personality

In a continuing attempt to apply these approaches to develop a structural model of personality, a series of experiments has been carried out more recently at Michigan. The general three-phase paradigm is outlined below.

First, the general method outlined in the tray-anchor experiment was repeated in a number of modalities in an attempt to find the limits of "functional similarity" and to develop a standard set of verbal and attitudinal stimuli for judgment. Throughout this phase of the research, the interest centered on arriving at reliable and standard judgment situations in which it was possible to manipulate group ALs by manipulation along dimensions of similarity as discussed above. Several pilot studies have been carried out in the past years using a wide variety of physical and social stimuli.

Once the dimension of similarity was established, the second phase of the work began. This approaches the problem of isolating the dimensions along which cognitive systems are differentiated, integrated, and changed as a function of stimulus conditions. Here the focus was on dimensions along which a range of individual differences could be reliably generated.

The assumption is that individuals differ in their preference for and ability to combine sets of stimuli into single systems, on the one hand, and to separate them out, on the other. A typical pilot study that has been conducted involved the judgment of the weights of a series of seven like-appearing objects. The two weights at the low end of the series had a yellow band around them, while the two at the upper end had a green band. The three middle weights had a green band 50% of the time or a yellow band 50% of the time. The subjects worked under the following conditions: (a) applying the judgment scale without mention of the color; (b) applying the scale separately to the two sets of weights identified by the two colors; and (c) judging only one of the sets in the randomly distributed series.

The degree to which the subjects can consistently integrate or separate these systems in several different modalities, including verbal attitudinal stimuli, is taken as a measure along defining cognitive dimensions. In all conditions the specificity or generality of the system operating in the subject at the moment of judgment is systematically tested on the standard stimuli developed in phase one.

Other pilot studies have been done using methods similar to Klein's studies of levelers and sharpeners. Here a shifting series of weights was used and the consequent shifts in ALs for the subjects was studied. In a further study, attitudes of differing levels of agreement toward social questions were used with similar results. The subjects perform reliably in both types of tasks—either shifting very rapidly as the actual stimuli change, shifting only after the new mean of the series has been well established, or never shifting after the original level is reached. It is hypothesized that each of these types of subjects will show consistent but different patterns on measures of similarity groupings of stimuli and measures of category width.

Once a standard set of stimuli was identified along which a reliable range of individual differences could be found, it was possible to enter into the third phase—the development of a cognitive or personality typology based on the degree to which the subjects can separate and combine cognitive systems along the dimensions that are found in the second phase.

STUDIES OF CROSS-MODALITY CATEGORIZATION

Richard Kubo, Carol Reich, Richard Fuller, Robert Goldberg, and I have been carrying out the following program based on the assumption that it is possible to advance a theory of personality in which individual differences in categorizations across several modalities can be grouped around the stable cognitive characteristics of subjects.

Helson (1955) regards personality as "the pooled effects of stimulus, background, and residual factors manifesting itself in characteristic patterns of behavior [p. 98]." Personalities differ in the weightings given to various classes of stimuli—immediate and past, internal and external, near and far—and degree of significance or value. The crucial interest of personality theory lies in the development, control, and change of residuals. Berkowitz (1960) advocates a judgmental approach to personality description, and for a start outlines the dynamics of paranoia in terms of self-as-an-anchor and contrast effects.

An even more basic approach is to begin a study of personality with the functioning of cognitive systems in general, rather than with the influence of specific stimuli. One important variable of functioning is system flexibility: the capacity of an individual to change AL because of experience with new stimuli, and the extent to which he can differentiate among stimuli and form independent systems.

This is difficult to measure because of the residuals which develop from past experience and exert so strong an influence on contemporary behavior. However, by requesting a subject to make comparison judgments of stimuli using the entire scale, it is possible to limit the stimuli entering into AL formation to the immediate stimulus and context.

Although Helson and others have recognized the possibility of a personality theory, to date no systematic work has been done in this area. The present experimental series is, hopefully, a start.[3] Using the concept of system

---

[3] The following experiment was largely carried out by Carol Reich. It has since been refined and successfully replicated by Richard Fuller, to avoid scaling problems which reduced the differences in the original, and by Robert Goldberg, in an attempt at relating the cognitive flexibility concept to clinical types.

flexibility, it is an attempt to assess the validity of individual differences across situations.

Parts I and II below are psychophysical judgment situations with weights. Parts III and IV are translations of Parts I and II, respectively, into verbal material. The general hypothesis is that a subject's level of system flexibility is a general cognitive trait that operates in all types of behavioral settings.

METHOD AND DATA ANALYSIS

Subjects

Sixty undergraduate students comprised the sample. Each subject participated in all four experimental situations and served as his own control.

PART I

Materials

The stimulus materials were ten graduated weights increasing in units of .70 just noticeable difference (JND) and ranging from 80 to 230 gm. The weights were constructed by filling medicine bottles with paraffin and lead shot, and painting them a flat black.

Procedure

The Ss were presented with the weights in a shifting series of six blocks. The random presentation of all weights in the current series comprised one trial. The five lightest weights (weights 1–5) presented for five trials comprised the 25 judgments of block 1. In block 2 (judgments 26–50) weight 1 was omitted and weight 6 was added. Block 3 used weights 3–7; block 4, weights 4–8; block 5, weights 5–9; and block 6, weights 6–10. In each block, Ss judged the heaviness of the weights on a 5-point scale and recorded their own judgments. Most Ss were run in small groups of five to ten, seated around a large table. The experimenter sat at one end of the table with the weights concealed behind a screen and placed each weight in order in front of the S to his immediate right. The Ss handled the weights by passing them counterclockwise around the table. A few Ss were run individually, and E recorded their verbal judgments.

The Ss were given instructions as follows:

> We are doing an experiment in judging the weight of a number of objects. We are going to do this in a group, and the weights will move counterclockwise around the circle. With your right elbow on the table, grasp the top of the object in front of you with your fingers. Lift it and set it down in front of the person to your right. Then judge

its weight on a 5-point scale where "1" is the lightest and "5" the heaviest. You can think of the points on the scale as meaning "very light," "light," "medium," "heavy," and "very heavy." However, always use numbers in making your judgment.

Judge how much the object seems to weigh in comparison with the other objects. After lifting each object, write your judgment on the sheet. Be careful to record your judgment in the proper space on the sheet. Several times during the session we will check that everyone is working on the correct number.

I will begin by giving the first object to the person on my right. You will have to wait to begin your judgments until it is passed to you. In making your judgments try to use the whole range from "very light" to "very heavy," that is, from "1" to "5." Just relax, and judge quickly and spontaneously where each object seems to fall on the scale.

Analysis and Results

In this task the subjects formed an AL for a series of weights whose values soon changed, and continued changing throughout the session. To what extent did the subjects change AL with change in the series?

Generally, there are two types of performance. At one extreme are those who failed to change AL at all and increasingly clustered their judgments at the high end of the judgment scale. At the other extreme are the subjects who changed AL a great deal. With each change in the values of the weights, change in AL occurred, and judgments were always distributed evenly over the entire scale. The actual performance of any subject lay somewhere between these two types and is a compromise weighting of past and present experience.

The data analysis reported represents a crude attempt to measure the subjects' performance flexibility. The statistic chosen for part I was the regression line (Guilford, 1956, p. 366), which is the best representation of change in Y over all X values—in this case the change in judgment value over trials. The slope of the line is given by the formula

$$b = \frac{\sum(XY) - NM_XM_Y}{\sum X^2 - NM_X^2},$$

where X values are the judgment numbers beginning with judgment 6 and continuing to judgment 150. Calculation began with judgment 6, because inspection of the data indicated that the subjects had stabilized their judgments by that point, leaving 145 trials ($N = 145$). The Y values are judgment values.

After the slope has been calculated, the Y value corresponding to any X value is given by the equation for a straight line, $Y = bX + a$, where $a = M_Y - M_Xb$. Here, M_Y is the mean judgment, and M_X is the mean trial number.

For a notion of the average performance and the range of performance, Table I gives the slope and initial and terminal Y values for the group as a whole and for the most and least flexible Ss in the group as a whole and in the interquartile range. The $Y(6)$ and $Y(150)$ are the calculated judgment values at the end points of the series.

TABLE I

Slope of Regression Line and End Points for Part I

Subjects	Slope[a]	$Y(6)$	$Y(150)$	Y difference
Group mean	5.269	3.214	3.972	.758
Least flexible S	15.442	2.520	4.744	2.224
(no. 28)				
Most flexible S	−2.366	3.893	3.553	−.340
(no. 49)				
Interquartile range				
least flexible	7.491	3.424	4.502	1.078
(no. 40)				
most flexible	2.071	3.528	3.826	.298
(no. 23)				

[a] All slope values x 10^{-3} throughout.

Values in Table I indicate that the subjects noticeably shifted AL with changing experience. Average judgment only increased by about .75 scale unit from beginning to end of the judgment series. The least flexible subject raised his average judgment by over 2 scale units. At the end of the session he was responding almost exclusively with judgments of "4" or "5." The most flexible performer actually decreased his average judgment by about .33 scale unit. This means that his judgments became more isomorphic to the actual weight distributions within any one block than they were in the initial block. However, this subject had an unusually high mean judgment in block 1.

The interquartile range is a better indicator of the effective range of performance. Lowest flexibility here is indicated by a judgment shift of about 1 unit and high flexibility by a shift of only .33 unit.

Part II

Materials

The stimulus materials consisted of the first seven weights used in part I. Weights 1 and 2 were always yellow; weights 6 and 7 were always green. Weights 3, 4, and 5 were yellow 50% of the time and green 50% of the time.

Procedure

Section 1. The method of presenting the weights was the same as in part I. All seven weights were presented over eight trials, comprising a total of 56 judgments. Color was not mentioned. The Ss were told to judge the weights on a

7-point scale ranging from "very, very light" to "very, very heavy." Directions were as follows:

> This is also an experiment in judging the weight of a number of objects. We will pass the weights counterclockwise around the circle as we did in the last session involving weights. Handle the weights and record your judgments the same way as you did then.
>
> This time, however, there will be one change. Instead of using five categories, use the following seven categories running from "very, very light" to "very, very heavy." You can think of the seven categories as meaning 1, very, very light; 2, very light; 3, light; 4, medium; 5, heavy; 6, very heavy; 7, very, very heavy. Judge how much each object seems to weigh in comparison with the other objects.
>
> Do not be too careful. Great accuracy is not required. Just relax. Judge quickly and spontaneously where each object seems to fall on the scale.

Section 2.   After the eight stabilization trials, Ss were given a new set of instructions with color relevant. They were told to compare each weight only to members of its own color series and to spread their judgments of each color series over the entire judgment scale:

> Now I would like you to judge the objects somewhat differently. You notice that some of the objects are yellow and others are green. They will be presented to you in random order as before, but this time judge each object only in comparison to members of its own color series. Spread your judgments of each color series over the entire judgment scale of seven categories. Judge how much each yellow object seems to weigh in comparison with the other yellow objects using the 7-point scale. Do the same with each green object.

Analysis and Results

As in part I, the subjects were asked to establish an AL for a series of weights and then change that AL in a systematic way. In this case the change was related not to new values of the stimulus, but to a previously irrelevant attribute, namely, color.

During the stabilization trials, differences between the judgments of the yellow and green weights should be maximal. If judgment is completely isomorphic to the distribution of weight values, the average judgment for yellow weights (weights 1–5) should be 3.0 and for the green weights (weights 3–7) it should be 5.0. The difference between the two averages is -2.0 (d_s).

On the test trials, a completely inflexible subject should give the same average judgment to the yellow and green weights as he did in the stabilization trials. Yellow weights would again receive an average judgment of 3.0, and green weights 5.0, with a difference of -2.0 (d_t). A perfectly flexible subject would give each color series an average judgment of 4.0 with a difference of 0.0. The difference between d_s and d_t (D) serves as an overall measure of flexibility.

Table II gives the average judgments, d_s, d_t, and D, for the group as a whole and for the most and least flexible subject in the group as a whole and in the interquartile range. As seen in Table II, the average judgment of the yellow weights was slightly higher than if color were completely ignored and for the green weights it was slightly lower. Average judgment of the two color series was about 1.5 scale units apart instead of the ideal of 2 units. However, this probably indicates a reluctance on the part of the subjects to use the extreme ratings, rather than an initial separation of the weights on the basis of color. This tendency was noted in a pilot test of part II.

TABLE II

Mean Judgments of Green and Yellow Weights on Part II[a]

Subjects	Stabilization trials				Test trials		
	$\bar{X}_y$	$\bar{X}_g$	d_s	$\bar{X}_y$	$\bar{X}_g$	d_t	D
Group mean	3.18	4.73	−1.55	3.69	4.79	−1.09	− .46
Least flexible S							
(no. 6)	3.58	4.85	−1.27	3.56	5.43	−1.87	.60
Most flexible S							
(no. 16)	2.60	4.61	−2.01	4.15	4.16	−0.01	−2.00
Interquartile range							
least flexible							
(no. 20)	2.96	4.37	−1.41	3.50	4.89	−1.39	−0.02
most flexible							
(no. 48)	2.64	4.12	−1.48	3.65	4.30	−0.65	−0.73

[a] $d_s = \bar{X}_g - \bar{X}_y$ on stabilization trials; $d_t = \bar{X}_g - \bar{X}_y$ on test trials; $D = d_s - d_t$; $\bar{X}_g$ is the average judgment of green weights; $\bar{X}_y$ is the average judgment of yellow weights.

Instructions to separate the weight series into two independent series on the basis of color brought the average judgment of the yellow and green weights about .5 scale unit closer together. On the average, then, the subjects showed a small degree of flexibility.

With this measure, the most flexible subject achieved a practically perfect separation of the color series. Average judgments of the yellow and green weights on the test trials were almost identical. The least flexible subject, on the other hand, separated the average judgment of the two color series even more. Judgments of the yellow weights were clustered even more toward the low end of the scale and vice versa with the green weights. The significance of this is not clear. The subject's posttest questionnaire indicated that he did understand the task.

Confining analysis to the interquartile range reduces the range of behavior by about a factor of three.

PILOT STUDY FOR PARTS III AND IV

Materials, Procedure, and Analysis

Parts III and IV of this study use trait-descriptive adjectives instead of weights. To ensure that the adjectives presented to the subjects would be evenly distributed over all scale positions, a pilot study was conducted. Twenty undergraduate students rated 300 trait-descriptive adjectives on a scale from 1 to 10 according to how favorable they judged the words to be. They were told to record their own opinions.

The 300 words were written in small spiral notebooks in large print, one word to a page. Each subject leafed through the series of notebooks and recorded his own judgment.

From these ratings, the 10 adjectives most frequently rated at each of the 10 scale positions were chosen, for a total of 100 words. These words comprised the list used in part III, section 1.

PART III

Section 1. Part III was a direct translation of Part I into verbal materials. In the judgments of Parts I and II, the weights provided an objective scale. This is not true with words. This section is a procedure to establish an independent scale of words on the judged dimension.

Cowen and Stiller (1959) were able to show context effects in rating the social desirability of trait-descriptive terms. However, only a nonparametric directional analysis yielded significant results. The reason probably lay in their use of group means. It was hoped that the design of this study, using norms established individually for each subject, would be more sensitive to both context and individual differences.

Unlike weights, words have no absolute meanings. Cowen and Stiller found correlations of .80 and .82 among the ratings given adjectives in widely differing contexts. However, asking Ss to rate the adjectives in comparison only to others on the list should minimize the effects of residuals.

Materials and Procedure

The Ss were asked to rate the 100 trait-descriptive adjectives chosen in the pilot study on a 10-point unfavorable–favorable dimension. There were five trials for a total of 500 judgments. The words were presented as in the pilot study. Directions to Ss were as follows:

> This experiment is a study of how people feel about personality characteristics that many individuals have. We are interested in how favorable or unfavorable they will judge a list of personality traits.

You have been given a series of notebooks. Each page contains a common term which is used to describe people. Read each one and assign it a rating from 1 to 10 which indicates how unfavorable or favorable you think that term is; 1 is the least favorable rating, 10 is the most favorable. Record the number of your judgment in the correct space on the rating sheet.

Remember, we are interested in your opinion. How favorable or unfavorable do you think each trait is in comparison to the other traits? Work carefully, but do not take a great deal of time with each term. It is very important that you do not return to previous parts of the list, either to recall what words were given there or to change ratings.

Analysis

Arithmetic and modal means were found for each subject's ratings of the 100 adjectives, and an individual stimulus series was constructed for each subject. The series was composed of the three adjectives "closest" to each of the ten scale positions for a total of 30 words. "Closest" was defined by the following algorithm:

1. Adjectives with high modal ratings at a scale position were chosen to represent that position. Adjectives with a judgment frequency of 5 were chosen first, then 4, then 3.

2. This usually left a few positions vacant. Adjectives were then chosen for those which, although lacking a modal judgment at a particular position with a frequency of 3 or more, had the closest arithmetic mean judgment.

3. In a few cases even this did not complete the stimulus series. In such cases, adjectives were chosen according to which ones were most frequently rated at the desired scale position in the pilot sample. The result was a list formally similar to the ten-member weight series used in Part I.

Materials and Procedure

Section 2. This section was administered several weeks after Section 1. The stimulus materials were the individual lists of 30 adjectives evenly distributed over the 10-point rating scale. A shifting series was constructed that was directly analogous to part I. Block 1 was composed of the three adjectives at scale positions 1-5 presented in random order over five trials for a total of 75 judgments. The scale positions for the remaining blocks were: block 2, 2-6; block 3, 3-7; block 4, 4-8; block 5, 5-9; block 6, 6-10. This was a total of 450 judgments.

The words were presented as in Section 1 with similar instructions. However, instead of judging the adjectives on a 10-point scale, Ss were told to judge them on a scale of 1-5. The change in instructions was:

Read each one (adjective) and assign it a rating from 1 to 5 which indicates how favorable or unfavorable you think that term is in comparison with the other terms. You can think of the points of the rating scale as meaning 1, very unfavorable; 2, unfavorable; 3, neither unfavorable nor favorable; 4, favorable; 5, very favorable.

Analysis and Results

The analysis of data was similar to that in Part I. Table III gives the slopes and calculated Y values. The last column of Table III gives the difference between the end points of the regression lines from Table I for Part I. A comparison of

TABLE III

Slope of Regression Line and End Points for Part III

Subjects	Slope[a]	$Y(16)$	$Y(450)$	Y difference	Part I−Y difference
Group mean	5.432	1.967	4.324	2.357	.759
Least flexible S (no. 5)	7.559	1.856	5.137	3.280	2.223
Most flexible S (no. 36)	1.192	3.055	3.573	.518	−.341
Interquartile range					
least flexible (no. 6)	6.291	1.726	4.456	2.730	1.079
most flexible (no. 40)	4.777	2.198	4.271	2.073	.323

[a] All slope values × 10^{-3} throughout.

these differences in Parts I and III shows that the subjects shifted a great deal more with the verbal material. However, there are still differences in performance among subjects. The sample as a whole shifted almost 2.5 scale units. The least flexible S shifted over 3 units, and the most flexible subject shifted only .5 unit. Values for the least and most flexible subjects of the interquartile range are almost .75 scale unit apart.

PART IV

Part IV is an attempt to replicate Part II using verbal materials. The essential feature of Part II was that the subjects were asked to establish one AL for the stimuli as a whole, and then to separate the stimuli into several classes, establishing an independent AL for each class.

Materials and Procedure

From the norms established for each S in Section 1 of Part III, three subsets of twelve adjectives were individually constructed according to the following criteria. Subset 1 was composed of adjectives with the following distribution of ratings: four adjectives at scale position 1, three at 2, three at 3, and one each at

8 and 9. The algorithm for choosing adjectives was the same as used previously. Subset 2 had three adjectives at scale position 4, three at 5, three at 6, and three at 7. Subset 3 had four adjectives at scale position 10, three at 9, three at 8, and one at 2. Subset 1 then was mainly composed of adjectives previously rated as unfavorable (mean = 3). Favorable adjectives (mean = 8) comprised subset 3, and subset 2 was neutral (mean = 5.5). The overall average rating of the 36 adjectives was 5.5.

The technique used to make the subsets psychologically differentiated for the subjects was to associate each one with a hypothetical person:

Person 1 is harsh	Person 2 is clever	Person 3 is nice
Person 1 is unkind	Person 2 is relaxed	Person 3 is smart
etc.	etc.	etc.

The presentation and judgments of adjectives in Section 1 of Part III corresponds to the presentation of weights without mention of color in Section 1 of Part II. Corresponding to the second section of Part II, presentation of weights with color relevant, the 36 sentences formed by the three adjective subsets were presented five times each in random order. The Ss were instructed as follows (each S recorded his own judgments):

> Again we are interested in how people view certain personality characteristics. You have been given a pack of cards. On each card is a short description of a particular person who is identified only by number. There are several descriptions of each person. The entire pack of cards describes three persons with three different sets of traits. Read each sentence and judge how favorable or unfavorable you think each trait is *in comparison with the other traits that person has.*
>
> Spread your judgments of the traits of each person over the entire judgment scale. A person's worst trait should be labeled "1" and his best trait "10." In judging the traits of one person, it is not necessary to use all the scale positions nor for you to assign an equal number of traits to each scale position.
>
> It is very important that you do not return to previous parts of the list either to recall what traits were listed there or to change ratings.

Analysis and Results

A complete analysis of Part IV should use the difference between the subjects' ratings of each adjective in the unified condition and the separated condition (IV). This is essentially what was done in Part II. For this preliminary analysis, however, a much simpler measure has been used, the difference among the average ratings given each subset, with the following assumptions: Extremely flexible subjects should spread the ratings of each subset over the entire judgment scale, minimizing the differences among average subset ratings.

Inflexible subjects should continue to judge the adjectives with reference to the unified list. Adjectives in subset 1 would all continue to be judged unfavorable. Adjectives in subset 3 would be judged favorable, and subset 2 adjectives would be judged neutral.

The difference among the means is defined as

$$D = (\bar{X}_3 - \bar{X}_1) + (\bar{X}_3 - \bar{X}_2) + (\bar{X}_2 - \bar{X}_1).$$

The $\bar{X}_2$ terms cancel out, leaving

$$D = 2(\bar{X}_3 - \bar{X}_1).$$

Since only rank order is of interest, the equation can be further simplified to

$$D = \bar{X}_3 - \bar{X}_1.$$

Table IV gives the average rating of each subset and the difference (D) for the group as a whole as well as for the most and least flexible subjects in the group and in the interquartile range. As seen in this table, the group as a whole performed quite inflexibly. The least flexible subject came fairly close to the theoretical ideal ($D = 0$). Performance within the interquartile range was heavily skewed toward inflexibility.

TABLE IV

Average Subset Ratings and Differences for Part IV

Subjects	Subset 1	Subset 2	Subset 3	D
Group	3.491	5.465	7.448	3.957
Least flexible S (no. 3)	2.083	4.208	8.938	6.855
Most flexible S (no. 34)	5.229	5.521	5.688	.459
Interquartile range				
least flexible (no. 44)	3.313	5.729	8.000	4.687
most flexible (no. 40)	3.333	5.771	6.583	3.250

These studies have been replicated with more careful controls, and the results are more encouraging, but not yet reportable. Currently, we are testing groups of obsessive and hysterical Ss with hypotheses derived from clinical theory with respect to their expected cognitive flexibility. The hope is to make a virtue of individual differences and experimental error.

ACKNOWLEDGMENT

The senior author wishes to express his appreciation to Richard Fuller, Robert Goldberg, Richard Kubo, and Carol Reich for their assistance.

REFERENCES

Asch, S. *Social psychology.* New York: Prentice-Hall, 1952.
Berkowitz, L. The judgmental process in personality functioning. *Psychological Review,* 1960, **67,** 130–142.
Brown, D. R. Stimulus similarity and the anchoring of subjective scales of judgment. *American Journal of Psychology,* 1953, **66,** 199–214.
Brown, D. R., & Bass, M. Judges' displacement of items on a Thurstone equal-appearing interval scale as a function of judges' position, intensity, and information level on the domain. Paper presented at Eastern Psychological Association, Spring, 1962.
Bruner, J. On perceptual readiness. *Psychological Review,* 1957, **64,** 123–152.
Cowen, E. L., & Stiller, A. The social desirability of trait descriptive terms: Order and context effects. *Canadian Journal of Psychology,* 1959, **13,** 193–199.
Davidon, R. S. Relevance and category scales of judgment. *British Journal of Psychology,* 1962, **53,** 373–380.
Fillenbaum, S. How fat is fat? Consequences of similarity between judge and judged object. *Journal of Psychology,* 1961, **52,** 133–136.
Gleitman, H., & Hay, G. The effect of instruction on positive time-errors in successive comparison. *American Journal of Psychology,* 1964, **78,** 286–290.
Guilford, J. P. *Fundamental statistics in psychology and education.* New York: McGraw-Hill, 1956.
Helson, H. Adaptation level as a basis for a quantitative theory of frames of reference. *Psychological Review,* 1948, **55,** 297–313.
Helson, H. An experimental approach to personality. *Psychiatric Research Reports,* 1955, **no. 2,** 89–99.
Hovland, C. I., & Sherif, M. Judgmental phenomena and scales of attitude measurement: Item displacement in Thurstone scales. *Journal of Abnormal and Social Psychology,* 1952, **47,** 822–832.
Kind, B., & Brown, D. R. Time-error and the separation of cognitive systems. *Journal of Personality,* 1966, **34,** 569–576.
Klein, G. S. Perception, motives and personality. In Z. L. McCary (Ed.), *Psychology of personality.* New York: Logos, 1956.
Klein, G. S., & Krech, D. The problem of personality and its theory. *Journal of Personality,* 1951, **20,** 2–23.
Krech, D., & Crutchfield, R. S. *Theory and problems of social psychology.* New York: McGraw-Hill, 1948.
Levy, L. H. Adaptation, anchoring, and dissipation in social perception. *Journal of Personality,* 1961, **29,** 94–104.
Lewin, K. *Dynamic theory of personality.* New York: McGraw-Hill, 1947.
MacLeod, R. B. The phenomenological approach to social psychology. *Psychological Review,* 1947, **54,** 193–210.
Parducci, A. An adaptation-level analysis of ordinal effects in judgment. *Journal of Experimental Psychology,* 1959, **58,** 239–246.

Perloe, S. I. Assimilation as a consequence of categorization. *Journal of Personality,* 1961, **29,** 148–166.

Rappaport, D. The structure of psychoanalytic theory: A systematizing attempt. In S. Koch (Ed.), *Psychology: A study of a science.* Vol. 3. New York: McGraw-Hill, 1959.

Sanford, R. N. Personality: Its place in psychology. In S. Koch (Ed.), *Psychology: A study of a science.* Vol. 5. New York: McGraw-Hill, 1963.

Tajfel, H. The anchoring of value in a scale of judgments. *British Journal of Psychology,* 1959, **50,** 294–304.

White, R. W. Motivation reconsidered: The concept of competence. *Psychological Review,* 1959, **66,** 297–333.

COMMENT[1]

Howard Egeth

I find myself in almost total sympathy with the goals of Brown's research, and so my discussion will consist largely of some suggestions for further work on the separation and integration of cognitive systems. However, I do have one cautionary comment on the preceding contribution.

I am concerned that the ways in which subjects may have interpreted their judgmental tasks may not have been considered carefully enough, especially in experiments I and III. In those studies, after stabilization trials, the stimulus series was gradually increased in either weight or favorableness. Brown found that the subjects differed from one another in the extent to which they shifted their ALs as the overall level of the series shifted. Although such individual differences clearly have a cognitive basis, it is not so clear that they should be taken as an index of flexibility.

The problem, as I see it, is that the demand characteristics of the experimental situation are ambiguous. I suspect that all subjects were aware of the shifting level of the stimuli. But each subject had to decide for himself how, if at all, to adjust his responses, taking into account what he thought the experimenter wanted him to do. The subjects that Brown called "flexible" allowed their "subjective midpoints" to increase over trials. However, it is possible to make at least as strong a case that the subjects whose ALs remained the same were actually the flexible ones. For AL to remain fixed in these experiments means that over trials more and more stimuli must be given "high" ratings. However, as Parducci (1965) has pointed out, there is a strong tendency for the subjects in rating experiments to use categories equally often. As the strategy of keeping AL constant requires violation of this habitual tendency, might this not as well be called flexibility?

Let me turn now to some of the possibilities for further research. Separation and integration of cognitive systems can be studied with a wide variety of experimental tasks. More important, it *should* be so studied to get some idea of

[1] Preparation of this article was supported by a grant from the U.S. Office of Education.

233

the generality of the phenomenon. I shall return to this point at the conclusion of my discussion.

Brown has already described the use of tasks that are intimately related to AL notions. I will briefly mention some other kinds of paradigms that might prove useful.

1. Selective attention tasks are important in the present context because they suggest the extent to which the contents of cognitive systems can be kept separate from one another or integrated with one another at the input stage of information processing. Although quite a bit has been learned about the properties of attention in the past few years, the study of individual differences in attention is still largely uncharted territory. However, some of the existing work suggests how fruitful further research may be. For example, Smith and Klein (1953) demonstrated that individual differences in the ability to devote sustained attention in Stroop's color-naming task is correlated with ability to perform in a variety of perceptual and cognitive tasks. One of those tasks is essentially the same as the shifting series paradigm Brown and Reich used in Parts I and III; another was the Gottschaldt embedded-figures test.

Others have investigated the effects of drive level and anxiety on selective attention in the Stroop test as well as in other attention-demanding tasks. It would be most interesting to determine the generality of these motivational manipulations on a variety of other tasks that require the separation or integration of multiple sources of information.

In an unpublished experiment, I used an attention paradigm to determine under what conditions the left and right hands feed into separable cognitive systems. (I believe you will notice a family resemblance to Brown's examination of whether his yellow and green weights fed into separable cognitive systems.)

The task was the classical one of weight discrimination. The subjects lifted, in order, a standard, an interpolated weight, and then a comparison weight. They always had to judge the comparison weight with respect to the standard weight. Half were instructed to lift the interpolated (middle) weight with the same hand they used to lift the standard and the comparison, while the other half were instructed to use the opposite hand. Moreover, half of each group of subjects were instructed simply to lift the interpolated weight, but to ignore it, because it would only serve to confuse them. The remaining subjects were required to render a judgment on the interpolated weight. This was accomplished by using three fairly similar interpolated weights. On each trial the subject had to indicate which of the three had actually been presented. Each subject served as his own control in another session with no interpolated weight.

One of the chief differences between this experiment and Brown's research is that the dependent variable of major interest to me was the difference limen (DL) rather than the point of subjective equality (PSE). It seemed that a measure of accuracy such as DL might have certain advantages over a measure of

AL such as the PSE. For example, suppose I had thoughtlessly selected interpolated weights at about the AL of the series on which the subjects were making their paired-comparison judgments. This would have had no effect on the AL calculated from their judgments (via PSE) but it still might have had a substantial effect on DL and thus indicated interference of one task with the other. For this reason I decided that the accuracy measure might be of greater usefulness.

The results indicated that the presence of an interpolated weight was interfering and that actual judging of the interpolated weights resulted in greater interference than passive lifting. Most important, however, was the evidence that the kinesthetic memory systems of the left and right hands were separable, as indicated by the fact that DLs were considerably larger when the interpolated weights were lifted with the same hand as the standard and comparison rather than the opposite hand. Finally (to my surprise), the degree of separation was the same regardless of whether the interpolated weights were attended to or ignored.

2. In the field of memory, such phenomena as release from proactive inhibition (PI) when stimulus material is changed in the course of an experiment (a change, say, from digits to consonants) provides a likely starting place for investigation. Cognitive control over interference effects may prove to be an even more relevant means of studying the structural properties of mind. I am thinking here of research by Bjork, LaBerge, and Legrand (1968) on "drop" instructions in short-term memory research. They have found that the subjects, when instructed partway through a list to forget the previous items because they will not be tested on them, remember the subsequent part of the list better than if there had been no instruction to forget. The instruction to forget reduces PI, although the mechanism for this reduction has not yet been identified. An interesting footnote to this research is that PI is reduced even though subsequent interrogation indicates that the subjects actually did not forget the items that they were told they could forget. Surely, individual differences in the ability to reduce PI voluntarily must be closely related to what Brown is studying, and would probably repay careful investigation in that framework.

Another useful kind of memory study is called *keeping track*. Yntema and Mueser (1962), Monty (1968), and others have studied the ability to keep track of the current status of several variables simultaneously. Some people are very impressive indeed in their ability to keep track of several things at once. For example, the chess master Najdorf was able to play 40 games of chess simultaneously. What makes this especially interesting is that he was blindfolded at the time, and thus truly had to keep the status of all the boards in mind at once. Najdorf's accomplishment may be taken to be an example of flexibility on a grand scale, and this leads me to think that he would have made a very interesting subject for Brown's studies.

3. Speaking of interesting kinds of subjects brings me directly to a third field of study that could be investigated within the framework of mental structure. Multilingual persons have highly elaborated cognitive systems corresponding to the languages they speak. Kolers' (1963) research suggests that in some respects the two language systems of bilinguals are unified, but in other respects they are separate. I would think that intensive investigation of this special kind of subject population could provide some useful insights into the more general topic of cognitive structure. A more accessible subject population might prove to be of even greater practical value, namely, students learning a second language. The detailed investigation of positive and negative transfer during second-language learning would be one way of moving out of the laboratory into a useful real-life situation that demands both an ability to keep separate and an ability to integrate relevant kinds of information.

The last point I would like to make does not concern an experimental paradigm, but instead is a suggestion about data analysis. It seems to me that a serious attempt to factor analyze the data resulting from the use of a wide variety of tasks is necessary. I do not think it will be sufficient in the future to show that there is a tendency for subjects to keep roughly the same rank order when a few closely related tasks are used. It seems unlikely to me that flexibility will prove to be a unitary concept as the domain of tasks is extended. As Brown has pointed out, subjects probably differ on their propensity to separate or integrate as well as their ability to do so. Furthermore, in a factor analysis, I would expect to find that content would be of considerable importance and that no single factor would account for the data. As an example, I do not think that flexibility as defined in the weight-lifting experiment will necessarily be closely related to a person's flexibility with respect to new social ideas.

REFERENCES

Bjork, R. A., LaBerge, D., & Legrand, R. The modification of short-term memory through instructions to forget. *Psychonomic Science,* 1968, **10,** 55–56.

Kolers, P. A. Interlingual word associations. *Journal of Verbal Learning and Verbal Behavior,* 1963, **2,** 291–300.

Monty, R. A. Spatial encoding strategies in sequential short-term memory. *Journal of Experimental Psychology,* 1968, 77, 506–508.

Parducci, A. Category judgment: A range-frequency model. *Psychological Review,* 1965, **72,** 407–418.

Smith, G. J. W., & Klein, G. S. Cognitive controls in serial behavior patterns. *Journal of Personality,* 1953, **22,** 188–213.

Yntema, D. B., & Mueser, G. E. Keeping track of variables that have few or many states. *Journal of Experimental Psychology,* 1962, **63,** 391–395.

CONTEXT EFFECTS IN COMMUNICATION

DETERMINANTS OF VERBAL OUTPUT AND REFERENTIAL DECODING[1]

Melvin Manis

One of the most replicable findings in the literature on subjective judgments is the fact that the individual's response to any given stimulus is partly determined by the total array of stimuli to which he has recently been exposed, not just by the stimulus then being judged. This contextual effect usually takes the form of an apparent *contrast* between the overall stimulus array and the individual test items. For example, Campbell, Hunt, and Lewis (1958a) have shown that in evaluating the degree of disorganization and eccentricity of thought implied in a series of vocabulary definitions, judges who have been primarily exposed to "high-pathology" definitions· rate midscale items as indicating *less eccentricity* than do those who have been predominantly exposed to "low pathology" definitions. Similar effects have been reported in studies dealing with judgments of weights (Heintz, 1950), length of lines (Krantz & Campbell, 1961), and a variety of other psychophysical and social continua (Helson, 1964; Bevan, 1968).

PERCEPTUAL VERSUS SEMANTIC INTERPRETATIONS

Despite the reliability and generality of this phenomenon, the basic data in these experiments can frequently be interpreted in two rather distinct ways. Some researchers have offered a *perceptual* interpretation, based on the assumption that contextual stimuli affect the *subjective impression* elicited by the various test items. This would imply, for example, that in assessing vocabulary definitions, a judge who has mainly had experience with pathological items will spontaneously "see" midscale items as being relatively well organized

[1] This research was supported in part by the Veterans Administration and in part by NSF Grant GS-1116.

237

and lacking in eccentricity. This interpretation has generally been accepted by investigators working in the adaptation-level (AL) tradition.

There is, however, a compelling alternative explanation for the contrast phenomenon (Campbell, Lewis, & Hunt, 1958b; Krantz & Campbell, 1961; Stevens, 1958; Upshaw, 1962, 1969; Volkmann, 1951). According to this view, changes in context do not affect the judge's subjective experience, but instead influence the *language* that he uses in describing this experience. The contrast effect is thus assumed to be *semantic,* rather than *perceptual,* in origin. For example, consider a judge who attempts to rate the thought pathology implied by various definitions that range from *moderate* to *extreme* disorganization; assume that he is to use a 9-category response scale with "totally disorganized" and "well organized" as end points. Since the definitions that are to be evaluated cover a narrower range of the subjective continuum than the available response categories (that is, none of the definitions that he has been given are really *free* of pathological indicators), the judge may redefine the category "well organized," to make the bounds of his subjective scale more congruent with the definitions that he *is* shown. Such a shift would, of course, result in a repositioning of *all* the category boundaries, since the experimenter's instructions normally indicate that the subjective continuum should be divided into categories of equal breadth. Figure 1 presents these alternative explanations for the contrast phenomenon, where (a) the perceptual interpretation is

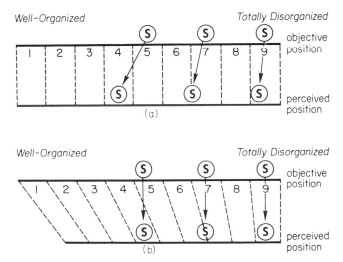

Fig. 1. Two conflicting interpretations for the phenomenon of context-induced contrast effects: (a) perceptual interpretation, based on an assumed *perceptual* effect; (b) *semantic* explanation.

depicted, and (b) the underlying assumptions of the semantic-shift idea is illustrated. It is important to recognize that both these theories are completely consistent with most of the experimental observations in this field. That is, both theories can readily accommodate the fact that neutral stimuli typically elicit judgments that *contrast* with the bulk of the rater's prior experience.

In discussing these conflicting interpretations, Campbell *et al.* (1958b) suggest that shifts in the meaning of the various response alternatives (as in Fig. 1b) may be particularly likely when the judge is required to use a response language that the researcher "creates" for the experiment, for this typically results in a language that is novel, arbitrary, and relativistic. The novelty of the language implies that the respondent must learn the proper meaning for the different response categories as he becomes familiar with the stimuli that are to be judged, and the results of this learning process might quite plausibly be affected by systematic changes in the stimulus array. The *relativity* of the typical response language produces similar problems. In the words of Campbell *et al.* (1958b):

> Terms like *heavy* and *light* are in their proper semantic usage situationally relative, i.e., they convey no absolute meaning apart from a comparative setting. We can speak of a heavy truck, a heavy.suitcase, or a heavy fish line. In such usage, terms like *heavy* and *light* contrast with "absolute" terms like *one ounce, ten pounds,* or *three kilos,* which, in dealing with the same attributes of physical objects, have become extricated from specific immediate comparisons and are understood to be invariant attributes of the objects, appropriately descriptive of it no matter what its setting [pp. 220–221].

In brief, given the typical vague characterizations for the various response categories in a rating task, there is little to prevent the judges from privately defining the various alternatives to "fit" the range of stimuli with which they are presented.

To demonstrate the validity of this argument, Campbell and his associates have conducted two experiments in which judgmental shifts associated with contextual differences are compared in two situations: (*a*) when subjects are instructed to rate the stimuli using response categories that are clearly anchored and thus relatively unsusceptible to redefinition, and (*b*) when the response categories are less well defined. In one study (Campbell *et al.*, 1958a), the subjects rated the amount of disorganization present in a series of vocabulary definitions. For those in the "detailed" condition, each of the 9 points on the response scale was defined explicitly (for example, category 3 was to be used for definitions showing "very slight traces of disorganization and eccentricity"); for subjects in the "simple" condition, however, only the end categories were explicitly defined. In another study (Krantz & Campbell, 1961) the subject's task was to judge the length of a series of white lines projected on a screen. Some subjects used a familiar absolute, and presumably stable response language, making their judgments in inches; other subjects were instructed to use an "artificial," relativistic language, in which the response "100" was to represent lines of "average" length, "95" was reserved for "less-than-average" lines, and so forth. In both studies, biases in the stimuli presented for judgment produced marked contrast effects when the response alternatives were unfamiliar and loosely defined; by comparison, contextually induced contrast effects were reduced (but not eliminated) when the subjects used a more firmly established set of responses. The demonstration of statistically reliable contrast effects even when the subjects used a relatively unambiguous response scale argues against the claim that contrast effects are solely attributable to differences among the subjects in their labeling of the subjective continuum; instead, these data support the notion of a true perceptual effect, independent of semantic (labeling) processes.[2]

Contrast and Communication

These results appear to have direct implications for the process of communication. In a typical communicative episode the sender tries to convey information to his receiver by constructing an appropriate message; the receiver, on the other hand, tries to infer the referent that the communicator had "in mind." Consider a hypothetical case in which a college senior applies to graduate school and submits letters of reference from two professors. One professor, a faculty member at a junior college where the student was formerly enrolled, might characterize him in glowing, enthusiastic terms, having observed his performance within a class of only moderately talented people. The second professor might describe him more cautiously, having observed this same student within the context of an honors seminar at a highly selective, prestigious university. As this hypothetical example suggests, there is some reason to believe that the contrast phenomenon may affect verbal output in a variety of naturally occurring communication settings.

The contrast effect may also have implications for the interpretative behavior of message *receivers*. As noted above, the receiver often has the task of trying to infer the referent that the message sender is attempting to transmit. As in the method of single stimuli, the message (stimulus) must be assigned to one of several categories, with each category representing a particular referent. If the contrast effect is indeed perceptual in origin, then by biasing the receiver's prior experience, it should be possible to affect his choice from a set of *potential* referents, even though the available alternatives are reasonably familiar, unambiguous, and extraexperimentally anchored (and hence resistant to the forms of displacement that are normally assumed in semantic-shift explanations).

[2] Also see Campbell *et al.* (1958b) for a demonstration of contrast effects using an absolute and extraexperimentally anchored response language.

In the experiments described below,[3] the subjects were required either (*a*) to *describe* a series of posed emotional expressions, or (*b*) to *decode* others' descriptions of these emotions. Figure 2 shows a collection of the referent emotions used in these experiments. Previous research (Schlosberg, 1952) has shown that posed emotions vary along several reasonably distinct dimensions. In the present studies, we were mainly concerned with the dimension of *pleasantness* (although this fact was never mentioned to any of the subjects). Accordingly, the photographs shown in Fig. 2 have been drawn from all regions of the pleasantness continuum.

Experiment I

The first experiment was focused on the decoding process. A group of college students was presented with a series of written messages, each describing one of the posed emotions from the set shown in Fig. 2. After reading each passage, the respondents were to choose the photograph (referent) that the writer was attempting to describe; in brief, they were to *decode* his message. The respondents' choices were made from a set of 11 photographs that were randomly arranged and which spanned the pleasantness continuum.

One group of Ss was given a series of descriptions based primarily on pleasant poses; a second group received mainly unpleasant descriptions, while a third group was given an unbiased set of descriptions based on photographs from all regions of the pleasantness continuum. In addition to these *context* passages, all Ss received a common set of 12 *test* descriptions, based on essentially neutral expressions. The test descriptions, which were presented intermittently throughout the experimental session, served as a common standard for comparing the decoding behavior of the three groups; in scoring the Ss' responses to the test descriptions, their choices were converted into a numerical scale, based on the pleasantness of the selected photographs (as scaled by Schlosberg, 1952).

For comparative purposes, two additional groups of Ss served in a parallel *rating* experiment. These Ss were presented with either the pleasant or unpleasant context passages, together with the neutral test descriptions; their task was simply to rate the pleasantness of each emotional state, "as it would be experienced by the person being described." We fully expected to find the classic contrast effect when the rating groups were compared, since the procedures employed in this phase of the study closely paralleled those that have traditionally been used in AL studies. The more critical question, however, revolved about the results obtained in the decoding task. If the contrast

[3] Detailed descriptions of Experiments I and II appear in publications by Manis (1967) and Manis and Armstrong (1971).

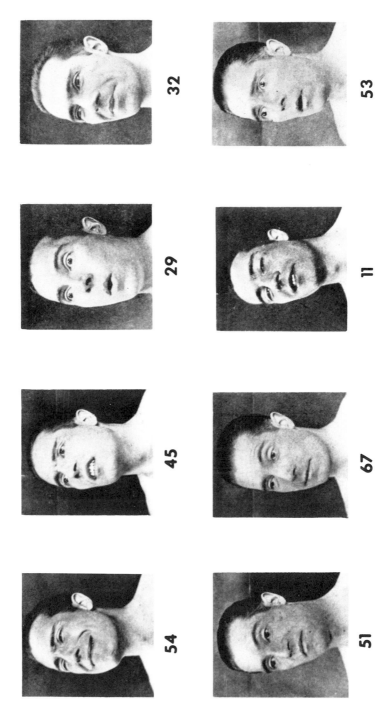

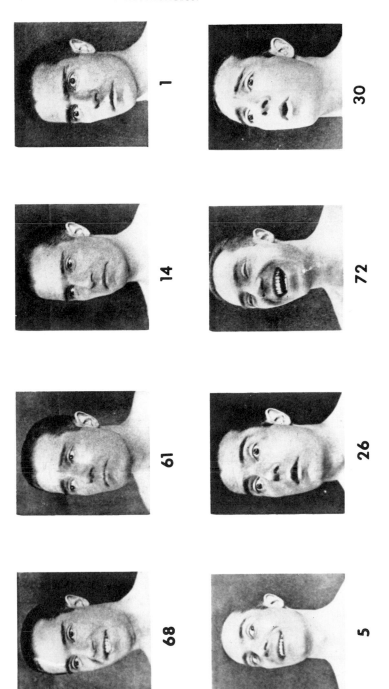

Fig. 2. A collection of posed emotions that were used in this program of research.

phenomenon was due mainly to semantic readjustments of the various rating categories, this effect might be virtually eliminated when the Ss' reactions were assessed within the *decoding* paradigm, where the significance of the different response alternatives (photographs) was now presumably more palpable and clear-cut. Thus, in contrast to the rating task, where the selection of a given response alternative (for example, category 3) might signify different things for different respondents, the decoding task seemed less ambiguous. We reasoned that if contrast effects were obtained, despite the presumed stability of the response alternatives (photographs), this would constitute important evidence favoring the *perceptual* interpretation of contrast.

Data was analysed by combining the results from adjacent test items. The results from the decoding task are shown in Fig. 3, while in Fig. 4 a summary of the results obtained with the traditional rating procedure is given. In both cases, there was consistent evidence of contrast. The subjects assigned to the pleasant context responded to the test items in less favorable terms than did those assigned to the unpleasant context; moreover, within the decoding task, subjects who were assigned to the *unbiased* condition followed the expected pattern by generally falling between the two extreme groups.

Discussion

Perhaps the main virtue of the decoding procedure was the fact that it involved relatively unambiguous response alternatives; regardless of the context group to which a subject had been assigned, the choice of a particular picture simply meant that this was the respondent's best guess as to the photograph the communicator was attempting to describe. The directness of this interpretation weakened the applicability of the semantic-change hypothesis. The contrast effects obtained in the decoding task thus suggested that the recipient's understanding of a freely composed message (that is, the referent which he assumes guided the communicator's verbal output) may be significantly affected by prior exposure to a biased sample of messages.

On thinking the matter over, however, it seemed conceivable that the results obtained in the decoding experiment might partly have reflected an implicit attempt to use the various response alternatives with *equal frequency*. Although our respondents had all been assured that the various response alternatives (photographs) would not necessarily be "called for" equally often, and that some of the photographs might *never* seem appropriate in decoding the writers' passages, there is no guarantee that those instructions were completely effective. A respondent who was concerned about distributing his responses relatively "evenly" might, when in doubt, select that photograph (from the set of plausible alternatives) that he had chosen *least often* in the past. Such a process would automatically generate a contrastlike effect. For example, suppose that a given

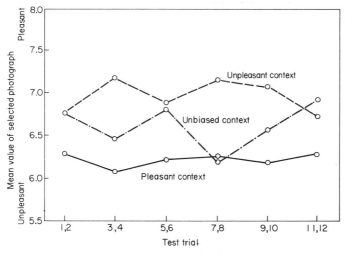

Fig. 3. The effects of extreme contexts on the *S*'s response to the decoding task.

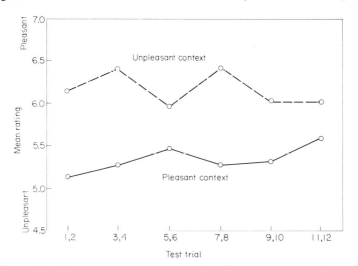

Fig. 4. The effects of extreme contexts on the *S*'s response to the rating task.

passage seemed equally descriptive of two photographs, one depicting a mildly pleasant emotion, and the other an emotion that was mildly unpleasant. The equal-frequency principle suggests that a recipient whose assignment to the more pleasant context had resulted in the selection of the more pleasant of these photographs on several preceding trials might be inclined to "even things up," by now choosing the *less* pleasant of the two; for someone assigned to the unpleasant context, on the other hand, the equal-frequency bias would lead to a choice of the *more* pleasant photograph. The second experiment in this series was designed, in part, to correct this deficiency.

Experiment II

Experiment II had two main goals: (*a*) to explore the contrast phenomenon in a setting that would eliminate the equal-frequency principle along with the semantic-change hypothesis as a viable interpretation for the results; (*b*) to study the impact of divergent contexts on *verbal output* (in contrast to Experiment I, which was solely concerned with the *decoding* process).

In essence, Experiment II compared descriptive passages that were written by respondents who had been exposed to contrasting arrays of *potential* referents (for example, photographs of predominantly pleasant or unpleasant emotional expressions), but who had been instructed to write about the same subsample of neutral *test* referents. If the overall array mainly included pleasant emotional expressions, the contrast hypothesis suggests that neutral emotions should be described in relatively unpleasant terms; analogously, a writer who was assigned to an unpleasant context should produce relatively pleasant test messages, while those who were assigned to a full-range context (including photographs from all regions of the pleasantness continuum), would be expected to write messages falling somewhere between these extremes.

The passages produced by the various writers in Experiment II were converted into a common quantitative system by means of a rating procedure, in which a group of judges assessed the "pleasantness–unpleasantness" of the emotional experiences that were described. These ratings of course, were collected without telling the judges about the diverse experimental conditions under which the different messages had been produced.

The design of this experiment seemed to eliminate several methodological problems. For one thing, since the writers were permitted to express themselves freely, using a perfectly familiar means of expression, it seemed reasonable to assume that many of the problems associated with novel response languages (see above) might be avoided. The equal-frequency principle also seemed less relevant in this setting, for it appeared unlikely that the writers would attend to the number of pleasant versus unpleasant emotions they had recently seen (or described), given the innumerable ways in which the photographs and messages differed from one another. Moreover, since the experimenters' interest in the pleasantness dimension was never explicitly mentioned to the writers, it seemed highly unlikely that they would be concerned with producing equal numbers of pleasant and unpleasant passages.

An analysis of the judges' ratings indicated that the three groups of writers had indeed produced systematically different descriptions. The obtained pattern of results was fully consistent with theoretical expectations, for there was an inverse relationship between the pleasantness of the photographs that provided the contextual background, and the rated pleasantness of the writers' test messages. That is, writers who were assigned to the pleasant array of photographs produced the *least pleasant* test messages (with a mean rating of 4.1 on a 9-point scale), followed by the full-range group (mean rating = 4.7), and finally those writers who were assigned the unpleasant array, whose descriptions of the neutral test photographs were judged to be most pleasant of all (mean rating = 5.1).

EXPERIMENT III

Experiment II showed that the verbal reactions elicited by various posed emotions could be systematically affected by the array of *other* photographs (pleasant or unpleasant) with which they appeared. Experiment III was concerned with the possibility that similar effects might be produced if the writers merely read *descriptions* of biased arrays, without actually viewing the photographs themselves. We expected to find further evidence of contrast, with exposure to "unpleasant" reading materials (for example) leading to relatively pleasant test descriptions.

The overall design of this experiment was relatively simple. One group of Ss read an extended series of descriptive passages concerned with pleasant emotions, while another group read descriptions of unpleasant emotions; to ensure careful reading, the Ss rated each passage in terms of its "ability to communicate." The impact of these divergent reading experiences was assessed by intermittently having all Ss write descriptive test passages based on the "mood, feelings, or thought" portrayed in 15 photographs from the Frois–Wittman series. To determine the degree of pleasantness that each message conveyed, the individual test descriptions were rated by a group of judges who were unaware of the contextual variations involved in the study.

The first five photographs that were described all depicted emotions that were essentially *neutral* with respect to pleasantness–unpleasantness. Neutral photographs were used here because we were fearful that any effects produced by the Ss' biased reading experiences might be eliminated once they were exposed to expressions that covered the full spectrum, from very *pleasant* to very *unpleasant* emotions. The data from this first part of the experimental session were in general accord with the contrast hypothesis, but the obtained differences were not statistically significant. That is, writers who were assigned to the unpleasant context showed an increasing tendency to write test passages that were rated as *more* pleasant than the passages produced within the unpleasant context, although this effect was of uncertain replicability.

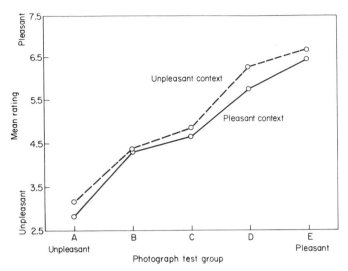

Fig. 5. Rated pleasantness of test passages produced in response to different types of photographs; data are plotted separately for *S*s assigned to the pleasant and unpleasant contexts.

Figure 5 presents the mean ratings that were obtained during the latter part of the experimental session, when the subjects wrote passages describing the *full range* of emotional expressions. The photographs that were described in these passages reflected five different degrees of pleasantness, and when considered as an overall set, they spanned the entire pleasantness continuum. As the graph indicates, the results of this experiment revealed a consistent (and statistically reliable) contrast effect; writers who had read about unpleasant emotions consistently produced passages that were rated as more *pleasant* than those written within the unpleasant context.

Discussion

All things considered, the results of Experiment III closely paralleled the results obtained in Experiments I and II. Exposure to contrasting sets of written descriptions had a modest but consistent impact on the subjects' *own* written descriptions. These results extend the generality of earlier research and show that *verbal* stimuli can establish a context that may affect the individual's subsequent response to *nonverbal* referents (photographs). It appears that the contexts established by the assigned reading materials produced a cognitive impact much like the one observed in Experiment II, where exposure to biased arrays of photographs (rather than written descriptions) led to contrast in the respondents' subsequent descriptions.

It is interesting to note that the results of this experiment are in striking disagreement with what might be termed the *priming* hypothesis, since reading about unpleasant emotions (for example) could plausibly be expected to trigger additional unpleasant associations and verbal reactions when the writers were called upon to produce their own descriptions. The failure to obtain this "reasonable" pattern of results may simply reflect the potency of the contrast phenomenon.

Experiment III revealed one further result that is worthy of comment: The contrast effects produced by divergent reading experiences were essentially constant, regardless of the pleasantness value of the various test photographs. Note, that in Fig. 5 the difference between the two groups was relatively unaffected by the pleasantness values of the particular photographs that they were describing. These results are inconsistent with the pattern that might be anticipated from theories that focus on the discrepancy between some *prevailing* level of stimulation, and the respondent's assessment of an incoming *focal* stimulus. An extrapolation from the theory outlined by Sherif and Hovland (1961), for example, suggests that assimilation (rather than *contrast*) might be produced when a writer describes a photograph that is rather similar to the various descriptions he has recently read. Operationally, this would be reflected in a reduced difference between the two groups, when the writers described extremely pleasant and extremely unpleasant test photographs. For example, in describing a very pleasant photograph, the assimilation that might be expected from writers who had read about pleasant emotions would essentially "cancel" the contrast effects that would be anticipated from those assigned to the unpleasant context. There is, however, no evidence of such a trend in the data from Experiment III.

THE ROSENBERG-COHEN HYPOTHESIS

Experiments II and III both indicated that a communicator's freely produced descriptions may be systematically affected by the context to which he has been exposed; a given referent may thus be described in rather different terms, depending upon contextual factors. To account for these results, a straight-forward application of AL theory (Helson, 1964) would focus on the perceptual effects that may be produced through contextual influences. This would imply that in Experiments II and III, the variations in context were instrumental in affecting the subjective impressions that the various photographs evoked, which in turn were reflected in the writers' descriptions. Thus, when embedded in an array of pleasant photographs, a neutral picture might simply *look* less pleasant than it would under other circumstances, and it would, as a result, be described in relatively unpleasant terms.

An alternative explanation would emphasize the context as a *direct* determinant of the writer's descriptions. Explanations of this type are basically semantic in character, for they focus on the labeling systems that are utilized under divergent contextual circumstances. A well-developed theory of this sort, with particular relevance for the present experiments, may be found in Rosenberg and Cohen's analysis (1966) of the referential process (also see Rosenberg & Gordon, 1968). These theorists suggest that when a speaker is faced with the task of describing a given referent, the message that he ultimately generates will be partly determined by a *comparison process,* which leads him to inhibit certain descriptions that have implicitly been evoked, but must be rejected as unsuitable because they are associated both with the speaker's intended referent, and with various nonreferents with which it might be confused. According to this view, contextual influences may affect the writer's overt description by inducing him to inhibit verbalizations that might be freely emitted in other circumstances.

The Rosenberg–Cohen account can be most readily applied to Experiment II, where the respondent would presumably avoid descriptive comments that might be relevant to several of the photographs in his assigned array. For example, given a predominantly *pleasant* set of photographs, a writer might conclude that a neutral test picture could best be distinguished from the others in the array by emphasizing its unpleasant aspects. This hypothesized selection process seems particularly plausible in view of the instruction to the writers that each description should be "clear enough so that someone else would know which picture you have written about."

The results of Experiment III, on the other hand, seem less directly related to the Rosenberg–Cohen approach, although here, too, their analysis may be applicable. In this experiment the writers were simply asked to describe the various test photographs. Nothing was said about the desirability of generating passages that would permit a clear discrimination between the emotions that the writers read about (the context), and those that served as referents for their own descriptions. Despite this, the writers produced passages that were systematically contrasted "away" from the descriptions that they had read. The Rosenberg–Cohen theory may apply here as well, however, if we emphasize the possibility that in screening implicit verbalizations that have been stimulated by a given referent, the writer may be significantly affected by the salience of various nonreferents that operate at a purely symbolic level. Thus, by having the writer read about different emotional expressions, we may strengthen his awareness ("remind" him) of certain *nonreferent* emotions, and induce him to inhibit ambiguous descriptions that might otherwise be freely emitted.

EXPERIMENT IV

In Experiment III we were mainly concerned with assessing the impact of what our subjects had *read* upon the content of their *written* descriptions.

Experiment IV followed the reverse of this pattern, evaluating the effects of the subjects' *writing* experiences on their subsequent attempts to decode descriptions that had been written by others.

The design of Experiment IV included two main groups of students, who were instructed to write descriptions of several photographs from the Frois–Wittman series. One group wrote about predominantly pleasant emotional expressions, while the other wrote about unpleasant emotions. Our main goal was to assess the impact of these contrasting writing assignments on the subjects' *decoding* behavior, when they attempted to identify the various referents (photographs) that were described in a series of passages which were intermittently presented.

The first eight messages that Ss were to decode all described neutral photographs, since we were fearful that exposure to the *full range* of descriptive passages might eradicate any displacement effects that had been generated by Ss' biased writing assignments (pleasant or unpleasant). In the second part of the experimental session Ss decoded eight different sets of descriptions, with each set spanning the entire pleasantness continuum. To quantify the Ss' decoding performance, each response (picture choice) was converted into a numerical score based on the pleasantness value of the chosen photograph.

The results of this experiment indicated that the subjects who were assigned to the pleasant context generally selected photographs that were *more pleasant* than those selected within the unpleasant context. Despite the seeming consistency of this trend, the difference between the divergent context groups was *not* statistically significant during the initial (neutral) test series. An analysis of the test data collected in the latter part of the experimental session, however, indicated that this initial trend was maintained (and *strengthened*) when the respondents attempted to decode messages based on the *full range* of emotional expressions, for the difference between the two context groups was now statistically significant.

Figure 6 presents the results from this latter, full-range test series. The plotted points represent the mean pleasantness value for the referent photographs that were selected in each of the eight test cycles. In six of the eight test cycles, the subjects who had been assigned to the pleasant context selected photographs that had higher pleasantness values (on the average) than those selected by the subjects in the unpleasant context group. Inspection of Fig. 6 indicates, moreover, that the only exceptions to this trend appeared toward the end of the experimental session (in test cycles 5 and 7), after the divergent contextual influences had been removed (by no longer requiring the subjects to write descriptive passages based on emotions from their assigned pool of photographs).

It may finally be noted that, as in Experiment III, the results of this experiment were relatively *independent* of the pleasantness value of the various test messages. That is, the displacement effects produced by the subjects' divergent writing experiences were essentially unaffected by the discrepancy

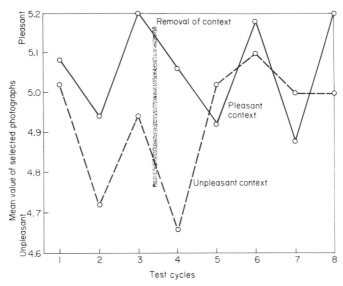

Fig. 6. The effect of divergent writing experience on subsequent response to a full range of test passages in the decoding task.

between their assigned contextual background, and the content of the messages that they decoded.

Discussion

The overall results of Experiment IV were generally consistent with earlier findings in demonstrating systematic context effects within a communication paradigm. This experiment was unique, however, in that unlike the earlier studies in this series, the structure of the experimental task resulted in a displacement toward the "context" side of the continuum; for example, those subjects assigned the task of describing *unpleasant* photographs tended to select relatively *unpleasant* photographs as referents for the various test messages. In Experiments I, II, and III, on the other hand, those subjects assigned to the unpleasant context typically selected responses from the "opposite" (or pleasant) side of the continuum. Experiment IV can, nevertheless, be interpreted within the general framework of Helson's AL theory (see Fig. 7).

Figure 7 was designed to illustrate the dynamics presumed to underlie the results of Experiment IV. In this diagram, the decoding of a descriptive message is assumed to depend in part on a "matching" of (*a*) messages with (*b*) referents (photographs) of similar perceived pleasantness; this is symbolized by the ellipses in the diagram. The diagonal arrows that slant up from left to right represent a hypothesized displacement process, in which prior exposure to predominantly

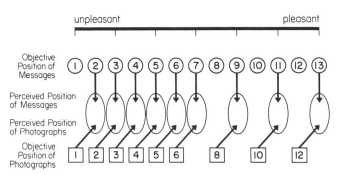

Fig. 7. A schematic diagram showing the impact of a biased (unpleasant) writing experience on subsequent decoding performance.

unpleasant photographs (during the course of the writing task) has produced a perceptual shift of the overall array of emotions toward the pleasant pole of the continuum; in brief, we are assuming that exposure to a series of unpleasant emotional poses has made the overall set of pictures *look* more pleasant. The vertical arrows symbolize the assumption that the messages that were to be decoded maintained a relatively *fixed* position. The figure suggests that as a consequence of these two assumptions, a subject assigned to the unpleasant writing condition should select relatively unpleasant referents (photographs) in decoding the various test messages. For example, a photograph with an objective pleasantness value of 4 is presumably displaced toward the pleasant pole, so that it is perceived as expressing a somewhat more pleasant emotion. A message describing an emotion with an objective pleasantness value of 5 might, as a consequence, lead to the erroneous selection of this photograph, which has migrated from its "proper" location in category 4, into category 5. The net result is that the exposure to an unpleasant context has led our hypothetical subject to choose a referent (photograph) that is less pleasant than the one he should have chosen. By similar reasoning, we would anticipate that those subjects exposed to a predominantly pleasant array of photographs would choose referents that were "too pleasant." The combination of these effects would lead to the overall results shown in Fig. 6, in which the subjects who had viewed (and written about) a predominantly *pleasant* array of emotions selected photographs that were *more pleasant* than those chosen by subjects assigned to the *unpleasant* condition.

This analysis of Experiment IV is based on the assumption that the *viewing* of contrasting emotional photographs (rather than the act of *writing* about them) was of critical importance in the results that were obtained. This assumption is consistent with incidental results obtained in Experiment II, which showed that there was no discernible difference between the neutral test messages produced by writers who had merely *viewed* the contextual photographs in their assigned array, and those who had, in addition, *described* the critical context emotions (pleasant or unpleasant).

CONCLUSION

This program of research was motivated, in part, by an interest in studying contrast phenomena in a setting that would (hopefully) eliminate semantic explanations for the obtained results. The stability of our findings suggests, at the very least, that the contrast effect is not dependent on the subject's use of an unfamiliar and hence unstable rating-scale response language, nor does it appear to depend on his implicit attempt to use each element in a limited response array with equal frequency. A less cautious conclusion would involve a forthright acceptance of the perceptual theory of contrast. The conflict between semantic and perceptual theories is, however, complex and possibly insoluble in any truly *definitive* sense. Nevertheless, the present results appear to be most readily explained within a perceptual frame of reference, mainly because of the varied forms in which the semantic argument must be cast in order to make it applicable from one experiment to the next. This writer is also impressed by the apparent continuity between the results obtained in human studies of contextual phenomena, and those obtained with infrahuman organisms (see Adamson's article in this volume; Bevan, 1968). Since semantic explanations for contrast seem clearly inapplicable in work with animals, it would seem unparsimonious to explain the infrahuman results using a *perceptual* model, while simultaneously favoring a semantic explanation to account for similar effects in humans.

The present results testify to the significance of contextual stimuli as determinants of natural language behavior, a phenomenon of obvious importance and generality. Our results suggest that when A speaks to B concerning some external referent, the information that is conveyed may be significantly affected by the contexts to which these individuals have previously been exposed.

The robustness of the contrast phenomenon across a wide range of experimental settings and methodologies suggests that it reflects a basic behavioral principle; the present results indicate that it plays a significant role in communication, and quite possibly in other cognitive activities as well.

ACKNOWLEDGMENT

The research that is described here was carried out with the able assistance of Arnold Weingarden, Gregory Armstrong, and Stephanie Riger.

REFERENCES

Adamson, R. Contrast effects and reinforcement. Pages 159–168 of this volume.

Bevan, W. The contextual basis of behavior. *American Psychologist,* 1968, **23,** 701–714.

Campbell, D. T., Hunt, W. A., & Lewis, N. A. The relative susceptibility of two rating scales to disturbances resulting from shifts in stimulus context. *Journal of Applied Psychology,* 1958, **42,** 213–217.   (a)

Campbell, D. T., Lewis, N. A., & Hunt, W. A. Context effects with judgmental language that is absolute, extensive, and extra-experimentally anchored. *Journal of Experimental Psychology,* 1958, **55,** 220–228.   (b)

Heintz, R. K. The effect of remote anchoring points upon the judgments of lifted weights. *Journal of Experimental Psychology,* 1950, **40,** 584–591.

Helson, H. *Adaptation-level theory: An experimental and systematic approach to behavior.* New York: Harper, 1964.

Krantz, D. L., & Campbell, D. T. Separating perceptual and linguistic effects of context shifts upon absolute judgments. *Journal of Experimental Psychology,* 1961, **62,** 35–42.

Manis, M. Context effects in communication. *Journal of Personality and Social Psychology,* 1967, **5,** 326–334.

Manis, M., & Armstrong, G. W. Contrast effects in verbal output. *Journal of Experimental Social Psychology,* 1971, **7,** 381–388.

Rosenberg, S., & Cohen, B. D. Referential processes of speakers and listeners. *Psychological Review,* 1966, **73,** 208–231.

Rosenberg, S., & Gordon, A. Identification of facial expressions from affective descriptions: A probabilistic choice analysis of referential ambiguity. *Journal of Personality and Social Psychology,* 1968, **10,** 157–166.

Schlosberg, H. The description of facial expressions in terms of two dimensions. *Journal of Experimental Psychology,* 1952, **44,** 229–237.

Sherif, M., & Hovland, C. I. *Social judgment: Assimilation and contrast effects in communication and attitude change.* New Haven, Connecticut: Yale University Press, 1961.

Stevens, S. S. Adaptation level vs. the relativity of judgment. *American Journal of Psychology,* 1958, **71,** 663–647.

Upshaw, H. S. Own attitude as an anchor in equal-appearing intervals. *Journal of Abnormal and Social Psychology,* 1962, **64,** 85–86.

Upshaw, H. S. The personal reference scale: An approach to social judgment. *Advances in Experimental Social Psychology,* 1969, **4,** 315–371.

Volkmann, J. Scales of judgment and their implications for social psychology. In J. H. Rohrer & M. Sherif (Eds.), *Social psychology at the crossroads.* New York: Harper, 1951. Pp. 273–294.

COMMENT

Alice H. Eagly

It has often been demonstrated that systematic shifts in the judgment of stimuli occur as a function of changes in the total set of stimuli to which an individual is exposed. Though the phenomenon of such context effects is well established, its interpretation has generated considerable debate between those who claim that context has an impact on what a person actually experiences or perceives and those who favor the view that a context effect represents merely a difference in semantics. This debate has appeared in many guises—as perceptual effect versus semantic effect, psychological level versus response level (Bieri *et al.,* 1966), quantity versus scale (Upshaw, 1969), and sensory adaptation versus the relativity of judgment (Stevens, 1958). The series of experiments carried out by Manis and his associates (described in the preceding contribution) brings this issue into sharp focus through the use of a set of dependent variables that makes possible a relatively strong inference concerning perceptual versus semantic contributions to context effects with complex social stimuli.

The typical experiment in this area (see, for example, Sherif, Taub, & Hovland, 1958) has demonstrated a judgmental contrast effect—a displacement of the stimulus series away from an anchor stimulus—with the dependent variable consisting of ratings of stimuli on a numerical response scale or of descriptions of stimuli in terms of a categorical response language provided by the experimenter. Though one interpretation of such a contrast effect is that the subjects perceive the stimuli differently, one must deal with the alternative interpretation that differences in the distribution of stimuli in the set affect the subject's use of the response language that he has available, rather than his perception.

The relevance of Manis' work to this issue arises in his very interesting choice of dependent variables. Yet Manis himself cautiously and properly points out that his own evidence on the issue is not *completely* unambiguous, and one wonders if any completely unambiguous demonstration of the perceptual origin of context effects is possible within the type of experimental situation that he created. Still, it is relatively difficult to claim that the response alternatives in his matching task were merely reinterpreted or redefined as a function of exposure to a biased context. Very special arguments concerning selectivity in responding must be invoked to give a semantic interpretation to his free-response data.

But to gain more perspective on the perceptual vs. semantic issue, Manis' studies need to be examined in the context of a variety of kinds of evidence that may bear on the issue. Thus, one gains confidence that the origin of context effects is perceptual to the extent that several sorts of criteria are met (for example, that the response scale is unrestricted; that scales with absolute zero points and unambiguous units, such as inches, are employed; that context effects are demonstrated in lower animals). No single method of dealing with the issue is likely to leave us thoroughly convinced that we have solved it in a general sense.

The particular type of dependent variable that Manis has chosen focuses our attention on some of the social consequences of context effects. He has shown that biased contexts create inaccuracy in a matching task—that is, bias in one's past history makes it likely that an individual will incorrectly interpret descriptions of stimuli (if these descriptions were not generated by persons who are products of similarly biased environments). Furthermore, he has shown that persons exposed to one context give a verbal description of stimuli different from the descriptions provided by persons exposed to different contextual stimuli and that context influences the manner in which subjects decode descriptions written by other people.

One must conclude from Manis' demonstrations that differences in context—and the associated differences in AL that are created—cause *real* difficulties in communication. Thus, if my experience in a given realm is different from yours in a way that creates a difference in AL, we will not see things in the same way, and we may accuse each other of nonveridicality. We match the same stimulus with different referents, and we describe the same stimulus differently when we are given a chance to use our own verbal labelings. That such phenomena occur in everyday life is apparent enough—the man who is a "cowardly draft dodger" when viewed from the right is a "hero committed to higher principles" when viewed from the left. That these differences in how one perceives events contribute to social conflict is also apparent. An AL interpretation of these differences in judgmental behavior—an interpretation in terms of one's point of psychological neutrality—exposes the source of the conflict in differences in the kind and range of stimuli that one has experienced and is experiencing. In a general way, AL theory also points toward a part of what needs to happen if such differences in how people perceive events are to be reduced—namely, persons' experiences need to become more equivalent, or, at least, differences in experience should be the kind that cancel one another in the pooling process so that the outcome of pooling brings about roughly equivalent ALs. Unless such equivalence is established, accusations of nonveridicality seem inevitable, and Manis' work is consistent with the view that we cannot remove the conflict by the claim that we really see things the same but use words differently.

In looking at our society, we can point out both mechanisms creating greater equivalence of experience between subgroupings and mechanisms creating greater differences. On the one hand, we have the mass media—the tremendous equivalence of exposure created by television and mass-circulation newspapers. On the other hand, however, we have the increased ghettoization of American society, with the continued flight of white people from the central city to the suburbs and, to look at one special context, the establishment of increasingly large, isolated middle-class ghettos of the intelligentsia in university communities. If one were to hazard a social policy recommendation on the basis of the principles of perception to which we are addressing ourselves here (though to do this without taking into account a myriad of other variables is probably simplistic), this recommendation would be a mixing of society in order to create the kind of equivalence of experience that would enable us to give the same interpretation to events.

It is almost inevitable that Helson's work is of considerable interest to social psychologists because of the traditional importance within social psychology of concepts pointing to the fact that an individual's past and present experience in a realm establishes a standard in terms of which he perceives and evaluates present stimuli. Sherif (1936), for example, writing extensively in terms of a "frame-of-reference" concept, argued that behavior becomes predictable only through taking into account its antecedent background and present context. Sherif considered any internalized standard (be it one's own attitude, a norm, a custom, or a value) to be an instance of frame of reference. In addition, social psychology has a whole family of concepts (such as reference group, distributive justice, equity) that amplify the notion that one's own outcomes are judged in relationship, not just to one's own past outcomes, but to the outcomes that other people are perceived to be experiencing.

Though many social psychologists have been explicit about acknowledging the fact that an individual's past and present experience affects his perception of stimuli—and therefore his behavior—theoretical amplification of this position by social psychologists has tended to remain, for the most part, rather global. To help us to move beyond the mere recognition of the fact that the context establishes a standard for judgment, AL theory offers a quantitative approach to specifying the way in which experience is pooled to establish a frame of reference. The AL approach has exerted an explicit influence on Thibaut and Kelley's exchange-theory concept of comparison level, which is a standard that a person engaged in social interaction uses in judging the adequacy of the outcomes that he receives. Thus, for Thibaut and Kelley (1959), comparison level is "some modal or average value of all the outcomes known to the person, each outcome weighted by its salience [p. 81]." Yet this idea that comparison levels operate in social situations remains largely unexplored in any systematic fashion, and the most popular experimental paradigms for investigating the concepts of exchange theory (the minimal social situation and two-person bargaining situation) have not yet provided an empirical avenue for investigating the relativity of outcomes. Clearly, a tremendous amount of careful work is in order before we can systematically incorporate into our theories of social interaction a precise conceptualization of how experience is pooled to create adaptation or comparison levels. However, the fact that Helson in his own writing has pointed to the relevance of AL theory to social psychology has certainly helped to stimulate thinking in these directions.

One other general point concerning the impact of AL theory on social psychology should be made. Helson's work, rooted as it is in the study of psychophysical phenomena, provides us with one illustration of the position that social perception does not require a set of explanatory principles different from those that apply to other perceptual phenomena. Though social psychologists are often very receptive to ideas from other areas of psychology, the notion that social and thing perception will be incorporated under one set of principles is by no means generally accepted by social psychologists, at least some of whom are fond of pointing to a set of crucial differences between the two processes (see, for example, Tagiuri, 1969). However, the burden of proof lies with those who vote against parsimony and prefer to use new and more complex principles for understanding social perception. Accordingly, if the principles of AL theory apply to social stimuli, such as those investigated by Manis, we have the beginnings of a stronger linkage between general and social psychology.

Manis' careful examination of the perception-versus-labeling issue constitutes an empirical demonstration of the applicability of AL theory to social psychology. In further applications of the principles of AL theory to complex social stimuli, it may be possible to predict the magnitude of contrast effects from knowledge of the shift of context. When we can make predictions for the perception of complex social stimuli at this level of precision, we will be able to evaluate more fully the success with which we can import general judgmental principles into social psychology.

References

Bieri, J., Atkins, A. L., Briar, S., Leaman, R. L., Miller, H., & Tripodi, T. *Clinical and social judgment: The discrimination of behavioral information.* New York: Wiley, 1966.
Sherif, M. *The psychology of social norms.* New York: Harper, 1936.
Sherif, M., Taub, D., & Hovland, C. I. Assimilation and contrast effects of anchoring stimuli on judgments. *Journal of Experimental Psychology,* 1958, 55, 150–155.
Stevens, S. S. Adaptation-level vs. the relativity of judgment. *American Journal of Psychology,* 1958, 71, 633–646.

Tagiuri, R. Person perception. In G. Lindzey & E. Aronson (Eds.) *Handbook of social psychology*. Vol. 3. Reading, Massachusetts: Addison-Wesley, 1969. Pp. 395–449.

Thibaut, J. W., & Kelley, H. H. *The social psychology of groups*. New York: Wiley, 1959.

Upshaw, H. S. The personal reference scale: An approach to social judgment. In L. Berkowitz (Ed.), *Advances in experimental social psychology*. Vol. 4. New York: Academic Press, 1969. Pp. 315–371.

LEVELS OF COGNITIVE FUNCTIONING AND THE AUDITORY–VISUAL DIFFERENCES IN HUMAN TIMING BEHAVIOR[1]

Sanford Goldstone and William T. Lhamon

INTRODUCTION

For some reason or other, a program of research which was always intended to focus primarily upon the psychopathology of time judgment has been persistently sidetracked by basic psychophysical issues; the one which has consumed more of our effort than any other is the comparison of auditory and visual temporal behavior. Although this would appear to be a natural consequence of studying man's *time,* his only panmodal sensory dimension that permits direct comparison across the senses through common intraorganismic temporal norms, we have tried to remain true to our prime interest in psychopathology, only to stumble across mysterious intersensory differences when least expected. Since we can trace the diversion and victimization by cross-modal serendipity to an old visit from Helson, it seemed fitting that we review our work on auditory–visual differences in human timing behavior in this volume. Indeed, the fact that we came across another of these differences at the time of the original symposium while looking for something else was regarded as an omen that we could not ignore. Hence, we will take this opportunity to summarize briefly previous work on intersensory differences in human timing behavior, report a new auditory–visual difference, and speculate about possible implications of these findings for models of healthy and deviant cognitive functioning and temporal information processing.

Exactly 15 years ago, Helson offered to help us in our beginning program of research on human timing behavior and psychopathology. We had just completed a study (Lhamon & Goldstone, 1956) from which we developed a simple theory postulating a general alteration in the internal clock in schizophrenics. Helson introduced us to the notions of relativity of

---

[1] This research was conducted at the Edward W. Bourne Behavioral Research Laboratories, New York Hospital, Westchester Division.

psychophysical judgment and the contextual basis of behavior, but cautioned us about hasty generalizations.

Our subsequent researches indicated that patient-control difference in time judgment was dependent on many contextual factors (Webster, Goldstone, & Webb, 1962; Lhamon, Goldstone, & Goldfarb, 1965; Wright, Goldstone, & Boardman, 1962). We achieved consistent results from the healthy human timer, but stable findings about psychopathology eluded us. By absolute methods, we found that sounds were judged longer than lights (Goldstone, Boardman, & Lhamon, 1959a; confirmed independently by Behar & Bevan, 1961). We then explored the auditory–visual difference in average response level of time judgment using other psychophysical methods, and the intersensory difference in reaction time (Goldstone, 1968b).

A more recent study (Goldstone, in press) suggested that the processes of encoding within the schizophrenics' informational analytic systems were more likely to be producing the cognitive deficits in temporal functioning than any specific error in the sensory systems of the timepiece (Venables, 1964). By use of the statistical tools of information theory (Garner, 1962) to reexamine old data, a new auditory–visual difference in the amount of information transmitted was revealed.

Review

In the first study comparing auditory with visual time judgment using the absolute method (Goldstone *et al.,* 1959a), the subjects described durations as *more* or *less* than one clock second. The point that was reported as *more* and *less* 50% of the time was designated as the *second estimation point* (SEP). Auditory SEPs were always longer than visual SEPs. When attention was focused selectively, the SEP was auditory or visual (depending on which stimulus was more intense) regardless of visual target size (Goldstone, Jernigan, Lhamon, & Boardman, 1959b). Behar and Bevan (1960, 1961) confirmed these findings in two studies of heteromodal anchoring effects.

An inquiry into the effects of various contextual factors upon intersensory time judgments (Goldstone & Goldfarb, 1964a) confirmed the finding of shorter judgments of visual duration.[2] Frequency of light and sound had no apparent effect (Behar & Bevan, 1961; Goldfarb & Goldstone, 1964), but more intense visual stimuli were judged to be slightly longer than weaker ones. The auditory–visual difference can be attenuated but not eliminated with practice (Goldstone & Kirkham, 1968). Most surprising, the auditory–visual effect is present with the absolute method even for empty intervals bounded by clicks or flashes (Goldstone & Goldfarb, 1963), although this finding vanished when vacant intervals bounded by clicks or flashes were used (Goldstone, 1964) with

[2] Henceforth all studies comparing auditory and visual timing behavior employed lights and sounds of equivalent subjective intensity.

the method of direct comparison. However, Tanner, Patton, and Atkinson (1965) found no auditory–visual difference in a two-category, forced-choice direct comparison.

The relationship between time judgment and sense modality seems to be very complex indeed.

In an attempt to avoid the limitations of a single system of representation, namely, category scaling, Goldstone (1968a) asked his subjects to produce a signal of specified duration or to reproduce a given signal within and between sense modes. This experiment again demonstrated the auditory–visual difference.

The studies cited above indicate a stable and pervasive phenomenon independent of context. Goldstone and Goldfarb (1966), however, found that developmental factors influenced the ability to make absolute judgments of duration, since auditory temporal judgment seems to develop before visual.

This suggested the application of Ribot's law (Lhamon & Goldstone, 1970) in studying time judgment in brain-damaged and aging subjects.

The auditory–visual difference was found for healthy and retarded children (Goldstone, 1964), for various socioeconomic factors in adolescents (Rutkin, 1966), and for subjects who had been administered sedatives or stimulants (Ehrensing, Stokes, Pick, Goldstone, & Lhamon, 1970; Goldstone, 1964; Goldstone & Kirkham, 1968).

While schizophrenics retained the auditory–visual difference (Goldfarb, 1963), they showed a reduction of cross-modal transfer effects and successive pooling (Goldstone, 1964).

Reaction time (RT) to signal onset is generally agreed to be faster for sounds than for lights (see Woodworth & Schlosberg, 1954; Elliott, 1968). Comparison of RT to onset and cessation of signals within and across modes, in an attempt to determine whether the auditory–visual differences for time judgment and RT are related, has not produced consistent results (Wells, 1913; Woodrow, 1915; Johnson, 1923; Woodworth & Schlosberg, 1954; Teichner, 1954).

Studies by Grier (1966a, b), Sticht (1964), and Sticht and Foulke (1966a, b) indicate that the speed to peak intensity and from peak to disappearance may be basic to the presence and direction of an onset–termination difference.

Using the same rapid rise and decay signals as in the time-judgment experiments, Goldstone (1968b) found the auditory–visual difference for onset and termination RT, with the latter slightly greater, indicating that a slower response at the periphery cannot account for the intersensory difference in time judgments. Onset RT was faster than termination RT for both modes. Again this was true for a wide range of social, mental, and pharmacologic conditions (Goldstone, 1964; Rutkin, 1966).

These last experiments seem to indicate a more central relative slowness for visual processing as the explanation of the intersensory difference. It appears that the auditory–visual difference both in RT and in duration judgment remain separate psychotemporal facts.

THE NEW INTERSENSORY DIFFERENCE: MORE INFORMATION IS TRANSMITTED WITH AUDITORY THAN WITH VISUAL TIME JUDGMENTS

During the investigation of temporal judgment and psychopathology, we chanced upon another intersensory difference in human timing behavior. We had become interested in the excessive intrasubject response variability that consistently accompanied schizophrenic patients to the laboratory, and we had speculated about the possible presence of greater cognitive deficit in visual judgments by schizophrenic patients than those derived from auditory input (Goldstone, in press; Lhamon & Goldstone, 1970). The measure of *information transmission* or *uncertainty reduction* was used to study the amount of correspondence in the input–output matching by schizophrenic and healthy subjects.

First, we reexamined the direct comparison data by computing *information transmission*[3] $[U(x:y)]$ measures for each of the mixed intramodal and cross-modal conditions by patient and control subjects, using three standard-variable interduration intervals ranging from 1.00 to 4.00 sec. It was hypothesized that (*a*) schizophrenic patients would show a deficit in information transmitted; (*b*) the patients would show a greater relative deficit in $U(x:y)$ with visual judgments; and (*c*) there would be more $U(x:y)$ with intramodal than with cross-modal judgments (Lhamon & Goldstone, 1970). A general and pervasive intersensory difference in $U(x:y)$ appeared immediately upon examination of the control data and is reported in Experiment 1.

Second, Experiment 2 was undertaken as a replication with new data that included only intramodal judgments and extended the standard-variable interduration interval range (.50–6.00 sec.). We wished to determine if the observed auditory–visual difference in $U(x:y)$ would be present in the replication and if the intersensory difference would be consistent across an extended range of interduration intervals which changes the temporal properties of storage.

Finally, Experiment 3 investigated the question of whether the amount of stimulation was a primary determinant of the amount of auditory and visual information transmission; the $U(x:y)$ was studied with the direct comparison of vacant intervals bounded by clicks and flashes. As reported earlier, the direct comparison of vacant intervals failed to reproduce the intersensory difference in average response level (Goldstone, 1964) obtained with the direct comparison of durations filled with continuous stimulation (Goldstone & Goldfarb, 1964b). We

---

[3] Notational system after Garner (1962).

now wished to determine if the intersensory difference in $U(x:y)$ would be eliminated in the judgment of vacant intervals where the lights and sounds are simply marker signals.

METHODS

Electronic systems activated and controlled auditory and visual signals that provided durations filled with continuous light or sound, or empty intervals bounded by flashes or clicks with an accurate and reliable range of .01–1.99 sec. Experiments 1 and 3 used a preset counter to control the timing of filled and vacant intervals, and the clicks and flashes were produced by a mercury-wetted contact relay with an approximate make–break speed of $500\,\mu sec$. The filled durations of Experiment 2 were programmed by a magnetic tape which contained the sequence of durations in the form of 10-kHz trigger signals recorded from a low-frequency function generator turned on and off by a universal counter–timer. An audiooscillator and low-frequency function generator produced 1-kHz tones at 84 and 82 dB (.0002 $dyne/cm^2$), respectively, for Experiments 1 and 2; the clicks which enclosed the vacant intervals were produced by a 1.5-V battery through a 100-Ω resistor. Sounds were delivered through high-fidelity headphones. The lights were produced by four 4-W fluorescent tubes which illuminated a 1-inch opal glass circular target 43 inches from the subjects' eyes; this produced a blue-white light of approximately 5.5 and 3.0 apparent footcandles for Experiments 1 and 2, respectively. The lights and sounds for Experiment 1 were equated for subjective intensity with different subjects, using a cross-modality matching technique; in Experiment 2 the sounds were subjectively slightly more intense than the lights. The same light source provided the illumination for the visual filled and unfilled conditions, but the light flashes for the visual unfilled intervals appeared dimmer because of their very brief exposure.

The experiments employed 140 volunteer subjects (63 female; 77 male), respectively, between the ages of 16 and 27 years for Experiment 1 (median, 20 years) and Experiment 3 (median 23 years), and between the ages of 19 and 51 years for Experiment 2 (median 27 years). All had at least a high-school education.

The experiments used a 9-category response scale, and the subjects judged the second and variable member of a pair of durations as *less, equal,* or *more* than the first and standard member; these durations consisted of continuous and filled auditory or visual signals, or vacant and unfilled intervals bounded by discrete light flashes or sound clicks. All three experiments employed a 1.00-sec. standard duration, followed by a constant interduration interval and a variable duration of .60, .80, 1.00, 1.20, or 1.40 sec. The subjects compared the second variable duration with the first standard duration using the following 9-category response scale: 1, very much shorter or less; 2, much shorter or less; 3, shorter or less; 4, slightly shorter or less; 5, equal; 6, slightly longer or more; 7, longer or more; 8, much longer or more; 9, very much longer or more.

A stimulus–response (S–R; x–y) matrix was constructed for each condition for every subject, and measures of information transmission or contingent uncertainty $[U(x:y)]$ were computed. The $U(x:y)$ measures were treated with analysis of variance procedures.

Experiment 1 (Filled Durations)

This experiment explored the intersensory difference in information transmission with cross-modal and intramodal comparisons of filled durations separated by 1.00, 2.00, or 4.00 sec.; all cross-modal and intramodal conditions were included haphazardly in a single block of 200 pairs and each S received only one of the three interduration intervals. The five standard-variable combinations were presented ten times for each of the following four sense-mode orders: audition, standard-audition variable; vision, standard-vision variable; audition, standard-vision variable; vision, standard-audition variable. All pairs were separated by a 5-sec. interval. Sixty Ss were divided into three equal groups with a standard-variable interduration interval of either 1.00, 2.00, or 4.00 sec. Analysis of variance included *interduration interval* (1.00, 2.00, 4.00 sec.) as the between-Ss factor and *sense mode* (audition or vision judged) and *sense-mode sequence* (cross-modal–intramodal) as within-S factors (Table I).

TABLE I

Summary of Analysis of Variance: Experiment 1 (Filled Durations)

Source of variation	df	MS	F
Interduration interval (*I*)	2	0.5848	3.08
Error (*b*)	57	0.1901	
Sense mode (*M*)	1	1.8529	65.71*
Intramodal–Cross-modal (*Y*)	1	0.8712	35.56*
M x *Y*	1	0.3463	14.67*
I x *M*	2	0.0108	0.38
I x *Y*	2	0.0127	0.52
I x *M* x *Y*	2	0.0338	1.43
Error$_1$ (*w*) *M/I*	57	0.0282	
Error$_2$ (*w*) *Y/I*	57	0.0245	
Error$_3$ (*w*) *MY/I*	57	0.0236	

*$p < .001$.

Experiment 2 (Filled Durations: Replication)

This experiment was an attempt to replicate Experiment 1 with a sufficient alteration of design to allow more credible generalization from a confirming result. Here Ss received only audition–audition or vision–vision pairs using the same five standard-variable combinations; no cross-modal judgments were obtained, and Ss were tested with just one sense. A control interduration interval (2.00 sec.) in common with Experiment 1 was included for all Ss to allow direct comparison of results; the range of interduration intervals was extended with a short (.50 sec.) and long (6.00 sec.) interval. The Ss received 100 pairs of either the .50 or 6.00-sec. interval and 100 pairs of the 2.00-sec. control interval successively with the order counterbalanced. The five standard-variable combinations were presented haphazardly 20 times for each of the following four interduration interval orders: .50 followed by 2.00 sec.; 2.00 followed by .50 sec.; 6.00 followed by 2.00 sec.; 2.00 followed by 6.00 sec. All pairs were separated by a 10-sec. interval.

Forty Ss were divided into two equal groups: audition, standard-audition variable, and vision, standard-vision variable. These groups were subdivided further into four five-S groups for each sense mode representing the four

TABLE II

Summary of Analysis of Variance: Experiment 2 (Filled Durations: Replication)

Source of variation	df	MS	F
Sense mode (M)	1	1.7468	13.55*
Long–short interval condition (I)	1	0.0300	0.23
Control interval position (O)	1	0.6516	5.06
M × I	1	0.0122	0.10
M × O	1	0.0875	0.68
I × O	1	0.1053	0.82
M × I × O	1	0.0514	0.40
Error (b)	32	0.1289	
Long–short or control interval (C)	1	0.0053	0.23
C × M	1	0.0199	0.87
I × C	1	0.0045	0.20
O × C	1	0.0207	0.90
M × I × C	1	0.0028	0.12
M × O × C	1	0.0044	0.19
I × O × C	1	0.0046	0.20
M × I × O × C	1	0.0012	0.05
Error (w)	32	0.0229	

* $p < .001$.

interduration interval orders. The analysis of variance included *sense mode* (audition, vision), *long–short interduration interval* (.50 + 2.00 sec., 6.00 + 2.00 sec.), and *position of control interval* (2.00 sec. first, 2.00 sec. last) as between-*S* factors, and *interduration interval* (long–short, or control) as the within-*S* factor (Table II).

Experiment 3 (Unfilled Intervals)

This experiment was conducted to determine whether the findings of Experiments 1 and 2 were dependent upon the presence of continuous stimulation. The five standard-variable combinations were delivered exactly as in Experiment 1, but here *S*s judged silence or darkness bounded by clicks or flashes within and between sense modes. Forty *S*s were divided into two equal groups with a standard-variable interduration interval of either 2.00 or 4.00 sec. The analysis of variance included the 2.00- and 4.00-sec. interduration interval groups of Experiment 1 with the similar data from Experiment 3 to permit comparison of filled and unfilled conditions; *filled–unfilled* and *interduration interval* were the between-*S*s factors and *sense mode* and *sense-mode sequence* were the within-*S* factors (Table III).

TABLE III

Summary of Analysis of Variance: Experiment 3 (Unfilled Intervals)

Source of variation	df	MS	F
Filled–Unfilled (F)	1	2.4194	11.33**
Interduration interval (I)	1	0.2926	1.60
$F \times I$	1	0.1835	0.86
Error (b)	76	0.2135	
Sense mode (M)	1	1.8001	72.88***
Intramodal–cross-modal (Y)	1	1.2508	40.61***
$M \times Y$	1	0.4585	19.27***
$F \times M$	1	0.0989	4.00*
$I \times M$	1	0.0003	0.01
$F \times I \times M$	1	0.0167	0.68
$F \times Y$	1	0.0007	0.02
$I \times Y$	1	0.0010	0.03
$F \times I \times Y$	1	0.0510	1.66
$F \times M \times Y$	1	0.0438	1.84
$I \times M \times Y$	1	0.0047	0.20
$F \times I \times M \times Y$	1	0.0214	0.90
Error$_1$ (w) M/FI	76	0.0247	
Error$_2$ (w) Y/FI	76	0.0308	
Error$_3$ (w) MY/FI	76	0.0238	

* $p < .05$.　　** $p < .005$.　　*** $p < .001$.

RESULTS

Figure 1 displays the *mean U(x:y)* for all conditions of Experiment 1 which studied information transmission in the comparative judgment of durations filled with continuous lights and sounds using intramodal and cross-modal judgments and three interduration intervals. More information was transmitted with auditory judgments ($F_{1/57}$ = 65.71, p < .001) with both the intramodal and cross-modal comparisons for the three interduration intervals. As expected, $U(x:y)$ was greater for intramodal than for cross-modal judgments ($F_{1/57}$ = 35.56, p < .001), and the intersensory difference was larger within than between sense modes (*sense mode* × *intramodal–cross-modal,* $F_{1/57}$ = 14.67, p < .001). The intramodal comparisons produced an intersensory difference in $U(x:y)$ that ranged from .20 to .30 bit, while the cross-modal difference between

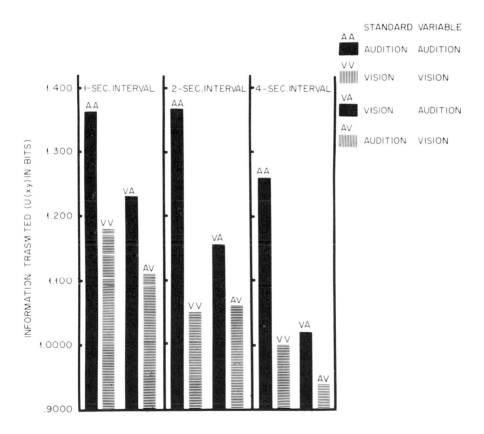

Fig. 1. Mean information transmitted in bits for the intramodal and cross-modal judgments of each interduration interval for Experiment 1 (filled durations).

the senses was about .10 bit. It is especially interesting to note that 17 of the 20 subjects in the 1.00-sec. interduration interval group, all 20 subjects in the 2.00-sec. group, and 17 of the 20 subjects in the 4.00-sec. group revealed the intersensory difference in $U(x{:}y)$ for the intramodal judgments. This reexamination of old data showed in striking fashion that auditory temporal processing was more efficient than visual; auditory input–output matching resulted in a more consistent representation of the temporal magnitude of the signal.

The second experiment was conducted as a replication of the first with the range of interduration intervals extended from 1.00–4.00 sec. to .50–6.00 sec., thereby altering the temporal characteristics of storage. Only the subjects' intramodal judgments were studied. Significant intersensory differences in $U(x{:}y)$ ($F_{1/32} = 13.55$, $p < .001$) were again found which, as in Experiment 1, were independent of interduration interval conditions. In Fig. 2 the *mean $U(x{:}y)$* measures of Experiments 1 and 2 for the intramodal judgments combined over all interduration interval conditions are compared. The results of the two experiments are similar, revealing an approximately .30-bit difference between the senses, which confirms an auditory–visual difference in $U(x{:}y)$ for comparative judgments of filled durations.

The third experiment was undertaken to examine the importance of the temporal magnitude of stimulation in determining the amount of information transmitted in comparative judgments of time, as well as in producing the auditory–visual difference in $U(x{:}y)$.

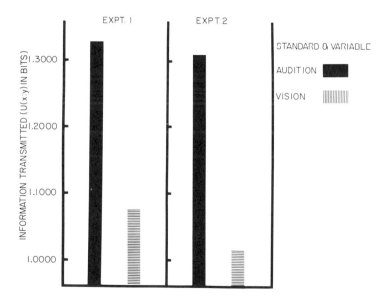

Fig. 2. Mean information transmitted in bits for the intramodal judgments of Experiment 1 (filled durations) and Experiment 2 (filled durations: replication) combined over all interduration intervals.

We sought to determine whether this intersensory difference is a product of a peripheral level of processing associated with the registration and regulation of input, or of a more central property of processing at a higher level of cognitive analysis. The subjects compared vacant intervals bounded by clicks and flashes within and between sense modes using two interduration intervals (2.00 and 4.00 sec.) identical with those employed in Experiment 1; data from Experiment 1 were combined with those of Experiment 3 to permit the comparison of $U(x{:}y)$ for filled and vacant time.

The *mean* $U(x{:}y)$ for the intramodal and cross-modal unfilled judgments of Experiment 3 is given in Fig. 3. It was surprising to discover that the judgment of empty intervals bounded by clicks and flashes was accompanied by greater $U(x{:}y)$ than the judgment of durations of continuous stimulation ($F_{1/76} = 11.33$, $p < .005$); a comparison of Figs. 1 and 3 shows that this filled–unfilled difference was present for all experimental conditions. It is also apparent from Fig. 3 that the auditory–visual difference in $U(x{:}y)$ was present for unfilled as well as filled time ($F_{1/76} = 72.88$, $p < .001$), although the intersensory difference was slightly greater for the durations filled with continuous stimulation (*sense mode* x *filled–unfilled*, $F_{1/76} = 4.00, p < .05$).

More information was transmitted when judgment was based upon input initiated along the auditory channel than when based upon visual stimulation,

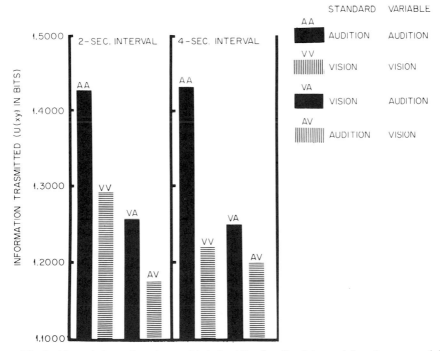

Fig. 3. Mean information transmitted in bits for the intramodal and cross-modal judgments of both interduration intervals for Experiment 3 (unfilled durations).

regardless of whether the temporal magnitude of the stimuli consumed the entire duration processed, or whether the stimuli merely acted as signal markers which defined the boundaries of vacant judged intervals. Indeed, the unexpected finding that the empty durations produced greater $U(x:y)$ than did the filled intervals suggests the possibility that the temporal processing of continuous auditory and visual input involves more noise in the analytic system than when stimulation is limited to marking boundaries.

Also, in confirmation of the first experiment, more information was transmitted within than between sense modes ($F_{1/76}$ = 40.61, $p <$ .001) and the intersensory difference in $U(x:y)$ was greater for intramodal than for cross-modal judgments (*sense mode* x *intramodal–cross-modal, $F_{1/76}$* = 19.27, $p <$ .001); these findings were independent of the filled or unfilled status of the durations processed.

These three studies point to the presence of a third auditory–visual difference in human temporal functioning; more information is transmitted with comparative judgments of the duration of sounds than with comparative judgments of lights. That this is an independent finding and not a direct product of the intersensory difference in average response level is shown by the facts that (*a*) it is largest for intramodal judgments which did *not* produce the other auditory–visual difference, and (*b*) it was present for unfilled intervals bounded by light and sound signal markers, while the other intersensory difference vanished under the same conditions.

This new auditory–visual difference has been demonstrated at present only with the method of comparison using healthy adult subjects. It was confirmed recently with the same psychophysical procedure using ambulatory and hospitalized schizophrenic patients as well as healthy subjects who had ingested 200 mg. of secobarbital (Lhamon & Goldstone, 1970). It has not been established clearly that the auditory–visual difference in information transmitted would be obtained as generally with the method of absolute judgment, however. In the only study along this line (Lhamon & Goldstone, 1970) the intersensory difference was attenuated with the absolute method for healthy adults but not with schizophrenic patients. Since these two psychophysical contexts involve different processing requirements, it would be of interest to study the developmental unfolding of this auditory–visual difference in information transmission using both the comparison and absolute methods. One could speculate, for example, that the difference between the senses using the method of single stimuli is greatest for the youngest children, gradually diminishing with development, while the comparison method is less influenced by age.

COMMENT

Now we have three auditory–visual differences in human timing behavior without an obvious explanation, where once we had only two that we did not understand, adding another cross-modal curiosity to our list. It is distinctly possible that we are dealing with little more than some trivial, unrelated temporal properties of audition and vision limited to the narrow set of stimulating conditions which defined the contexts of the experiments here cited. We do not think that this is the case. The fact that people judged short sounds as longer than physically equivalent lights seemed to withstand the test of varied contextual and organismic factors, and the auditory–visual difference in simple RT seems to have withstood the test of time; it is too early to speculate about the generality of the new intersensory difference in the amount of information tranmitted, but it is there.

Rather than take these three intersensory differences as separate unrelated facts, let us consider the possibility that they may be connected functionally in the information-processing systems that combine to produce temporal cognition. It is possible that we are seeing sense-mode related levels of cognition that may differ functionally in quality, efficiency, and complexity.

A first assumption, which seems credible on the basis of available evidence, is that these auditory–visual differences are produced at central processing levels which yield sense-mode-specific auditory–cognitive analyses and visual–cognitive analyses that may be functional. It is less likely that these intersensory differences are determined by peripheral sensory factors located at the level of input information registration and regulation; these differences seem to be sense-mode specific but cognitive in nature. Hence, the sense-mode-related cognitive systems can be present, intact, and operating, while the input information is lacking, as in dreams or in people born blind who demonstrate the capacity for typical visual–cognitive processing (Kielkopf, 1969).

In attempting to interpret these findings, one is struck with the fact that the intersensory differences in RT and information transmission suggest greater auditory efficiency in processing. This suggests that the auditory modality may be a more effective and even a superior entrance to the temporal analyzer and that unpatterned sound may be a more adequate, natural, and appropriate stimulus for temporal processing than unpatterned light. Indeed, one could make a good case for affirmation of the first point outside the dimension of time; recent studies of short-term memory have consistently shown a superiority for auditory presentation using verbal information (Murdock, 1969).

While we may be able to accept greater efficiency of function with aural presentation, the issue of superiority is another question. Our intuition tells us that the visual–cognitive systems involve processing at more complex and more abstract analytic levels. The lower efficiency seen in slower RT and less information transmitted may be the consequence of additional steps and potential noise in a more complex, higher-resolution cognitive system. The following general ideas will be proposed as points of departure: First, temporal cognition is primarily a product of information processing at the auditory–cognitive level; second, visual temporal processing requires transformation from the visual to the auditory–cognitive system for analysis requiring more steps and involving a less direct route; third, the more direct and less complex auditory system develops first and suffers last and least due to pathologies of information processing (for example, organic brain disease, schizophrenia). In general it is assumed that visual information processing involves a higher, more complex, and more abstract cognitive level (a) requiring more time for processing (longer RT), (b) involving more noise which may trim input information magnitude (lights shorter than sounds), and (c) involving more steps and noise and thus reducing the information transmitted [less $U(x:y)$].

There seems to be enough evidence at present (Norman, 1969) to support the idea that visual processing is less direct than auditory, involving separate storage, and requiring the additional steps of transformation or conversion back through auditory storage; the intersensory differences in human timing behavior seem compatible with this point of view.

As a result of our initial attempts to apply these findings to a schema of sense-mode-related levels of cognitive functioning we found ourselves thinking about the senses in a rather clinical fashion. Since man's capacity to deal with input information is so very limited in contrast to his capacity to analyze stored data, it seemed rather foolish to have different senses as doorways for input entrance that were functionally equivalent from a cognitive standpoint, and that acted merely as specialized receivers and transducers. While logically equivalent auditory and visual durations probably end up in a similar format, it would seem desirable that the two senses have a nonredundant capability. It appears unreasonable to assume that the senses are functionally redundant and it is unsafe to dismiss the possibility that the properties of processing are dependent upon signal modality and stimulus characteristics.

The metaphorical expression of cognitive analyses that portray high levels of abstraction such as appreciation, understanding, and agreement seem to employ "visual" language (that is, "men of vision," "I see," "look at it this way," "don't plunge into it blindly," "these are my views,"); one of the few aural expressions involves "telling time." The measurement of intelligence, personality, and neuropathology typically involves tests of visual cognition, and Guilford (1967) has suggested that *sense mode* may be required as another dimension of intelligence to account for separate auditory, visual, and kinesthetic factors. Finally, it seems as if vision holds a supraordinate position in the determination of truth, and there appears to be a tendency to transform information into visual form to achieve higher levels of cognitive resolution—the oscilloscope and the visual model are examples from science, while the precedence of the eyewitness over hearsay in the courtroom is an example from public policy.

In development, acoustic language is learned first and unfolds in a natural fashion without requiring formal education, and verbal–aural concepts seem to be more effectively processed at early stages of language development, as seen in the "bow-wow," "tick-tock," and "choo-choo." Our time studies (Goldstone & Goldfarb, 1966) showed (*a*) that auditory-temporal judgment appeared prior to visual judgment, and (*b*) that there is a prior auditory-to-visual cross-modal transfer effect. It is as if an earlier auditory–cognitive system is the necessary requirement for the development of subsequent visual processing; it seems reasonable that the system which appears first (audition) should be less complex with fewer steps and less potential clutter than the later cognitive system (vision), which may require the participation of those structures which emerged earliest.

This led us to wonder about the efficiency of auditory temporal processing which yielded more information transmitted. It seemed sensible to assume that the more efficient system of the two, which also developed first, was the simpler system, and that increased complexity of processing included added steps and more elaborate rules of analysis. While resolution could be at a higher level of abstraction, this would be at the expense of additional processing time and greater potential noise. The price paid for the higher level of analysis may be a cognitive system in a more delicate balance with greater vulnerability to interference from external and internal sources. If this is the case, then interference due to schizophrenia and organic brain disease should show a predominant deficit in the visual–cognitive system when processing required this level of analysis. This position is in substantial accord with Ribot's law regarding the course of deterioration—interference should reverse the process of development, with those functions suffering first and most being those that either matured or were learned last.

Although it has been suggested (Venables, 1964) that schizophrenia is accompanied by a relatively greater disturbance in the auditory sphere, this conclusion was based upon the results of simple sensory–motor studies such as flash-and-click thresholds, simple reaction time (Sutton, Hakarem, Zubin, & Portnoy, 1961), and physiologic orienting responses (Zahn, Rosenthal, & Lawler, 1962), rather than upon higher levels of cognitive functioning that might require visual processing. Also, the predominance of auditory hallucinations in schizophrenic patients is often viewed as evidence of an auditory–cognitive deficit. However, if one postulates a derangement of the more complex, higher-resolution visual–cognitive system with schizophrenia, then the auditory hallucinations may be taken as an attempt at restitution at a more primitive and regressed level of information processing and display.

A recent study (Lhamon & Goldstone, 1970) showed the greatest impairment of information transmission in schizophrenic patients with the absolute judgment of visual durations using dense stimulus series and narrow input ranges. Unfortunately, no differential effect due to sense mode was obtained with the method of comparison. Hence, partial confirmation of the predicted greater visual impairment was obtained, but the relationship between schizophrenia and sense-mode-related cognitive functioning is determined in part by the psychophysical context.

Only one study has been completed with patients suffering from organic brain disease. Schwartz (1965) compared auditory and visual timing behaviors of victims of a St. Louis viral encephalitis epidemic with those of schizophrenic patients and healthy controls, using the methods of production, reproduction, and reaction time. He found that the patients with brain disease had more significantly impaired reaction time to the visual signals, and revealed greater intrasubject response variability in the production and reproduction of visual durations than did the other two groups; the schizophrenics also differed more from the healthy controls in visual production and reproduction, although both sense modes yielded greater variability with both patient groups. This again suggests greater interference with visual cognition accompanying both schizophrenia and organic brain disease.

To pursue the functional and clinical implications of these temporal intersensory differences further, additional research is required that will undoubtedly keep us in the cross-modal business for some time to come. The new auditory–visual difference in information transmission has particular appeal because of its relevance to the cognitive impairment which we know accompanies pathology. At the very basic level, it will be necessary to learn about the specific effects of altered context upon this new auditory–visual difference (for example, stimulus intensity, psychophysical method, stimulus range and density, the number of stimulus and response elements in the input–output matrix). Cross-modal pooling can be studied through concurrent and successive presentation of auditory and visual durations with stimulus intensity and attention focus varied.

If our speculations about Ribot's law have any merit, visual cognition should reveal earlier and more severe impairment than auditory with natural and premature aging; children with maturation disorders which are typically diagnosed as minimal brain dysfunction or congenital dyslexia should also show a relative deficit in visual–cognitive processing. It would be of particular interest to us to follow-up on the lead which suggests a possibility that there may be something similar about the cognitive impairment in schizophrenia and the deficit noted in patients with organic brain disease. Finally, we would like to examine the effects of drugs upon auditory and visual temporal cognition.

At this point it appears as if these auditory–visual differences in human timing behavior may be related to levels of cognition in such a way that they may provide a vehicle for our reentry into the field of temporal psychopathology. This would complete a full circle, return us to our original intent, and reverse the process of serendipity.

References

Behar, I., & Bevan, W. Analysis of the prime psychophysical judgment. *Perceptual and Motor Skills,* 1960, **10,** 82.

Behar, I., & Bevan, W. The perceived duration of auditory and visual intervals: Cross-modal comparison and interaction. *American Journal of Psychology,* 1961, **74,** 17–26.

Ehrensing, R. H., Stokes, P. E., Pick, G. R., Goldstone, S., & Lhamon, W. T. The effect of alcohol on auditory and visual time perception. *Quarterly Journal of Studies in Alcoholism,* 1970, **31,** 851–860.

Elliott, R. Simple visual and simple auditory reaction time: A comparison. *Psychonomic Science,* 1968, **10,** 335–336.

Garner, W. R. *Uncertainty and structure as psychological concepts.* New York: Wiley, 1962.

Goldfarb, J. L. Time judgment and schizophrenia: Intersensory factors. Unpublished doctoral dissertation, University of Houston, 1963

Goldfarb, J. L., & Goldstone, S. Properties of sound and the auditory-visual difference in time judgment. *Perceptual and Motor Skills,* 1964, **19,** 606.

Goldstone, S. The time sense in normal and psychopathologic states. Multilithed report of progress, USPHS Grant MH 01121, October 1964.

Goldstone, S. Production and reproduction of duration: Intersensory comparisons. *Perceptual and Motor Skills,* 1968, **26,** 755–760.　(a)

Goldstone, S. Reaction time to onset and termination of lights and sounds. *Perceptual and Motor Skills,* 1968, **27,** 1023–1029.　(b)

Goldstone, S. The variability of temporal judgment in psychopathology. In M. Keitzman & J. Zubin (Eds.), *Objective indicators of psychopathology.* New York: Academic Press, in press.

Goldstone, S., & Goldfarb, J. L. Judgment of filled and unfilled durations: Intersensory factors. *Perceptual and Motor Skills,* 1963, **17,** 763–774.

Goldstone, S., & Goldfarb, J. L. Auditory and visual time judgment. *Journal of General Psychology,* 1964, **70,** 369–387.　(a)

Goldstone, S., & Goldfarb, J. L. Direct comparison of auditory and visual durations. *Journal of Experimental Psychology,* 1964, **67,** 483–485.　(b)

Goldstone, S., & Goldfarb, J. L. The perception of time by children. In A. H. Kidd & J. L. Rivoire (Eds.), *Perceptual development in children.* New York: International Universities Press, 1966.

Goldstone, S., & Kirkham, J. E. The effects of secobarbital and dextroamphetamine upon time judgment: Intersensory factors. *Psychopharmacologia,* 1968, **13,** 65–73.

Goldstone, S., Boardman, W. K., & Lhamon, W. T. Intersensory comparisons of temporal judgments. *Journal of Experimental Psychology,* 1959, **57,** 243–248.　(a)

Goldstone, S., Jernigan, C., Lhamon, W. T., & Boardman, W. K. A further note on intersensory differences in temporal judgment. *Perceptual and Motor Skills,* 1959, **9,** 252.　(b)

Grier, J. B. Auditory reaction time as a function of stimulus intensity and rise time. *Psychonomic Science,* 1966, **6,** 307–308.　(a)

Grier, J. B. Reaction time to "tone-off". *Psychonomic Science,* 1966, **5,** 385–386.　(b)

Guilford, J. P. *The nature of human intelligence.* New York: McGraw-Hill, 1967.

Johnson, H. M. Reaction time measurements. *Psychological Bulletin,* 1923, **20,** 562–589.

Kielkopf, C. F. The pictures in the head of a man born blind. *Philosophical and Phenomenological Research,* 1969, **28,** 501–513.

Lhamon, W. T., & Goldstone, S. The time sense: Estimation of one second durations by schizophrenic patients. *Archives of Neurology and Psychiatry*, 1956, **76**, 625–629.

Lhamon, W. T., & Goldstone, S. Temporal information processing in schizophrenia. Paper presented at the annual meeting of the American Psychiatric Association, San Francisco, California, May, 1970.

Lhamon, W. T., Goldstone, S., & Goldfarb, J. L. The psychopathology of time judgment. In P. H. Hoch & J. Zubin (Eds.), *The psychopathology of perception.* New York: Grune & Stratton, 1965.

Murdock, B. B. Where or when: Modality effects as a function of temporal and spatial distribution. *Journal of Verbal Learning and Verbal Behavior*, 1969, **8**, 378–383.

Norman, D. A. *Memory and attention.* New York: Wiley, 1969.

Rutkin, R. Time judgment of delinquent and neglected children. Unpublished doctoral dissertation, University of Houston, 1966.

Schwartz, J. T. Sequelae of St. Louis Viral Encephalitis: Psychomotor and time judgment measures. Unpublished manuscript, Baylor University College of Medicine, Spring 1965.

Sticht, T. G. Reaction time to cutaneous onset and offset stimulation. *Perceptual and Motor Skills*, 1964, **19**, 611–614.

Sticht, T. G., & Foulke, E. Reaction time to the onset and offset of electrocutaneous stimuli as a function of rise and decay time. *Perception and Psychophysics*, 1966, **1**, 361–362. (a)

Sticht, T. G., & Foulke, E. reaction time to electrocutaneous onset and offset stimulation. *Psychonomic Science*, 1966, **4**, 213–214. (b)

Sutton, S., Hakarem, G., Zubin, J., & Portnoy, M. The effect of shift of sensory modality on serial reaction-time: A comparison of schizophrenics and normals. *American Journal of Psychology*, 1961, **74**, 224–232.

Tanner, T. A., Patton, R. M., & Atkinson, R. C. Intermodality judgments of signal duration. *Psychonomic Science*, 1965, **2**, 271–272.

Tanner, T. A., Patton, R. M., & Atkinson, R. C. The effect of signal intensity on comparative judgments of auditory durations. *Psychonomic Science*, 1966, **4**, 353–354.

Teichner, W. H. Recent studies of simple reaction time. *Psychological Bulletin*, 1954, **51**, 128–149.

Venables, P. H. Input dysfunction in schizophrenia. In B. Maher (Ed.), *Progress in experimental personality research.* Vol. 1. New York: Academic Press, 1964.

Webster, F. R., Goldstone, S., & Webb, W. W. Time judgment and schizophrenia: Psychophysical method as a relevant contextual factor. *Journal of Psychology*, 1962, **54**, 159–164.

Wells, G. R. The influence of stimulus duration on reaction time. *Psychological Monographs*, 1913, **15**, No. 5.

Woodrow, M. Reactions to the cessation of stimuli and their nervous mechanism. *Psychological Review*, 1915, **22**, 423–452.

Woodworth, R. S., & Schlosberg, H. *Experimental psychology.* (Rev. ed.) New York: Holt, 1954.

Wright, D. J., Goldstone, S., & Boardman, W. K. Time judgment and schizophrenia: Step interval as a relevant contextual factor. *Journal of Psychology*, 1962, **54**, 33–38.

Zahn, T. P., Rosenthal, D., & Lawler, W. G. G.S.R. Orienting reactions to visual and auditory stimuli in chronic schizophrenia and normal subjects. Paper presented to Society for Psychophysiological Research, Denver, Colorado, 1962.

COMMENT

Joseph A. Steger

As Goldstone and Lhamon point out, Helson's notions of relativity of judgment and his emphasis on contextual factors, as well as his personal advice early in their research, led them to expand their experimental efforts to the systematic and vigorous program of research it is today. Because I worked as Helson's research assistant for several years, I know well his conviction that one must explore all the stimulus dimensions in a wide range of values and not generalize from single experiments. However, because the studies on which I am to comment are so extensive, I am obliged to limit my discussion to only a few aspects of their findings and theorizing.

Goldstone and Lhamon have demonstrated with several response techniques, time durations, intensities, and subject populations that sounds having temporal intervals equal to those of lights are judged to be of a longer duration than lights. More recently they have demonstrated that the auditory channel is more efficient than the visual channel in judgments of temporal duration. What does one make of this apparent inherent difference in our ability to estimate time durations via different sensory modes?

The authors suggest that these differences in temporal judgment are sense-mode related but reflect a *central* processing difference. They accentuate this position by the use of the terms "auditory-cognitive" and "visual-cognitive" system. They theorize that the visual information processing is more complex and abstract and requires more time for processing than the auditory. They have also demonstrated that the auditory system unfolds prior to the visual, and they suggest that the earlier development of the auditory-cognitive system is a prerequisite to the development of the visual-cognitive system. Their research and theory has implications for many areas of psychological research.

Let us consider first the relation of Goldstone and Lhamon's findings in timing behavior to adaptation-level (AL) theory. It is apparent that when one conducts research using cross-modal comparisons, one is dealing with at least two ALs. There is, however, another consideration. Since the auditory system has been shown to develop earlier, there is a more well-established AL for timing auditory judgments than for judging visual duration. Let us assume that this well-established normative AL interacts with the specific AL for the experimental condition. I am postulating that we have a kind of residual AL, in Helson's terms (or personal AL, as Bevan has suggested), that interacts with the focal AL, and well may partly establish the specific AL for the given focal conditions. This personal AL is not well established for judgments of duration of visual stimuli until a chronological age later than that at which the personal auditory AL develops. There is support for this notion in the research reported by Goldstone and Lhamon showing that children who received the auditory followed by visual materials performed much better on the visual judgments than did children who received the visual first, then the auditory materials. In fact, the visual–auditory testing sequence impaired the performance on the auditory time-estimation task.

In summary, I am arguing that the results of these studies of Goldstone and Lhamon, as well as some of the work of Bevan (Turner & Bevan, 1962) and myself (Steger & O'Reilly, 1970) suggest the expansion of AL theory in the direction of multiple anchoring or multiple ALs. Not only simultaneously interacting situational ALs, but also personal or residual ALs must be taken into account in future research in judgment.

I would like now to consider another implication of the Goldstone–Lhamon research. They argue that the difference in time estimation is largely a central processing phenomenon. They relate this argument to such clinical phenomena as dyslexia, in that the dyslexic child should have a relatively poorer visual-cognitive processing ability than his normal counterpart. I would like to add support to their notion that the difference in timing judgment is centrally produced and not a function of end-organ specificity. However, I am going to differ with them in suggesting that it is not simply a loss in visual-cognitive ability that seems to define the dyslexic, nor for that matter most reading difficulties, but instead it is a poor *interaction* between the visual–cognitive and auditory–cognitive systems. Some asynchronism appears to be occurring between the inputs of these sense–cognition systems.

The finding, referred to earlier, that the children who received the visual–auditory sequence in Goldstone and Lhamon's experimental procedure had extremely poor performance, offers some evidence to support the notion that it is the *integration* of these systems and not just the absolute level of functioning of either the auditory or visual system that determines the overall performance. I am not arguing that if one of these sense-cognition systems is poorly developed, performance in reading will be normal. I am rather arguing that the *interaction* of these systems accounts for more of the failure to learn to read than the absolute ability in either the visual– or auditory–cognitive systems.

Two studies that have just been completed in conjunction with my colleague Vellutino (Steger & Vellutino, 1970) present, I believe, evidence in support of such an auditory–visual interaction hypothesis. In the first study, we had dyslexic and normal readers, ages 9 to 14 years, view simple black-and-white designs—a psi, a triangle, etc.—and three-digit numbers at 600 msec. in a tachistoscope. Each child was instructed to copy or draw what he saw. After he copied all the figures and numbers, he was tested on three-, four-, and five-letter words. Again, he was simply to copy, not read, these words. After he finished running through the list of 12 words, the words were shown again, and each child was asked to read them out loud. I shall not belabor you with all the experimental controls; suffice it to say that we used 34 normal and 34 dyslexic subjects.

The results of the design and number reproduction tasks are clear-cut. There was no difference between the normal or dyslexic children's performance. Thus, the visual–cognitive systems of both normals and dyslexics seem to be functioning equally well. However, as usual with much research, the question is not that easily answered. The analysis of the word reproduction showed that the normal readers' performance was better at copying the words than that of the poor readers. Hence, the results are somewhat equivocal in terms of answering whether it is the sensory deficit or central integration that is the locus of the reading disability. We felt, however, from the evidence that every dyslexic subject could correctly copy 3–4 times as many words as he could read, that we were still on the right track. We hypothesized that the dyslexic subject's performance on the word stimuli was hampered by his normal negative emotional reaction to verbal materials.

It should also be added that the normal readers had a decided advantage in the word-copying task, since they were familiar with most of the words.

Our second experiment was designed to get around the use of verbal materials and to test the auditory–visual integration hypothesis. In this paired-associates (PA) experiment, we designed geometric symbols that had no correspondence to our alphabet. We ran both dyslexic and normal subjects under three conditions of PAs. The first was visual–visual, where two geometric symbols were paired. Each subject was given seven associate trials for five symbol pairs. The second condition was auditory–auditory, where two sounds, such as a click and a pure tone, were paired. The same experimental trials were run as with the visual–visual condition. The third was the visual–auditory condition, where a geometric symbol was paired with a sound. Again, the same experimental trials as in the visual–visual were used. In summary then, each subject was run in a visual–visual, auditory–auditory, and visual–auditory PA task.

The results are very simple indeed. There was no difference in performance between the normal and dyslexic subjects in the visual–visual or auditory–auditory PA tasks. But there was a difference in performance in the visual–auditory task in that the normal subjects did perform significantly better than the dyslexic subjects. This, coupled with the finding that dyslexics could copy numbers and designs as well as normals, we see as evidence that dyslexia is not simply the result of a disability in the visual–cognitive system, but is a disability in the *integration* of the visual– and auditory–cognitive systems.

I think it is apparent how Helson's influence has manifested itself in Goldstone and Lhamon's work as well as in our research. This influence extends beyond theoretical issues and has its foundation in Helson's ability to define research problems and teach research skills.

REFERENCES

Steger, J. A., & O'Reilly, E. Simultaneously contrasting anchors. *Perception and Psychophysics,* 1970, **7,** 281–283.
Steger, J. A., & Vellutino, F. Two studies. Mimeographed manuscripts, State University of New York, 1970. (Copies available from J. A. Steger, SUNY at Albany, Department of Psychology, Albany, New York 12203.)
Turner, E. D., & Bevan, W. Simultaneous induction of multiple anchor effects in the judgment of form. *Journal of Experimental Psychology,* 1962, **64,** 589–592.

VI

Implications and Applications

INTRODUCTION

M. H. Appley

The contribution which follows was prepared after, rather than before, the symposium on AL theory. It is, in a sense, the joint product of the indicated authors and all the symposium participants. Campbell presented an outline of his intentions during the final session of the symposium and invited the participants to help him write the article. Whether due to his inspired leadership or the unusual nature of the group, a highly spirited 2-hr discussion ensued. The transcript of this discussion then formed the basis for the article that Brickman and Campbell prepared.

As the reader will soon discover, the authors focus upon political–economic–social implications and applications and present a highly imaginative blueprint for transforming laboratory-derived principles into possible real-world practices. They challenge society to "undertake an explicit, experimental commitment to maximize the greatest subjective good [read happiness] for the greatest number." Brickman and Campbell examine a number of social problems and a variety of social psychological, sociological, economic, and political theories in order to show how they might be illuminated by the application of hedonic AL theory. At the same time, they are careful to point out the possible pessimistic as well as optimistic implications of the relativistic interpretation of subjective experience and the need to consider possible nonrelativistic solutions to the "problem of happiness."

The provocative discussion by Brickman and Campbell, as McClelland so enthusiastically remarks in his later comments, provides any number of meaningful hypotheses for exploration by social scientists and planners and leaves little excuse for them to ignore the findings of psychologists as having no relevance for problems in the real world.

HEDONIC RELATIVISM
AND PLANNING THE GOOD SOCIETY[1]

Philip Brickman and Donald T. Campbell

In specifying only the *pursuit* of happiness as an inalienable right of man, the writers of our Declaration of Independence may well have expressed an intuitive understanding of adaptation-level (AL) theory (Helson, 1964), as indeed have certain philosophers since the time of the Stoics and the Epicureans. While happiness, as a state of subjective pleasure, may be the highest good, it seems to be distressingly transient. Even as we contemplate our satisfaction with a given accomplishment, the satisfaction fades, to be replaced finally by a new indifference and a new level of striving. This is, of course, a derivation from the fundamental postulate of AL theory, namely, that the subjective experience of stimulus input is a function not of the absolute level of that input but of the discrepancy between the input and past levels. As the environment becomes more pleasurable, subjective standards for gauging pleasurableness will rise, centering the neutral point of the pleasure–pain, sucess–failure continuum at a new level such that once again as many inputs are experienced as painful as are pleasurable (see for example, Beebe-Center, 1932).

In making this derivation, one must assume that the same laws governing the experience of specific sensations will also govern the experience of generalized symbolic rewards (namely, money, prestige), and also even the experience of qualitative pleasures that lack clear external or extrinsic reference scales. Not all these assumptions have been subject to test. It should be noted, however, that this derivation does *not* rest on the assumption that an increase in the input level for a given good must lead to a further increase in the level of aspiration (LA) for that good, as in achievement tasks (Lewin, Dembo, Festinger, & Sears, 1944). Even if LA does not increase, the important AL principle remains: Habituation will produce a decline in the subjective pleasurableness of the input.

If the planning of a society in which people are happy is a task of Sisyphus, it would seem no wonder that the only societies which have set themselves this

[1] Work on this article was supported in part by a grant from the Russell Sage Foundation and in part by National Science Foundation Grant GS-28178.

goal are the fictional creations called (sometimes scornfully) utopias. Interestingly enough, one of the main criticisms raised about proposals for ideal societies is that the utopias themselves are too static, too unchanging, too unchallenging, and that the inhabitants would soon grow bored and restless with the "ideal" conditions the authors find so desirable (see Dahrendorf, 1958). We may take it as given that if a society in which people are happy is possible at all, it will be possible only if it incorporates an understanding of AL phenomena, an understanding which past writers appear to have lacked.

And yet there is some sense in which society, without any such understanding of AL effects, has already begun this task of Sisyphus. Society has committed itself to providing for its members certain minimal levels of goods and services, for example, minimal levels of income and education. These levels may not be explicitly justified in terms of providing for happiness. Instead, mention may be made of fairness or equity, which, as we shall see, are related concepts. Where hedonic value is invoked to justify social programs, the value is much more likely to be one of minimizing discontent, which may be quite different from maximizing happiness. Thibaut and Kelley (1959) draw a distinction between comparison level for outcomes and comparison level for alternatives. A person will be satisfied if his outcomes are above his comparison level for outcomes (which may also be his general AL); however, even if his outcomes sink below this level and he becomes unhappy, he will not necessarily become violently discontent. That will occur only if his outcomes also sink below his comparison level for an alternative society, or a violent revolution. Thus, society's present commitment seems only to be keeping people above their comparison level for violent (or nonviolent) revolution, and not to keeping them above their AL for hedonic satisfaction. However, it is still true that the satisfaction with the level of goods society seeks as a minimal goal for all its members will decrease as a result of habituation, even if this subjective decrease does not bring it below people's comparison level for alternative societies. Thus, the long-term effects of any societal program to ameliorate the general condition or the specific condition of particular groups cannot be understood without reference to the temporal course of subjective AL, even if the specific programs limit themselves to talking about objective quantities like tons of food or number of available jobs.

Economists have long been very gloomy about measuring and comparing the subjective satisfactions that people derive from goods (see Mishan, 1960, for a review of the relevant area of welfare economics), because such measurement would involve assumptions that they feel are untenable (such as that people have equal capacity for satisfaction). But social psychologists have long been committed to trying to assess such satisfactions in laboratory settings and recently have shown interest in trying to assess more general satisfactions with the "quality of life" (see for example, Bradburn & Caplovitz, 1965). One of the purposes of this article will be to demonstrate that social psychology has accumulated enough knowledge in this regard to at least ask some of the right questions. This article will attempt to organize what we already know about the determinants of hedonic ALs, to assess the implications for social planning, and to point out new areas of relevant research.

Throughout this article there will run two themes: a pessimistic one, and an optimistic, or at least an ameliorative, one. The pessimistic theme is that the nature of AL phenomena condemns men to live on a hedonic treadmill, to seek new levels of stimulation merely to maintain old levels of subjective pleasure, to never achieve any kind of permanent happiness or satisfaction. The optimistic theme is that regardless of this ultimate impossibility, there are still wise and foolish ways to pursue happiness, both for societies and for individuals, and, from a planner's point of view, there are certain distributions of goods over time, persons, and modalities that will result in greater happiness than others. The pessimistic theme is that subjective pleasure is, as a state, by its very nature transient, and, as a goal, an ever-receding illusion. The optimistic theme is that society is overdue to undertake an explicit, experimental commitment to maximize the greatest subjective good for the greatest number. Whether the reader resonates more to the pessimistic theme or the optimistic theme is probably in large part a matter of his own philosophical bent. This article does not reconcile these two conflicting themes, except to the extent that it argues that no planning for the good society (a task for optimists) can be successful unless it is done by people who thoroughly understand the relativistic and elusive character of subjective pleasure (an understanding of pessimism).

It is important here to enter a disclaimer on the question of who should make decisions about the distribution of rewards. This article limits itself to a treatment of the probable consequences of different distributions. We do not mean to imply that social scientists should make the decisions as to which of these are preferable. Indeed, it may well be that the question of how decisions about the distribution of rewards are made is more important in determining satisfaction with outcomes than the nature of the particular decisions, that is, people will be satisfied with allocations of resources to the extent that they participate in the allocation decisions. Even here, however, it should be noted that how satisfied people are with their participation in decision making will itself be a function of an AL for participation. It may also be that certain distributions of rewards that satisfy our demands for maximizing general hedonic satisfaction will not work because they will self-destruct, in other words, a particularly ill-favored group will seek violent redress, or a particularly well-favored group will move to seek still further reward. This alerts us to a further issue not treated in this article, that differences in rewards are not merely a matter of hedonic satisfaction with present states, but also a serious issue of social power to affect future states. A man's wealth or his prestige affects not only his satisfaction but also his ability to influence others, and this too must be considered.

The present authors believe that all members of society should participate in making these decisions about the distribution of rewards, both as regards their own individual states and as regards the interrelationships among everyone. What this would lead to can only be speculated about at the present time. As will be discussed, there are some grounds for believing that people will prefer a system in which everyone is equal, but there are also grounds for believing that they will prefer a system in which people are rewarded differentially according to merit. And indeed, they might even prefer a system in which people were rewarded differentially by chance, for example, in which monthly or yearly lotteries decided who lived extravagantly and who lived in genteel poverty.

There are in general two possible solutions to the problem of keeping stimulus levels above ALs so that the stimulus levels continue to be experienced as pleasurable. The first is to continually increase stimulus levels in some fashion so as to keep them above the hedonic AL. For a variety of reasons—limited resources, declining marginal utilities for goods, and social comparison complexities (to be discussed)—this seems an impractical solution in the general case. This article will concentrate on the second possible solution, preventing hedonic ALs from continuously rising, or specifying situations in which AL phenomena either do not hold or can be modified. Let us first consider the various factors that determine hedonic ALs and how these might be manipulated.

Temporal Comparison: Discrepancy between Present and Past Rewards

The first mechanism for establishing AL (Helson, 1964) is temporal pooling of stimuli, or, for hedonic AL, the individual history of reward. Temporal comparison may be considered to involve a person's comparing his level of reward at the present time t_n with his level of reward at time t_{n-1}, or with some temporally weighted average of his rewards over all times up to t_n. It has been demonstrated that past experiences of rewarding or punishing sensation are pooled and that stimuli are most effective as reinforcers when they depart most strongly from the level of past experience (Bevan, 1963; McHose, 1970; Quinsey, 1970). It has also been shown that people typically set their LA slightly above their past performance level (Lewin et al., 1944).

While a strict AL theory would predict that the larger the positive discrepancy between reward and AL, the greater the pleasurable sensation, there is considerable evidence from a variety of domains that outcomes very much in excess of AL may not be positively reinforcing (Lewin et al., 1944; McClelland, Atkinson, Clark, & Lowell, 1953; Aronson & Carlsmith, 1962). While this issue is not fully settled, because there is also evidence that outcomes far above AL are primary sources of elation and pleasure (Dittes, 1959; Verinis, Brandsma, & Cofer, 1968), we are probably safe in following the lead of Siegel (1957), who showed that outcomes above the LA might produce further increments in satisfaction, but none so great as that produced by reaching the LA.

This leads to the first important implication of hedonic AL theory, namely that we can most efficiently allocate goods to produce satisfaction by first trying to give everyone the minimum above his AL that brings him to his LA. Indeed, this principle has been suggested as the basis for proportional or progressive taxation (Duesenberry, 1949; Vertinsky, 1969). As ALs continue to rise, however, society is then faced with the problem of trying to simultaneously increase its inputs to everyone. Doing this, that is, expanding production, rather than redistributing goods, has been the historic secret of the success of capitalism (Galbraith, 1958), although there are limits on the expansion of production such as the accumulation of hidden costs in the form of pollution and the finite nature of natural resources. Society is given a break in this process, however, by the fact that members with high consumption functions or high ALs are continually dropped out of the picture (through death), while new members starting with low ALs are added (through birth). Thus, society may manage something very much like the continual pacing of stimulus inputs ahead of AL across the individual life cycle, by increasing the monetary rewards, freedom of choice, and social status that accrue to the individual as he gets older just fast enough to keep his inputs above his AL. Indeed, apart from the frustrations of living, one of the reasons that people may not be much attracted by the idea of living their lives over is that such a renewal would mean starting with rewards that are much below the standards to which they have been accustomed. And one of the basic, though often unrecognized, factors in today's "generation gap" may be that the continuity of the incremental reward function with age has been disrupted, so that the younger generation is seen as getting "too much, too soon," and are themselves strongly challenged by having to cope with their disproportionate affluence.

There are, of course, some difficulties with taking reward according to AL as an explicit principle of distribution. A teacher who was limited in the number of high grades she could give out might know that she could maximize satisfaction in the class by giving each person just what the person expected and no more (and it might be hypothesized that teachers seek to learn student expectancies for precisely this reason). However, the moment the students learned that this was her grading principle, they would take great pains to state as high expectancies as possible, and to escalate their demands even beyond normal AL effects. It would seem difficult to recommend as a basis for social organization a principle that could succeed only if members of the social system remained in ignorance of it. The only alternative, however, would be to devise a system in which it was truly to people's advantage over the long run to state only their "honest" ALs and LAs.

Next we might consider the related question of how shifts in level of reward should be managed. Should an upward shift be made gradually or suddenly in order to maximize the satisfaction gained from the new level of reward? Adaptation-level theory and evidence (see, for example, Quinsey, 1970) are unequivocal in predicting that the affective value of the final level of reinforcement will be reduced if the transition is gradual rather than sudden. This by itself would argue that we should try to avoid too much "smoothing out" of positive transitions, while conversely making negative transitions as smooth as possible. Dissonance theory, on the other hand, would suggest that subjects are much more likely to accept new levels of reward without dissonance if these new levels are not sharply discrepant with their expectancy levels, that is, if the transition to a higher level of reward is gradual (Aronson & Linder, 1965) versus if the transition is sudden (Aronson & Carlsmith, 1962). It should be noted that this question cannot be answered by considering the affective value of the reward level alone, but must also take into account the satisfaction experienced by the person over the whole series of rewards, where the sum total of rewards received over all points in time is equal in all conditions. The evidence reviewed earlier would seem to suggest that a series of gradual increments would be preferable to an alternative series, equal in total reward, that delayed the person longer at his initial level and then jumped him all at once to his final level.

If overall shifts are to be gradual, is there any way we can preserve the virtues of sudden discrepancies, without at the same time drastically affecting the gradual course of the AL? We may now mention a second implication of AL theory for the societal scheduling of rewards that society has already discovered: the use of periods of abstinence and periods of special indulgence. Adaptation-level theory would suggest that periods of abstinence could serve the very useful function of lowering AL in certain areas and thus permitting future rewards to be experienced with greater satisfaction. These periods of abstinence must be clearly connected to the ordinary course of events. On the other hand, it would be equally useful to allow periods of special indulgence that are specifically *defined* as special, and hence not allowed to affect the ordinary AL, much as the tray lifted in the middle of a series of weights does not affect the AL for judging the heaviness of the weights (Brown, 1953). Both these practices are features of traditional religion which have become less common as traditional religion has lost its central place in society. It might be well both to gear some of our future research to understanding the effects of these practices, and to consider whether they might be reintroduced into social custom with a new rationale.

Finally, besides manipulating AL through programming variations in current experience, for example, introducing recurrent periods of abstinence, we might consider achieving comparable effects by playing with memory functions. Adaptation-level theory would suggest that there is an optimal degree of recollection for past sadness. It would not recommend that people dwell on past unhappy states, for that would probably cause them to assimilate current events to past levels. On the other hand, AL theory would not recommend that people forget or suppress entirely these sad times, for the measure of their present happiness is the contrast with the less pleasurable past. Thus, perhaps the happiest adult is one who had a moderately unhappy childhood. Since there is good evidence that people ordinarily forget unhappy memories faster than they do happy ones (Holmes, 1970), AL theory would suggest that we employ occasional reminders of such events.

Spatial Comparison: Discrepancy between Areas of Competence

The second mechanism for establishing AL in perceptual experiments is the spatial pooling of stimuli, or the averaging of the stimuli received from the synchronous background. With regard to hedonic AL, spatial comparison may be somewhat loosely taken to refer to a person comparing his level of reward on dimension A with his simultaneous level of reward on dimension B, or with some weighted average of his rewards on all other dimensions. The literature which has been most nearly devoted to this topic is the literature on status incongruence or status inconsistency (see Sampson, 1963, for a review). Status incongruence exists when a man's standing on one dimension is discrepant with his standing on another dimension, for instance, when a man's occupational prestige is higher or lower than his income level. Though here again there are conflicting findings (Lenski, 1967; Segal, Segal, & Knoke, 1970), much of the work in this area has demonstrated that status incongruence is a source of activation, strain, and discontent. Thus, Lenski (1967) reports that people with discrepant status inputs are more likely to support radical political parties that promise to help secure their status at a favorable level. In part, then, it seems that stimulus inputs on the more favorable dimension may come to serve as AL for the inputs on other dimensions, thereby greatly increasing discontent, not unlike the golfer who allows a once-in-a-blue-moon score in the 80s to make him thereafter unhappy with his usual 110s.

Traditionally, societies have coped with the potential problems of discrepant status inputs for individual ALs in several different ways. One solution refuses to allow status inconsistencies to arise in the first place—the definition of a caste society, in which an individual's placement in one status category automatically determines his location on all other dimensions. The other logical solution permits status inconsistencies to be fully resolved, in whatever fashion, by social mobility processes. Of most interest for our purposes, however, is an intermediate course, in which such inconsistencies are allowed to arise and to persist without resolution; yet comparison among these dimensions is mitigated or prevented, for example, by role segregation. In this manner society may even be able to turn the multidimensional nature of status and prestige to its advantage. For instance, lower participants may be "cooled out" (Goffman, 1952) by having their attention diverted to relatively satisfactory returns they may be receiving on unimportant dimensions, on which higher-status persons are much more likely to make concessions (Jones, Gergen, & Jones, 1963).

Research in the area of status incongruence has not been couched in an AL framework, and it is not fully possible to assess the hedonic implications of the research at this point. Instead it may be more appropriate here simply to phrase some of the relevant questions. It would seem rare for an individual to be outstanding on all dimensions, so as to receive top rewards in all areas. The question then arises as to whether it would be more satisfying for a person to be outstanding on dimension A and relatively poor on dimension B, or to be located at an intermediate (fairly good) positon on both A and B. Or, in a case involving social comparison, would two people together derive more satisfaction if each were superior on one dimension and inferior on the other, or if both were identical (at some intermediate position) on both dimensions? Is it possible that receiving a varied pattern of rewards—including at least one domain in which the individual is in a steady state of high reward, and one in which he is experiencing sharply rising rewards—can protect a person from dissatisfaction due to an unsatisfactory level of reward in other areas—that is, a low level or even a declining level of reward? Or will it be true, as some of the status-incongruence literature implies, that the added dissatisfaction from the lower levels will more than counterbalance the added satisfaction from the higher levels?

Social Comparison: Discrepancy between Self and Similar Others

The third and perhaps most potent mechanism for establishing hedonic AL is social comparison, or the comparing of the rewards accruing to oneself with the rewards accruing to a relevant other person, or to some weighted average of the rewards accruing to all relevant others. Social comparison may of course have both temporal and spatial components. The literature on social comparison has established that the reward levels of various others will contribute to the person's hedonic AL for his own rewards to the extent that these others are seen as similar to the person seeking comparison (see Latané, 1966; Festinger, 1954). In one of the best studies on this point, Hoffman, Festinger, and Lawrence (1954) found that subjects were less likely to compete with an opponent who had gained a head start if that opponent were defined as superior to them in ability than if he were defined as similar in ability. Much the same findings on this important point have been obtained on a societal level. Stern and Keller

(1953) and Runciman (1961) found that it was relatively rare for respondents in France and England, respectively, to take as standards for comparison persons who were perceived as belonging to different social classes than their own.

The concept of "relative deprivation" (Merton & Kitt, 1950) was evolved to explain why in a number of instances persons who were objectively better off appeared to be more discontent with their lot. Studies of the American soldier in World War II, for instance, found that soldiers with more education were significantly less content with their chances of being promoted—even though they had significantly better chances of being promoted than did the less well-educated soldiers. The better-educated soldiers were not comparing themselves to their less well-educated peers, however, but to others who were similar to them in education but were getting better treatment (others who were officers). Since then, the notion of relative deprivation has been used to explain why people may become less satisfied, rather than more satisfied, as their objective condition improves—because the improvement of their condition raises their comparison AL at an even faster rate. Thus, Pettigrew (1964) discusses the psychological losses that accompany the actual gains achieved by the Negro civil rights movement, and Sears and McConahay (1970) explain the fact that Northern-born Negroes are both more optimistic in their aspirations and also more discontented and more likely to participate in riots than their Southern-born neighbors.

Loose application of the concept of relative deprivation in explaining the dynamics of social change can make those whose lot is improving seem relatively ungrateful and short-sighted. Thus, it may be well to say a word in passing about other possible interpretations of these data. As Sawyer (1971) points out, the notion that the improvement has stimulated a sense of relative deprivation, on the basis of present data, cannot be distinguished from the possibility that the improvement has activated a general desire to make all men equal. Thus, it may be unnecessary to assume that the improvement results in a shift in AL (resulting from a shift in social comparison), but merely that the improvement generates well-known goal gradient effects as a long-standing goal comes nearer (see Brown, 1961). The effects of blocking efforts to reach a goal are greatly enhanced when the goal is close versus when it is far off (Haner & Brown, 1955), a fact that has been incorporated in the theory of revolution (Brinton, 1938; Davies, 1962).

Also in passing, it might be noted that there is no parallel concept of "relative enrichment," or at least no concept that implies that overreward can present a similar danger to a social system. Indeed, giving people more than they deserve may be seen as an effective way of inducing them to increase their commitment to the system, much as Adams (1965) found that subjects worked harder when they were overpaid in order to "justify" their level of reward. But we may suspect that overreward too can result in discontent, especially when it cannot be made up for or justified by extra work. That some members of the privileged classes perceive such inequity and are not satisfied to deal with it by the traditional gestures of charity has meant that a small but historically important group of revolutionaries has always come from the upper classes. The American New Left is the latest case in point (Franks & Powers, 1970).

The first major implication of hedonic AL theory in the area of social comparison is simply that we should recognize the importance of allowing people to maintain favorable comparisons and to protect themselves from unfavorable comparisons. Thus we might note that traditional society encouraged covert comparison with those less fortunate in the form of "counting one's blessings." Charity simultaneously provided an occasion for comparing one's own lot with those worse off and at the same time worked to relieve the guilt that might come from such comparison. And we should consider the possibility that Castro may have raised the psychic well-being of the Cubans simply by getting rid of the rich tourists who came in numbers sufficient to constitute a very unfavorable comparison group. An unrestricted range of social comparison may itself have detrimental effects on hedonic ALs, as in the case of academic conventions in which the vast number of similar others set hedonic ALs very high. Ideally, one principle of freedom that a good society might embody is freedom of comparison, both in the sense of allowing a person to seek comparison where and when he chooses, and in allowing him to protect himself from comparison where and when he chooses.

The principle of equity (Adams, 1965) or of distributive justice (Homans, 1961) specifies the most important dimension people use in comparing their own rewards with those of others: their relative merits, or inputs. The equity principle implies that if people are unequal in their abilities or their past accomplishments or in what they contribute to a job, we would prefer to see them rewarded unequally, and indeed, to see them rewarded in direct proportion to their merits. Thus, Exline and Ziller (1959) found that groups in which members had power or status directly proportionate to their skills were more satisfying than groups in which such resources were allocated in inverse proportion to merit.

From all this we may draw a second major conclusion for the allocation of rewards with regard to social comparison ALs: Rewards should be allocated so as to be congruent with these comparison ALs, and thus to be perceived as fair, equitable, and legitimate. They should neither be allowed to fall below these levels nor to rise above them (in contrast to the situation for temporal ALs) and, if it is important to conserve the supply of available resources, these comparison ALs should be lowered by reducing people's perceptions of what they deserve.

The control of perceptions of similarity and merit has of course been the principal means in traditional society whereby people were induced to accept discrepancies between wealth and poverty even more striking than those in modern industrial society. However familiar a servant might be with the standard of living in the castle, beliefs about differences in birth, breeding, and station protected the servant (and the master) from the servant's taking life in the castle as the basis for his own hedonic AL. No such inhibitions are imposed in the descriptions of how other people live by our own egalitarian media—especially movies and television. By choice or necessity—perhaps the media are the message—these emphasize the common humanity of people rather than their class or regional differences. This has had the momentous consequence of making the range of social comparison wider—rendering similar more and more others who were believed to be dissimilar (and hence perhaps deserving of dissimilar rewards). The erosion of the traditional controls on social comparison is of course the so-called "revolution of rising expectations" that is shaking the world today, a revolution that many of us would judge good, many would judge inevitable, and all would agree is highly explosive.

Interestingly, as the perception of similarity has become more important, the desire to control information about rewards as a means of minimizing discontent from social comparison has probably increased. Experienced interviewers know that people are even more reluctant to reveal their incomes than to reveal their sexual habits. A study by Lawler (1965), however, indicates that secrecy may not work to minimize dissatisfaction but just the opposite. Lawler found that managers overestimated the pay of subordinates and peers and thus saw their own pay as too low by comparison. However, abandoning secrecy about rewards in the face of increasing perceived similarity would increase pressure for full equality, perhaps even regardless of equity.

There is reason to hypothesize that the principle of equality will tend to gain strength simply as information about rewards and decisions about rewards become more public. It is interesting to note the contrast between the division of reward on athletic teams in salaries (which each player negotiates individually with management) versus prize money or bonuses for winning (which the players as a whole allocate by vote). Salaries are of course traditionally highly uneven, with players receiving what it is believed that their skills deserve. Prize money, on the other hand, is traditionally divided into equal shares and given to all members of the team regardless of their contributions to winning. Recently, as players have begun to hire agents to bargain for them at salary time, one general manager (Editors of *Sport*, 1970) has had the thought (not serious) of telling the agents and the players: "Look—here's what the club can afford for salaries. You divide it." If the players were called upon to divide salary money as they are to divide prize money, would they preserve the traditional equity principle or would we see a sharp swing toward equality? If there were a shift toward equality, would the overall satisfaction of members (averaging those receiving less than "equity" with those receiving more than "equity") be enhanced or decreased? While no general manager of a professional team is likely to try this experiment in the near future, there is no reason social psychologists should not pursue this question in their own territory.

Finally, it is most important to note that the distinction between a preference for equality and a preference for equity takes on additional importance when it is realized that assigning rewards on the apparently fair principle of equity strongly biases against the possibility that people will ever achieve equality by handicapping further those who begin with lesser abilities or accomplishments. For example, by giving the most promising and most accomplished new graduate students the most attractive forms of aid (fellowships or prestigious research assistantships), while the less accomplished ones are given less attractive forms of aid (teaching assistantships or perhaps no aid), we thereby help to ensure that those who have done better in the past will continue to do better in the future. (We ignore for the moment the narrow perspective of competing systems, each concerned with attracting the best talent.) Thus, the principle of merit, or to each according to his achievement, directly contradicts the principle of welfare, or to each according to his need—which may be one reason why this country has found it so difficult to design truly effective compensatory education and welfare programs.

We must discover the limits of Homans' distributive justice principle, or the principle of assigning rewards in direct proportion to merit (thus far called "the" equity principle, but there is in fact no reason to give this principle a monopoly on the word "equity"). We must discover when people will accept either the principle of assigning rewards in inverse proportion to accomplishment (the compensatory equity principle) or the principle of assigning rewards equally irrespective of merit (the equal equity principle). Beck (1967) suggests that labeling is the crucial difference, and that welfare will work (in the sense of benefitting or rehabilitating its recipients) only when it is not called welfare.

THE GREATEST GOOD FOR THE GREATEST NUMBER

The question of hedonic relativism has been largely—though not entirely—ignored in welfare economics (see Duesenberry, 1949; Brown, 1952; Mishan, 1960). The relativistic perspective considerably complicates the question of whether a given distribution of welfare is optimal or not, that is, maximizes the greatest possible good for the greatest number. The most basic and enduring optimality principle was formulated by Pareto and is called "Pareto optimality." This principle states that a given distribution is optimal if there is no change that will make any person better off without also making somebody worse off—or, conversely, a change is to be preferred if it makes at least one person better off without making anyone worse off, or (in subsequent versions) if the gain to the first party is such that he can compensate the second party for the loss and still have some left over. In any event, we should note that the idea that utilities for goods change over time as AL changes, or the idea that increases for certain parties may automatically produce decrements either for others or for themselves by changing social comparison ALs, materially complicates the task of defining optimal distributions. But welfare economics is already so overburdened by abstract complications [for example, an unwillingness to assume that utility or satisfaction can be compared across persons, or the demand that there exist unequivocal social choice functions for all possible combinations of individual preference orders (Arrow, 1951)] that it seems unfair to add to its theoretical problems. Instead what we recommend, both for welfare economics and for social psychology, are empirical studies of the effects of various distributions of goods over times, modes of competence, and persons.

Even without any theoretical underpinning at all, it would seem most useful simply to map out, empirically, how not only the mean but also the variance and the skewness of a distribution of rewards affects satisfaction. This should be done for each of the distributions discussed (temporal, spatial, social). If we remove all variance from such a distribution, do we thereby destroy that distribution as a basis for satisfaction? If we make all people equal, do we thereby destroy social comparison as a basis for satisfaction? Or do we thereby maximize satisfaction, or minimize dissatisfaction—which may be quite different things? If we insist on an unequal distribution of rewards, should the range be wide or narrow? Should the distribution be negatively skewed (so that most people lie above the mean, but a few lie far below it), positively skewed (so that most people lie below the mean, but a few lie far above it), or bimodal (haves and have-nots)?

It would also seem useful to know whether temporal discrepancies, "spatial" or status discrepancies, or social discrepancies are most influential in determining AL. Given the general importance of social factors in the conception of self (see Jones & Gerard, 1967), we might think that social comparison would be the most important determinant. Yet Fishbein, Raven, and Hunter (1963) found that students preferred to use their own past performances rather than social comparison information in setting their aspirations and expectancies for a future performance. Clearly this too is an area that needs more work.

Finally, it should be noted that AL theory has something very important to say about how the evaluations of the success or failure of social programs should be conducted: It tells us that we must be aware of and indeed explore the subtle effects that may be generated by implicitly evoking one or another AL in our questionnaires. At the same time, evaluative research may itself be a very handy arena for building our knowledge about the effects of AL on judgments about the goodness of life.

GETTING OFF THE HEDONIC TREADMILL

In closing, it may be well to return once again to the pessimistic theme, the theme that the relativistic nature of subjective experience means there is no true solution to the problem of happiness. It should be remembered, however, that there are nonrelativistic elements that enter into pleasure, and that there is, in addition, a view that "true happiness" does away with all relativistic perspectives. The nonrelativistic elements are those that come from the satisfaction of recurrently renewed need cycles, like hunger; though we may satiate (and raise our hedonic AL) each time we eat, nature has arranged it so that the effects of this reinforcement dissipate over time and that we will be satisfied with the same level of reinforcement 6 hours later. On this level, we should not ignore the possibility of a purely physical or physiological and nonrelativistic solution to the problem of happiness. There may be a new drug, a method of brain stimulation, or a happiness pill that will move people to any level of good feeling they choose whenever they choose. Short of this, however, there may be no way to permanently increase the total of one's pleasure except by getting off the hedonic treadmill entirely. This is of course the historic teaching of the Stoic and Epicurean philosophers, Buddha, Jesus, Thoreau, and other men of wisdom from all ages. Unfortunately, renouncing the hedonic treadmill is a very difficult thing for men to do at least until, like St. Augustine, they have travelled the full path from innocence to corruption. Even in renouncing the pleasures of the flesh, however, men may experience AL phenomena in their pursuit of piety or saintliness.

Truly renouncing the hedonic treadmill may mean abandoning all evaluative judgments and even all questions about happiness in pursuit of the notion that happiness is unselfconscious and that when a person is happy he is unaware of it. It may be, however, that evaluative judgments, and AL and LA phenomena, are necessary to the restlessness and the searching that have made human life what it is; perhaps the absence of such phenomena is to be found only in people who are resigned to an oppressive existence or have surrendered even the basic competence motivation (White, 1959); but if we are to prevent this restlessness from wreaking its most destructive consequences we must acquire new, humane means of controlling rising ALs.

REFERENCES

Adams, J. S. Inequity in social exchange. In L. Berkowitz (Ed.), *Advances in experimental social psychology*. Vol. II. New York: Academic Press, 1965.

Aronson, E., & Carlsmith, J. M. Performance expectancy as a determinant of actual performance. *Journal of Abnormal and Social Psychology*, 1962, **65**, 178–182.

Aronson, E., & Linder, D. Gain and loss of esteem as determinants of interpersonal attraction. *Journal of Experimental Social Psychology*, 1965, **1**, 156–171.

Arrow, K. J. *Social choice and individual values.* New York: Wiley, 1951.

Beck, B. Welfare as a moral category. *Social Problems,* 1967, **14**, 258–277.

Beebe-Center, J. G. *Pleasantness and unpleasantness.* Princeton, New Jersey: Van Nostrand, 1932.

Bevan, W. The pooling mechanism and the phenomena of reinforcement. In O. J. Harvey (Ed.), *Motivation and social interaction, cognitive determinants.* New York: Ronald Press, 1963.

Bradburn, N. M., & Caplovitz, D. *Reports on happiness.* Chicago: Aldine, 1965.

Brinton, C. C. *The anatomy of revolution.* New York: Norton, 1938. Later editions, Englewood Cliffs, New Jersey: Prentice-Hall, 1957; New York: Random House, 1965.

Brown, D. R. Stimulus-similarity and the anchoring of subjective scales. *American Journal of Psychology,* 1953, **66,** 199–214.

Brown, J. S. *The motivation of behavior.* New York: McGraw-Hill, 1961.

Brown, T. M. Habit persistence and lags in consumer behavior. *Econometrica,* 1952, **20,** 355–371.

Dahrendorf, R. Out of Utopia: Toward a reorientation of sociological analysis. *American Journal of Sociology,* 1958, **64,** 115–127.

Davies, J. C. Toward a theory of revolution. *American Sociological Review,* 1962, 27, 5–18.

Dittes, J. E. Attractiveness of group as a function of self-esteem and acceptance by group. *Journal of Abnormal and Social Psychology,* 1959, **54,** 77–82.

Duesenberry, J. S. *Income, saving, and the theory of consumer behaviour.* Cambridge, Massachusetts: Harvard University Press, 1949.

Editors of *Sport.* Four general managers sound off: How to make money, win, and keep the peace. *Sport,* 1970, **50,** 46.

Exline, R. V., & Ziller, R. C. Status congruency and interpersonal conflict in decision-making groups. *Human Relations,* 1959, **12,** 147–162.

Festinger, L. A theory of social comparison processes. *Human Relations,* 1954, 7, 117–140.

Fishbein, M., Raven, B. H., & Hunter, R. Social comparison and dissonance reduction in self evaluation. *Journal of Abnormal and Social Psychology,* 1963, **67,** 491–501.

Franks, L., & Powers, T. Dianna: The making of a terrorist. *Chicago Daily News,* 1970, September 14–18.

Galbraith, J. K. *The affluent society.* Boston: Houghton, 1958.

Goffman, E. On cooling the mark out: Some aspects of adaptation to failure. *Psychiatry,* 1952, **15,** 451–463.

Haner, C. F., & Brown, P. A. Clarification of the instigation to action concept in the frustration-aggression hypothesis. *Journal of Abnormal and Social Psychology,* 1955, **51,** 204–206.

Helson, H. *Adaptation-level theory: An experimental and systematic approach to behavior.* New York: Harper, 1964.

Hoffman, P. J., Festinger, L., & Lawrence, D. H. Tendencies toward group comparison in competitive bargaining. *Human Relations,* 1954, 7, 141–159.

Holmes, D. S. Differential change in affective intensity and forgetting of unpleasant personal experience. *Journal of Personality and Social Psychology,* 1970, **15,** 234–239.

Homans, G. C. *Social behavior: Its elementary forms.* New York: Harcourt, Brace & World, 1961.

Jones, E. E., & Gerard, H. B. *Foundations of social psychology.* New York: Wiley, 1967.

Jones, E. E., Gergen, K. J., & Jones, R. G. Tactics of ingratiation among leaders and subordinates in a status hierarchy. *Psychological Monographs,* 1963, **77,** Whole No. 566.

Latané, B. Studies in social comparison—Introduction and overview. *Journal of Experimental Social Psychology,* 1966, **Supplement 1,** 1–5.

Lawler, E. E., III. Managerial perceptions of compensation. Paper presented at the Midwestern Psychological Association Convention, Chicago, April, 1965.

Lenski, G. Status inconsistency and the vote: A four-nation test. *American Sociological Review,* 1967, **32**, 298–301.

Lewin, K., Dembo, T., Festinger, L., & Sears, P. Level of aspiration. In J. McV. Hunt (Ed.), *Personality and the behavior disorders.* New York: Ronald Press, 1944.

McClelland, D. C., Atkinson, J. W., Clark, R. A., & Lowell, E. L. *The achievement motive.* New York: Appleton, 1953.

McHose, J. H. Relative reinforcement effects: S_1/S_2 and S_1/S_1 paradigms in instrumental conditioning. *Psychological Review,* 1970, **77**, 135–146.

Merton, R. K., & Kitt, A. S. Contributions to the theory of reference group behavior. In R. K. Merton & P. F. Lazarsfeld (Eds.), *Continuities in social research: Studies in the scope and method of "The American Soldier".* Glencoe, Illinois: Free Press of Glencoe, 1950.

Mishan, E. J. A survey of welfare economies, 1939-59. *The Economic Journal,* 1960, **70**, 197–265.

Pettigrew, T. F. *A profile of the Negro American.* Princeton, New Jersey: Van Nostrand, 1964.

Quinsey, V. L. Some applications of adaptation-level theory to aversive behavior. *Psychological Bulletin,* 1970, **73**, 441–450.

Runciman, W. G. Problems of research on relative deprivation. *European Journal of Sociology,* 1961, **2**, 315–323.

Sampson, E. E. Status congruence and cognitive consistency. *Sociometry,* 1963, **26**, 146–162.

Sawyer, J. Relative deprivation: A politically-based concept. *Psychiatry,* 1971, **34**, 97–99.

Sears, D. O., & McConahay, J. B. Racial socialization, comparison levels, and the Watts riot. *Journal of Social Issues,* 1970, **26**, 121-140.

Segal, D. R., Segal, M. W., & Knoke, D. Status inconsistency and self-evaluation. *Sociometry,* 1970, **33**, 347–357.

Siegel, S. Level of aspiration and decision making. *Psychological Review,* 1957, **64**, 253–262.

Stern, E., & Keller, S. Spontaneous group reference in France. *Public Opinion Quarterly,* 1953, **17**, 208–217.

Thibaut, J. W., & Kelley, H. H. *The social psychology of groups.* New York: Wiley, 1959.

Verinis, J. S., Brandsma, J. M., & Cofer, C. N. Discrepancy from expectation in relation to affect and motivation: Tests of McClelland's hypothesis. *Journal of Personality and Social Psychology,* 1968, **9**, 47–58.

Vertinsky, A. Research note: The use of aspiration-level behavior models in political science. *American Behavioral Scientists New Studies,* 1969, May–June, NS9-NS12.

White, R. W. Motivation reconsidered: The concept of competence. *Psychological Review,* 1959, **66**, 297–333.

COMMENT

David C. McClelland

Brickman and Campbell have presented a fascinating article of the type I wish psychologists would produce more often. They have taken some findings from laboratory psychology and shown how they illuminate problems of society. In one striking instance after another, they illustrate how findings on hedonic adaptation level (AL) and level of aspiration (LA) should be taken into account in planning for happiness and the good society. Too often economists, sociologists, and planners have neglected some of the most elementary principles of hedonic AL. Now they have no excuse. We psychologists do have something to contribute to questions of how various distributions of rewards will be received in society, and Brickman and Campbell have done a very perceptive job of suggesting what it is.

Having said all that and meant it, I have to confess to a nagging doubt, as they do, as to whether what we have to say is all that useful. After all, did not William James say similar things about the relativity of satisfaction? What have we accomplished in the meantime? A number of elegant experiments have been performed in which the parameters can be much more precisely defined and even written in terms of mathematical formulas. But when we try to apply this knowledge to questions involving the groups of others with which people in real life will compare themselves, we feel lost and uncertain—no longer in very good "control" of the variables that will affect the outcome. I doubt if further precision in the controlled experiment will help us much. The only answer seems to be to *do* the studies in real life, as they suggest, but there the simplicities of some of our generalizations appear to fade away. Still we just have not done enough work out in the world to know *where* we stand, and Brickman and Campbell's contribution should be a useful encouragement to get to work on answering the questions they so cogently raise.

My one other reaction to their article stems from the fact that I have lately become very sensitized to the way in which we behavioral scientists tend almost unconsciously to think of people as *S*s or pawns to be manipulated. Brickman and Campbell fall easily into this posture. They seem to look at society as if it were some great watch and their task as watchmakers were to use knowledge of hedonic principles to set up the parts of the watch in such relationship to each other as to maximize satisfaction or minimize dissatisfaction. To be sure, they are worried about who has the power to make such decisions about how to put such a watch together, but in a sense even this question flows from a viewpoint which I would regard as misleading at the outset. Instead of seeing themselves as gods outside the machine (society) arranging things so that pawns will be kept happy, they might better regard themselves as insiders giving information to others like themselves who are active agents (or origins) who can then use the information to plan their lives (and society) to make themselves happier. If they are active agents, why not assume that those to whom they are talking are, also? This may sound like a trivial difference in viewpoint—and they probably would not object to my way of putting it—but I am not sure it is trivial in its effects on what we do with knowledge. Too often we talk as if psychological "laws" (generalizations) *determine* behavior. A deprived background *makes* people low achievers. Watching the media *makes* us compare ourselves with everybody. People are pawns or victims of psychological "laws." But surely there is an element of choice here. The knowledge of these findings can be used to free a person from their tyranny. A man can be taught the laws of hedonic relativism and learn how to gain greater satisfaction from life. He can choose his own goals and comparison groups and use all that we know about how to minimize dissatisfaction or maximize satisfaction to make a better life for himself and others. That seems to me a much safer, saner, and better way to make a better world than to try to think in terms of rigging things so that masses of human pawns will willy-nilly be happier than they would have been without our intervention,

VII

Tributes to Harry Helson

HARRY HELSON—AN APPRECIATION[1]

Deane B. Judd

I am happy that, because of my long friendship and collaboration with Dr. Helson, I have the privilege of introducing him to you.

Dr. Helson received his degree of Doctor of Philosophy from Harvard University in 1924. His thesis was on the psychology of Gestalt, and for me the important part of this psychology is summarized by the statement that all the parts of the environment combine to influence the responses that are observed, and that the form in which the parts are combined may be crucial. A corollary to this statement is that to analyze the environment into parts, each to be studied separately, is often foredoomed to failure because it may not be possible to synthesize the responses to the separate parts in order to predict the response to the total situation. Adaptation level (AL) conforms to the idea that the situation must be evaluated as a totality.

I met Helson in the autumn of 1924 at Cornell University where he was an instructor in the Department of Psychology and I was a graduate student of physics. There, Harry and I carried out our first collaborative work, a study of photopic adaptation. Since that time, there have been four other collaborations, one on object-color perception, two on object-color changes caused by change in the illuminant, and finally a recent collaboration on the pleasantness of object–background color combinations.

Following our first collaboration at Cornell in 1924, Dr. Helson has spent 46 years as a professor of psychology at one or another of the following institutions: University of Kansas, Bryn Mawr College, University of Texas, Brooklyn College, Leland Stanford University, York University (Canada), and, since 1968, at the University of Massachusetts. During World War II (1942–1944) he was in charge of research for the National Defense Research Committee on visual tracking at the Foxboro Company in Massachusetts, and

---

[1] Based on a citation of Harry Helson for the 1969 Godlove Award of the Inter-Society Color Council.

later (1952–1954), he served as director of the U.S. Air Force Radiobiological Laboratory at the University of Texas. He held the editorship of the *Psychological Bulletin* from 1958 to 1964. In 1959 he received the Howard Crosby Warren Medal of the Society of Experimental Psychologists; and in 1962, the Distinguished Scientific Contribution Award of the American Psychological Association.

Last year it was my privilege to read the citation for Dr. Helson when he was presented with the 1969 Godlove Award of the Inter-Society Color Council for distinguished contributions to the knowledge of color. The chief contribution for which the award was made is Dr. Helson's development of the theory of adaptation level and its application to color perception. I had to explain to members and delegates of the Inter-Society Color Council, including artists, engineers, chemists, and physicists, who had never heard of it, why adaptation level is important. It seemed appropriate at that time to start the citation by quoting from Dr. Helson's book, *Adaptation-Level Theory* (1964), a statement of the principle of adaptation level. Now here, in a volume dedicated to Dr. Helson and to the continuing development of adaptation-level theory, it seems appropriate to end my comments with the same quotation:

> In every situation confronting the organism there is established an adaptation level that is a weighted mean of focal, background, and residual stimuli. Adaptation level represents the zero of function, and, since it is always associated with positive values of stimulation, stimuli below as well as above level exert positive effects on behavior. Responses to stimulation are manifestations of positive or negative gradients from level [pp. 62–63].

REFERENCE

Helson, H. *Adaptation-level theory: An experimental and systematic approach to behavior.* New York: Harper & Row, 1964.

HARRY HELSON–SCIENTIST'S SCIENTIST

William Bevan

I first met Professor Helson in 1955 at the annual meeting of the Southern Society for Philosophy and Psychology held in New Orleans. I was there to report a study (Bevan & Darby, 1955) that had been designed to test the predictive limits of AL theory in the judgment of lifted weights. When I arrived at the meeting, I was told that there was a real likelihood that Professor Helson would be in the audience. It furthermore was emphasized—with, I suspect, some relish—that his scientific standards were most exacting, indeed. Thus I approached zero hour with more than the usual apprehensiveness. I was relieved and delighted when his response to our work was favorable. He and I had what was for me a very rewarding conversation and followed it up with correspondence on our shared psychological interests that has continued ever since. During my tenure at Kansas State University, Dr. Helson came as Visiting Professor of Psychology and subsequently stayed on as John C. Peterson Regents' Professor of Psychology, the first holder of a named chair in the University's history. This made possible for me a much-cherished opportunity for collaborative work, and our sharing of interests assumed greater proportions.

In point of fact, I have been a Harry Helson fan for most of my life in psychology. My 1943 Master's thesis research, an investigation of the influence of residuals upon the threshold perception of forms (Bevan & Zener, 1952), was directly influenced by Helson's work (Helson & Fehrer, 1932) on the perception of emerging visual forms, and that of his student, Henle (1942), on the role of past experience as a determinant of visual form perception.

Harry Helson is one of three persons whose influence on my life as a psychologist has been most profound. Paul Whitely, who introduced me to psychology, was—and still is—a magnificent teacher with a special facility for transmitting to his students an enthusiasm for our science that is independent of the affection and respect we feel for him as our teacher. Professor Whitely had taken his degree with Carr at Chicago, and the psychology that came through in his courses was an updated functionalism which treated behavior in terms of adaptive activity with both utilitarian implications and a broadly biological flavor.

Karl Zener taught best through the dialog of the laboratory. He was a compulsive perfectionist who constantly emphasized the need to replicate one's observations, to strive for a more precise definition of problems, and to continue to improve one's empirical procedures. My understanding of the relational and interactive nature of behavioral phenomena was enhanced by a better understanding of Gestalt psychology, gained in my work with Zener, and by my becoming acquainted about the same time with Cannon's principle of homeostasis in physiology.

The advent of Harry Helson's adaptation-level (AL) theory provided the consolidating principle for which I had been searching. At once it accommodated the basic character of perception and, at the same time, reconciled these facts with those of learning and motivation. Furthermore, it emphasized the fundamentally psychological basis of all behavior while at the same time being objective, analytical, and quantitative. Thus, with it one could be scientific without being physicalistic in the narrow, conventional way that the earlier generation of American experimentalists had been. Through AL theory I could bring together what I had absorbed of both the functionalist and the Gestalt approaches and, in addition, achieve the kind of rigor in quantification characteristic of the psychophysical tradition in which Zener had trained me.

My involvement with AL theory over the last 20 years has been a matter of total immersion. The appeal of the AL principle is many-faceted. It is a formal, rather than a substantive, concept. As such, it renders irelevant some of the issues on which other theoretical approaches have foundered. For the same reason it is capable of encompassing a wide variety of phenomena for which the underlying physiological mechanisms may differ substantially. As a systematic approach, it is metaphysically neutral. Thus such issues as the relative importance of conscious and unconscious determinants of behavior or of immediately given and learned behavioral attributes are matters to be resolved empirically in particular behavioral settings. Adaptation level is functional in that it identifies the interaction of several classes of variable in the generation of specific responses; it is quantitative in that it provides for the assessment of the contribution of each of these classes to the response. Furthermore, the distinction that it forces between definitions of stimuli in simplistic physical terms and in terms of behavioral effectiveness provides a flexibility not inherent in traditional stimulus–response formulations.

Although we have collaborated over the years on several research papers and in the editing of a book, my relationship with Professor Helson has been more than that of two professional colleagues. We have from the beginning been close friends. Hence, I think it important to say something about his personal qualities.

More than anyone I know, he has a deep belief in the rewards of faith and hard work. He has always displayed a genuine independence in both his personal and professional life that results from a conviction that good work will survive and have an impact upon the field. Thus he has refused to involve himself in the power politics of our profession but has stuck steadfastly to the laboratory. In moments of discouragement about the significance of my own work, I have always found him ready with an eloquent statement of this philosophy. At the same time, he is modest about his own accomplishments.

He is a scientist's scientist. Everything he does–whether it involves a decision in the laboratory, the formation of a political opinion, or the purchase or sale of securities–is done with the rationality of the scientist. As far as I know, he has no hobbies, except perhaps to play the violin occasionally; his whole life is taken up by his science. And he pursues his scientific interests with an intensity and vigor not often found even among our younger colleagues–and in the face of what, over the years, has been a series of serious medical problems. One need only review the number of his publications that appear and the number of lectures and seminars he presents year after year to be convinced of this.

He is youthful in spirit. While he is not swayed by fads in psychology, his research interests and methods stay abreast of current trends. Our group at Kansas State University was a young group–our average age in the early 1960s was in the low 30s. We were eager, ambitious, hardworking–and Professor Helson was at the center of everything. He was not only a willing participant in all aspects of the department's educational program, but he and Mrs. Helson were actively involved in the department's social life as well.

He is a patient counselor, generous to a fault with his time and energy. His students and his colleagues invariably find him prepared to guide and to help whenever they seek him out. And his advice is sought on matters of a personal as well as a professional nature. I, for one, have been privileged to consult him at a number of major decision points in my life. Although I have not always followed his advice, it has continued to be a significant element in my choice of a course of action. He has been more than generous, over the years, in his support of the career advancement of those who have closely associated with him.

When I was young, I believed that the end of science-making was the substantiation of theory: Experiments were done to yield data which determined the status of current explanatory models. Today, I have come to the understanding that theories are only devices that help in the uncovering of new scientific facts. I am fully confident that the judgment of history will place Harry Helson among the major figures of twentieth-century psychology, not because he created a phrase that has now become a psychological household word, but because he has enunciated a principle that has contributed substantially to the factual repertoire of psychology.

References

Bevan, W., & Darby, C. L. Patterns of experience and the constancy of an indifference point for perceived weight. *American Journal of Psychology*, 1955, 68, 575–584.

Bevan, W., Jr., & Zener, K. Some influences of past experience upon perceptual thresholds of visual form. *American Journal of Psychology,* 1952, **65,** 434–442.

Henle, M. An experimental investigation of past experience as a determinant of visual form perception. *Journal of Experimental Psychology,* 1942, **30,** 1–22.

Helson, H., & Fehrer, E. V. The role of form in perception. *American Journal of Psychology,* 1932, **44,** 79–102.

HARRY HELSON—VERSATILE INNOVATOR

J. P. Guilford

From the time of our first meeting as newcomers at Cornell University in the fall of 1924, and through the years as friends, I have continued to be impressed with the contributions of a man who epitomizes what it means to be intellectually alive. I shall never forget his enthusiasms on his encountering new experiences and his immediate, active responses in the way of seeing significant implications. That is what it means to see problems, in the life of a truly creative person. His highly alert disposition accounts for the versatility of his attention to varied areas within his chosen science, and his flair for fresh approaches to those areas. His greatest contribution, of course, has been his monumental adaptation-level (AL) theory, but that achievement should not be permitted to obscure his other numerous innovations.

A look at Helson's bibliography will show considerable breadth of interest, from psychological history and theory to color conversion and the tau effect. The subject of adaptation level, first announced in 1947,[1] accounts for approximately 16% of the titles in his list of publications. But over nearly 50 years of a creative career, studies in perception account for 26% and history and theory for 21%. Special studies of color phenomena and preferences comprise about 12% of the total, the remaining titles distributed mostly among the subjects of psychophysical methods and laws, psychomotor phenomena, neurology, and the surprisingly distant subjects of personality and social behavior. In all these areas he left models for new thinking and procedures.

Helson's *"The Psychology of Gestalt"* (1925, 1926) was based on his unusual doctoral dissertation at Harvard. It opened up to the English-reading psychologists a radically new point of view and presented a large store of supporting evidence. To this day, Helson has been the leading interpreter and critic of the Gestalt point of view. The Gestalt insistence on the lack of constant relations between stimulus and perception was undoubtedly a key to his later development of AL theory, which brought relativity into psychology in a

---

[1] See Bibliography (p. 317) for all references to Helson's works in this article.

comprehensive and systematic way. Thus, he profited by adopting one of the important cornerstones of *Gestalttheorie* while also recognizing its faults. Psychology has had few, if any, laws of universal scope, such as Newton's laws of motion, for example, but AL principles come close to qualifying. Helson's book (1964) goes a long way toward pointing out their broad sphere of application to behavior.

In this limited space, it is possible to cite only a few of the more noteworthy contributions from Helson's long list. His psychophysical contributions include a reformulation of Fechner's law (1949), a reconciliation of that law with data obtained from ratio judgments (1954), a theory of time-order error (1954), and the introduction of a new "comparative rating scale" (1954), which calls for direct, quantitative judgments of differences.

His studies of physiological problems included a demonstration of afferent functions of the sympathetic nervous system (1932), of the correlation between visual sensitivity and pigmentation of the iris (1933), and of correlation between skin temperature and emotion (1934). There was also a study of pupillary and consensual reflexes (1935).

From his many studies of color perception, Helson arrived at his principle of color conversion (1938), which covers some nine cases of complementarism and the Land colors, among other things. There were studies of color illumination (1938, 1940) and of color changes for objects under different illuminations. The latter line of research led to a very comprehensive investigation of color preferences as functions of color properties of objects under different illuminations (1970). There were also studies of color constancy (1943, 1968) and of reversals of color contrast (1959, 1962, 1963).

In a wartime interlude, at the Foxboro Company, Helson's studies of tracking operations and of design of equipment so as to optimize human adaptation and control could be cited as pioneering work in what became known as "human engineering" or "human-factors" psychology.

Showing that he could readily adapt experimental method in the area of social behavior, Helson collaborated in studies of attitudes and their formation, and of social conformity in behavior (1955, 1957, 1958). The experimental designs could serve well as models in their area.

A little further afield was Helson's excursion into theorizing about personality. One effort was a review of the relationships of personality to perceptual processes, prepared for the U.S. Air Force (1953). Another was his theorizing as to the relevance of AL for personality, as developed in his book (1964).

In the general area of perception, again, a few somewhat isolated problems were investigated. There was a demonstration of the extent to which light perception can be produced by stimulation within the blind spot. There was an experiment showing that the phi phenomenon bears no relation to eye movements and therefore cannot be attributed to them. And there was a novel approach to the tau effect.

Thus, no matter what the area of investigation and no matter what the problem, we see how an active, fertile mind responds and how the science of psychology has thereby been enriched.

HARRY HELSON–BIOGRAPHICAL NOTES[1]

Harry Helson was born in Chelsea, Massachusetts, on November 9, 1898. He received the B.A. degree (*magna cum laude*) at Bowdoin College in 1921 and the Ph.D degree at Harvard University in 1924. He was Instructor in Psychology at Cornell University, 1924–1925; at the University of Illinois, 1925–1926; Assistant Professor at the University of Kansas, 1926–1928; Associate Professor and Director of the Psychology Laboratory at Bryn Mawr College, 1928–1933 and Professor and Chairman of the Department, 1933–1949; Professor and Chairman at Brooklyn College, 1949–1951; Professor at the University of Texas, 1951–1961; John C. Peterson Regents' Professor at Kansas State University, 1961–1967; and Distinguished Visiting Professor at York University, 1967–1968. He has been Professor at the University of Massachusetts since 1968. During 1948–1949, while on leave from Bryn Mawr College, he was Thomas Welton Stanford Fellow and Acting Professor at Stanford University. In World War I, he was in the Naval Unit of the Student Army Training Corps at Bowdoin College, and in World War II (1942–1944), he was Co-Director of the antiaircraft fire-control laboratories at the Foxboro Company (Foxboro, Massachusetts) studying handwheel controls and sighting devices in antiaircraft firing and tracking equipment under the auspices of the National Defense Research Committee. He was Director of the Radiobiological Laboratory of the University of Texas and the U.S. Air Force, 1952–1954. He has served on advisory committees for the Office of Naval Research, the Air Force Office of Scientific Research, and the National Science Foundation. During the year 1956–1957, he was Hogg Foundation Research Scholar. He was awarded the Howard Crosby Warren medal of the Society of Experimental Psychologists in 1959, the Distinguished Scientific Contribution Award of the American Psychological Association in 1962, and the I. H. Godlove Award of the Inter-Society Color Council in 1969.

Helson was Editor of the *Psychological Bulletin* from 1959–1964, and has been or is currently cooperating or consulting editor of the following journals:

---

[1] The material in this biography is adapted, in part, from that appearing in the *American Psychologist* 1962, 17, 895–896.

American Journal of Psychology, Journal of Experimental Psychology, Psychological Review, and the *Journal of General Psychology.*

He is a Fellow of the Society of Experimental Psychologists, American Psychological Association (President, Division 1, 1959; Division 10, 1965), and the American Association for the Advancement of Science (Council, 1941–1942, 1950–1951, 1970–1971), has served a term as a member of the National Research Council, and is now a member of the Midwestern Psychological Association, the Psychonomic Society, the Optical Society of America, the American Association of University Professors, Phi Beta Kappa, and the Society of the Sigma Xi. He is a Delegate from the American Psychological Association to the Inter-Society Color Council and is a member of the U.S. Delegation to the International Commission on Illumination (CIE).

HARRY HELSON—BIBLIOGRAPHY

1925

The psychology of *Gestalt. American Journal of Psychology,* 1925, **36,** 342–370, 494–526.

1926

The psychology of *Gestalt. American Journal of Psychology,* 1926, **37,** 25–62, 189–223.

1927

Insight in the white rat. *Journal of Experimental Psychology,* 1927, **10,** 378–396.
Some anomalies in nerve regeneration. *Psychological Bulletin,* 1927, **24,** 192–193.

1929

The effects of direct stimulation of the blind-spot. *American Journal of Psychology,* 1929, **41,** 345–397.
the effects obtained from rotation of irregularly formed regions. In *Proceedings of the 9th International Congress of Psychology.* Princeton, New Jersey: Psychological Review, 1929. Pp. 219–220.
A modified kinohapt. In *Proceedings of the 9th International Congress of Psychology.* Princeton, New Jersey: Psychological Review, 1929. Pp. 67–68. (With S. H. Bartley)
Eye-movements and the phi-phenomenon. *American Journal of Psychology,* 1929, **41,** 595–606. (With J. P. Guilford)

1930

A new visual phenomenon—the cigarette illusion. *Psychological Review,* 1930, **37,** 273–275.
The *Tau* effect—an example of psychological relativity. *Science,* 1930, **71,** 536–537.
The nature and problem of perception. In R. H. Wheeler (Ed.), *Readings in psychology.* New York: Crowell, 1930. Pp. 389–408.

1931

The *Tau* effect: An example of psychological relativity. *Journal of Experimental Psychology,* 1931, **14,** 202–217. (With S. M. King)
New experiments upon photopic adaptation and the classic laws of adaptation. *Psychological Bulletin,* 1931, **28,** 709–710.
Group presentation in the method of constant stimuli as a time-saving device. *American Journal of Psychology,* 1931, **43,** 422–433. (With D. J. Shaad)
The cigarette 'illusion': A case of color transformation. *American Journal of Psychology,* 1931, **43,** 691–700.

1932

Studies in the theory of perception. I. The clearness-context theory. *Psychological Review*, 1932, **39**, 44–72.

The role of form in perception. *American Journal of Psychology*, 1932, **44**, 79–102. (With E. V. Fehrer)

A study in photopic adaptation. *Journal of Experimental Psychology*, 1932, **15**, 380–398. (With D. B. Judd)

The part played by the sympathetic system as an afferent mechanism in the region of the trigeminus. *Brain*, 1932, **55**, 114–121.

1933

The fundamental propositions of Gestalt psychology. *Psychological Review*, 1933, **40**, 13–32.

A child's spontaneous reports of imagery. *American Journal of Psychology*, 1933, **45**, 360–361.

Dr. Wilcox on "The rôle of form in perception." *American Journal of Psychology*, 1933, **45**, 171–173.

The relation of visual sensitivity to the amount of retinal pigmentation. *Journal of General Psychology*, 1933, **9**, 58–76. (With J. P. Guilford)

1934

Changes in skin temperature following intense stimulation. *Journal of Experimental Psychology*, 1934, **17**, 20–35. (With L. Quantius)

The relation between instructions and past experience in a simple observational task. *Journal of Educational Psychology*, 1934, **25**, 29–38.

How do we see in the blind spot? *Journal of Experimental Psychology*, 1934, **17**, 763–772.

1935

Demonstration of pupillary, accommodative, and consensual reflexes through changes in apparent size of a pinhole. *Journal of General Psychology*, 1935, **13**, 186–188.

1936

Prediction and control of judgments from tactual single-point stimulation. *American Journal of Psychology*, 1936, **48**, 609–616. (With R. H. Burgert)

On statistical methods of comparing heavy mineral suites (An answer to Mr. Churchill Eisenhart). *American Journal of Science*, 1936, **32**, 392–395.

Size-constancy of the projected after-image. *American Journal of Psychology*, 1936, **48**, 638–642.

An experimental and theoretical study of changes in surface colors under changing illuminations. *Psychological Bulletin*, 1936, **33**, 740–741. (With D. B. Judd)

1937

Tri-dimensional analysis and the non-film modes of color appearance. *Journal of the Optical Society of America*, 1937, **27**, 59.

A self-calibrating time-control for multiple circuits. *American Journal of Psychology*, 1937, **49**, 109–113. (With N. Powell)

1938

Fundamental problems in color vision. I. The principle governing changes in hue, saturation, and lightness of non-selective samples in chromatic illumination. *Journal of*

Experimental Psychology, 1938, **23,** 439–476.

Color constancy, conversion, contrast and adaptation. *Psychological Bulletin,* 1938, **35,** 672–673.

1939

Effects of certain variables on hue, lightness, and saturation of samples having identical trilinear coordinates. *Journal of the Optical Society of America,* 1939, **29,** 260.

Color tolerances as affected by changes in composition and intensity of illumination and reflectance of background. *American Journal of Psychology,* 1939, **52,** 406–412.

1940

Fundamental problems in color vision. II. Hue, lightness, and saturation of selective samples in chromatic illumination. *Journal of Experimental Psychology,* 1940, **26,** 1–27. (With V. B. Jeffers)

Some implications of recent psychology. *Phi Kappa Phi Journal,* 1940, **20,** 139–144.

1941

Color perception. Acuity and space perception. S. W. Fernberger (Ed.). *Psychological Bulletin,* 1941, **38,** 433–440.

1942

Multiple-variable analysis of factors affecting lightness and saturation. *American Journal of Psychology,* 1942, **55,** 46–57.

A study of factors determining accuracy of tracking by means of handwheel control. Report 3451. Washington, D.C: Office of Scientific Research and Development, 1942. (With W. H. Howe)

A supplemental study of factors determining accuracy of tracking by means of handwheel control. Report 3452. Washington, D.C.: Office of Scientific Research and Development, 1942. (With W. H. Howe)

Handwheel speed and accuracy of tracking. Report 3453. Washington, D.C.: Office of Scientific Research and Development, 1942. (With W. H. Howe)

Inertia, friction and diameter in handwheel tracking. Report 3454. Washington, D.C.: Office of Scientific Research and Development, 1942. (With W. H. Howe)

Relative accuracy of handwheel tracking with one and both hands. Report 3455. Washington, D.C.: Office of Scientific Research and Development, 1942. (With W. H. Howe)

Tracking with illuminated and non-illuminated oscilloscopes. Report 3608. Washington, D.C.: Office of Scientific Research and Development, 1942. (With W. H. Howe)

1943

Some factors and implications of color constancy. *Journal of the Optical Society of America,* 1943, **33,** 555–567.

Thinking: Some problems and solutions. *Bulletin of the Wagner Free Institute of Science,* 1943, **18,** 9–18.

1945

Psychological aspects of some post-war problems. *Bulletin of the Wagner Free Institute of Science,* 1945, **20,** 5–15.

1946

Some common features of concrete and abstract thinking. *American Journal of Psychology,* 1946, **59,** 468–472. (With H. B. Helson)

1947

Adaptation-level as frame of reference for prediction of psychophysical data. *American Journal of Psychology,* 1947, **60,** 1–29.
Changes in hue, lightness, and saturation of surface colors in passing from daylight to incandescent-lamp light. *Journal of the Optical Society of America,* 1947, **37,** 387–395. (With J. Grove)

1948

The effect of chromatic adaptation on achromaticity. *Journal of the Optical Society of America,* 1948, **38,** 1025–1032. (With W. C. Michels)
Adaptation-level as a basis for a quantitative theory of frames of reference. *Psychological Review,* 1948, **55,** 297–313.

1949

A reformulation of the Fechner law in terms of adaptation-level applied to rating scale data. *American Journal of Psychology,* 1949, **62,** 355–368. (With W. C. Michels)
Design of equipment and optimal human operation. *American Journal of Psychology,* 1949, **62,** 473–497.

1951

Theoretical foundations of psychology. Princeton, New Jersey: Van Nostrand, 1951. (Editor)
Perception. In H. Helson (Ed.), *Theoretical foundations of psychology.* Princeton, New Jersey: Van Nostrand, 1951. Pp. 349–389.

1952

Vision. *Annual Review of Psychology,* 1952, **3,** 55–84.
Object-color changes from daylight to incandescent-filament illumination. *Illuminating Engineering,* 1952, **47,** 221–233. (With D. B. Judd & M. H. Warren)

1953

Perception and personality—a critique of recent experimental literature. *United States Air Force School of Aviation Medical Reports,* Project 21-0202-0007, Report 1, 1953.
Man as a meter. *Physics Today,* 1953, **6,** 4–7. (With W. C. Michels)

1954

Der Mensch als physikalisches Messinstrument. *Physikalische Blätter,* 1954, **10,** 114–118. (With W. C. Michels)
Color and vision. *Illuminating Engineering,* 1954, **49,** 92–93.
The use of comparative rating scales for the evaluation of psychophysical data. *American Journal of Psychology,* 1954, **67,** 321–326. (With W. C. Michels & A. Sturgeon)
A quantitative theory of time-order effects. *American Journal of Psychology,* 1954, **67,** 327–334. (With W. C. Michels)
A reconciliation of the *VEG* scale with Fechner's law. *American Journal of Psychology,* 1954, **67,** 677–683. (With W. C. Michels)

1955

An experimental approach to personality. *Psychiatric Research Reports,* 1955, No. 2, 89–99.
Color and seeing. *Illuminating Engineering,* 1955, **50,** 271–278.

Un planteamiento experimental del estudio de la personalidad. *Revista de psicologia general y aplicada (Madrid)*, 1955, **10**, 5–24.

A short method for calculating the adaptation-level for absolute and comparative rating judgments. *American Journal of Psychology*, 1955, **68**, 631–637. (With P. Himelstein)

1956

Color rendition with fluorescent sources of illumination. *Illuminating Engineering*, 1956, **51**, 329–346. (With D. B. Judd & M. Wilson)

Attitudes as adjustments to stimulus, background, and residual factors. *Journal of Abnormal and Social Psychology*, 1955, **52**, 314–322. (With R. R. Blake, J. S. Mouton, & J. A. Olmstead)

Quantitative denotations of common terms as a function of background. *American Journal of Psychology*, 1956, **69**, 194–208. (With R. S. Dworkin & W. C. Michels)

1957

The generality of conformity behavior as a function of factual anchorage, difficulty of task, and amount of social pressure. *Journal of Personality*, 1957, **25**, 294–305. (With R. R. Blake & J. S. Mouton)

1958

An experimental investigation of the effectiveness of the "big lie" in shifting attitudes. *Journal of Social Psychology*, 1958, **48**, 51–60. (With R. R. Blake & J. S. Mouton)

A study of the Witte–König paradoxical fusion-effect. *American Journal of Psychology*, 1958, **71**, 316–320. (With A. E. Wilkinson)

Petition-signing as adjustment to situational and personal factors. *Journal of Social Psychology*, 1958, **48**, 3–10. (With R. R. Blake & J. S. Mouton)

1959

Adaptation-level theory. In S. Koch (Ed.), *Psychology: A study of a science.* Vol. I. New York: McGraw-Hill, 1959. Pp. 565–621.

A quantitative study of reversal of classical lightness-contrast. *American Journal of Psychology*, 1959, **72**, 530–538. (With F. H. Rohles, Jr.)

Psychological Bulletin, 1959, **56**, 1–470. (Editor)

1960

Anchor, contrast, and paradoxical distance effects. *Journal of Experimental Psychology*, 1960, **59**, 113–121. (With M. C. Nash)

Psychological Bulletin, 1960, **57**, 1–532. (Editor)

1961

A study of coloured shadows. Abstract of a paper presented at the Maxwell Colour Centenary. London: The Royal Institution and the Imperial College, 1961, 23–24. (With C. Self)

The pleasantness of color: Object, source, and background. *Western Architectural Engineering*, 1961, **221**, 35–37.

Psychological Bulletin, 1961, **58**, 1–514. (Editor)

1962

Domains of lightness assimilation and contrast. *Psychologische Beiträge*, 1962, **6**, 405–415. (With V. L. Joy)

On the inhibitory effect of a second stimulus following the primary stimulus to react. *Journal of Experimental Psychology,* 1962, **64**, 201–205. (With J. A. Steger)

Psychological Bulletin, 1962, **59**, 1–532. (Editor)

1963

The influence of context upon the estimation of number. *American Journal of Psychology,* 1963, **76**, 464–469. (With W. Bevan & R. A. Maier)

Studies of anomalous contrast and assimilation. *Journal of the Optical Society of America,* 1963, **53**, 179–184.

Psychological Bulletin, 1963, **60**, 1–575. (Editor)

1964

Current trends and issues in adaptation-level theory. *American Psychologist,* 1964, **19**, 26–38.

Competing theories of receptor excitation in the retina: A symposium. *Psychological Bulletin,* 1964, **61**, 241.

Adaptation-level theory: An experimental and systematic approach to behavior. New York: Harper, 1964.

An investigation of variables in judgments of relative area. *Journal of Experimental Psychology,* 1964, **67**, 335–341. (With W. Bevan)

Psychological Bulletin, 1964, **61**, 1–468. (Editor)

Psychological Bulletin, 1964, **62**, 1–428. (Editor)

Reflections of the retiring editor. *Psychological Bulletin,* 1964, **62**, 427–428.

1965

Torque: A new dimension of tactile-kinesthetic sensitivity. *American Journal of Psychology,* 1965, **78**, 271–277. (With B. Woodruff)

1966

A quantitative study of relevance in the formation of adaptation levels. *Perceptual and Motor Skills,* 1966, **22**, 743–749. (With W. Bevan & H. G. Masters)

A study of inflection-points in the locus of adaptation-levels as a function of anchor-stimuli. *American Journal of Psychology,* 1966, **79**, 400–408. (With H. G. Masters)

Anchor-effects in pitch-localization. *American Journal of Psychology,* 1966, **79**, 458–463. (With E. D. Rubin & M. E. Ware)

The two-point threshold as a function of position in the dermatome. *Journal of Comparative and physiological Psychology,* 1966, **62**, 314–316. (With C. K. Adams)

Some problems in motivation from the point of view of the theory of adaptation level. In D. Levine (Ed.), *Nebraska Symposium on Motivation, 1966.* Lincoln: University of Nebraska Press, 1966. Pp. 137–182.

1967

Some remarks on Gestalt psychology by Kurt Koffka. *Journal of the History of the Behavioral Sciences,* 1967, **3**, 43–46.

Perception. In H. Helson & W. Bevan (Eds.), *Contemporary approaches to psychology.* Princeton: Van Nostrand, 1967. Pp. 311–343.

Contemporary approaches to psychology, Princeton: Van Nostrand, 1967. (Editor with W. Bevan)

Autobiography. In E. G. Boring & G. Lindzey (Eds.), *A history of psychology in autobiography.* Vol. V. New York: Appleton, 1967. Pp. 195–220.

Stimulus generalization as a function of contextual stimuli. *Journal of Experimental Psychology*, 1967, 73, 565–567. (With L. Avant)

Torque sensitivity as a function of knob radius and load. *American Journal of Psychology*, 1967, 80, 558–571. (With B. Woodruff)

1968

Perceptual constancy. In D. L. Sills (Ed.), *International encyclopedia of the social sciences.* New York: MacMillan and Free Press, 1968. Pp. 544–546.

Anchor effects using numerical estimates of simple dot patterns. *Perception and Psychophysics*, 1968, 4, 163–164. (With A. Kozaki)

Effects of duration of series and anchor-stimuli on judgments of perceived size. *American Journal of Psychology*, 1968, 81, 291–302. (With T. Kozaki)

Comments on McFarland's paper. In K. W. Schaie (Ed.), *Theory and methods of research on aging.* Morgantown: West Virginia University Press, 1968. Pp. 53–55.

1969

A study of visual temporal size contrast. *Perception and psychophysics*, 1969, 5, 239–240. (With T. Kozaki)

Why did their precursors fail and the Gestalt psychologists succeed? Reflections on theories and theorists. *American Psychologist*, 1969, 24, 1006–1011.

1970

The role of spectral energy of source and background color in the pleasantness of object colors. *Applied Optics*, 1970, 9, 1513–1562. (With T. Lansford)

The perception of Gestalt-1969. *Annals of the New York Academy of Sciences*, 1970, 169, 654–663.

E.G.B.: The early years and change of course. *American Psychologist*, 1970, 25, 625–629.

1971

Kurt Koffka. *Dictionary of International Biography.* (In press)

Theories of perception. In B. J. Wolman (Ed.), *Handbook of general psychology.* Englewood Cliffs, New Jersey: Prentice-Hall. (With L. Avant) (In press)

A salute to J. P. Guilford. In P. R. Merrifield (Ed.), *Experimental and factor-analytic measurement of personality.* Kent, Ohio: Kent State University Press. (In press)

APPENDIX

JACK E. CAPEHART: A MEMORIAL NOTE

John A. Hebert

    Jack E. Capehart, who died unexpectedly in June of 1969, was an invited participant to the symposium on adaptation-level (AL) theory. He would have been pleased to participate in honoring Helson and his work. As Jack's former student and co-worker, I can testify that the symposium would have been the richer for his participation. Although Jack was a very kind man with many outstanding personal qualities both as a colleague and as a friend, the best tribute one could pay him would be to describe his science and the kind of scientist he was. What follows is an attempt to present what might have been his contribution to the symposium, pieced together from papers that I have examined. Any lack of clarity in the following pages should be attributed to the present author, not to the originator of the research.

    Jack was, first of all, a theoretician. His central scientific activity, it is fair to say, was thinking about theory (AL theory in particular) and devising experiments to test theoretical predictions. He had that rare capacity to devise elegant little experiments—that is, small experiments that could answer relatively large numbers of questions. These questions or hypotheses usually followed very directly from theoretical constructs and assumptions by means of "public steps of inference." His considerable expertise in research design and statistics convinced Jack that it was preferable to employ no more than two experimental variables within a single experiment. He was pleased if simple ordinal predictions could be verified. In short, his approach to science was one of artful craftsmanship leading to solid, if small, gains in knowledge. His paper on the effects of context on a conditional discrimination (Capehart & Pease, 1968) is a good example of an elegant little experiment. The recently published theory of stimulus equivalence (Capehart, Tempone, & Hebert, 1969) is good testimony to his ability to integrate theory and data.

325

The studies reported below are seen as attempts to extend and verify this stimulus-equivalence theory.

Two Generalization Experiments

The theory states that if the subject is presented with a single stimulus value in training, his AL is at that value. In a voluntary stimulus-generalization study, the subject is told to "remember" the single training stimulus and to identify it in a subsequent test series. Since the subject receives only one stimulus in training (and AL is, therefore, at that value), he (or she) is said to learn that "the AL value is correct," not "the stimulus of value X is correct." If some reason (for example, context, frequency, or recency effects) the AL value shifts during testing, then the theory predicts a concomitant shift in the subject's judgment. Thus, stimuli are said to be equivalent with respect to a potentially changing AL, not to a fixed physical value.

In the first study 10 Ss were asked to lift a 350-gm. weight seven times and were instructed to identify it in an immediately following test series of weights ranging from 275 to 425 gm. in 25-gm. steps, 350 gm. being the middle value. Each of the seven test stimuli was presented once within a block of seven trials, for seven blocks or a total of 49 trials. The original training stimulus was to be identified by pressing a "yes" response key, while stimuli judged as not the original were identified by pressing a "no" response key. Decision time (time between the lift and the key press) was recorded for all responses. One might expect that the 350-gm. weight would be most often chosen as the original stimulus, other stimuli being chosen as a function of their similarity to 350 gm., in other words, the typical bidirectional gradient of generalization. However, AL theory predicts a different outcome, that 325 gm. will be most often chosen as the original, even more often than 350 gm. In addition, stimuli will be chosen on the basis of similarity to 325 gm., not 350 gm. This unorthodox prediction rests on the following rationale: If the subject assumes that the AL weight is correct as stated above, then in testing he should choose that stimulus closest in value to the prevailing AL. An *a priori* estimate of the AL of the test series can be obtained from a modification of Helson's (1964) formula for lifted weights:

$$\log(\mathrm{AL} + .75d) = \sum \log S_i/n,$$

where S_i represents the test values, d the interval between values, and n their number. Using this empirically derived formula, the AL of the test series in this study is calculated to be approximately 328 gm. Since it is closest to the AL value, the prediction is that 325 gm., not 350 gm., will be chosen most frequently, given *sufficient test experience*. This last qualifier is necessary since AL is said to be at 350 gm. at the conclusion of training, and will shift toward 328 gm. (that is, 325 gm.) during testing. Forty-nine test trials (versus seven training trials) was considered sufficient test exposure. Inspection of Fig. 1 clearly shows that the 325-gm. weight is chosen most often (dotted line) as the original training stimulus, and that the frequency of choice is related to similarity of a given stimulus to 325 gm., confirming the AL prediction. In addition, the decision time (solid line) was longest at 325 gm. and is highly correlated with the choice data. This correlation of choice and latency of response leads to an interesting notion: Given this particular set of operations (a voluntary stimulus-generalization study) the stimulus most often chosen as the original and the stimulus associated with the longest latency of response will be the same. Furthermore, both measures will indicate the approximate location of AL. With this situation, then, choice and latency of response are thought of as *indicators* of AL. This assertion has further support from a previous study of voluntary stimulus generalization (Hebert & Capehart, 1969).

The second experiment takes advantage of the latency measure as an indicator of AL to make an interesting comparison between the two experiments. The procedure for Experiment II was identical to that for Experiment I except in one important respect: the subjects were trained on 325-gm. weights instead of 350-gm. weights. For these subjects AL should do very little shifting, since training AL (325 gm.) and testing AL (328 gm.) are virtually identical. Stable responses in terms of choice and latency are expected from the beginning of testing, since no shift in AL is predicted. In Fig. 2 the latency of response in the first part of testing (test cycles 1–3) is compared with the second part of testing (test cycles 4–7) for both experiments. Note that in Experiment I, latency peaks at the value of the original training stimulus (350 gm.) in the first part of testing but shifts to 325 gm. for the latter part of testing. By contrast, in Experiment II, latency peaks at 325 gm. initially and remains there throughout testing. The results, of course, are consistent with the notion of a shifting AL in Experiment I and a stable AL in Experiment II.

Another prediction is made concerning the overall latency of response: Since the situation was made relatively stable for the subjects in Experiment II, one might expect quicker responses over test cycles. In Experiment I, on the other hand, the shifting AL might result in slower response over test cycles and then, if AL stabilizes, a subsequent increase in speed of response. These expectations are confirmed, as shown in Fig. 3. The long latency for Experiment I on the first test cycle can be accounted for in terms of familiarization with the test procedure. Cycles 2–5 for this group suggest increasing confusion (created by a shifting AL?), and cycles 6 and 7 suggest a stabilization of AL by the reversal of the trend. The latency pattern in Experiment II is quite different: Long latencies grow progressively shorter as test cycles continue. Trend analysis indicates a significant cubic trend ($p < .001$) in Experiment I and no other trend; both a significant linear trend ($p < .001$) and a quadratic trend ($p < .05$) are indicated in Experiment II. These two experiments taken together give good support to the AL approach to stimulus generalization (Capehart *et al.,* 1969).

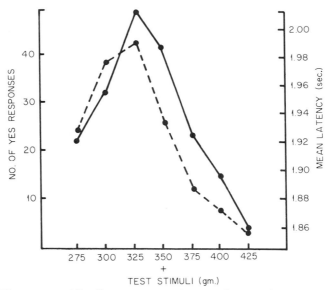

Fig. 1. The number of "yes" responses and the mean latency of response as a function of stimulus weights: (– – –) choice; (———) latency.

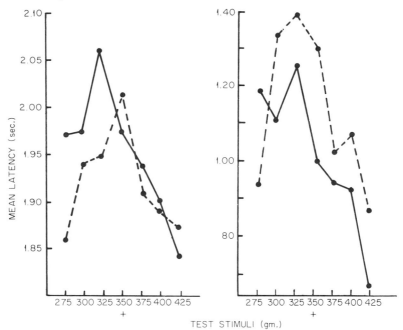

Fig. 2. Mean latencies to stimulus weights in the first part (test cycles 1–3) and second part (test cycles 4–7) of testing, for (a) Experiment I and (b) Experiment II: (– – –) cycles 1–3; (———) cycles 4–7.

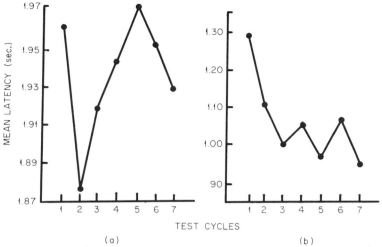

TEST CYCLES

(a)   (b)

Fig. 3. Mean latencies combined across stimuli as a function of test cycles for (a) Experiment I and (b) Experiment II.

A CONSTRUCT VALIDATION

The close correspondence of choice and latency data in the above studies, as well as their usefulness as indicators of the location of AL raises an interesting question. Is the concept referred to in this article the same as Helson's (1964) AL? Although a modification of Helson's empirical formula is used, one must remember that it is *not* a formal operational definition, but rather a statement based on a set of operations that, for Helson, defines AL: namely, the value rated as neutral on a category rating scale. If it could be shown in a given experiment that choice, latency, and category rating all indicated the same value for AL, this would provide a sort of construct validation of AL. The following study is an attempt at such validation. Through our correspondence, Capehart had told me that he had done such a study and had found the three "indicators" of AL to agree. Unfortunately, these data have not been found and may be permanently lost. However, Frank McGuirk and I had independently conducted a very similar study in our laboratory, and these data are reported below.

Ten Ss were asked to lift a 150-gm. weight and were told to "remember" it because they were to identify it in an immediately following test series of weights (100, 125, 150, 175, and 200 gm.). The procedure was essentially the same as in the above two studies. That is, Ss were told to press a "same" key if they felt a test weight was the same as the original and a "different" key if they felt it was not the same as the original. As before, latency of response (decision time) was recorded as the time between the lift and the key press. However, following each response in testing, S was asked to rate the heaviness of the weight he had just lifted on a 7-point category rating scale. The categories ranged

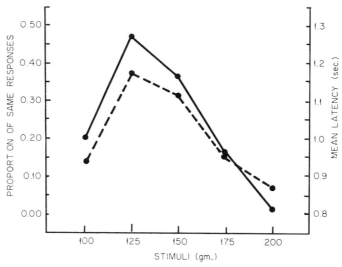

Fig. 4. Proportion of same responses and mean latency of response as a function of stimulus weights: (– – –) latency; (———) choice.

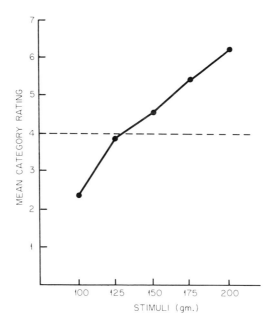

Fig. 5. Mean category ratings as a function of stimulus weights.

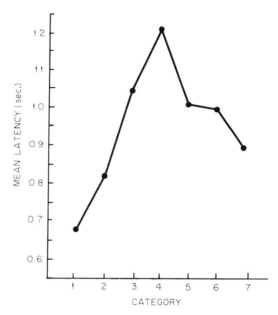

Fig. 6. Mean latency of same–different responses arranged according to subsequent category rating.

from 1, very light, to 7, very heavy, with the neutral category being 4, neither light nor heavy. Although Ss were required to use numbers in their ratings, a display of the verbal equivalents was directly in front of them. (It should be noted that no suggestion by E was ever made as to the appropriate scale value of the training stimulus.) The pattern of choice and latency of response to the test stimuli is illustrated in Fig. 4. As in the previous two studies, the stimulus chosen most often is also associated with the longest latency of response. The indicators suggest that AL is closest to 125 gm., not to 150 gm., and since the calculated AL is 128 gm., this amounts to a replication of Experiment I with different stimulus values.

More important in this study is the relationship of category rating to choice and latency measures. In Fig. 5 it is clearly indicated that AL is closest to 125 gm., since the average rating for that stimulus was closest to the neutral value 4. Using linear extrapolation and dropping a perpendicular from the dotted line (at the point at which the response line crosses it) to the abscissa, an AL of 130 gm. is found, not too far off from the value of 128 gm. calculated from the formula. Thus three logically independent indicators all suggest that AL is close to the same point: 125 gm. Since the experimenter made no suggestion to the subject that the correct stimulus is, say, 4 in terms of heaviness, this must be taken as solid evidence that the subject does learn that "the AL value is correct" by virtue of the single-stimulus training procedure. As a final piece of evidence, the decision times according to how they were subsequently rated is depicted in Fig. 6. It appears that long latency decisions are associated more with a rating of 4 than with any other. This does not necessarily demonstrate that it would take longer to rate a stimulus in category 4, since the latencies shown are not based on the time from lift to category choice, but from lift to the same–different response.

REFERENCES

Capehart, J., & Pease, V. An application of adaptation-level theory to transposition responses in a conditional discrimination. *Psychonomic Science,* 1968, **10,** 147–148.

Capehart, J., Tempone, V. J., & Hebert, J. A theory of stimulus equivalence. *Psychological Review,* 1969, **76,** 405–418.

Hebert, J. A., & Capehart, J. E. Generalization of a voluntary response as a function of presentation frequency of the training stimulus in testing. *Psychonomic Science,* 1969, **16,** 315–316.

Helson, H. *Adaptation-level theory: An experimental and systematic approach to behavior.* New York: Harper, 1964.

AUTHOR INDEX

Numbers in italics refer to the pages on which the complete references are listed.

333

SUBJECT INDEX

A

Absolute judgements, method of, 27, 32, 33, 36, 176, 264, 274
Absolute method, *see* Absolute judgements, method of
Abstinence, 292
Activation, 293
Adaptation, 5, 6, 15, 20, 23, 43, 74, 78, 129, 210, 305
  chromatic, 110
  reflectance, 136
  spatial, 23, 24, 74, 78, 110, 117
Adaptation level (AL), 10, 11, 15, 21–23, 24, 27, 29, 32–36, 40, 44, 45, 51, 55, 56, 59, 84, 97, 101, 102, 104, 106, 130–133, 137, 179, 216, 221, 223, 227, 233, 258, 282, 291–293, 300, 305, 326, 327
  hedonic, 289, 290, 293, 294, 296, 297, 300, 303
Adaptation-level (AL) theory, 1, 2, 5, 6, 8, 9, 11, 12, 13, 14, 19, 24, 37, 38, 45, 46, 49, 50, 57, 62, 66, 68, 71, 75, 77, 93, 101, 113, 117, 129, 130, 131, 133, 136, 137, 143, 144, 148, 149, 154, 155, 157, 168, 170, 171, 175, 197, 203, 204, 205, 207, 208, 211, 249, 252, 259, 260, 281, 285, 287, 290, 291, 294, 299, 306, 307, 308, 311, 325
Adaptation theory, 78
Adaptive behavior, *see* Adaptation
Additive constant, 29, 33, 40
Affect, 11, 15, *see also* Emotion
Age, 52, 278
Anchor (effects), 6–8, 13, 14, 21, 22, 34–36, 81, 82, 92, 106, 109, 111, 113, 119, 158, 167, 179, 180, 183, 184, 187, 188, 204, 210, 216, 217, 219, 239, 240, 257, 282

heteromodal, 264
Anticipation, method of, 176, 180
Anxiety, 234
Apparent cold, 41, 43–45
Apparent distance, 23, 71–74, 77, 78
Apparent length, 61, 113
Apparent magnitude, 19, 24
Apparent shape, 106
Apparent size, 75, 89
Apparent space, 102
Apparent warmth, 41, 44, 45
Aspiration, 299, *see also* Level of aspiration (LA)
Assimilation (effects), 8, 22, 23, 114, 115, 143, 216, 249
Attention, 56, 59, 82, 167, 234, 264, 278
Attitude(s), 20, 50, 207, 209, 210, 217, 218, 312
Audition, 119, 268–270
Auditory behavior, 263
Auditory cognitive system, 275, 277, 281, 282
Auditory temporal judgment, 277, 278
Auditory–visual differences, 263–266
Aversive stimulation, *see* Avoidance
Avoidance, 165–167

B

Background (effects), 7, 8, 56, 58, 105, 130, 133, 136, 140–142, 149, 151, 153–155
Behaviorism, 5, 6
Bowing, 40, 41, 46
Brain damage, 211, 265
Breadth, 91, 95
Brightness, 36, 55, 66, 135–137, 139, 140, 142, 144, 176, 178, 189, 194–197

339